OS X
Mountain
Lion

MARIA LANGER

Visual QuickStart Guide

OS X Mountain Lion

Maria Langer

Peachpit Press
www.peachpit.com

To report errors, please send a note to errata@peachpit.com.
Peachpit Press is a division of Pearson Education.

Editor: Clifford Colby
Production Coordinator: David Van Ness
Copyeditor: Scout Festa
Technical Editor: Clifford Colby
Compositor: Maria Langer
Indexer: Julie Bess
Cover Design: RHDG / Riezebos Holzbaur Design Group, Peachpit Press
Interior Design: Peachpit Press
Logo Design: MINE™ www.minesf.com

Notice of Rights

Notice of Liability

Trademarks

ISBN-13: 978-0-321-85788-0
ISBN-10: 0-321-85788-7

9 8 7 6 5 4 3 2 1

Printed and bound in the United States of America

Dedication

To Michael Chilingerian,

for finally giving me
freedom without guilt.

Special Thanks:

To Cliff Colby, who has been working with me on *Mac OS Visual Quick-Start Guides* forever and a day. Cliff deserves special thanks this year for being so unbelievably understanding during a difficult time in my life. I know I let him down this time around, but he had the courtesy not to remind me about it.

To David Van Ness, production editor extraordinaire! David not only did a great job making this book look picture perfect, but he sent me chocolate and soothing words when I needed them most.

To Scout Festa, copy editor, brand new to the OS X VQS team. Scout did a great job catching all my typos and helping to make sure that my text was as clear and understandable as it could be.

To Julie Bess, for her seemingly infinite bank of patience. She waited a very long time for my manuscript pages this time around and still got the index done on time.

To Don McAllister, Michael Rose, Miraz Jordan, and John Aabbott for helping me with a few screen shots that were difficult (or downright impossible) for me to get on my own.

Speaking of screen shots, to the folks at Ambrosia Software, for developing and supporting Snapz Pro X. I could not have taken the 2,000+ screen shots in this book without that great application. A big thanks to the development team for quickly getting me on the beta program when I was having trouble getting Snapz to work with Mountain Lion.

To the Mac OS development team at Apple, for continuing to refine and improve the world's best operating system. I didn't think they could make it any better but they proved me wrong.

And to my very, very good friends, for giving me moral support when I needed it most. This includes, but is certainly not limited to, Pete and Katie Beaumont, Jim and Teresa Van Sky, Don and Jonnie Johnson, Kathy Kiefer, Shirley Kaiser, Ruth Kneale, Barbara Gavin, Keith Gill, Paula Williams, Janet LeRoy, Ann Torrence, Megg Morin, Tom and Tammy Heffernan, Melissa Brooks, Jeane Vogel, Mike Rose, Ronda Johnson, Mike Muench, Pam Baker, Jim Ferman, Jeff Noreman, Mark Orenzow, Greg Glockner, Steve Greenheck, Mike Sullivan, Tom Negrino, Cheri Herrmann, Mike and Cheryl Tragarz, Esther Schindler, Ryan Keough, Richard Kitos, Pete and Judy Vergalla, Jan Kabili, Dallas Brown, Irene Hoffman, and Brett Campany.

Contents at a Glance

Table of Contents

Introduction

OS X Mountain Lion is the latest version of the computer operating system that put the phrase *graphic user interface* in everyone's vocabulary. With OS X, you can point, click, and drag to work with files, applications, and utilities. Because the same intuitive interface is utilized throughout the system, you'll find that a procedure that works in one program works in virtually all the others.

Using This Book

This Visual QuickStart Guide will help you learn OS X Mountain Lion by providing step-by-step instructions, plenty of illustrations, and a generous helping of tips. On these pages, you'll find everything you need to know to get up and running quickly with OS X—and a lot more!

This book was designed for page flipping. Use the table of contents or index to find the topics you need help for, learn what you need to know, and get on with your work. If you're brand new to OS X, however, I recommend that you begin by reading at least Part I of this book. In those chapters, you'll find basic information about techniques you'll use every day with your computer.

If you're interested in information about new OS X features, be sure to browse through this Introduction. It'll give you a good idea of what you can expect to see on your computer.

But Wait, There's More!

Although this book is almost 650 pages long, it doesn't cover every single aspect of using OS X. You can find additional material that didn't make it into this book—including content about features that were just being announced when this book went to press—on my book support website, **www.MariasGuides.com**.

Visual QuickStart Guides are now even more visual: Building on the success of the top-selling Visual QuickStart Guide books, Peachpit now offers Video QuickStarts. As a companion to this book, Peachpit offers more than an hour of short, task-based videos that will help you master Mountain Lion's top features and techniques; instead of just reading about how to use a tool, you can watch it in action. It's a great way to learn all the basics and some of the newer or more complex features of the program. Log on to the Peachpit site at **www.peachpit.com/register** to register your book, and you'll find a free streaming sample; purchasing the rest of the material is quick and easy.

New Features in OS X Mountain Lion

OS X Mountain Lion includes several brand new features, as well as a handful of interface and functionality improvements and "under-the-hood" changes to improve performance.

Here's a look at some of the new and revised features you can expect to find in OS X Mountain Lion; most of these features are covered in detail throughout the pages of this book.

TIP You can learn more about the new features of OS X Mountain Lion on Apple's Web site at www.apple.com/osx/.

Brand New Features

- Notification Center Ⓐ offers a customizable interface for receiving notifications from a wide range of applications.

- A new Share button Ⓑ enables you to share items with a variety of appropriate services and apps, including Twitter, Flickr, AirDrop, and Mail.

- Dictation makes it possible to dictate text anywhere it can be typed in.

- Messages Ⓒ combines the features of the old iChat app with the ability to send and receive text messages to other Macs and iOS devices.

Ⓐ Notification Center can display a wide range of notification types in a variety of ways.

Ⓑ Click the new Share button to access a menu full of sharing options that vary depending on the item you're working with.

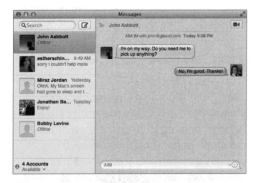

Ⓒ Messages combines text messaging with chat features into one interface.

D Reminders lets you create to-do lists full of tasks.

E Notes offers a simple interface for entering and saving freeform notes.

F Game Center makes it easy to find and compete with friends.

- The new Reminders app **D** makes it possible to track to-do items with reminders based on dates, times, and locations—and sync them via iCloud with other Macs and iOS devices on your Apple ID.

- The new Notes app **E** offers a simple but effective interface for keeping freeform notes—and syncing them via iCloud with other Macs and iOS devices on your Apple ID.

- The new Game Center app **F** enables you to personalize your gaming experience by adding friends and tracking your performance on a leaderboard.

- iCloud enables you to store documents and data in "the cloud," making it easy to synchronize them between computers and devices.

- Gatekeeper enables you to limit the sources of applications you install to help prevent the installation of malware.

- OS X now supports AirPlay Mirroring, so you can wirelessly display what's on your Mac to Apple TV.

- Twitter and Facebook integration make it possible for you to set up your Twitter and Facebook accounts once and access them from almost any window or app.

System & Finder Improvements

- Finder copying now displays progress bar for each file being copied, right on the icon.

- Auto Save has been improved to be more intuitive, offer title bar document renaming, and support iCloud for saving documents.

- Launchpad can now be searched **G** to find applications quickly.

- Screen Saver **H** includes new slide show options that include a Photo Stream module.

- Software Update has been integrated into the Mac App Store so you can update all your Apple software and App Store purchases from one screen.

- OS X now checks for security updates every day to keep your Mac secure.

- Power Nap enables your computer to download and install important updates and perform Time Capsule backups while your Mac sleeps.

G You can now search for apps within LaunchPad.

H Screen Saver has been completely revised to include more photo screen saver modules.

I Calendar's new date picker makes it easy to enter a date.

J In Calendar, you can now display groups in a column on the left side of the window.

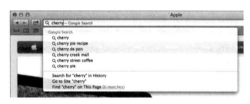

K You can now use the address bar for entering URLs or search phrases.

Other Improved Features

- Calendar (formerly iCal) now displays a list of all your calendars in a convenient sidebar. A new date picker **I** makes it easier than ever to enter dates.

- Contacts (formerly Address Book) has an improved interface that unifies groups **J** and contacts onto one screen.

- Mail now lets you tag certain people as VIPs and organizes messages from them into a VIPs smart folder.

- Safari's address bar and search box are now combined into one field **K** that you can use to search for Web content or go right to a URL.

- TextEdit now supports a pinching gesture to zoom.

- Dashboard has a new widget browser to make it easier to find widgets when you need them.

- The Dictionary app now supports swiping between pages and includes new dictionaries for Chinese, Spanish, and German.

- Time Machine supports multiple backup locations.

- The Accessibility preferences pane has been improved to add more features and make it easier to customize them.

Getting Started with OS X

In This Part

Setting Up OS X Mountain Lion

Before you can use OS X Mountain Lion, you must install it on your computer and configure it to work the way you need it to. These are two separate steps and you may not need to do both.

- If you purchased a new computer with OS X Mountain Lion already installed, you won't need to install it, so you can skip the first half of this chapter. When you start your computer for the first time, it'll open the Setup Assistant to step you through the process of configuring your computer. This is discussed in the second half of this chapter.

- If you are upgrading a Mac you already own to OS X Mountain Lion, you'll need to install Mountain Lion on your computer as discussed in the first half of this chapter. Once that's done, your Mac shouldn't need any additional configuration, so you can skip the second half of this chapter.

With all that in mind, this chapter covers how to install and configure OS X Mountain Lion.

Installing OS X Mountain Lion

OS X's installer application handles all aspects of an OS X installation. When you open it, it prompts you for some information, then restarts your computer and installs the software. When the installation process is finished, the installer automatically restarts your computer from your hard disk and, if necessary, displays the Setup Assistant so you can configure OS X Mountain Lion for your use.

OS X Mountain Lion is available as an App Store download. Because of this, you'll need a few things to purchase, download, and install the software:

- **A Macintosh computer with one of the following Intel processors: Core 2 Duo, Core i3, Core i5, Core i7, or Xeon.** Older Macintosh models cannot run Lion.

- **OS X Snow Leopard 10.6.7 or later.** This is the first version of OS X that supports the App Store, which you'll need to get the OS X Mountain Lion installer. If you don't have a recent enough version of OS X installed on your computer, you'll need to run Software Update to get it.

- **An Apple ID.** This is the same account you might already use for the App Store, iTunes Store, or iCloud. If you don't have an Apple ID, you'll need to sign up to get one; it's free.

- **An Internet connection.** Since you'll be downloading OS X Mountain Lion and the file is large, you'll want the fastest Internet connection possible.

This part of the chapter explains how to prepare for and install OS X Mountain Lion.

TIP The installation instructions in this chapter assume you know basic OS X techniques, such as pointing, clicking, double-clicking, dragging, and selecting items from a menu. If you're brand new to the Mac and don't know any of these techniques, skip ahead to Chapter 2, which discusses OS X basics.

TIP If your computer is brand new and you haven't even started it yet, chances are you have OS X Mountain Lion installed. When you start your computer, it'll display the Setup Assistant. Skip ahead to the section titled "Configuring OS X Mountain Lion" on page 9.

TIP The OS X Lion installer is more than 4 GB in size and can take quite some time to download, even over a fast connection. Don't even *think* about downloading it using a dialup or mobile hotspot connection to the Internet.

TIP If you don't have a fast Internet connection, consider taking your Mac to an Apple Store or somewhere else where a fast connection is available. If that's not possible, contact Apple at 1-800-MY-APPLE for advice or assistance.

A Choose About This Mac from the Apple menu.

B The About This Mac window provides information about the currently installed version of OS X and your computer's processor, among other things.

To learn your computer's processor & OS X version:

1. Choose Apple > About this Mac **A**.

2. In the About This Mac window that appears **B**, consult the Version number and Processor information.

3. Click the window's close button to dismiss it.

TIP Remember, you need Version 10.6.7 and an Intel Core 2 Duo, Core i3, Core i5, Core i7, or Xeon processor.

To update to the latest version of Snow Leopard or Lion:

1. Use one of the following techniques to open Software Update:

    ▸ Choose Apple > Software Update.

    ▸ In the About This Mac window **B**, click the Software Update button.

2. Wait while Software Update checks for new software.

3. Install all Mac OS updates listed in the Software Update window.

TIP It's best to install *all* updates that Software Update finds.

To set up an Apple ID:

1. Click the App Store icon in the Dock to open the App Store application.

2. Follow the instructions in the section titled "To get an Apple ID" on page 171.

TIP If you already have an Apple ID, you don't need to do this.

To buy OS X Mountain Lion:

1. Follow the instructions in Chapter 13 to open the App Store, sign in, and search for OS X Mountain Lion.

2. Click the $19.99 buy button near the Mountain Lion icon.

3. Follow the prompts that appear to complete the purchase.

   Your computer should begin downloading OS X Mountain Lion immediately. If it does not, follow the instructions in the section titled "To download OS X Mountain Lion" below to download it.

4. When the download is complete, continue following the instructions in the section titled "To install OS X Mountain Lion" on page 7.

To download OS X Mountain Lion:

1. If you have already purchased Lion but have either not downloaded it or want to download it again for another computer, click the Purchases button in the App Store application.

   A list of all your purchased software appears .

2. Click the Install button on the right end of the line for OS X Mountain Lion.

   Your computer should begin downloading OS X Mountain Lion immediately.

3. When the download is complete, continue following the instructions in the section titled "To install OS X Mountain Lion" on page 7.

TIP You can download and install OS X Mountain Lion on any Macintosh you own.

C The Purchases screen lists all App Store purchases for your Apple ID.

The OS X Mountain Lion installer icon looks like this.

Install OS X Mountain Lion

E The first installer screen.

F The Software license agreement.

G Confirm that you want to install on the displayed disk...

To install OS X Mountain Lion:

1. Do one of the following:

   ▸ If the OS X Mountain Lion installer opened automatically after it was downloaded, skip ahead to step 2.

   ▸ If the OS X Mountain Lion installer did not automatically open, double-click its icon **D**. You should find it in the Applications folder on your hard disk.

2. An Install OS X window appears **E**. Click Continue.

3. A software license agreement appears next **F**. Read the contents of this dialog, click Agree, and then click Agree again in the smaller confirmation dialog that appears.

4. The next dialog indicates which hard disk OS X will be installed on **G**:

   ▸ To install on the hard disk displayed in the window **G**, click Install.

   ▸ To install on another hard disk that's connected to your computer but not displayed, click Show All Disks. Then select the disk in the list that appears **H** and click Install.

continues on next page

H ...or choose a different disk attached to your computer.

5. A password dialog appears next . Enter an administrator name and password and click OK.

6. Wait while the OS X Mountain Lion installer installs the software. You should see the following processes:

   ▸ The installer prepares to install . This includes checking the downloaded file to make sure it is problem-free.

   ▸ Your computer restarts.

   ▸ The installer installs OS X. This can take 30 minutes or more, depending on your computer.

   ▸ Your computer restarts again.

7. When the installation is finished, one of two things happens:

   ▸ If you are updating an existing OS X installation, a Thank You message appears. Click Start Using Lion to quit the installer. If prompted, log in to go to the Finder desktop. You're finished.

   ▸ If you have installed OS X on a hard disk that did not already contain an OS X installation, the first screen of the Setup Assistant appears. Continue following instructions in the section titled "Configuring OS X Mountain Lion" on page 9.

TIP In step 3, if you click the Disagree button, you will not be able to install OS X.

TIP The password dialog ❶ prevents someone without administrator privileges from installing system software. This is especially important on a computer accessible to others.

TIP Software Update (page 583) may run right after installing OS X Mountain Lion. If any software updates are available for your computer, a dialog with update information appears.

Install OS X Mountain Lion wants to make changes. Type your password to allow this.

Name: Maria Langer
Password:

Cancel   OK

❶ Enter an administrator name and password in this dialog to continue the installation.

Install OS X

OS X Mountain Lion
Preparing to install. Your computer will restart automatically.

Macintosh HD

About 11 minutes remaining

Cancel

❶ The installer prepares to install OS X.

Configuring OS X Mountain Lion

The OS X Setup Assistant uses a simple question-and-answer process to get information about you and the way you use your computer. The information you provide is automatically entered in the various System Preferences panes of OS X to configure your computer for OS X.

TIP The OS X Setup Assistant automatically opens when you first start a new computer or a computer with a new OS X installation.

TIP If the OS X Setup Assistant does not appear, OS X is already configured. You can skip this section.

TIP Although I'm pretty good at getting screenshots for my books, I was unable to capture images of OS X's Setup Assistant. Try to follow along with the text. As you'll see, the process is pretty self-explanatory.

To configure OS X:

1. In the Welcome window that appears after installing OS X, select the name of the country you're in. Click Continue.

2. In the Select Your Keyboard window, select a keyboard layout. Click Continue.

3. In the Select Your Wi-Fi Network window, do one of the following:

   ‣ If the network you connect to is listed, select it, enter a password if necessary, and click Continue.

   ‣ If you connect to a network or the Internet using a different method, click Other Network Options, select one of the options in the How Do You Connect? window, and click

Continue. The OS X Setup Assistant may prompt you for more information. Follow the prompts.

4. In the Transfer Information to This Mac window, select one of the options and click Continue:

   ‣ **From another Mac** enables you to connect your Mac to another Mac and transfer configuration settings and data from the other Mac. If you choose this option, continue following the instructions that appear onscreen. You should be able to skip most of the rest of these steps.

   ‣ **From a Windows PC** enables you to connect your Mac to a Windows PC and transfer configuration settings and data from the PC. If you choose this option, continue following the instructions that appear onscreen. You should be able to skip most of the rest of these steps.

   ‣ **From another disk** enables you to configure your Mac from a Time Machine backup or another attached disk. If you choose this option, continue following the instructions that appear onscreen. You should be able to skip most of the rest of these steps.

   ‣ **Not now** does not transfer any configuration information. Continue following these steps.

5. In the Enable Location Services window, turn on the check box if you want to allow apps to gather and use information about your Mac's location. If you prefer not to enable this feature, leave the check box turned off. Click Continue.

continues on next page

6. In the Apple ID window, you have three main options:

   ▸ If you have an Apple ID, enter it and your account password and click Continue.

   ▸ If you don't have an Apple ID and want one, click the Create a Free Apple ID button and follow the prompts that appear to create one.

   ▸ If you don't have an Apple ID and don't want one, click the Skip button to continue without an Apple ID.

7. In the Terms and Conditions window, read the information in each part of the screen and click Continue. You'll also have to click Agree in the small dialog sheet that appears.

8. If you provided or created an Apple ID, the Set Up iCloud window appears next. To set up iCloud on your Mac, turn on the check box; otherwise, turn it off. Click Continue. If you enabled iCloud, you'll also have to click Continue in a small dialog sheet that appears.

9. If you enabled iCloud, the Use iCloud for Find My Mac window appears. To enable this feature, turn on the check box; otherwise, turn it off. Click Continue. If you enabled Find My Mac, you'll also have to click Allow in a small dialog sheet that appears.

10. If you did not provide or create an Apple ID, a Registration Information window may appear. Fill in the form. You can press Tab to move from one field to the next. When you're done, click Continue.

11. In the Create Your Computer Account window, fill in the form to enter information to set up your OS X account:

    ▸ **Full Name** is your name.

    ▸ **Account Name** is a short version of your name used for networking. This name is also used to label your Home folder. I usually use my first initial followed by my last name: *mlanger*.

    ▸ **Password** is a password you want to use with your account. Enter the same password in each box.

    ▸ **Allow my Apple ID to reset this user password** enables you to reset your password on your computer if you forget it by entering your Apple ID.

    ▸ **Require password when logging in** requires that you enter your password when starting up or logging in to your computer. This, in effect, disables automatic login.

    When you're finished entering account information, click Continue.

12. The Select Your Time Zone window may appear. Click the world map to set your approximate location, then choose a city from the Closest City pop-up menu. Click Continue.

13. If you do not have an Internet connection, the Set Date and Time window may appear. Set the date and time and click Continue.

14. In the Register window, click Continue to register your computer or click Skip to skip registration.

15. In the Thank You, window, Click Start using your Mac. If prompted, log in to go to the Finder desktop. You're finished.

TIP In step 1, if you wait long enough, you'll hear your Mac provide some instructions using its VoiceOver feature (page 390). You can also press the Esc key to get VoiceOver instructions for configuration.

Finder Basics

The Finder is an application that is part of OS X. You use the Finder's graphic user interface to open, copy, delete, list, organize, and perform other operations on computer files.

The Finder is a special application that starts when you turn on your computer and is always open while your computer is running. In fact, under normal circumstances, you cannot quit it.

This chapter provides important instructions for using the Finder and its interface elements, including the desktop, windows, menus, and Dock. It's important that you understand how to use these basic Finder techniques, since you'll use them again and again every time you work with your Mac.

In This Chapter

The Finder & Desktop

The Finder's interface includes a number of elements, most of which are illustrated here **A**.

- **Menu bar** (page 15) offers access to all the Finder's menus.

- **Window** (page 23) displays the contents of a folder or search results.

- **Icon** (page 19) represents a document, folder, application, or other file on your computer.

- **Pointer** enables you to work directly with items you see onscreen. You control the pointer with your mouse, trackpad, or other pointing device (page 13).

- **Dock** (page 34) offers quick access to applications, documents, folders, or other items you use often.

- **Desktop** is an image or colored background for the Finder.

As you work with OS X, you'll find that these basic Finder elements appear over and over in all applications.

A Basic Finder interface elements.

The pointer usually looks like an arrow pointer when you are working in the Finder.

B A USB Apple Mouse (left) and **C** a Bluetooth Magic Mouse (right).

D Laptops such as a MacBook Pro have a built-in trackpad.

Trackpad

E Apple's Magic Trackpad is a multi-touch trackpad.

The Mouse & Trackpad

OS X uses a *mouse* or *trackpad* as an input device to manipulate an onscreen *pointer* **A**.

A **mouse** works by moving the mouse on your work surface or mouse pad to move the pointer on your screen. You can then press the mouse or use its button(s) to click, double-click, or drag. Macs work with a variety of mouse models, including the **Apple Mouse B** and **Magic Mouse C**.

A **trackpad** works by moving your finger along the surface of the trackpad to move the pointer on your screen. You can then press the trackpad or its button to click, double-click, or drag. Laptop computers such as the **MacBook Pro** and **MacBook Air** have a trackpad built in **D**; Apple's **Magic Trackpad E** is another example of a trackpad that works with Mac computers.

There are several basic techniques you must know to use your computer (**Tables 2.1** and **2.2**):

- *Point* to a specific item onscreen.
- *Click* an item to select it.
- *Right-click* an item to display options for it.
- *Double-click* an item to open it.
- *Drag* to move items or make selections.

In addition to these techniques, you can also use *gestures* on a *multi-touch* device such as a trackpad or Magic Mouse to work with items onscreen.

TIP Use the Mouse and Trackpad preferences panes (pages 530 and 532) to customize the functionality of your mouse or trackpad.

TIP The tip of the pointer **A** is its "business end."

TABLE 2.1 Mouse Techniques

Task	One-button mouse	Two-button mouse	Buttonless mouse
Point	Move the mouse on the work surface or mouse pad until the tip of the pointer's arrow is on the item you want to point to **F**.		
Click	Press (and release) the mouse button.	Press (and release) the left mouse button.	Press (and release) the top-left corner of the mouse **G**.
Right-click	Hold down the Control key and press (and release) the mouse button.	Press (and release) the right mouse button.	Press (and release) the top-right corner of the mouse **G**.
Double-click	Click twice quickly.		
Drag	While holding the button down, move the pointer.		

TABLE 2.2 Trackpad Techniques

Task	Trackpad with a button	Buttonless trackpad
Point	Move the tip of one finger on the surface of the trackpad until the tip of the pointer's arrow is on the item you want to point to **F**.	
Click	Press (and release) the button.	Press (and release) the bottom of the trackpad.
Right-click	Hold down the Control key and press (and release) the mouse button.	Use two fingers to click.
Double-click	Click twice quickly.	
Drag	While holding the button down, move the pointer.	

About Stacks.pdf

F Move the pointer so the arrow's tip is on the item you want to point to.

Click here

Right-click here

G "Button" locations on a Magic Mouse.

A The menu bar offers pull-down menus.

B A submenu appears when you choose a menu option with a right-pointing triangle beside it.

C To display a pop-up menu, click it.

D A contextual menu appears when you right-click certain items.

Menus

The Finder—and most other OS X applications—offers menus full of options. There are four types of menus in OS X:

- A pull-down menu appears on the menu bar at the top of the screen **A**.
- A submenu appears when a menu option with a right-pointing triangle is selected **B**.
- A pop-up menu appears within a window or dialog **C**.
- A contextual menu appears when you right-click an item **D**.

Here are a few things to keep in mind about menus:

- A menu option followed by an ellipsis (...) **A B C D** displays a dialog (page 166).
- A menu option that is dimmed or gray cannot be chosen. Command availability varies based on what is selected.
- A menu option preceded by a check mark **A B** is enabled, or "turned on."
- A menu option followed by a series of keyboard characters **A B** has a keyboard shortcut (page 18).
- Contextual menus **D** only display options that apply to the item you are pointing to.

TIP Menus and the menu bar are slightly translucent, making it possible to see the desktop picture or open windows beneath them. To keep the screenshots cleaner looking for this book, most screenshots were created with a plain white desktop.

To use a menu:

1. Point to the name of the menu **E**.

2. Click.

   The menu opens, displaying its options **F**.

3. Point to the menu option you want **G**.

4. Click to choose the option.

   The menu disappears.

TIP OS X's menus are "sticky menus"—a menu opens and stays open when you click its name.

TIP To close a menu without choosing an option, click outside the menu.

TIP This book uses the following notation to indicate menu commands: *Menu Name* > *Sub-menu Name* (if necessary) > *Command Name*. For example, the instructions for choosing the Size command from the Clean Up By submenu under the View menu **B** would be: "choose View > Clean Up By > Size."

To use a contextual menu:

1. Point to the item on which you want to act.

2. Right-click.

   A contextual menu appears **D**.

3. Click the menu option you want.

TIP Contextual menus are similar to the Action pop-up menu (page 30).

 Finder File Edit View Go Window Help

E Point to the menu name.

File	
New Finder Window	⌘N
New Folder	⇧⌘N
New Folder with Selection	^⌘N
New Smart Folder	⌥⌘N
New Burn Folder	
Open	⌘O
Open With	▶
Print	⌘P
Close Window	⌘W
Get Info	⌘I
Compress "Applications"	
Duplicate	⌘D
Make Alias	⌘L
Quick Look "Applications"	⌘Y
Show Original	⌘R
Add to Sidebar	⌘T
Move to Trash	⌘⌫
Eject	⌘E
Burn "Applications" to Disc...	
Find	⌘F
Label:	
✕ ● ● ● ● ● ● ●	

F Click to display the menu.

File	
New Finder Window	⌘N
New Folder	⇧⌘N
New Folder with Selection	^⌘N
New Smart Folder	⌥⌘N
New Burn Folder	
Open	⌘O
Open With	▶
Print	⌘P
Close Window	⌘W
Get Info	⌘I
Compress "Applications"	
Duplicate	⌘D
Make Alias	⌘L
Quick Look "Applications"	⌘Y
Show Original	⌘R
Add to Sidebar	⌘T
Move to Trash	⌘⌫
Eject	⌘E
Burn "Applications" to Disc...	
Find	⌘F
Label:	
✕ ● ● ● ● ● ● ●	

G Click to choose the menu option you want.

TABLE 2.3 Special Character Keys

Key	Function
Enter	Enters information or "clicks" a default button.
Return	Begins a new paragraph or line or "clicks" a default button.
Tab	Advances to the next tab stop or the next item in a sequence.
Delete	Deletes a selection or the character to the left of the insertion point.
Del	Deletes a selection or the character to the right of the insertion point.
Esc	"Clicks" a Cancel button or ends the operation currently in process.

TABLE 2.4 Modifier Keys

Key	Function
Shift	Produces uppercase characters or symbols. Also works with the mouse to extend selections.
Option	Produces special characters.
Command	Accesses menu commands via keyboard shortcuts.
Control	Modifies the functions of other keys and displays contextual menus.
Fn	Switches F-keys between System and user-assigned functions.

TABLE 2.5 Dedicated Function Keys

Key	Function
Help	Displays onscreen help.
Home	Scrolls to the beginning.
End	Scrolls to the end.
Page Up	Scrolls up one page.
Page Down	Scrolls down one page.
Up, Down, Left, Right	Moves the insertion point or changes the selection.

The Keyboard

The keyboard offers another way to communicate with your computer. In addition to typing text and numbers, you can use it to choose menu commands.

There are three types of keys on an OS X keyboard:

- **Character keys**, such as letters, numbers, and symbols, are for typing information. Some character keys have special functions, as listed in Table 2.3.

- **Modifier keys** alter the meaning of a character key being pressed or the meaning of a mouse or trackpad action. Modifier keys are listed in **Table 2.4**.

- **Function keys** perform specific functions in OS X or an application. Dedicated function keys, which always do the same thing, are listed in **Table 2.5**. Function keys labeled F1 through F12 (or higher) on the keyboard—which are sometimes referred to as *F-keys*—can be assigned specific functions by applications.

TIP The key with the Apple on it is called the *Command* key—not the Apple key.

TIP On some keyboards, the Control key is labeled Control, while on others it is labeled Ctrl. Throughout this book, I'll use Control to refer to the Control key, no matter how it might be labeled on your computer's keyboard.

TIP The Del key does not appear on all keyboards.

To use a keyboard shortcut:

1. Hold down the modifier key(s) in the sequence. This is usually Command, but can be Option, Control, or Shift or a combination of any of these.

2. Press the letter, number, or symbol key in the sequence.

   For example, to choose the Open command, which can be found under the File menu **Ⓐ**, hold down the Command key and press O.

TIP You can learn keyboard shortcuts by observing the key sequences that appear to the right of some menu commands **Ⓐ**.

TIP Some commands include more than one modifier key. You must hold all modifier keys down while pressing the letter, number, or symbol key for the keyboard shortcut.

TIP Some applications refer to keyboard shortcuts as *keyboard equivalents* or *shortcut keys*.

TIP You can add or modify keyboard shortcuts for the Finder and other applications in the Keyboard preferences pane (page 526).

File	
New Finder Window	⌘N
New Folder	⇧⌘N
New Folder with Selection	⌃⌘N
New Smart Folder	⌥⌘N
New Burn Folder	
Open	⌘O
Open With	▶
Print	⌘P
Close Window	⌘W
Get Info	⌘I
Compress "Applications"	
Duplicate	⌘D
Make Alias	⌘L
Quick Look "Applications"	⌘Y
Show Original	⌘R
Add to Sidebar	⌘T
Move to Trash	⌘⌫
Eject	⌘E
Burn "Applications" to Disc…	
Find	⌘F
Label:	

Ⓐ When available, keyboard shortcuts appear to the right of menu commands.

TextEdit   **Preview**   **iPhoto**

Ⓐ Application icons.

Letter to Cliff Flying Facts Butterfly

Ⓑ Document icons often display a preview of the document's first page.

Applications   System   Letters

Ⓒ Folder icons.

Macintosh HD   Jump Disk   Multimedia

Ⓓ Three different volume icons: hard disk, USB thumb drive, and an external USB hard disk.

Ⓔ The three faces of the Trash icon in the Dock: empty, full, and while dragging removable media.

Icons

OS X uses icons to graphically represent files and other items on the desktop, in the Dock, or within Finder windows:

- **Applications Ⓐ** are programs you use to get work done. Chapters 11 through 18 discuss working with applications.

- **Documents Ⓑ** are the files created by applications. Chapters 11 and 14 cover working with documents.

- **Folders Ⓒ** are used to organize files. Chapters 3 and 6 discuss using folders.

- **Volumes Ⓓ**, including hard disks, CDs, DVDs, iPods, USB thumb drives, and network disks, are used to store data. Chapter 8 covers working with volumes.

- **The Trash Ⓔ**, which is in the Dock, is for discarding items you no longer want and for ejecting removable media. Using the Trash is covered on page 48.

TIP **Icons can appear a number of different ways, depending on the view and view options chosen for a window. You can learn more about working with windows starting on page 23 and about window views in Chapter 4.**

To select, deselect & move icons:

- To select an icon, click the icon that you want to select. A gray shaded box appears around the icon and its name becomes highlighted **F**.

- To deselect an icon, click anywhere in the window or on the desktop other than on the selected icon.

- To select multiple icons by clicking, click the first icon that you want to select **F**, then hold down the Command key and click another icon that you want to select **G**. Repeat this process to add additional icons to the selection.

- To select multiple icons by dragging, drag a box around the icons you want to select **H**.

- To select all icons in a window, choose Edit > Select All **I**, or press Command-A.

- To deselect one icon in a multiple icon selection, hold down the Command key while clicking the icon that you want to deselect.

- To move an icon, drag the icon to the new location **J** and release it **K**.

TIP You can also select an icon in an active window by pressing the keyboard key for the first letter of the icon's name or by pressing any arrow key until the icon is selected.

TIP Icons that are part of a multiple selection must be in the same window **G H**.

TIP To select multiple icons by dragging **H**, the icons must be adjacent.

TIP You move icons to rearrange them in a window or on the desktop or to copy or move the items they represent to another folder or disk. You can learn about copying and moving items in Chapter 3.

F To select an icon, click it.

G Hold down the Command key while clicking other icons to add them to a multiple icon selection.

H Drag to draw a shaded selection box around the icons that you want to select.

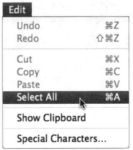

I Choose Select All from the Edit menu to select all items in the active window.

J Drag the icon to a new position.

K Release the button to complete the move.

L Choose Open from the File menu.

TIP Your ability to reposition icons within a window is limited by the view settings for that window. For example, you cannot drag to reposition icons within windows set to list, column, or Cover Flow view. You can learn about window views in Chapter 4.

TIP You can also move multiple icons at once. First, select the icons. Then drag any one of the selected icons. All selected icons move together.

TIP To force an icon to snap to a window's invisible grid, hold down the Command key while dragging it. The grid (page 477) ensures consistent spacing between icons so your window looks neat.

To open an icon:

1. Select the icon you want to open **G** .

2. Choose File > Open **L**, or press Command-O.

Or:

Double-click the icon you want to open.

TIP Only one click is necessary when opening an item in a Finder window's sidebar (page 31) or the Dock (page 34).

TIP To open a folder or disk in a new Finder window, hold down the Command key while opening it.

TIP The File menu's Open With submenu (page 139) enables you to open a document with a specific application.

Opening Icons

What happens when you open an icon depends on the type of icon you open. For example:

- Opening a disk or folder icon displays the contents of the disk or folder in the same Finder window.

- Opening an application icon launches the application that so you can work with it.

- Opening a document icon launches the application that created the document and displays the document so you can view or edit it.

- Opening the Trash displays items that will be deleted when you empty the Trash.

To use enhanced icon view:

1. Point to the icon for a multiple-page document or QuickTime movie.

   Controls appear on the icon **M N**.

2. Do one of the following:

   ▸ To scroll through the pages of a document in its icon, click the right arrow. The icon changes to display the next page **O**. You can use the arrows to scroll forward or backward through the pages of the document.

   ▸ To play a movie in its icon, click the arrow. The movie plays **P**. You can click again to stop movie play.

TIP Enhanced icon view works for compatible multiple-page documents or QuickTime movies that are displayed in icon, column, or Cover Flow view as previews.

TIP Viewing the contents of a document in enhanced icon view works best when the icon size is large or you are viewing the icon in Cover Flow (page 61).

SouthwestCircle.pdf

M When you point to a preview icon for a multi-page PDF file, page scrolling buttons appear.

Exploring Sedona.mp4

N When you point to a preview icon for a QuickTime movie, a play button appears.

SouthwestCircle.pdf

O Clicking the right arrow button for a document displays the next page of that document.

Exploring Sedona.mp4

P Clicking the Play button plays the movie.

Close button
Minimize button
Zoom button Toolbar Title bar Search field

Sidebar   Status bar   Icon size control

A A Finder window in icon view on a MacBook Air.

Column heading Scroll bars

B The same Finder window as **A**, but in list view with an Apple Mouse attached to the computer.

Windows

OS X makes extensive use of windows for displaying icons and other information in the Finder and documents in other applications. Each window includes a variety of controls that you can use to manipulate it **A** **B**:

- The **close button** closes the window.

- The **minimize button** collapses the window to an icon in the Dock.

- The **zoom button** toggles the window's size between full size and a custom size.

- The **toolbar** displays buttons and controls for working with Finder windows.

- The **title bar** displays the window's icon and name.

- The **search field** enables you to search for files using Spotlight.

- The **sidebar** shows commonly accessed folders, volumes, and searches.

- The **status bar** provides information about items in a window and space available on disk.

- The **icon size control** makes it easy to change the size of icons.

- **Column headings** (in list and Cover Flow views only) display the names of columns and let you sort by a column.

- **Scroll bars** scroll the contents of the window.

TIP By default, when you open a folder or disk icon, its contents appear in the active window. You can set Finder preferences (page 464) to open folders in new windows.

TIP Scroll bar display is determined by General preference settings (page 494) and the type of pointing device you are using.

TIP Learn more about views in Chapter 4.

To open a new Finder window:

Choose File > New Finder Window , or press Command-N.

A new Finder window appears .

TIP By default, when you use the New Finder Window command, OS X displays the All My Files window (page 41) . You can use Finder preferences (page 464) to specify which folder should open when you use this command.

To open a folder or volume in a new Finder window:

Hold down the Command key while opening a folder or volume icon.

A new window containing the contents of the folder or volume appears.

To close a window:

Click the window's close button **A**, or choose File > Close Window **E**, or press Command-W.

To close all open windows:

Hold down the Option key while clicking the active window's close button **A**, hold down Option while choosing File > Close All **F**, or press Option-Command-W.

TIP Close Window/Close All **E F** are examples of dynamic menu items—pressing a modifier key (in this case, Option) changes the menu command from Close Window **E** to Close All **F**.

C To open a new window, choose New Finder Window from the File menu.

D By default, the All My Files window opens.

E Choose Close Window from the File menu...

F ...or hold down Option and choose Close All from the File menu.

Window	
Minimize	⌘M
Zoom	
Cycle Through Windows	⌘`
Bring All to Front	
✓ All My Files	
Documents	

G Use the Window menu to perform a number of tasks with open Finder windows.

H The active window appears atop all other windows. The buttons on the left end of the active window's title bar appear in color.

To activate a window:

Use one of the following techniques:

- Click anywhere in or on the window you want to activate.
- Choose the name of the window you want to activate from the list at the bottom of the Window menu **G**.

TIP Make sure the window you want to work with is active before using commands that work on the active window—such as Close Window, Select All, and View menu commands.

TIP You can distinguish between active and inactive windows by the appearance of their title bars; the buttons on the left end of an active window's title bar are in color **H**. In addition, a check mark appears beside the active window's name in the Window menu **G**.

TIP When two or more windows overlap, the active window will always be on top of the stack **H**.

TIP You can use the Cycle Through Windows command **G** or its shortcut, Command-`, to activate each open window, in sequence.

To bring all Finder windows to the top:

Choose Window > Bring All to Front **G**.

All open Finder windows that are not minimized are moved in front of any windows opened by other applications.

TIP Finder windows can be intermingled with other applications' windows. The Bring All to Front command gathers the windows together in the top layers. This command is especially useful when working with many windows from several different applications.

To move a window:

1. Position the pointer on the window's title bar **I** or status bar (if displayed).

2. Press the button and drag the window to a new location.

   As you drag, the window moves along with the pointer.

3. When the window is in the desired position, release the button.

To resize a window:

1. Do one of the following:

   ▸ To change just the height of the window, position the pointer on the top or bottom edge of the window.

   ▸ To change just the width of the window, position the pointer on the left or right edge of the window **J**.

   ▸ To change both the height and width of the window, position the pointer on a corner of the window.

   The pointer turns into a two-headed arrow that indicates which direction the edge or corner can be dragged **J**.

2. Press the button and:

   ▸ To make the window smaller, drag toward the center of the window.

   ▸ To make the window larger, drag away from the center of the window.

   As you drag, the edge or corner of the window moves with the pointer, changing the size and shape of the window **K**.

3. When the window is the desired size, release the button.

I You can move a window by dragging its title bar.

J When you position the pointer on the edge of a window, it turns into a two-headed arrow.

K Drag the window's edge or corner to resize it.

○ A minimized window shrinks down into an icon in the Dock.

Window	
Minimize	⌘M
Zoom	
Cycle Through Windows	⌘ `
Bring All to Front	
✓ All My Files	
Applications	
◆ Documents	

○ A diamond beside a window name indicates that the window has been minimized.

To minimize a window:

Use one of the following techniques:

- Click the window's minimize button **○**.
- Choose Window > Minimize **○**, or press Command-M.

The window shrinks into an icon and slips into the Dock at the bottom of the screen **○**.

TIP To minimize all Finder windows, hold down the Option key and choose Windows > Minimize All, or press Option-Command-M.

TIP You can set an option in the General preferences pane (page 494) so that double-clicking a window's title bar minimizes it.

To redisplay a minimized window:

Use one of the following techniques:

- Click the window's icon in the Dock **○**.
- Choose the window's name from the Window menu **○**.

To zoom a window:

Click the window's zoom button **○**.

Each time you click the zoom button, the window's size toggles between two sizes:

- **Standard state size** is the smallest possible size that would accommodate the window's contents and still fit on your screen.
- **User state size** is the custom size you specify by dragging a window's edge or corner.

To scroll a window's contents with the scroll bar:

Use one of the following techniques to scroll a window's contents up, down, left, or right:

- Drag a scroller along the scroll track .

- Click in the scroll track on either side of the scroller 🅝.

TIP You cannot scroll a window if all contents are already displayed.

TIP The scrollers 🅝 are *proportional*—this means that the more of a window's contents you see, the more space the scroller will take up in its scroll bar.

TIP If you're using OS X with a Multi-Touch device such as a trackpad or Magic Mouse, the scroll bars may not appear in the window. You can display them by using gestures, as discussed next, or by setting General preferences (page 494) to always display them.

To scroll a window's contents with gestures:

1. Position the pointer anywhere within the window you want to scroll.

2. On your Multi-Touch device, use two fingers to push the contents of the window up, down, left, or right.

Scroll bars

Scroll tracks

🅝 Scroll bar components.

Back &
Forward
buttons

View
buttons

Action pop-up menu
Arrange pop-up menu
Share menu
Search field

A The toolbar.

B The Action pop-up menu offers commands for working with selected items in a window.

C The Sharing pop-up menu offers a number of options for sharing selected items with others.

D When the window is narrow, some toolbar items may be hidden; click the double arrow to display a menu of hidden items.

The Toolbar

The toolbar **A** offers navigation tools and view buttons within Finder windows:

- The **Back button** displays the previous window's contents.

- The **Forward button** displays the window that was showing before you clicked the Back button.

- **View buttons** (Chapter 4) enable you to change the window's view.

- The **Action pop-up menu** **B** offers commands for working with an open window or selected object(s) within the window.

- The **Arrange pop-up menu** (Chapter 4) offers commands for arranging icons in the window.

- The Share pop-up menu **C**, which is new in OS X Mountain Lion, offers commands for sharing selected items with others.

- The **Search field** (Chapter 7) enables you to quickly search for a file.

If the window is not wide enough to show all toolbar buttons, a double arrow appears on the right side of the toolbar. Click the arrow to display a menu of missing items **D** and select the one you want.

TIP The toolbar can be customized to show the items you use most (page 483).

TIP Does the Action pop-up menu **B** look familiar? It should! It's very similar to the contextual menu shown on page 15.

To hide or display the toolbar:

Choose View > Hide Toolbar **E**, View > Show Toolbar, or press Option-Command-T.

One of two things happens:

- If the toolbar is displayed, it disappears **F**.
- If the toolbar is not displayed, it appears **A**.

TIP Options on the View menu **E** vary depending on whether the toolbar is displayed or hidden.

TIP Hiding the toolbar also hides the sidebar (page 29). If the status bar (page 33) is set to display in all windows, it moves right beneath the title bar. With the toolbar and sidebar hidden, the window is smaller **F**.

To use a toolbar button:

Click the button once.

To use a toolbar pop-up menu:

1. If necessary, select the items you want to work with.
2. Click the pop-up menu to display a menu of commands.
3. Choose the command you want to use.

E To hide the toolbar, choose Hide Toolbar from the View menu.

F Hiding the toolbar also hides the sidebar, making the window smaller.

A The sidebar appears on the left side of a Finder window.

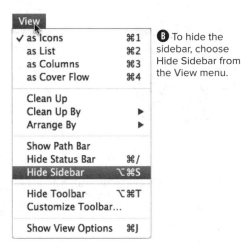

B To hide the sidebar, choose Hide Sidebar from the View menu.

C Hiding the sidebar does not hide the toolbar.

The Sidebar

The sidebar appears on the left side of Finder windows **A**. It offers quick access to the items you use most.

The sidebar has three sections:

- **Favorites** displays the All My Files smart folder (page 99), AirDrop (page 422), Desktop, your Home folder (page 38), several commonly accessed folders, and saved searches (page 99).

- **Shared** lists volumes available over your network (Chapter 24).

- **Devices** lists volumes that are accessible by your computer, such as your hard disk, iDisk, and optical discs (Chapter 8).

TIP You can customize the sidebar to add or remove items or change its width (page 485).

TIP When a window is resized, the size of the sidebar may also change. If the sidebar is too short to display its contents, a vertical scroll bar can appear within it.

To hide or display the sidebar:

Choose View > Hide Sidebar **B**, View > Show Sidebar, or press Option-Command-S.

One of two things happens:

- If the sidebar is displayed, it disappears **C**.

- If the sidebar is not displayed, it appears **A**.

TIP Options on the View menu **B** vary depending on whether the sidebar is displayed or hidden.

TIP The toolbar (page 29) must be displayed to show the sidebar.

To use the sidebar:

Click the icon for the item you want.

One of two things happens:

- If the item is a volume or folder, the window's contents change to display the contents of the item you clicked **A**.

- If the item is an application or document, the item opens in its own window.

To show or hide sidebar sections:

1. Point to the sidebar section heading.

   A Hide **D** or Show button appears to the right of the heading in the sidebar.

2. Do one of the following:

   ▸ To hide the items in the section, click the Hide button. The section heading collapses and the items disappear from view **E**.

   ▸ To show the items in the section, click the Show button. The section expands and the items within it appear.

TIP You can customize the sidebar (page 485) to permanently remove items from it.

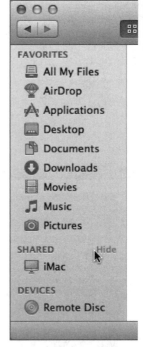

D When you point to a sidebar heading, a Hide or Show button appears beside it.

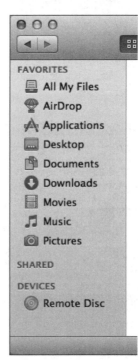

E Clicking the Hide button collapses the heading so the items within it no longer display in the sidebar.

When the toolbar is displayed, the status bar appears at the bottom of the window.

When the toolbar is hidden, the status bar appears beneath the title bar.

The status bar displays a write-protected icon if the window's contents cannot be changed.

To hide the status bar, choose Hide Status bar from the View menu.

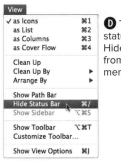

A window looks barren without a toolbar, sidebar, or status bar.

The Status Bar

The status bar is an area of a window with information about the window's contents. It can appear two different places:

- If the toolbar is displayed, the status bar appears at the bottom of the window .

- If the toolbar is hidden, the status bar appears just beneath the window's title bar .

What displays in the status bar depends on what is selected in the window:

- If nothing is selected, the status bar indicates how many items are in the window and how much disk space is available on that volume .

- If one or more items are selected, the status bar indicates how many items are selected and how much disk space is available on that volume.

- If the window is on a volume that cannot be written to, such as a CD, the status bar displays a write-protected icon .

- The status bar also includes a slider you can use to change the size of icons in the window .

To hide or display the status bar:

Choose View > Hide Status Bar , View > Show Status Bar, or press Command-/.

One of two things happens:

- If the sidebar is displayed, it disappears .

- If the sidebar is not displayed, it appears .

The Dock

The Dock **A** offers easy access to often-used applications and documents, as well as minimized windows.

TIP You can customize the Dock (page 468) to add or remove items and set a number of preferences.

To identify items in the Dock:

Point to the item.

The name of the item appears above the Dock **B**.

To open an item in the Dock:

Click the icon for the item you want to open. One of five things happens:

- If the icon is for an application that is running, the application becomes the active application.

- If the icon is for an application that is not running, it launches. Its icon in the Dock bounces so you know something is happening.

- If the icon is for a minimized window (page 27), the window is displayed.

- If the icon is for an unopened document, the document opens in the application that created it.

- If the icon is for a folder, the folder's contents appear using the Stacks feature.

TIP You can use a contextual menu for items on the Dock. Right-click the Dock icon to display the menu **C** and choose the option you want.

A The Dock.

B Point to an icon to see what it represents.

C You can use a contextual menu on a Dock item.

A The Apple menu includes three commands for changing the work state of your computer.

B This dialog appears when you press the power key on your keyboard (if you have one) or hold down Control while pressing the Media Eject key.

Sleeping, Restarting & Shutting Down

The Apple menu **A** offers several options that change the work state of your computer:

- **Sleep** puts the computer into a state where it uses very little power. The screen goes blank and the hard disk may stop spinning.

- **Restart** instructs the computer to shut down and immediately start back up.

- **Shut Down** closes all open documents and programs, clears memory, and cuts power to the computer.

OS X's Resume feature can restore your applications exactly as they were before restarting or shutting down. This means that applications that were running are automatically restarted and all open document windows reopen when your computer starts up.

TIP You can press your keyboard's power key (if it has one) or hold down the Control key while pressing the Media Eject key to display a dialog with buttons for the Restart, Sleep, and Shut Down commands **B**.

TIP Do not restart or shut down a computer by simply flicking off a power switch. Doing so prevents the computer from properly closing files, which may result in file corruption and related problems.

TIP OS X includes a screen saver (page 499), which automatically starts when your computer is inactive for a while. Don't confuse the screen saver with System or display sleep—it's different.

To put your computer to sleep:

Choose Apple > Sleep **A**.

TIP Sleep mode is a good way to conserve laptop battery power without turning it off.

TIP By default, OS X automatically puts a computer to sleep when it is inactive for a while. You can customize this in the Energy Saver preferences pane (page 523).

To wake a sleeping computer:

Press any keyboard key.

You may have to wait several seconds for the computer to fully wake.

TIP It's much quicker to wake a sleeping computer than to start a computer that has been shut down.

To restart your computer:

1. Choose Apple > Restart **A**.

   A dialog appears **C**.

2. To restore all applications and documents to the way they currently appear, select the Reopen windows when logging back in check box.

3. Click Restart, press Return or Enter, or simply wait until your computer restarts on its own.

To shut down your computer:

1. Choose Apple > Shut Down **A**.

   A dialog appears **D**.

2. To restore all applications and documents to the way they currently appear, select the Reopen windows when logging back in check box.

3. Click Shut Down, press Return or Enter, or simply wait until your computer shuts down on its own.

C A dialog like this appears when you choose the Restart command from the Apple menu.

D A dialog like this appears when you choose the Shut Down command from the Apple menu.

File Management Basics

If you think of your computer and its hard disk as a giant filing cabinet—one that could hold far more paper than any filing cabinet you've ever seen—you can begin to get an idea of how important it is to keep your files organized. After all, if you had a file cabinet with one giant drawer and just tossed all your files into it, how would you ever find a specific file when you need it?

In OS X, you use the Finder to organize and manage your files. You can:

- Rename items.
- Create folders to store related items.
- Move items stored on disk to organize them so they're easy to find and back up.
- Copy items to other disks to back them up or share them with others.
- Delete items you no longer need.

This chapter explores all of these tasks, but it starts with the basics: an overview of how OS X organizes its own files and provides a basic framework for organizing yours.

In This Chapter

OS X Disk Organization

Like most other computer operating systems, OS X uses a *hierarchical filing system* (*HFS*) to organize and store files, including system files, applications, and documents.

The top level of the filing system is the computer level **Ⓐ**. This level shows the computer's internal hard disk, any other disks the computer is connected to, the Network icon, and connected servers.

The next level down is the computer's hard disk level **Ⓑ**. You can view this level by opening the icon with the name of your hard disk—usually *Macintosh HD*, but it can be renamed (page 43). While the contents of your hard disk may differ from what's shown here **Ⓑ**, at least four folders should be the same:

- **Applications** contains OS X applications that are installed for all of the computer's users.

- **System** and **Library** contain the OS X system files. In general, you should not add or remove files in these folders; doing so could prevent your computer from operating properly.

- **Users** **Ⓒ** contains individual folders for each of the computer's users, as well as a Shared folder. This is where the computer's users store document files.

By default, an OS X hard disk is organized for multiple users. Each user has his or her own "Home" folder, which is stored in the Users folder **Ⓒ**.

TIP You can learn more about multiple users features of OS X, including the Home folder, in Chapter 10.

Ⓐ The top level of your computer shows all mounted disks and a Network icon.

Ⓑ A typical hard disk window might look like this.

Ⓒ The Users folder contains a Home folder for each user, as well as a Shared folder.

(A) The path bar that you can display at the bottom of a Finder window displays the complete path to a selected folder or file.

(B) You can also display a pop-up menu that shows all of a window's enclosing items.

Pathnames

A *path*, or *pathname*, is a kind of address for a file on disk. It includes the name of the disk on which the file resides, the names of the folders the file is stored within, and the name of the file itself. For example, the pathname for a file named *SWCircle.pdf* in the Documents folder of the mlanger folder **(A)** on my hard disk would be: `Macintosh HD/Users/mlanger/Documents/SWCircle.pdf`.

When entering a pathname from a specific folder, you don't have to enter the entire pathname. Instead, enter the path as it relates to the current folder. For example, the path to the above-mentioned file from the mlanger folder would be: `Documents/SWCircle.pdf`.

To indicate a specific user folder, use the tilde (~) character followed by the name of the user account. So the path to the mlanger folder would be: `~mlanger`. (You can omit the user name if you want to open your own user folder.)

To indicate the top level of your computer, use a slash (/) character. So the path to Maria's MacBook Air would be: `/`.

When used as part of a longer pathname, the slash character indicates the root level of your hard disk. So `/Applications/Utilities` would indicate the Utilities folder inside the Applications folder on your hard disk.

OS X offers two easy ways to learn the complete path to a specific file on your hard disk: the path bar **(A)**, which can be displayed at the bottom of any Finder window, and a pop-up path menu on a window's title bar **(B)**.

To show or hide the path bar:

Choose View > Show Path Bar **C** or View > Hide Path Bar.

One of two things happens:

- If the path bar is not displayed, it appears **A**. The path bar indicates the complete path from your computer to a selected file in the window.

- If the path bar is displayed, it disappears.

TIP Options on the View menu **C** vary depending on whether the path bar is displayed or hidden.

To display a window's path menu:

Hold down the Control or Command key and click the icon in a window's title bar.

A pop-up menu appears **B**. It indicates the enclosing folders, disk, and computer for the window.

TIP This technique works in the Finder as well as within most OS X applications that enable you to work with documents. For example, you can display the path menu for a document open in Preview **D**.

TIP You can use the path menu to open an enclosing disk or folder. Simply select its name from the menu.

C The View menu includes a command to show (or hide) the path bar.

D You can display the path menu for a document window within an application.

A The Go menu offers commands for quickly opening specific locations.

B The Recent Folders submenu on the Go menu lists folders you recently accessed, making them quick and easy to open again.

- **Utilities** (Shift-Command-U) opens the Utilities folder inside the Applications folder.

- **Recent Folders** displays a submenu of recently opened folders **B**.

- **Go to Folder** (Shift-Command-G) lets you open any folder your computer has access to.

- **Connect to Server** (Command-K) enables you to open a server accessible via a network (page 420).

The Go Menu

The Go menu **A** offers a quick way to open specific locations on your computer:

- **Back** (Command-[) displays the contents of the folder or disk you were looking in before you viewed the current folder or disk. This command is only active if the current window has displayed the contents of more than one folder or disk.

- **Forward** (Command-]) displays the contents of the window you were viewing before you clicked the Back button. This command is only available if a window is active and if the Back button has been clicked.

- **Enclosing Folder** (Command-Up Arrow) opens the parent folder for the active window. This command is only available if a window is active and was used to display the contents of a folder.

- **All My Files** (Shift-Command-F) opens the All My Files smart folder (page 99).

- **Documents** (Shift-Command-O) opens the Documents folder.

- **Desktop** (Shift-Command-D) opens your Desktop folder.

- **Downloads** (Option-Command-L) opens your downloads folder.

- **Home** (Shift-Command-H) opens your Home folder (page 125).

- **Computer** (Shift-Command-C) opens the top level window for your computer.

- **AirDrop** (Shift-Command-R) opens the AirDrop window (page 422).

- **Network** (Shift-Command-K) opens the Network window (page 419).

- **Applications** (Shift-Command-A) opens the Applications folder (page 133).

To open a Go menu item:

Choose the item's name from the Go menu or the Recent Folders submenu **B**, or use the appropriate keyboard shortcut.

TIP For OS X power users: Need to open the invisible Library folder inside your Home folder? Hold down the Option key and choose Go > Library.

To go to a folder:

1. Choose Go > Go to Folder **A**, or press Shift-Command-G.

2. In the Go to Folder dialog that appears **C**, enter the pathname for the folder you want to open.

3. Click Go.

4. One of two things happens:

   ▸ If you entered a valid pathname, the folder opens in a Finder window.

   ▸ If you did not enter a valid pathname, an error message appears in the Go to Folder dialog. Repeat steps 2 and 3 to try again, or click Cancel to dismiss the dialog.

TIP If a window is open when you use the Go to Folder command, the Go to Folder dialog will appear as a dialog sheet attached to the window. The pathname you enter must be from that window's folder location on your hard disk.

TIP OS X attempts to complete a path as you type it. Try it for yourself! Type part of a valid pathname and wait a moment. OS X will complete the path with a valid pathname. (Whether it's the one you want is another story.)

C Use the Go to Folder dialog to enter the pathname of the folder you want to open. In this example, I'm opening the Archives folder I've created within my Documents folder in my Home folder.

A Select the icon you want to rename.

B When you press Return an edit box appears around the item name and the name is selected.

C Type in a new name.

D When you press Return the new name is saved.

To rename an icon:

1. Click the icon to select it **A**.

2. Press Return.

   A box appears around the icon name and the name becomes selected **B**.

3. Type the new name.

   The text you type automatically overwrites the selected text **C**.

4. Press Return or Enter, or click anywhere else. The icon is renamed **D**.

Icon Names

OS X is very flexible when it comes to names for files, folders, and disks.

- A file or folder name can be up to 255 characters long.

- A disk name can be up to 27 characters long.

- A name can contain any character except a colon (:).

This flexibility makes it easy to give your files, folders, and disks names that make sense to you.

There are a few additional things to keep in mind when naming or renaming items:

- A lengthy item name may appear truncated when displayed in lists.

- No two items in the same folder can have the same name.

- Because slash characters (/) are used in pathnames, it's not a good idea to use them in names.

- It's generally not a good idea to rename applications or their supporting documents or items in your computer's System or Library folder.

TIP Note that in step 2, if the icon has a file name extension, that extension is not selected **B**. Do not change a file's extension unless you know what you're doing; making a mistake can render the file impossible to open on your computer.

TIP Not all icons can be renamed. If the edit box does not appear around an icon name in step 2, that icon cannot be renamed.

TIP You can also rename an icon in the Info window (page 88).

Folders

OS X uses folders to organize files and other folders on disk. You can create a folder, give it a name that makes sense to you, and move files and other folders into it. It's a lot like organizing paper files and folders in a file cabinet.

OS X supports three different kinds of folders :

- A standard *folder* is for manually storing files on disk. You create the folder, and then move or copy items into it. Throughout this book, I use the term *folder* to refer to this kind of folder.

- A *smart folder* (page 99) works with Spotlight, OS X's integrated searching feature, to automatically organize files and folders that meet specific search criteria.

- A *burn folder* (page 109) is for organizing items you want to save, or "burn," onto a CD or DVD.

This part of the book covers standard folders—the kind you'd use to organize your documents and other files. Because a folder can contain any number of files and other folders, you can easily create a filing system that works best for you.

Letters   Images   Backup

A OS supports three kinds of folders, each with its own icon: standard folder (left), smart folder (center), and burn folder (right).

TIP Your Home folder includes folders set up for organizing files by type. You'll find that these folders often appear as default file locations when saving specific types of files from within software applications (page 160).

TIP You can rename a folder the same way you rename any other icon (page 43).

B Choose New Folder from the File menu.

C A new untitled folder appears.

D Select the items you want to include in a new folder.

E Choose New Folder with Selection from the File menu.

To create a folder with the New Folder command:

1. Choose File > New Folder **B**, or press Shift-Command-N.

    A new untitled folder appears in the active window **C**.

2. While the edit box appears around the new folder's name **C**, type a name for it and press Return.

To create a folder with the Group as Folder command:

1. Select one or more icons you want to group together into a new folder **D**.

2. Choose File > New Folder with Selection **E**, or press Control-Command-N.

    A new folder appears in the active window and the items that were selected are moved into it **F**.

3. While the edit box appears around the new folder's name **F**, type a name for it and press Return.

TIP In OS X Lion, this was the Group as Folder command. It has the same functionality, despite the new name.

F A new folder appears and the items that were selected are moved into it.

Moving & Copying Items

In addition to moving icons around within a window or on the desktop (page 20), you can move or copy items to other locations on the same disk or other disks. This makes it possible to organize items into folders, make copies of items for safekeeping, and share items with others.

You can use drag and drop to move or copy an item by dragging it to a destination location:

- When you drag an item to a location on the same disk, the item is moved to that location. To force the item to be copied instead, hold down the Option key until you release the item in the destination location.

- When you drag an item to a location on another disk, the item is copied to that location. To force the item to be moved instead, hold down the Command key until you release the item in the destination location.

The next page explains how to move, copy, and duplicate items.

TIP You can move or copy more than one item at a time. Select all of the items that you want to move or copy, and then drag any one of them to the destination location.

TIP You can continue working with the Finder or any other application—even start more copy jobs—while a long copy job is in progress.

TIP You cannot move or copy items to a location that is write protected or for which you don't have write privileges (page 415).

A In this example, I'm dragging a file onto a folder icon to move it into that folder.

B In this example, I'm copying the same file into a folder window.

C You'll catch a glimpse of a dialog like this if it takes more than a few seconds to move or copy files.

D If an item with the same name already exists in the destination location, you'll see a dialog like this.

E Select the item you want to duplicate.

F Choose Duplicate from the File menu.

G A copy of the selected item appears with the original.

To move or copy an item:

1. Optionally, do one of the following:
   ▸ To copy the item to the same disk, press and hold the Option key.
   ▸ To move the item to a different disk, press and hold the Command key.

2. Drag the icon for the item that you want to move or copy as follows:
   ▸ To move or copy the item into a specific folder or volume, drag the icon onto the folder or volume icon **A**.
   ▸ To move or copy the item into a specific window, drag the icon into the window **B**.

3. Release the button (and then the Option or Command key, if held down). The item is moved or copied.

TIP If the item is being copied, a green + icon moves with the mouse pointer **B**.

TIP In step 3 you may see a progress dialog **C**.

TIP If an item with the same name already exists at the destination, an error dialog appears **D**. You have three choices: Keep Both Files moves or copies the file with a new name. Stop stops the move or copy. Replace replaces the original file with the one you are moving or copying.

To duplicate an item:

Do one of the following:

- Select the item you want to duplicate **E** and choose File > Duplicate **F**, or press Command-D.

- Hold down the Option key while dragging the item to a different place in the same window.

  A copy of the item you duplicated appears with the original. The word *copy* is appended to the file name **G**.

The Trash & Deleting Items

The Trash is a special place on your hard disk where you place items you want to delete. Items in the Trash remain there until you empty the Trash, which removes them from your disk. The Trash appears as an icon in the Dock .

The Trash icon's appearance indicates its status:

- If the Trash is empty, the Trash icon looks like an empty wire basket .

- If the Trash is not empty, the Trash icon looks like a wire basket with crumpled papers in it .

TIP You cannot move an item to the Trash if the item is locked (page 90) or on a write-protected disk (page 104).

To drag an item to the Trash:

1. Drag the icon for the item you want to delete to the Trash icon in the Dock.

   When the pointer moves over the Trash icon, the Trash icon becomes selected .

2. Release the button.

   The item moves into the Trash.

TIP You can delete more than one item at a time. Begin by selecting all the items you want to delete, and then drag any one of them to the Trash. All items are moved to the Trash.

TIP Dragging a disk icon to the Trash does not delete or erase it. Instead, it unmounts it (page 107).

A When there's nothing in the Trash, it looks like an empty wire basket.

B When there's something in the Trash, it looks like a wire basket with crumpled papers in it.

C When you drag an item to the Trash, the Trash icon becomes selected.

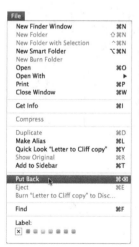

D The Move to Trash command moves selected items to the Trash.

E Opening the Trash displays the Trash window and its contents.

F You can use the Put Back command to take selected items out of the Trash and put them back where they were before you trashed them.

To use the Move to Trash command:

1. Select the item that you want to delete.

2. Choose File > Move to Trash **D**, or press Command-Delete.

    The item is moved to the Trash.

TIP You can delete more than one item at a time. Begin by selecting all the items you want to delete, and then use the Move to Trash command. All items are moved to the Trash.

To drag an item out of the Trash:

1. Click the Trash icon in the Dock to open the Trash window **E**.

2. Drag the item from the Trash window to the Desktop or to another window on your hard disk.

    The item is moved from the Trash to the window you dragged it to.

To use the Put Back command:

1. Click the Trash icon in the Dock to open the Trash window **E**.

2. Select the item you want to remove from the Trash.

3. Choose File > Put Back **F**, or press Command-Delete.

    The item is moved back to where it was before you moved it to the Trash.

To empty the Trash:

1. Use one of the following techniques:
   - ▶ Choose Finder > Empty Trash **G**, or press Shift-Command-Delete.
   - ▶ Click the Trash icon in the Dock to open the Trash window **E** and then click the Empty button.
   - ▶ Right-click the Trash icon to display a contextual menu **H** and then choose Empty Trash.

   A Trash warning dialog appears **I**.
2. Click Empty Trash to delete all items in the Trash.

> **TIP** If you hold down the Option key while emptying the Trash, the Trash is emptied without displaying the warning dialog **I**. You can use Finder preferences to disable the Trash warning (page 464).

To permanently remove items in the Trash from your disk:

1. Choose Finder > Secure Empty Trash **G**.

   A Trash warning dialog appears **J**.
2. Click Secure Empty Trash to permanently remove all items in the Trash.

> **TIP** The Secure Empty Trash command makes it impossible to use special data recovery software to unerase deleted files.

> **TIP** You may want to use the Secure Empty Trash command to erase personal files on a shared computer or a computer you plan to give away or sell.

> **TIP** Deleting files from disk with the Secure Empty Trash command may take longer than using the Empty Trash command, especially when deleting large files.

G The Finder menu includes two commands for emptying the Trash.

H The contextual menu for the Trash includes an Empty Trash command.

I The Trash warning dialog asks you to confirm that you really do want to delete the items in the Trash.

J Using the Secure Empty Trash command displays a warning dialog like this.

Window Views

The OS X Finder displays the contents of your hard disk and other accessible volumes in windows. A window can show the contents of a volume or folder.

OS X offers several different window views that make it easy to see and work with a window's contents. For example, you can view contents as icons or hierarchical lists that can be sorted any way you like. You can even use views that include previews of document contents so you can see a document without even opening it.

In this chapter, I tell you more about how to work with OS X's window views. By understanding how each view works and what features it offers, you should be able to decide which views work best for the things you need to do.

In This Chapter

Window Views

A Finder window's contents can be displayed using four different views:

- **Icon** displays the window's contents as icons . You can set the icon size and rearrange icons within the window.

- **List** displays the window's contents as a sorted list **B**. You can use disclosure triangles to hide or show folder contents.

- **Columns** displays the window's contents with a multiple-column format that shows the currently selected disk or folder and the items within it **C**. The right-most column displays a preview of a selected item.

- **Cover Flow** displays a folder's contents as preview images at the top of the window **D**. If you have a Multi-Touch device, you can use gestures to scroll through the preview icons.

You can switch from one view to another with the click of a button, making it easy to use any view you like for any window you're viewing. You can also set the view for each window separately.

A B C D OS X's four window views: icons view, list view, column view, and Cover Flow view.

Icons view   Columns view

List view   Cover Flow view

F Use the View buttons on the toolbar to switch from one view to another.

G Right-clicking in a window displays a contextual menu you can use to change the view. This is particularly handy when the toolbar is not showing.

E You can choose an option from the top of the View menu to change the active window's view.

To set a window's view:

1. If necessary, activate the window for which you want to change the view.

2. Do one of the following:

   ▸ Choose the view option you want from the View menu **E**, or press the corresponding shortcut key:
   Icon view: Command-1
   List view: Command-2
   Column view: Command-3
   Cover Flow view: Command-4

   ▸ Click the toolbar's view button for the view you want **F**. The button will appear "pushed in" when selected.

   ▸ Right-click in the window to display a contextual menu and choose the view you want from the View sub-menu **G**.

   The view of the window changes.

TIP Commands on the View menu **E** work on the active window only.

TIP A check mark appears on the View menu beside the name of the view applied to the active window **E**.

TIP If the toolbar is not showing for a window, you can choose View > Show Toolbar or press Option-Command-T to display it.

Working with Icon View

Icon view displays a window's contents as icons. Unlike some other views, a window in icon view displays the contents of only one disk or folder at a time.

As discussed on page 20, icons can be dragged to reposition them in a window. You can also use commands under the View menu to align icons in the window.

TIP Chapter 2 explains the basics of working with icons in the Finder.

To clean up a window:

1. Activate the window that you want to clean up .

2. Choose View > Clean Up 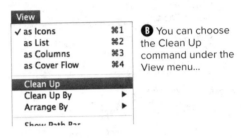.

   The icons are moved into the nearest unoccupied space in the window's invisible grid .

TIP A window's invisible grid (page 477) ensures consistent spacing between icons.

TIP You can manually position an icon in the window's invisible grid by holding down the Command key while dragging it within the window.

TIP If one or more icons in the window are selected when you display the View menu, the Clean Up command appears as Clean Up Selection. You can use this command to reposition just the selected icons in a window.

TIP You can use the Clean Up By submenu under the View menu to neaten up a window and place icons in a specific order at the same time.

Ⓐ Sometimes windows just get messy.

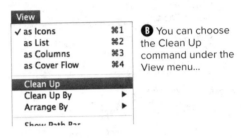

Ⓑ You can choose the Clean Up command under the View menu...

Ⓒ ...to move icons into the window's invisible grid.

Ⓓ The Clean Up By submenu under the View menu.

Sort Column

A Click a column heading to sort by that column.

B Click the same column heading to reverse that column's sort order.

Working with List View

List view displays a window's contents in an ordered list. Items cannot be manually moved around so there's no need for a Clean Up command.

Windows displayed in list view also have a feature not found in other views: They can display the contents of folders within the window as an outline. This makes it possible to see and select the contents of more than one folder at a time.

To sort a window's contents:

Click the column heading for the column you want to sort by.

The list is sorted by that column **A**.

> **TIP** You can identify the column by which a list is sorted by its colored column heading **A**.

> **TIP** You can reverse a window's sort order by clicking the sort column's heading a second time **B**.

> **TIP** You can determine the sort direction by looking at the arrow in the sort column. When it points up, the items are sorted in ascending order **B**; when it points down, the items are sorted in descending order **A**.

> **TIP** To properly sort by size, you must turn on the Calculate all Sizes option for the window (page 480).

> **TIP** You can specify which columns should appear in a window by setting view options (page 480).

To display or hide a folder's contents in outline list view:

- To display a folder's contents, use one of the following techniques:

  ▸ Click the right-pointing disclosure triangle beside the folder **C**.

  ▸ Click the folder once to select it, and press Command-Right Arrow.

  The items within that folder are listed below it, slightly indented **D**.

- To hide a folder's contents, use one of the following techniques:

  ▸ Click the down-pointing disclosure triangle beside the folder **E**.

  ▸ Click the folder once to select it, and press Command-Left Arrow.

  The outline collapses to hide the items in the folder **D**.

TIP You can use this technique to display multiple levels of folders in the same window **E**.

Disclosure triangles

C Disclosure triangles that point to the right indicate hidden content.

Disclosure triangle

D A disclosure triangle that points down indicates displayed content. In list view, this displays folder contents as an outline.

E In list view, you can display multiple levels of folders as an outline.

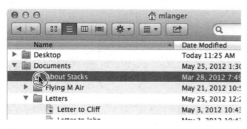

F Drag over the other icons you want to select.

G Select the first icon.

H Hold down Shift and click the last icon.

I Command-click additional icons to select them.

To select multiple contiguous icons in list view:

Use one of the following techniques:

- Position the pointer in front of the first icon and drag over the other icons you want to select **F**.

- Click to select the first icon **G**, hold down the Shift key, and click the last icon in the group you want to select **H**.

To select multiple noncontiguous icons in list view:

1. Click to select an icon **G**.

2. Hold down the Command key and click another icon.

   The icon is also selected **I**.

3. Repeat step 2 until all icons have been selected.

To deselect icons:

Click anywhere in the window other than on an icon's line of information.

To change a column's width:

1. Position the pointer on the line between the heading for the column whose width you want to change and the column to its right.

   The pointer turns into a vertical bar with two arrows **J**.

2. Press the button down and drag:

   ‣ To make the column narrower, drag to the left **K**.

   ‣ To make the column wider, drag to the right.

3. When the column is displayed at the desired width, release the button.

TIP If you make a column too narrow to display all of its contents, information may be truncated or condensed **K**.

To change a column's position:

1. Position the pointer on the heading for the column you want to move.

2. Press the button down and drag:

   ‣ To move the column to the left, drag to the left **L**.

   ‣ To move the column to the right, drag to the right.

   As you drag, the pointer turns into a grasping hand and the other columns shift to make room for the column you're dragging **L**.

3. When the column is in the desired position, release the button.

   The column changes its position **M**.

TIP You cannot change the position of the Name column.

J Position the pointer on the column border.

K When you press the button down and drag, the column's width changes.

L You can drag a column heading...

M ...to change the column's position.

A Clicking a folder name in one column displays the contents of that folder in the column to its right.

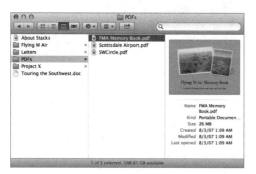

B Selecting a document in column view can display a preview and additional information in the column to the right.

C Scrolling to the left moves backward through the file hierarchy to display parent folders.

Working with Column View

Column view displays the contents of a window in multiple columns. Clicking a folder in one column displays the contents of that folder in the column to its right. Clicking a document or application in a column displays a preview or information about the item in the column to its right.

To display a folder's contents:

Click the name of the folder you want to view the contents of.

The contents of the folder appear in the column to the right of the one you clicked in **A**.

To display a document preview:

Click the icon for the document you want to preview.

One of two things happens:

- If a preview for the document is available, it appears in the column to the right of the one you clicked in, along with additional information about the file **B**.

- If a preview is not available, the icon for the item appears in the column to the right of the one you clicked.

To move through the folder hierarchy:

To move through the folder hierarchy, scroll left or right in the window using the scroll bar (page 28) or gestures (page 28):

- Scroll left to move backward and view parent folders **C**.

- Scroll right to move forward and view child folders.

To change column width:

1. Position the pointer on the divider between two columns or, if column scroll bars are displayed, on the handle at the bottom of the scroll bar between two columns.

   The pointer turns into a vertical line with two arrows **D** **E**.

2. Press the button down and drag:

   ▸ To make the column wider, drag to the right **F**.

   ▸ To make the column narrower, drag to the left.

3. When the column is the desired size, release the button.

To view more or fewer columns:

Change the width of the window (page 26):

   ▸ To show more columns, make the window wider **G**.

   ▸ To show fewer columns, make the window narrower.

D Position the pointer anywhere on a column border if scroll bars are not displayed...

E ...or on the column width handle at the bottom of the column if scroll bars are displayed.

F When you drag a border to the right, the column to the left of the border gets wider.

G You can view more columns by making the window wider.

Scroll bar scroller

A You can drag the scroll bar in the Cover Flow pane to flip through icons and previews.

B You can also flip through items in Cover Flow if scroll bars are not displayed.

Working with Cover Flow

Cover Flow splits the window into two panes:

- The Cover Flow pane at the top of the window displays each item in the window as an icon or a preview of its first page.

- The item list pane at the bottom of the window displays a sortable list of the items in the window.

When you select an item in the item list, its icon or preview appears in the Cover Flow pane.

You can use either pane to flip through the contents of a window to see item previews. This makes it possible to scroll through files to find one you're looking for, even if you don't know its name.

To flip through documents in Cover Flow:

Use one of the following techniques:

- If the scroll bar is displayed in the Cover Flow pane **A**, drag the scroller to the left or right to display different icons or previews.

- If you have a Multi-Touch device (page 13), use gestures to scroll icons and previews in the Cover Flow pane to the right or left. This works even if scroll bars are not displayed **B**.

- Click the icon or preview for an item in the Cover Flow pane.

- Select an item in the item list pane.

- Press the Up Arrow or Down Arrow key to display the previous or next item.

To change the size of the Cover Flow pane:

1. Position the pointer on the resize box beneath the scroll bar in the Cover Flow pane.

   The pointer turns into a hand.

2. Press the button and drag:

   - To make the Cover Flow pane smaller, drag up.

   - To make the Cover Flow pane larger, drag down .

   As you drag, the hand pointer seems to grasp the resize box **C** as the pane's bottom border moves.

3. When the pane is the desired size, release the button.

TIP The larger the Cover Flow pane is, the larger the icons and previews within it are **C**.

C Drag the resize handle down to make the Cover Flow pane larger, thus increasing the size of the icons and previews within it.

A In this example, the Documents folder is displayed in icon view and arranged by kind of file.

B Here's the Documents folder again, displayed in list view and arranged by date modified.

Arranging Window Contents

In addition to moving icons and sorting lists, you can also use menu commands to arrange window icons by specific fields of information, such as kind, size, or date. Items are then grouped in the window by the arrange field you chose **A****B****C****D**.

You can arrange a window's contents by nine different fields of information:

- **Name** (Control-Command-1) arranges items alphabetically by name.

- **Kind** **A** (Control-Command-2) arranges items alphabetically by the kind of file.

- **Application** arranges items alphabetically by the application that will open them.

continues on next page

Arranging vs. Sorting:

Although both the arranging and sorting feature put window icons in a specific order—usually the same order—there is a difference.

- *Arranging* groups items by the Arrange By option you specify. Within each group, items can also be sorted by another field. So, for example, you can arrange (and group) items by kind and, within each group, sort by name **A**.

- *Sorting* simply sorts items by the column or sort option you specify. There's no grouping. Sorting is most often done in list or Cover Flow view by clicking a column heading (page 480), but you can also sort a window's contents by choosing a command from the Sort By submenu under the View menu.

- **Date Last Opened** (Control-Command-3) arranges items in reverse chronological order by the date they were last opened.

- **Date Added** (Control-Command-4) arranges items in reverse chronological order by the date they were added.

- **Date Modified** (Control-Command-5) arranges items in reverse chronological order by the date they were last modified.

- **Date Created** arranges items in reverse chronological order by the date they were created.

- **Size** (Control-Command-6) arranges items in reverse size order. Folders have a size of 0 for this option unless you have set the window to calculate folder sizes (page 480).

- **Label** (Control-Command-7) arranges items by color-coded label (if applied; page 80).

- **None** (Control-Command-0) removes any applied arrangement option.

As shown on these pages, the Arrange feature works in all window views.

C The same Documents folder, this time in column view arranged by size.

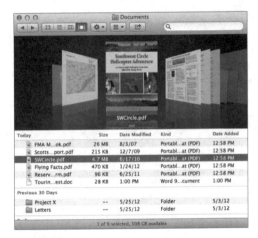

D In this example, the Documents folder is displayed in Cover Flow view and arranged by date added.

E The Arrange By submenu under the View menu.

F The Arrange menu on the toolbar.

To arrange window contents:

1. Activate the window you want to arrange.

2. Use one of the following techniques:

   ▸ Choose a command from the Arrange By submenu under the View menu **E**.

   ▸ Choose a command from the Arrange pop-up menu on the window's toolbar **F**.

   ▸ Press the appropriate keyboard shortcut (page 18).

   The icons are grouped in the window based on the Arrange By option you chose.

To remove arrangement settings from a window:

1. Activate the window you want to remove arrangement settings from.

2. Do one of the following:

   ▸ Choose View > Arrange By > None **E**.

   ▸ Choose None from the Arrange pop-up menu on the window's toolbar **F**.

   ▸ Press Control-Command-0 (zero).

To sort and arrange a window's contents:

1. Activate the window you want to sort and arrange.

2. Follow the instructions on page 65 to remove any arrangement settings applied to the window.

3. Hold down the Option key and choose an option from the Sort By submenu under the View menu .

   The items are sorted in the order you specified.

4. Follow the instructions on page 65 to apply an arrangement option to the window.

   The items are grouped by the arrangement option and, if possible, sorted within each group by the sort option you chose in step 3.

TIP This doesn't always work. It depends on which arrangement option is selected in step 4 and whether it allows sorting. For example, you can arrange by kind and, within each group, sort by name Ⓐ because the kind option has distinct groups and no sorting within each group. But you cannot arrange by size and then sort by another field because within each size group, OS X sorts by size Ⓒ.

TIP You can also sort a window's contents by pressing one of the Sort By shortcut keys Ⓖ.

TIP In icon view, you must disable the window's sort option by choosing None from the Sort By submenu Ⓖ to be able to move icons out of their sorted positions.

Ⓖ Holding down the Option key turns the Arrange By submenu into a Sort By submenu.

5

Getting Help

OS X offers two basic ways to get additional information and answers to questions as you work with your computer:

- **Help Tags** identify screen items as you point to them. This help feature is supported by many (but not all) applications.

- **Help Center** provides information about using OS X and its applications. This feature is accessible through commands on the Help menu. A great source of information, it is searchable and includes clickable links to content stored both on your Mac and online.

This chapter explains how to get help with OS X and applications when you need it. It also provides some tips for getting more information about your Mac, finding help, and troubleshooting problems.

In This Chapter:

Help Tags

Help Tags identify screen elements that you point to by providing information in small yellow boxes **Ⓐ****Ⓑ****Ⓒ**.

Help Tags are especially useful when first using a new application. Pointing at various interface elements and reading Help Tags is a great way to start learning about how an application works.

TIP Not all applications support the Help Tags feature. In addition, some applications have their own implementation of a similar feature that may work or look differently.

To use Help Tags:

Point to an item for which you want more information.

If a Help Tag is available for the item, it appears after a moment **Ⓐ****Ⓑ****Ⓒ**.

TIP Sometimes—but not very often—you can see an additional Help Tag if you press the Command key while a Help Tag is displayed.

Ⓐ A Help Tag in a Finder window,...

Ⓑ ...in a TextEdit window,...

Ⓒ ...and in a System Preferences pane window.

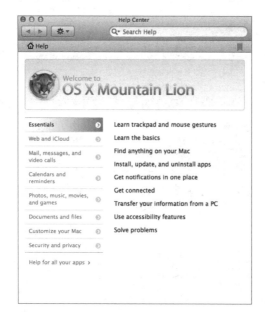

A The main Help Center window offers a table of contents with commonly used features and help topics.

Help Center

Help Center uses OS X's Help Viewer to display information about OS X or a specific application. It includes several features that enable you to find information—and use it—quickly:

- **Main Help Center window** provides a clickable table of contents for commonly used features and help topics **A**.

- **Search feature** enables you to search for topics containing specific words or phrases.

- **Related Topics links** enable you to move from one topic to a related topic.

- **Application links** enable you to open an application referenced by a help topic.

- **Online information links** enable you to get the latest information from Apple's website.

Help Center works for most Apple applications, as well as some OS X applications created by other software developers. It offers a standard interface for browsing, searching, and using help topics.

This section introduces you to Help Center and provides basic instruction for finding help when you need it. You can explore Help Center on your own to learn more about interface and features.

TIP If you are connected to the Internet when you access Help Center, the most up-to-date help information automatically appears, downloaded from Apple's servers on the Internet.

To open Help Center:

Do one of the following:

- In the Finder, choose Help > Help Center **B**.

- In an application, choose Help > *Application Name* Help **C**.

- In a window or dialog, click a Help button **D**.

The Help Center window appears **A** **E** **F**.

TIP You can only have one Help Center window open at a time. If the Help Center window is open for one application and you choose the Help command for another application, the second application's Help opens in the same window.

TIP If the application does not support Help Center but has a Help option on the Help menu, that application's onscreen help will open in its own window, which may not look or work like Help Center. For example, help for Microsoft Office applications opens it its own Help window.

E Opening the Help Center from within an application displays the main Help Center screen for that application.

B In the Finder, choose Help Center from the Help menu.

C In an application, the Help command starts with the name of the application.

Help button

D Some windows include a Help button.

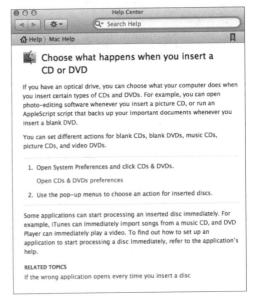

F Clicking a Help button in a window displays the appropriate help topic for that window.

G Help Center displays groups of icons for applications that support the Help Center interface.

H Clicking the Show all link expands the group to show all applications within it.

To open help for another application from within Help Center:

1. Open the main Help Center window **A**.

2. Click the Help for all your apps link at the bottom of the window.

   A screen with groups of application icons appears **G**.

3. If necessary, click the Show all link in the top of an icon group to expand the list and display all of the applications in that group **H**.

4. Click the icon for the application you want to open help for.

   The application's main Help Center screen appears **E**.

TIP This technique makes it possible for you to open an application's help without opening the application itself.

TIP An application may not be listed in Help Center until you've used that application or have accessed its Help window at least once.

TIP Onscreen help for applications that do not use the OS X Help Center interface is not accessible through this feature.

To browse help:

1. Click a link or button in a Help Center window.

   The window's contents change to view information related to the item you clicked **I**.

2. Continue clicking links or buttons to view related information **J**.

TIP Links in Help Center windows normally appear in blue type.

TIP You can backtrack through topics you have viewed by clicking the back button in the toolbar or by clicking one of the buttons in the Help Center path bar **I**.

TIP Clicking the bookmark button at the right end of the path bar **I** creates a bookmark that makes it easy to return to that topic later.

TIP To change the size of the text in Help Center's window, choose Make Text Smaller or Make Text Bigger from the Action pop-up menu in the Help Center toolbar **K**.

TIP To print a help topic, choose Print from the Action pop-up menu in the Help Center toolbar **K**. (Learn more about printing in Chapter 24.)

Path bar   *Bookmark button*

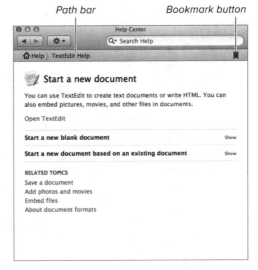

I Clicking the "Start a TextEdit Document" link in the main TextEdit Help Center window **E** displays this screen.

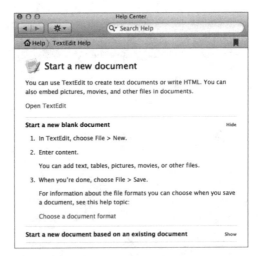

J Clicking the first Show link in the Start a TextEdit document help topic **I** expands the topic to provide detailed help information.

K The Action pop-up menu in the Help Center window.

L Help Center immediately matches what you type in the Help box.

M Clicking the Use an Apple wireless trackpad option on the Help menu **L** or in search results **N** displays this help topic.

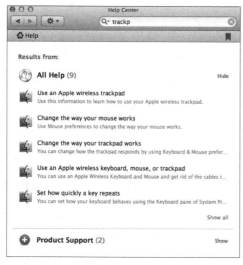

N A Help Center search results window.

To search help from the Help menu:

1. Click to display the Help menu.

2. In the search box, begin typing what you want to find help for.

   Help Center immediately begins listing help topics that match what you've typed so far **L**. You can continue typing, if necessary, to narrow down the search.

3. When you see the help topic you want on the menu, click it.

   Help Center displays the help topic you chose **M**.

TIP Clicking Show All Help Topics in the Help menu's search results **L** displays the Help Center window with search results displayed **N**.

To search help from the Help Center window:

1. Display any Help Center window.

2. In the search box on the toolbar, type what you want to find help for.

3. Press Return.

   A search results window with links to help topics appears **N**.

4. Click a link for the topic you want.

   Help Center displays the help topic you clicked **M**.

TIP In step 2, as you type, OS X will display a menu of recent search results that match what you're typing. You can click one of these to go directly to a previous search.

TIP Search results **N** can include help topics that reside on your computer as well as Support Articles that your Mac can retrieve from Apple's Product Support site if you have an Internet connection.

Help & Troubleshooting Advice

Here's some advice for learning more about your computer, getting help, and troubleshooting problems.

- **Join a Macintosh user group.** Joining a user group and attending meetings is probably the most cost-effective way to learn about your computer and get help. You can find a users' group near you by consulting the Apple User Group website, **www.apple.com/usergroups/**.

- **Attend free seminars at your local Apple Store.** You can learn more about Apple Stores and see a calendar of upcoming events at a store near you at **www.apple.com/retail/**.

- **Visit Apple's Support website.** You can find a wealth of information about your computer online. Start at **www.apple.com/support/** 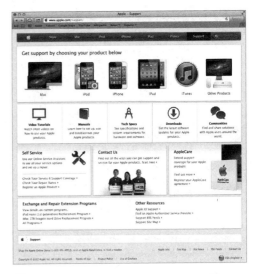 and search for the information you need.

- **Visit websites that offer troubleshooting information.** MacFixIt (**reviews.cnet.com/macfixit/**), The Unofficial Apple Weblog (**www.tuaw.com**), and OS X Hints (**hints.macworld.com**) are three excellent resources.

- **Visit the websites for the companies that develop the applications you use most.** A regular visit to these sites can keep you informed about updates and upgrades that can keep your software running smoothly. These sites can also provide technical support for problems you encounter while using the software. Learn the URLs for these sites by consulting the documentation that came with the software.

(A) Apple's support website includes a wealth of information about all Apple products—both hardware and software.

- **Read Macintosh magazines.** Several magazines, each geared toward a different level of user, can help you learn about your computer: *Macworld* (**www.macworld.com**) and *Mac|Life* (**www.maclife.com**) are two good ones. Avoid PC-centric magazines; the majority of the information they provide will not apply to your Macintosh.

- **Google the problem.** That seems like a common-sense approach to finding a solution for a problem, but it's surprising how few people do this. Enter a search phrase at **www.google.com** that describes the problem and you should come up with some search results to help guide you.

II

Managing Files

In This Part

Advanced Finder Techniques

In addition to the basic Finder and file management techniques covered in Chapters 2 through 4, OS X offers more advanced techniques you can use to work with files:

- Use spring-loaded folders to access folders while copying or moving items.
- Apply color-coded labels to Finder items.
- Use aliases to make frequently used files easier to access without moving them.
- Quickly reopen recently used items.
- Use Quick Look to view the contents of a file or folder without opening it.
- Use the Info window to learn more about an item or set options for it.
- Compress files and folders to save disk space or minimize data transfer time.
- Undo actions you performed while working with the Finder.

This chapter covers all of these techniques.

In This Chapter:

Spring-Loaded Folders

The spring-loaded folders feature lets you move or copy items into folders deep within the file structure of a disk—without manually opening a single folder. Instead, you simply drag icons onto folders and wait as they're automatically opened in the same window. When you drop the icon into the location you want, the item moves.

Here are a few additional things to keep in mind:

- To use spring-loaded folders, it must be enabled in Finder preferences (page 465). This feature is normally turned on by default.

- Using spring-loaded folders requires a steady hand, good mouse or trackpad skills, and knowledge of the location of folders on your disk.

- To use spring-loaded folders to move or copy more than one item at a time, select the items first, and then drag any one of them.

- The spring-loaded folders feature is sometimes referred to as *spring-open folders*.

TIP You can use spring-loaded folder techniques to work with folder icons (or stacks; page 250) on the Dock. So, for example, you can drag a PDF file icon from a Finder window onto the Applications stack to open the stack's window and then drop the file icon onto a compatible application to open it with that application.

A Drag an icon onto a folder and wait...

B ...until the folder opens in the same window.

C Continue to drag the icon onto a folder in that window and wait...

D ...until that folder opens in the same window.

E When you drop the icon into a window, the item moves there.

To move an item using spring-loaded folders:

1. Drag the item you want to move onto the folder you want to move it to **A**, but do not release the button. After a moment, the folder blinks and opens **B** in the same window.

2. Without releasing the button, repeat step 1. The destination folder becomes selected **C**, then blinks and opens **D**. Do this until you reach the final destination.

3. Release the button to place the item into the destination window **E**.

TIP In steps 1 and 2, to open a folder immediately, press the spacebar while dragging an item onto it.

TIP If you open the wrong folder and want to start over, without releasing the button, move the icon away from the window. The folders you opened close, returning you to the original window.

To copy an item using spring-loaded folders:

Hold down the Option key while following the above steps.

TIP If the destination folder is on another disk, it is not necessary to hold down the Option key to copy items; they're automatically copied.

Labels

OS X's Labels feature enables you to assign color-coded labels to Finder icons. You can then sort a window's contents by label or search for items based on the assigned label.

With a little imagination, labels can be a useful file management tool. For example, when I write a book and it goes through the editing process, I use labels to indicate each chapter's status. Yellow means it's a first draft, orange means it's a second draft, and green means it's final. This color-coding makes it possible for me to see a project's status just by looking inside a folder containing its files. (Imagine how good I feel when all of a book's chapter folders are green!)

TIP To sort a window's contents by label, you need to either use the **Sort By** submenu under the view menu (page 66) or, in list view, display the Labels column (page 480).

TIP You can use Finder Preferences to change the name associated with a label or its color (page 466).

Ⓐ Select the icon you want to apply a label to.

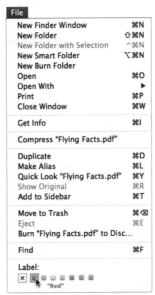

Ⓑ Choose a label color from the bottom of the File menu.

In icon view, the color you chose is applied to the icon's name.

In list view, the label color is applied to the entire line for the item.

Choosing the X under Label on the File menu removes the label from selected icons.

To assign a label to an item:

1. In a Finder window, select the icon(s) you want to apply a label to **Ⓐ**.

2. From the File menu, choose the color of the label you want to apply **Ⓑ**.

   In icon view, the name of the icon is enclosed in an oval in the color you chose **Ⓒ**; in other views, the item's entire line turns the color you chose **Ⓓ**.

TIP You can also assign a label to an item in its Info window (page 88).

TIP You use the same technique to change the label assigned to an item.

To remove a label from an item:

1. In a Finder window, select the icon you want to remove a label from.

2. From the File menu, choose the X beneath Label **Ⓔ**.

   The label is removed.

TIP If multiple icons are selected in step 1 and different labels are applied to them, all applied labels appear selected at the bottom of the File menu. Clicking the X removes them all.

Aliases

An *alias* is a pointer to an item. You can make an alias of an item and place it anywhere on your computer. Then, when you need to open the item, just open its alias.

You can move, copy, rename, open, and delete an alias just like any other file. By putting aliases of frequently used items together where you can quickly access them—such as on your desktop or in a stacks folder (page 250) in the Dock—you make the items more accessible without actually moving them.

It's important to remember that an alias is not a copy of the item—it's a pointer. If you delete the original item, the alias will not open.

Here are a few additional things to keep in mind about aliases:

- The icon for an alias looks very much like the icon for the original item but includes a tiny arrow in the bottom-left corner.

- You can name an alias anything you like, as long as you follow OS X file naming guidelines (page 43). An alias's name does not need to include the word *alias*.

- The sidebar (page 31), Dock (page 34), and recent items (page 85) features all work with aliases.

Ⓐ Select an icon you want to make an alias for.

Ⓑ Choose Make Alias from the File menu.

C The alias appears with the original item.

D Choose Show Original from the File menu.

To create an alias:

1. Select the item you want to make an alias for **A**.

2. Choose File > Make Alias **B**, or press Command-L.

   The alias appears right beneath the original item **C**.

3. While the alias file's name is selected **C**, you can rename it. Just type in a new name and press Return.

4. Move the alias icon as desired to another location on disk.

TIP You can also create an alias by holding down the Command and Option keys while dragging an item's icon to a new location on disk. The alias appears in the destination.

To find an alias's original file:

1. Select the alias's icon.

2. Choose File > Show Original **D**, or press Command-R.

   A window for the folder in which the original resides opens with the original item selected.

TIP If the original item cannot be found, OS X displays a dialog telling you so **E**. You can learn how to fix a broken alias on the next page.

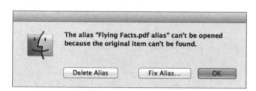

E If the original for an alias can't be found, a dialog like this appears when you look for its original or attempt to open it.

To fix a broken alias:

1. Select the alias's icon.

2. Do one of the following:

   ▸ Choose File > Show Original , or press Command-R.

   ▸ Open the alias icon.

   A dialog appears if the original can't be found ⓔ.

3. Click Fix Alias.

4. Use the Select New Original dialog that appears ⓕ to locate and select the item that you want to use as the original for the alias.

5. Click Open.

   The item you selected is assigned to the alias.

TIP The Select New Original dialog is similar to a standard Open dialog (page 158).

TIP If you would prefer to delete a broken alias instead of fixing it, click Delete Alias in the dialog that appears when you try to open it ⓔ.

TIP If an alias is not broken but you want to reassign it to a new original anyway, you can click the Select New Original button in its Info window (page 88).

ⓕ Use this dialog to select a new original item for an alias.

A Mac OS automatically tracks recent applications, documents, servers, ...

B ...and folders.

Recent Items

OS X automatically tracks the things you open. It creates submenus **A** **B** of the most recently opened items in four categories—applications, documents, servers, and folders—making it quick to open them again.

TIP You can specify how many recent items OS X tracks in the Recent Items submenu by setting options in the General preferences pane (page 494).

To open recent items:

Do one of the following:

- To open a recently used application, document, or server, choose its name from the Recent Items submenu under the Apple menu **A**.

- To open a recently used folder, choose its name from the Recent Folders submenu under the Go menu **B**.

TIP Recent Items works with aliases (page 82); OS X automatically creates an alias for each item you open and stores it in a hidden folder inside your Home folder.

To clear the Recent Items or Recent Folders submenu:

Choose Apple > Recent Items > Clear Menu **A** or choose Go > Recent Folders > Clear Menu **B**.

TIP Clearing the Recent Items or Recent Folders submenu does not delete any items.

Quick Look

Quick Look makes it possible to see what's in a file without actually opening it. Instead, Quick Look shows a preview of the item within a resizable window **A B C D**.

> **TIP** Quick Look is similar to enhanced icon view (page 21).

To view a file with Quick Look:

1. In a Finder window, select the item you want to view with Quick Look.

2. Choose File > Quick Look "*file name*" **E** or press Command-Y.

   A window displaying the item's contents **A B C** or icon **D** appears.

> **TIP** If you use Quick Look to view a multi-page document, you can scroll through the document or click thumbnail images **B** to view its pages.

> **TIP** If you use Quick Look to view a movie file, the movie begins playing immediately.

> **TIP** You can open an item from within Quick Look by clicking the Open button in the upper-right corner of the window **A B C D**.

> **TIP** OS X's new Share menu appears in the upper-right corner of the window **F**. Use it to share the item, as discussed on page 149.

To browse files with Quick Look:

1. Open a Finder window for the folder you want to browse.

2. Choose File > Quick Look "*file name*" **E** or press Command-Y to open the Quick Look window.

3. Select the items you want to view.

   Each time a different item is selected, the Quick Look window changes to display its contents **A B C** or icon **D**.

A The Quick Look window for a Rich Text Format document created with TextEdit.

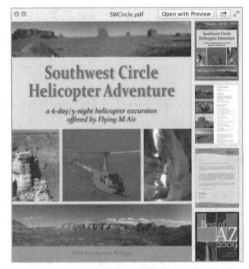

B The Quick Look window for a multi-page PDF.

C The Quick Look window for a JPEG image file.

D The Quick Look window for a folder.

E One way to open Quick Look is with a command on the File menu.

F The new Share pop-up menu makes it easy to share a document from the Quick Look window.

G An image file viewed in full screen mode in Quick Look.

Close
Exit Full Screen
Add to iPhoto

To switch to full screen view:

Click the Full Screen button at the top-right corner of a Quick Look window. The screen turns black and fills with the Quick View window **G**.

TIP Quick Look's full page view **G** is similar to OS X's Full-Screen Apps feature (page 142). The background is black and there are no menus.

To work with full screen view:

Click one of two or three buttons that may appear at the bottom of the screen **G**:

- **Add to iPhoto** adds a displayed image to your iPhoto library. This button only appears for image files if iPhoto is installed.

- **Play/Pause** plays or pauses a displayed movie. This button only appears for movie files.

- **Exit Full Screen** closes full screen view. You can also close full screen view by pressing the Esc key.

- **Close** closes Quick Look.

TIP If the button bar disappears, move the pointer to display it again.

TIP When viewing a movie with sound, a volume slider may also appear. You can use it to change the sound level for the movie as it plays.

To close the Quick Look window:

Use one of the following techniques:

- Click the Quick Look window's close button (a tiny X in the upper-left corner).

- Choose File > Close Quick Look, or press Command-Y.

The Info Window

You can learn more about an item by opening its Info window **ⓐⓑⓒⓓ**. Depending on the type of icon (disk, folder, application, document, alias, and so on), the General information in the Info window will provide some or all of the following:

- **Kind** or type of item.
- **Size** of item or contents (folders and files only).
- **Where** item is on disk (page 39).
- **Created** date and time.
- **Modified** date and time.
- **Version** number or **Copyright** date or both (disks and applications only).
- **Format** of item (disks only).
- **Capacity** of item (disks only).
- **Available** space on item (disks only).
- **Used** space on item (disks only).
- **Original** location on disk (aliases only; page 82).
- **Label** assigned to the item (page 80).
- **Shared folder** check box (disks and folders only) indicates whether the item is shared (page 418).
- **Open in 32-bit mode** check box (applications only) enables you to open the application in 32-bit mode rather than the default 64-bit mode.
- **Stationery pad** check box (documents only) to convert the file into a stationery format file, which is like a document template.
- **Locked** check box to prevent the file from being deleted or overwritten (folders and files only).

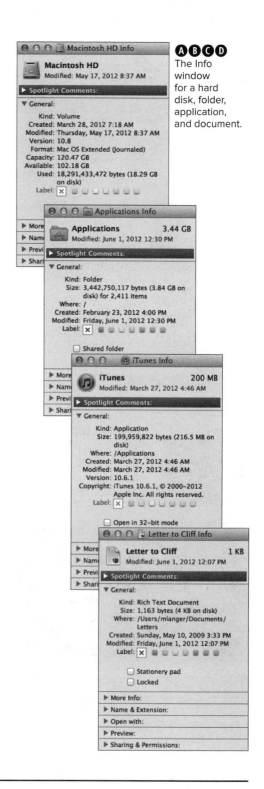

ⓐⓑⓒⓓ The Info window for a hard disk, folder, application, and document.

E Here's all the information you might find for a TextEdit document file.

In addition to the General category of information, the Info window offers additional categories **E**, depending on the type of item. You can click the disclosure triangle beside a category heading to display or hide the details for the category. Some of the categories include options that can be modified.

Some categories you might find in an Info window include:

- **Spotlight Comments** enable you to enter searchable comments or keywords for an item (page 90).

- **More Info** provides additional information about the file, including when the content was created and modified and when the item was last opened.

- **Name & Extension** displays an edit box you can use to change the file name (page 43) and its file name extension. A check box enables you to hide the extension in Finder windows.

- **Open with** (documents only) enables you to choose the application that should open the item and change the default application for all items of that type (page 139).

- **Preview** displays a preview for the item if one is available. Otherwise, it simply displays the item's icon.

- **Languages** (applications only; not shown in **C**) is a list of the languages built in to the application.

- **Sharing & Permissions** enables you to set file sharing permissions for the item (page 415).

TIP Changes you make in the Info window for an item are automatically saved.

To open the Info window:

1. Select the item you want to open the Info window for.

2. Choose File > Get Info **F**, or press Command-I.

   The Info window for that item appears **A** **B** **C** **D** **E**.

To enter Spotlight comments in the Info window:

1. Open the Info window for the item you want to enter comments for **A** **B** **C** **D** **E**.

2. If necessary, click the disclosure triangle beside Spotlight Comments near the top of the window. The window expands to show the Spotlight Comments box **E**.

3. Type your comments into the Spotlight Comments box **G**. They are automatically saved.

TIP You can use View Options to set a window's list view to display comments entered in the Info window (page 480).

To lock an application or document:

1. Open the Info window for the item you want to lock **A** **B** **C** **D** **E**.

2. Turn on the Locked check box.

TIP Locked items cannot be deleted or overwritten. They can, however, be moved.

F Choose Get Info from the File menu.

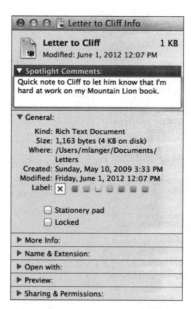

G You can type whatever you like into the Spotlight Comments box.

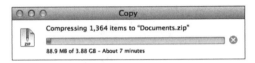

A Use the Compress command to compress one or more files into an archive file.

B This dialog may appear briefly as the selected item is compressed.

Documents   **Documents.zip**

C The compressed file appears in the same location as the original.

Compressing Files & Folders

OS X's file compression feature enables you to create compressed copies of items that are sometimes called *archived files* or *archives*. Compressed files take up less space on disk than regular files. You may find them useful for backing up files or for sending files to others over a network or via email.

The file compression feature uses ZIP format compression, which was originally developed as a DOS and Windows PC format. As a result, document archives created with this feature are fully compatible with Windows PCs.

To compress a file or folder:

1. Select the item you want to compress.

2. Choose File > Compress "*Item Name*" **A**.

3. Wait while your computer creates the archive. If it takes more than a few seconds, a Copy status dialog may appear **B**.

    When the process is finished, the archive file appears as a .zip file in the same location as the original file **C**.

TIP You can compress multiple items at once. Select the items, then choose File > Compress *n* Items (where *n* is the number of selected items). When the archive appears, it will be named Archive.zip.

To open a compressed file:

Double-click the compressed file. The file's contents are uncompressed and appear in the same window as the compressed file.

Undoing Finder Actions

The OS X Finder includes limited support for the Undo command, which can reverse the most recently completed action.

Say, for example, that you move a file from one folder to another folder. If you immediately change your mind, you can choose Edit > Undo Move of "*item name*" Ⓐ to put the file back where it was.

TIP Don't depend on the Undo command. Unfortunately, it isn't always available Ⓑ.

TIP The exact wording of the Undo command varies depending on the action and the item it was performed on. For example, the command shown in Ⓐ is Undo Move of "Letter to Cliff" because the last action was to move a document icon named Letter to Cliff.

TIP The Undo command is also available (and generally more reliable) in most OS X applications. You'll usually find it at the top of the Edit menu (page 164).

To undo an action:

Immediately after performing an action, choose Edit > Undo "*action description*" Ⓐ, or press Command-Z.

The action is reversed.

To redo an action:

Immediately after undoing an action, choose Edit > Redo "*action description*" Ⓑ, or press Shift-Command-Z.

The action is redone—as if you never used the Undo command.

TIP Think of the Redo command as the Undo-Undo command since it undoes the Undo command.

Ⓐ The Undo command enables you to undo the last action you performed.

Ⓑ In this example, I can redo the last thing I undid, but I can't undo anything.

Searching
for Files

OS X offers a number of search features you can use to find files or folders:

- Spotlight enables you to perform a search quickly, no matter what application is active. Search results appear in a Spotlight menu or in a search results window.

- A Finder window's Search field enables you to initiate a search based on file name or content from a Finder window. Search results appear within the window.

- The Find command takes Finder searching a step further by offering additional search options, including the ability to find files based on kind, dates, labels, and size.

- Smart folders make it possible to save your search queries. Repeating a query is as easy as opening a smart folder icon.

Once you have a list of found files, opening a file is as easy as double-clicking it.

This chapter takes a closer look at the search features in OS X.

In This Chapter:

The Spotlight Menu

The Spotlight menu on the right end of the menu bar makes Finder searching always available, no matter what application is active.

A Click the Spotlight icon on the far right end of the menu bar to display the Spotlight search box.

To use Spotlight, click the menu, enter a search word or phrase, and wait as Spotlight lists top search results. If you see the item you want on the menu, you can click it to open it. Otherwise, you can display all search results in a Finder window, choose the one you want, or begin a new search.

TIP The types of items found and the order in which they appear in search results depends on settings in the Spotlight preferences pane (page 514).

TIP Spotlight also works within certain OS X applications, such as System Preferences (page 490), as well as in standard Open (page 158) and Save (page 160) dialogs.

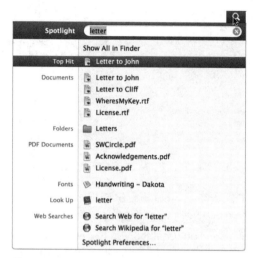

B As you enter a search word or phrase, Spotlight immediately lists matches, sorted by kind.

To find items with Spotlight:

1. Click the Spotlight icon on the right end of the menu bar or press Command-Space Bar.

   The Spotlight search field appears in a menu **A**.

2. Enter a search word or phrase in the search field.

   Spotlight immediately begins displaying matches for what you enter in a menu beneath the search field **B**.

C When you choose the Show All in Finder command from the Spotlight menu, it displays all search results in a Searching window.

To display all found items:

1. Follow the steps in the section titled "To find items with Spotlight" on the previous page to conduct a Spotlight search.

2. In the menu of search results **B**, click Show All in Finder.

   A Searching window full of search results appears **C**.

To open a found item:

Do one of the following:

- In the Spotlight menu of search results **B**, click the item you want to open.

- In the Searching window of found items **C**, double-click the item you want to open.

To perform a new search:

Do one of the following:

- Follow the instructions in the section titled "To find items with Spotlight" on the previous page. You may have to overwrite an existing search word or phrase with the new one.

- In the search box at the top of the Searching window **C**, enter a new search word or phrase.

TIP To quickly clear the contents of the search box, click the X button on its right side **B C**.

The Search Field

The Finder's Search field appears in the top-right corner of a Finder window's toolbar **A**. You can use it to initiate a search based on item name or contents. Simply enter a word or phrase in the field, and OS X displays a list of matches in the same window.

TIP A window's toolbar must be displayed (page 30) to use the Search field.

To find files with the Search field:

1. Click in the Search field of a Finder window to position the blinking insertion point there **A**.

2. Enter the word or phrase you want to search for.

   As soon as you begin typing, the window turns into a Searching window. OS X begins displaying results **B**.

3. When you finish typing, press Return.

   The search results for what you typed appear in the window **C**.

TIP Remember, this search feature searches by name or contents. If you're not sure of a file's name, search for some text you expect to find within it.

TIP To search based on file name only, before pressing Return in step 3, choose the Filename option in the menu beneath the search box **B**.

To return to the original window:

Click the back button on the toolbar.

The search box is cleared and the window that was open when you started the search reappears.

A The Search field appears in the toolbar on every Finder window.

B As you enter a search word, OS X immediately begins displaying search results.

C When you finish typing the word or phrase, the final search results appear. In this example, I searched for the word *white* and found 18 items that contain that word.

A The Find command displays the Searching window with some additional options.

B You can use the attributes pop-up menu to choose types of criteria to add.

C When you choose the Kind criteria, you can select from various types of items.

D Use this pop-up menu and the options with it to set the various date-related search criteria.

The Find Command

OS X's Find command also works with the Search field, but it automatically offers additional search options **A**:

- **Search locations** appear as buttons near the top of the window:
  - ▸ **This Mac**, which always appears, searches your entire computer.
  - ▸ "*Location name*" is the item that was selected or active when you chose the Find command.
  - ▸ **Shared** is any network volumes currently accessible to your computer.
- **Criteria filters** appear in rows above the search results area. You can set options with these filters to narrow down the search results. Use an attributes pop-up menu **B** to choose a search attribute and set up a filter:
  - ▸ **Kind** is the type of item to search for. Choose an option from the pop-up menu **C**.
  - ▸ **Last opened date**, **Last modified date**, or **Created date** are the date the item was last opened, last modified, or created. Use a pop-up menu **D** to set criteria options and set a date or date range. The options are the same for each attribute.
  - ▸ **Name** is the item's name. This tells Spotlight *not* to search the contents of an item to match text. If you choose this option, use a pop-up menu **E** and enter text to set criteria.
  - ▸ **Contents** is the contents of the item. This tells Spotlight *not* to search the name of the item to match text.
  - ▸ **Other** displays a dialog **F** that you can use to add additional search

continues on next page

attributes to the pop-up menu **B**. Turn on the check box beside each attribute you want to add.

You can add as many criteria filters as you like to fine-tune a search. OS X attempts to match *all* filters—thus, the more filters you add, the fewer search results will appear.

TIP To display criteria filters when using the Search field (page 96), click the Add (+) button near the top of the Searching window.

To find files with the Find command:

1. If necessary, activate the Finder.

2. To search a specific location on your computer, open a Finder window for that location.

3. Choose File > Find, or press Command-F.

   A Searching window appears **A**.

4. Enter a search word or phrase in the Search field.

5. Click a location button to choose one of the search locations.

6. Set up a criteria filter by choosing an option from the attribute pop-up menu **B** and setting related criteria options **G**.

7. To add additional criteria filters, click the Add (+) button at the right end of a criteria row. Then set options in the new row that appears **H**. Repeat this step to add as many filters as you need.

   Search results appear in the Searching window **G H** as you set search criteria.

TIP To remove a criteria filter, click the Remove (–) button at the right end of its row.

TIP Clicking the Save button near the top of the Searching window creates a smart folder (page 99).

E Use this pop-up menu to specify how a file name should match the criteria you enter.

F This dialog enables you to customize the Attributes pop-up menu **B**.

G In this example, I've entered a search word in the Search box and selected a search location.

H In this example, I've added two more criteria filters: Kind is PDF and Last opened date within last 3 days. This narrows down the search results.

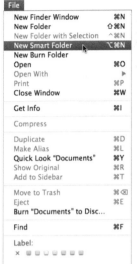

File

New Finder Window	⌘N
New Folder	⇧⌘N
New Folder with Selection	^⌘N
New Smart Folder	⌥⌘N
New Burn Folder	
Open	⌘O
Open With	▶
Print	⌘P
Close Window	⌘W
Get Info	⌘I
Compress	
Duplicate	⌘D
Make Alias	⌘L
Quick Look "Documents"	⌘Y
Show Original	⌘R
Add to Sidebar	⌘T
Move to Trash	⌘⌫
Eject	⌘E
Burn "Documents" to Disc...	
Find	⌘F
Label:	
× ⬜ ⬜ ⬜ ⬜ ⬜ ⬜	

A One way to create a smart folder is to choose New Smart Folder from the File menu.

B The New Smart Folder window looks just like the Searching window.

C In this example, I've searched my Mac for document files opened within the past 30 days.

Smart Folders

The smart folders feature takes the Find command one step further. It enables you to save search criteria as a special folder. Opening the folder automatically performs a search and displays matching items. The smart folder's contents always contain items that match search criteria, even if the files and folders on your computer change.

You can create a smart folder two ways:

- Use the New Smart Folder command under the Finder's File menu **A** to open a New Smart Folder window **B**, enter search criteria, and save the search.

- Click the Save button in the Searching window after performing a search you want to save, and save the search.

Either way, you'll create a smart folder with an interface that looks and works just like the Searching window that appears when you use the Search field (page 96) or Find command (page 97).

When you save a search, you can choose the location in which you want the smart folder saved. Although smart folders are normally saved in the Saved Searches folder in the invisible Library folder (page 42) in your Home folder (page 38), you can save a smart folder anywhere on disk. You can also toggle a check box to automatically place a smart folder in the sidebar when you create it.

TIP The All My Files item which appears under the Go menu and, by default, in the sidebar, is actually a smart folder with its criteria predefined by Apple.

To create a smart folder:

1. To create a smart folder that searches a specific location on your computer, open a Finder window for that location.

2. Choose File > New Smart Folder **Ⓐ**, or press Option-Command-N.

   A New Smart Folder window opens **Ⓑ**.

3. Follow steps 4 through 7 on page 98 to set up search criteria for the smart folder.

   The search results appear in the window **Ⓒ**.

4. Click the Save button near the top of the New Smart Folder window **Ⓒ**.

   The Save dialog (page 160) appears **Ⓓ** or **Ⓔ**.

5. Set options in the dialog:

   ▸ **Save As** is the name of the smart folder. Give it a name that describes what the folder will contain.

   ▸ **Where** is the location in which the smart folder will be saved. You can use the Where menu **Ⓓ** to choose a location or click the disclosure triangle beside the Save As box to expand the dialog **Ⓔ** and choose any location on disk.

   ▸ **Add To Sidebar** instructs OS X to add an alias of the folder to the sidebar **Ⓕ**.

6. Click the Save button.

   The name you gave the smart folder appears in the window's title bar **Ⓕ**, and the smart folder is saved for future use.

TIP If you create a smart folder by clicking the Save button in any Searching window, just follow steps 5 and 6 above.

Ⓓ The Save dialog might appear small, like this...

Ⓔ ...or expanded, like this.

Ⓕ When you save a smart folder, the name you gave it appears in its title bar when it's open. In this example, I've also added it to the sidebar, which is displayed here, too.

G A smart folder icon.

Recent Documents

H Choose Show Search Criteria from the Action pop-up menu in the window's toolbar.

I The search criteria reappears at the top of the window so you can modify it.

To open a smart folder:

Do one of the following:

- If the smart folder has been added to the sidebar, click its name in the sidebar **F**.

- If the smart folder has not been added to the sidebar, open its icon **G**.

  The contents of the smart folder appear in a window **F**.

To edit a smart folder:

1. Open the smart folder you want to edit **F**.

2. Choose Show Search Criteria from the Action pop-up menu in the window's toolbar **H**.

   The search criteria you used to create the smart folder appears at the top of the window **I**

3. Make changes as desired to the search criteria.

   The search results in the window change accordingly.

4. Click the Save button.

   The changes are saved to the smart folder's definition.

To delete a smart folder:

Drag the smart folder's icon **G** to the Trash (page 48).

TIP Deleting a smart folder does not delete the contents of the smart folder. It simply deletes the search criteria that displays those contents. The original items remain on disk.

Working with Search Results

No matter how you search for items, you will eventually wind up with a window full of found items . Because this window is very much like any other Finder window, you can:

- Change the window's view.
- Use menu commands on any selected item in the window.
- Open an item by simply double-clicking its icon.

Here are a two other things you can do with these windows.

TIP Consult Chapters 2, 3, and 4 for more information about using the Finder and working with windows.

To see where an item resides on disk:

In the search results window, select the item.

Its location on disk appears at the bottom of the window .

To open an item's parent folder:

1. In the search results window, select the item for which you want to open the parent folder.
2. Do one of the following:
   - ▶ In the directory path at the bottom of the window, double-click the folder listed to the left of the item name .
   - ▶ Choose File > Open Enclosing Folder , or press Command-R.

   The folder in which the item resides opens in a new window .

A Selecting one of your search results displays the path to that item in the path bar at the bottom of the window.

B Choose Open Enclosing Folder from the File menu to open a selected item's parent folder.

C The enclosing folder opens in a new window.

Storage Devices & Media

As you work with your Mac, humming away under its hood is some kind of storage device—most often a hard disk—that's giving you access to the applications, documents, and other files you and your computer need to get work done. Similarly, you might use other internal and external storage devices to open, save, organize, or archive your files.

This chapter explores some of the storage device that you might use with your Mac and OS X and explains how you can write data to recordable CDs and DVDs.

Storage Devices & Media

A Macintosh computer can read data from, or write data to, a wide range of storage devices and media, including:

- **Hard drive (HD)**—high capacity magnetic media made of spinning disks with movable read/write heads.

- **Solid state drive (SSD)**—similar to hard drives; high capacity storage media that uses semiconductors for storage.

- **Optical drives**—for recording data on high capacity, removable optical media such as CDs and DVDs.

- **SD cards**—small media cards supported by many digital cameras; some Mac models have SD card slots.

- **Flash, or "thumb," drives**—small USB devices commonly used to move files from one computer to another.

- **RAID devices**—extremely high capacity magnetic storage devices, normally used for servers or backup.

- Other legacy magnetic media, including floppy disks, or diskettes, and Zip disks.

Storage devices can be:

- **Internal**—inside your computer and not easily removed. All Macs have an internal HD or SSD. Most Macs also have an internal optical drive; the drive is internal and the disc is removable.

- **External**—attached to your computer by a cable. Most modern Mac models support FireWire, Thunderbolt, and USB connections for external devices.

To use storage media, it must be:

- **Mounted**—inserted, attached, or otherwise accessible to your computer.

- **Formatted** or **initialized**—specially prepared for use with your computer.

Storage media capacity is specified in terms of *bytes*, *kilobytes*, *megabytes*, *gigabytes*, and *terabytes* (**Table 8.1**). Terms for larger capacities do exist, but these are the only ones you need to know.

> **TIP** Don't confuse storage media with memory. The term *memory* usually refers to the amount of *RAM*, or *random access memory*, in your computer, not disk space. RAM is temporary high-speed data storage space used by apps that is erased when you shut down.

> **TIP** If a disk is write-protected or locked, files cannot be saved or copied to it. A pencil with a line through it appears in the status bar (page 33) of write-protected or locked disks **A**.

TABLE 8.1 Terminology for Storage Media Capacity

Term	Abbreviation	Size
byte	byte	1 character
kilobyte	KB	1,024 bytes
megabyte	MB	1,024 KB
gigabyte	GB	1,024 MB
terabyte	TB	1,024 GB

A A write-protected icon appears in the status bar for CD or DVD discs and other write-protected media.

A Here's a desktop and computer folder window with an internal hard disk, USB "thumb drive," network volume, and DVD disc inserted. The Network and Remote Disc icons offer access to networked disks that are not mounted.

Go	
Back	⌘[
Forward	⌘]
Enclosing Folder	⌘↑
🖥 All My Files	⇧⌘F
📄 Documents	⇧⌘O
🖥 Desktop	⇧⌘D
⬇ Downloads	⌥⌘L
🏠 Home	⇧⌘H
💻 Computer	⇧⌘C
📡 AirDrop	⇧⌘R
🌐 Network	⇧⌘K
📂 Applications	⇧⌘A
✂ Utilities	⇧⌘U
Recent Folders	▶
Go to Folder...	⇧⌘G
Connect to Server...	⌘K

B You can use the Go menu to open the top-level computer folder or connect to a server.

Mounting Disks

Mounting a disk makes it available for your computer to use. When a disk is mounted, your computer "sees" it and can access the information it contains. You must mount a disk to use it.

Mounted disks appear in the top-level window for your computer **A**. To display this window, choose Go > Computer **B** or press Shift-Command-C (page 42).

Mounted disks may also appear on the desktop **A**, depending on how Finder preferences (page 465) are set for the display of items on the desktop.

TIP To learn how to mount disks that are not specifically covered in this book, consult the documentation that came with the disk drive.

TIP You mount a network volume by using the Connect to Server command under the Go menu **B** or by browsing the network and opening the disk you want to mount. You can learn more in Chapter 26.

To mount a CD or DVD disc on a computer with a slot-loading optical drive:

Insert the CD or DVD disc into the CD/DVD drive slot.

After a moment, the disc icon appears in the top-level computer window **A**.

CAUTION Do not insert a mini CD or DVD disk into a slot-loading CD or DVD drive. Most Mac CD and DVD slot-loading drives do not support mini discs; inserting one can damage the drive mechanism.

To mount a CD or DVD disc on a computer with a tray-loading optical drive:

1. Press the Media Eject key on the keyboard to open the CD or DVD disc tray.

2. Place the CD or DVD disc in the tray or caddy, label side up.

3. Push the tray or caddy into the drive.

   After a moment, the disc icon appears in the top-level computer window **Ⓐ**.

TIP Although a Media Eject key appears on most Apple keyboards, it may not appear on a third-party keyboard.

To mount an external hard disk:

1. If necessary, connect the hard drive's power cord and plug it into a power outlet.

2. Connect the drive's FireWire, USB, or Thunderbolt cable to the drive and your computer.

3. If necessary, turn on the drive's power switch.

After a moment, the drive's hard disk icon should appear in the top-level computer window **Ⓐ**.

TIP Some external hard disk drives can draw their power from your computer via the connection interface cable. These drives do not require a power cord and do not have a power switch; you can skip steps 1 and 3.

TIP When you connect an external hard drive for the first time, a dialog may ask if you want to use the disk with Time Machine (page 115). If you don't, click Don't Use.

A Use the File menu's Eject command.

B An eject button appears on the sidebar beside each item that can be unmounted.

C When you drag a disk icon to the Trash, the Trash icon changes to an eject icon.

Unmounting & Ejecting Disks

When you *unmount* a disk, you make it unavailable for further use by the computer—until you mount it again. The disk disappears from the top-level computer window. Once a disk is unmounted, it can safely be ejected or removed.

There are several ways to unmount a disk and they work the same way, no matter what kind of disk is mounted. How the disk is removed, however, depends on the type of disk it is.

To unmount a hard disk:

Use one of the following techniques:

- Select the disk's icon and choose File > Eject "*Disc Name*" **A**, or press Command-E.

- Click the eject button to the right of the disc name in the sidebar **B**.

- Drag the disc's icon to the Trash. As you drag, the Trash icon turns into a rectangle with a triangle on top **C**. When the pointer moves over the Trash icon, release the button.

The disk's icon disappears from the computer window, desktop, and sidebar.

TIP You cannot unmount the startup disk.

To disconnect a hard disk:

1. Unmount the hard disk.

2. Disconnect the cable.

CAUTION Disconnecting a hard disk before it has been unmounted can cause data loss. Be sure to *always* unmount a disk before disconnecting it.

To unmount & eject an optical disc:

Use one of the following techniques:

- Select the disc's icon and choose File > Eject "*Disc Name*" **A**, or press Command-E.

- Click the eject button to the right of the disc name in the sidebar **B**.

- Drag the disc's icon to the Trash. As you drag, the Trash icon turns into a rectangle with a triangle on top **C**. When the pointer moves over the Trash icon, release the button.

- Press and hold the Media Eject key on the keyboard until the disc (or disc tray) slides out.

The disc's icon disappears from the computer window, desktop, and sidebar. Remove the disc from the drive slot or tray.

TIP Although a Media Eject key appears on most Apple keyboards, it may not appear on a third-party keyboard.

Burning CDs & DVDs

If your Macintosh includes a SuperDrive or Combo drive or you have a MacBook Air SuperDrive, you can write, or burn, files onto blank optical media. This is a good way to archive important files that you don't need on your computer's hard disk and to share files with other computer users.

The type of drive your computer has determines the type of media it can write to:

- A Combo drive can write to CD-R and CD-RW discs.

- A SuperDrive may be able to write to CD-R, CD-RW, DVD-R, DVD-W, DVD-RW, DVD+R, and DVD+RW discs.

The Finder offers three ways to burn a CD or DVD:

- Select a disc or folder and use the Burn command to burn its contents to a CD or DVD.

- Create a burn folder, fill the folder with the files you want to include on the CD or DVD, and use the Burn Disc command to burn the disc.

- Insert a blank CD or DVD, name it, and then drag the icons for the files you want to include on it onto its icon. Then use the Burn Disc command to burn the CD or DVD.

On the following pages, I explain how to use all three of these techniques.

TIP Not all SuperDrives can write to DVD+RW discs. You can use System Information (page 388) to see what formats your optical drive supports.

TIP You can also burn CDs or DVDs from within iTunes and iDVD (Chapter 17) or other third-party utilities, such as Roxio Toast.

To burn an existing folder or disc to CD or DVD:

1. Select the folder or disc you want to copy to a CD or DVD.

2. Choose File > Burn "*Folder or disc name*" to Disc .

   A Burn Disc dialog appears **B**.

3. Insert a CD or DVD in your computer.

   You may need to press the Media Eject button to open the media tray and then press it again to slide the tray and disc back into the computer.

   Another dialog appears **C**.

4. Set options as desired:

   ▸ **Disc Name** is the name you want to give the disc.

   ▸ **Burn Speed** is the speed your computer will use to burn the disc.

5. Click Burn.

   A Burn status dialog **D** appears as the disc is burned. When the dialog disappears, an icon for the CD or DVD appears in the computer window and in the sidebar. The disc is ready to use.

A The File menu includes commands for creating burn folders and burning discs.

B The Burn Disc dialog instructs you to insert a disc with enough capacity for the folder or disc you want to copy to a CD or DVD.

C You can use a dialog like this to enter a name for the new disc and set a burn speed.

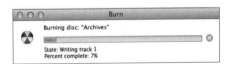

D A progress bar indicates the new disc is being prepared.

E An icon for the burn folder appears in the active window.

F The contents of a burn folder can include folders and aliases to files and folders.

Burn Folder: Keep or Delete?

When you're finished using a burn folder you can delete it or keep it:

- If you delete the burn folder, none of the original files are lost because the burn folder contains only aliases for original files.

- If you keep a burn folder, you can create new discs from it again and again in the future. Because the burn folder contains aliases rather than original files, the latest versions of the files will always be burned onto the disc.

To burn a CD or DVD from a burn folder:

1. Choose File > New Burn Folder **A**.

    A burnable folder icon named Burn Folder appears in the active window **E**.

2. While the folder name is selected, enter a new name for the folder and press Return.

    The folder's name changes.

3. Drag the files you want to include on the new CD or DVD to the burnable folder.

    You can create regular folders inside the burnable folder to organize the files you add to it **F**.

4. When you are finished adding files, do one of the following:

    ▸ Click the Burn button near the top of the folder's window **F**.

    ▸ Select the folder icon and choose File > Burn "*Folder name*" to Disc **A**.

    A Burn Disc dialog appears.

5. Follow steps 3 through 5 in the section titled "To burn an existing folder or disc to CD or DVD" on page 110.

TIP You can only create a burn folder in a window you have write permissions for.

TIP When you drag files to a burn folder, OS X creates aliases (page 82) to the original files. When it burns the disc, however, it copies the original files rather than the aliases to the disc.

TIP You might find a burn folder useful for periodically backing up important files. Fill a burn folder with the files you want to back up, and then burn a disc from that same burn folder every time you want to back up the files—OS X will automatically back up the latest versions of the files.

To burn files directly to a blank CD or DVD:

1. Insert a blank CD or DVD into your computer.

2. If a dialog appears , make sure Open Finder is chosen from the Action pop-up menu and click OK.

   An Untitled CD or Untitled DVD icon appears on the desktop and in the sidebar .

3. If desired, rename the icon.

   The icon name is the name that will be burned onto the disc.

4. Follow steps 3 and 4 in the section titled "To burn a CD or DVD from a burn folder" on page 111.

5. In the dialog that appears , set options as desired:

   ▸ **Disc Name** is the name you want to give the disc.

   ▸ **Burn Speed** is the speed your computer will use to burn the disc.

   ▸ **Save Burn Folder To** enables you to specify a name for a burn folder that will be created and saved to your computer.

6. Click Burn.

   A Burn status dialog **D** appears as the disc is burned. When the dialog disappears, the disc is ready to use.

TIP If you turn on the check box in step 5, the burn folder is saved to your desktop and a link to it appears in the sidebar. You can move the burn folder anywhere you like to save it on your computer. You can also remove it from the sidebar (page 486).

G A dialog like this appears when you insert a blank CD or DVD without being prompted to.

H The disc appears in the sidebar as a sort of burn folder.

I A dialog like this offers the usual options, along with the ability to save the disc contents as a burn folder.

Backup & Recovery Features

One of the most important things you can do to protect the applications and data on your computer's hard disk is to periodically back it up onto another device or media. OS X includes Time Machine, an application that can automate the backup process and make it easy to restore files that have been damaged or accidentally erased.

In the event that your computer's startup disk has serious problems, OS X has a feature that can really help: the recovery partition. It makes it possible for you to get a sick Mac started and troubleshoot its problems.

This chapter looks at both of these features and provides some tips for backing up your important data files.

Backup Basics

Backing up your computer refers to the process of making copies of important files onto some other storage device or media. This makes it possible to replace damaged files with the copies you've made in advance.

Everyone has his or her own strategy for creating and maintaining backups. Here are some things to consider when formulating yours:

- **Back up often.** The more often you back up your files, the more likely you are to have an up-to-date copy of a file if you need it. It follows that the more often a file changes, the more often it should be backed up.

- **Maintain multiple backups.** If the most recent backup copy of a file is also damaged, an older backup copy might not be. If you back up important data files to CD or DVD disc, keep as many backups as practical. Be sure to label the discs with the date so you know which one is most recent.

- **Keep important backups off-site.** If your computer is destroyed by flood or fire and your backups were stored with it, you've lost everything. By keeping a backup of your important files in a different location, you add an additional level of protection.

- **Consider backing up to "the cloud."** *Cloud computing* refers to the use of computing resources accessible on the Internet. Dropbox (**www.dropbox.com**) is an example of a free service that provides secure storage for files on a remote server.

- **Automate backups whenever possible.** You're far more likely to stick to a backup strategy if it's mostly or entirely automated. Time Machine (page 115) makes this very easy to do, but there are other third-party backup solutions, including SuperDuper (**www.shirtpocket.com/SuperDuper/**) and Carbon Copy Cloner (**www.bombich.com**).

- **Consider using iCloud to sync important data.** If you're an iCloud user, you can use its sync feature to automatically back up your calendar, contacts, mail accounts, and other data. Although this is intended primarily for syncing this data between two or more computers or devices, it can also be used as a simple, automated backup.

It's important to note that backup files can be maintained in two formats:

- Backup software, such as that used by Time Machine, creates a single backup file and multiple incremental backup files. To restore from a single backup file like this, you need the software that created the file.

- Finder copies, whether onto external hard disks or burned onto CDs or DVDs, maintain each file as a separate file—just as it is in the Finder. This makes it easy to restore an individual file—if that's all you need—even on another computer.

TIP I use a combination of backup techniques that include Time Machine, Finder backups to hard disk and DVD disk, off-site backups to another location, and backups to both iDisk and Dropbox. Of course, not *all* of my files are backed up this way; only Time Machine backs it all up. The other files are backed up based on their importance and use.

Ⓐ You turn on Time Machine in the Time Machine preferences pane.

Time Machine

Time Machine is an application that makes it easy to protect your computer's contents from loss due to accidental deletion or disk damage. It does this by keeping an up-to-date copy of everything on your Mac.

Unlike other backup software, Time Machine also remembers your system configuration on any given day, making it possible to go back in time (so to speak) to recover any of your files.

Time Machine is preconfigured to keep the following backups:

- Hourly backups for the past 24 hours.

- Daily backups for the past month.

- Weekly backups for all previous months until your backup disk is full.

Once you've created a Time Machine backup, you can restore individual files or restore your entire hard disk.

Time machine consists of two components:

- The Time Machine preferences pane **Ⓐ** (page 588) enables you to configure Time Machine so it works the way you want it to.

- The Time Machine application gives you access to Time Machine's backed up data.

In this part of the chapter, I explain how to enable and use Time Machine.

TIP If the backup disk is not available when Time Machine needs to back up, it postpones the backup until the disk is available.

TIP You can configure Time Machine to exclude certain folders from backups. This minimizes the amount of disk space needed and avoids backing up files you may not need backed up. Be sure to consult the information on page 588 about the Time Machine preferences pane to learn more.

To enable Time Machine:

1. Mount an external hard disk or network volume (page 105).

2. If a dialog asking if you want to use the disk or volume to back up with Time Machine appears **B**, click Use as Backup Disk and skip ahead to step 8.

3. Choose Apple > System Preferences and click the Time Machine icon in the System Preferences window that appears.

4. In the Time Machine preferences pane **A**, click the Select Disk button.

   A window listing available disks and mounted volumes appears **C**.

5. Select the disk you want to use as your Time Machine backup disk **C**.

6. If you want your backup encrypted, select the Encrypt backups check box.

7. Click the Use Disk button.

   The name of the backup disk appears in the Time Machine preferences pane window **D**.

8. If necessary, click in the slider control beside On to move the slider to the On position **D**.

9. Choose System Preferences > Quit System Preferences, or press Command-Q, to close Time Machine preferences.

   Time Machine begins backing up your hard disk within two minutes of enabling it. It displays a small progress dialog **E** as it works. You can continue working with your Mac.

TIP Time Machine's first backup can take a long time. Subsequent backups are much quicker.

B If this dialog appears when you connect the external hard disk you want to use for backup, click the Use as Backup Disk button.

C Choose a hard disk in this window.

D The backup disk's information appears in the Time Machine preferences pane.

E Time Machine displays a dialog like this as it creates its first backup.

F The Time Machine status menu.

G When you launch Time Machine, it begins by displaying the current window as it looks now.

H You can use the timeline on the right side of the screen to go back to a specific backup.

I When you see the item you want, select it.

J When you click Restore, the file is copied to its original location.

To restore a backed up file or folder:

1. Open the window for the disk or folder you want to restore.

2. Choose Enter Time Machine from the Time Machine menu **F**.

   The window's size reduces slightly and the desktop slides away. The Time Machine interface appears **G**.

3. Navigate to the version of the window that displays the contents you want to restore. You can do this in a number of ways:

   ▸ Click the backward or forward arrows in the lower-right corner of the screen to scroll through various versions of the window.

   ▸ Click along the timeline on the right side of the screen **H** to go to a specific backup.

   ▸ Click the title bar of the window version you want to see.

4. Select the item you want to restore **I**.

5. Click Restore.

   Time Machine displays an animation as it copies the file back to the folder and displays it in the Finder **J**.

TIP You can also use Time Machine with Spotlight (Chapter 7). Perform a search for the missing item, then launch Time Machine and browse backward through search results until it appears.

To restore a hard disk from a Time Machine backup:

1. Follow steps 1 through 3 in the section titled "To use the recovery partition" on page 119 and choose Restore From Time Machine Backup in the OS X Utilities dialog that appears.

2. Click Continue in the Restore Your System window.

3. In the Select a Backup Source screen that appears, select your Time Machine backup disk.

4. Click Continue and follow the instructions that appear onscreen to complete the restore process.

CAUTION Restoring your computer from a Time Machine backup erases the contents of your hard disk. This cannot be undone!

Recovery Partition

OS X automatically creates a *recovery partition* on your computer's hard disk. This is a special area on your computer's startup disk that stores a copy of the system software and some utilities that can help you troubleshoot and repair problems. The recovery partition can also be used to reinstall OS X or restore your computer from a Time Machine backup.

The recovery partition is not something for everyday use. Instead, you'd use it when you had a serious problem with your computer's startup disk—a problem that might make it impossible to start any other way. You can also use this feature to run Disk Utility.

This part of the chapter explains how to access and use the recovery partition feature of OS X. Unfortunately, because of the special access required to work with these features, it is not possible to create screenshots. Follow the instructions closely and you should be able to get the job done.

To use the recovery partition:

1. Restart your computer while holding down the Option key.

   Your computer starts and displays a screen with at least two options: your internal hard disk and Recovery-10.8.

2. Click the Recovery-10.8 icon to select it.

3. Click the arrow beneath the Recovery-10.8 icon to finish restarting your computer from the recovery partition.

continues on next page

The OS X Utilities dialog appears. It offers four options:

- **Restore From Time Machine Backup** enables you to restore your computer's hard disk from a Time Machine backup. If you select this option, you can follow steps 2 through 4 in the section titled "To restore a hard disk from a Time Machine backup" on page 118.

- **Reinstall OS X** reinstalls a new copy of OS X. For this option to work, you must be connected to the Internet.

- **Get Help Online** opens the Safari web browser (page 456) and takes you to the Apple Support website so you can search for help and troubleshooting information. You'll need an Internet connection to do this.

- **Disk Utility** launches the Disk Utility application (Chapter 25), which can verify and repair permissions and disks and might be able to resolve your problem.

4. Choose the option you want and click Continue.

5. Follow the instructions that appear onscreen or elsewhere in this book to complete the task you've selected.

TIP Starting your computer with the Option key held down is also a good way to choose a startup disk on the fly if more than one startup disk is available to your Mac.

10

Multiple Users

OS X is designed to be a multiple-user system. This means that different individuals can log in and use an OS X computer.

Each user can install his own applications, configure his own desktop, and save his own documents. User files and setup are kept private. When each user logs in to the computer with his account, he can access only the files that belong to him or are shared.

This chapter explains how to use OS X as a multiple-user system.

TIP Using a multiple-user operating system doesn't mean that you can't keep your computer all to yourself. You can set up just one user—you.

TIP Chapter 3 provides some additional information about how OS X's directory structure is set up to account for multiple users.

TIP You set up user accounts in the Users & Groups preferences pane (page 560).

Logging Out & In

If your computer is shared by multiple users, you'll probably want to log out when you're finished working. Logging out leaves the computer running but makes your account inaccessible until you log back in—thus keeping other users from accessing your files.

The Log Out command under the Apple menu closes your account on the computer. Then, when another user wants to access the computer, all she has to do is log in to her own account and she can get right to work.

The Finder can remember your workspace when you log out and restore it to the way it was when you log back in. So, for example, suppose you have three applications and six documents open on your Mac when you log out. If you indicate that this information should be saved, when you log back in, OS X will automatically reopen the same applications and documents so you can continue working where you left off.

In this part of the chapter, I explain how to log out and log in. Unfortunately, the limitations of my screenshot software make it impossible for me to illustrate the login window. Follow along carefully and you should have no trouble working with what you see onscreen.

TIP If you are your computer's only user, you'll probably never use the Log Out command. (I hardly ever do.)

TIP OS X's fast user switching feature (page 124) makes it quicker and easier to switch from one user account to another.

A The Log Out command is at the bottom of the Apple menu.

B A dialog like this one confirms that you really do want to log out.

To log out:

1. Choose Apple > Log Out *User Name* **A**, or press Shift-Command-Q.

   A confirmation dialog appears **B**.

2. To instruct OS X to remember the open documents and applications and reopen them when you log back in, select the Reopen windows when logging back in check box.

3. Click Log Out, press Return or Enter, or just wait for automatic logout.

   Your computer closes all applications and documents and then displays the login window.

TIP By default, the login window includes two buttons you can use to conserve power while the computer is idle: Sleep puts the computer to sleep and Shut Down turns the computer off. Sleep and Shut Down are discussed on page 35.

To log in:

1. Do one of the following:

   ▸ If the login window displays icons for user accounts, click the icon for your account.

   ▸ If the login window displays only Name and Password boxes, enter your full or short account name in the Name box.

2. Enter your password in the Password box.

3. Click Log In.

   Your OS X desktop appears. If you indicated that OS X should reopen windows when logging back in, all windows that were open when you logged out (or shut down) open.

TIP The appearance of the login window varies depending on how the Login Options of the Users & Groups preferences pane (page 569) has been configured by the system administrator.

TIP Your user name and short name are created when your account is created, either by the OS X Setup Assistant (page 9) or in the Users & Groups preferences pane (page 560). You can use either name to log in.

TIP If you enter an incorrect password in step 2, the login window will shake in step 3. Try again. If you enter an incorrect password three times in a row, the login window expands to display the password hint set up for your account. It also displays this hint if you click the Forgot Password button that may appear in the login window. You set up a password hint in the Users & Groups preferences pane (page 560).

Fast User Switching

Fast user switching enables one user to log in and use the computer without another user logging out. The main benefit to this is that it's fast—hence the name.

You access the fast user switching feature from a menu that appears on the right end of the menu bar **A**. There are a few things to keep in mind about this menu:

- The fast user switching menu is customizable, so it might not look exactly as you see it here. You can fine-tune its appearance by setting Login Options in the Users & Groups preferences pane (page 569).

- An orange check icon indicates which users are logged in.

- The name of the account that appears at the top of the menu is the account currently in use.

- You can also use the menu to display the login window (page 123) or open the Users & Groups preferences pane (page 560).

TIP Fast user switching is enabled by default. However, if it has been disabled, you can enable it in Login Options in the Users & Groups preferences pane (page 569).

To use fast user switching:

1. With the computer turned on and a user already logged in, choose a user account from the menu at the far right end of the menu bar **A**.

2. In the login window that appears, enter the account password and click Log In.

   The screen changes (using a rotating cube graphic effect) to the account you logged in to.

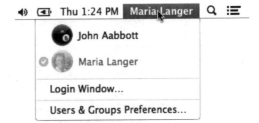

A Fast user switching puts a menu like this one on the right end of the menu bar.

A Home folders for all users can be found in the Users folder.

B Each user's Home folder has a number of preconfigured folders for storing specific types of files.

C Most folders inside another user's Home folder are locked and inaccessible to you.

The Home Folder

OS X creates a Home folder for each user account in the Users folder **A**, with the user's short name as the folder name.

The icon for the folder appears as a house for the user who is currently logged in and as a regular folder for all other users. Each user's Home folder contains folders for storing his files **B**:

- **Desktop** contains all items (other than mounted disks) on the user's desktop.

- **Documents** is the default file location for document files.

- **Downloads** is the default file location for downloaded files.

- **Movies**, **Music**, and **Pictures** are for storing video, audio, and image files.

- **Public** is for storing shared files.

- **Applications**, when present, is for storing applications installed by the user for his private use.

- **Library**, which is not normally visible, is maintained by OS X for storing various preferences files for your account.

Although a user can open another user's Home folder, he can only open the Public folder within that user's Home folder; all other folders are locked **C**.

TIP You can use the Go menu (page 42) to quickly open many folders, including your Home folder and some of the folders inside it.

Sharing Files with Other Users

OS X has three kinds of special folders that make it possible for multiple users of the same computer to share files with each other:

- The **Shared** folder in the Users folder **A** offers read/write access to all users.

- The **Public** folder in each user's Home folder **B C** offers read access to all users.

- The **Drop Box** folder in each user's Public folder **D E** offers write access to all users.

Read access for a folder enables users to open files in that folder. This means that all users can open files in the Shared folder **A** and individual users' Public folders **B C**. If you attempt to open a folder that you do not have read access for, OS X displays a dialog with an error message **F**.

Write access for a folder enables users to save files into that folder. This means that all users can copy files to the Shared folder **A** and individual users' Drop Box folders **D E**.

TIP Don't confuse multiple user file sharing with network file sharing. Multiple user file sharing shares files on the same computer. Network file sharing (page 418) and AirDrop (page 422) share files between multiple computers connected by a network.

A The Shared folder is accessible by all users.

B You can find your Public folder in your Home folder; anyone can open it and read its contents.

C You can also find a Public folder in another user's Home folder; anyone can open and read its contents.

D Your Public folder includes a Drop Box folder where other users can copy files for your use; only you can open this folder and read its contents.

E Although you can copy files into another user's Drop Box folder, you can't open it and read its contents.

F If you try to open a folder you don't have read access to, a dialog like this appears.

To make a file accessible to all other users:

Do one of the following:

- Place the file in the Shared folder in the Users folder **A**.

- Place the file in the Public folder in your Home folder **B**.

TIP If your computer is managed by a system administrator, check to see where the administrator prefers public files to be stored.

To access a file another user has made accessible to all users:

1. Find out where the user has put the file: in the Shared folder in the Users folder **A** or in the user's Public folder **C**.

2. Open the folder and move or copy the file to a folder in your Home folder.

TIP If you don't need a copy of the file, you don't have to move or copy it. You can simply open it from the folder in which it resides.

To make a file accessible to a specific user:

1. Drag the file's icon onto the Drop Box folder icon inside the Public folder in the user's Home folder **E**.

   A warning dialog appears **G**.

2. Click OK.

   The file moves into the Public folder.

CAUTION When you drag a file into a Drop Box folder, the file is moved—*not copied*—there. You cannot open someone else's Drop Box folder to remove its contents. If you need to keep a copy of the file, hold down the Option key while dragging the file into the Drop Box folder to place a copy of the file there. You can then continue working with the original.

TIP To use the Drop Box, be sure to drag the file icon onto the Drop Box folder icon **E**—not simply into the open Public folder. If you drag a file into another user's public folder, a warning dialog appears **H**. If you have an administrator account, you can click the **Authenticate** button and enter your user name and password in the dialog that appears **I** to override the warning and move the file.

To access a file another user has made accessible only to you:

Open the Drop Box folder inside your Public folder **D**. The file should be there.

TIP Remember, you are the only one who can open your Drop Box folder.

G OS X warns you when you try to put a file into a folder where it can't be retrieved.

H You can't place files into another user's Public folder or any other locked folder...

I ...unless you're an administrator.

Using Applications

In This Part

Application Basics

Applications, which are also known as *apps* or *programs*, are computer software packages you use to get work done.

For example, if you sit down at your computer to write a letter, you're likely doing it with a word processing application. If you spend some time browsing websites, you're using a web browser application. And if you import photos from your camera onto your computer and then email one of them to a friend, you might be using a photo management app and an email app.

Without applications, a computer would be pretty much useless—it simply wouldn't be able to *do* anything. OS X comes with some applications, most of which are discussed throughout this book. Your computer may have come with others, such as Apple's iLife suite of apps.

This chapter covers the basics of using applications, including multitasking, opening applications, and creating documents. Along the way, it'll show some new features in OS X Mountain Lion, including share sheets and changes to the Auto Save and Launchpad features.

In This Chapter:

Applications

Applications are often classified based on what they do. There are as many kinds of applications as tasks you can perform with your computer.

Here are some examples:

- **Word processors**, such as Text-Edit, iWork's Pages, and Microsoft Office's Word, are used to create letters, reports, and other text-based documents.

- **Spreadsheets**, such as iWork's Numbers and Microsoft Office's Excel, have built-in calculation features that are useful for creating number-based documents such as worksheets and charts.

- **Databases**, such as FileMaker Pro and Bento, are used to organize information, such as the names and addresses of customers or the artists and titles in a music collection.

- **Personal information management apps**, such as Contacts and Calendar, help you keep track of contacts and appointments.

- **Presentation apps**, such as iWork's Keynote and Microsoft Office's PowerPoint, are used to create presentations and animations.

- **Internet access apps**, such as the Safari and Firefox web browsers and the Mail and Microsoft Outlook email apps, let you access and share information on the Internet.

- **Photo and graphics apps**, such as Apple Aperture, iLife's iPhoto, and Adobe Photoshop, let you organize and edit images.

- **Movie editing apps**, such as iLife's iMovie and Apple Final Cut X, enable you to edit videos.

- **Utility apps**, such as Disk Utility and Activity Monitor, perform tasks to manage computer files or operations or keep your computer in good working order.

- **Games**, such as Angry Birds and Portal, let you use your computer for fun and relaxation.

These are just some examples. Nowadays, there's an app for just about anything you need to do.

TIP Unless you have Windows installed on your Mac, you need to make sure that the software you buy is OS X-compatible.

TIP A good source of OS X applications is the App Store, which is covered in Chapter 13.

A A typical installation of OS X installs 28 applications in the Applications folder...

B ...and another 21 in the Utilities folder within it.

OS X Applications

A standard installation of OS X installs about 50 applications on your computer's hard disk. These applications can be found in the Applications folder **A** and in the Utilities folder **B** within it.

Most of these applications and utilities are discussed in some level of detail throughout this book. Here's a quick summary of what you can find in the Applications folder and where you can learn more about it:

- **App Store** (Chapter 13) enables you to find, buy, install, and update OS X applications.

- **Automator** (Chapter 26) lets you automate repetitive tasks.

- **Calculator** (Chapter 16) enables you to perform calculations and conversions.

- **Calendar** (formerly iCal; Chapter 16) manages your appointments.

- **Chess** (chapter 16) is a computerized version of the game of chess.

- **Contacts** (formerly Address Book; Chapter 20) manages contact information for the people and organizations you know.

- **Dashboard** (Chapter 17) offers access to simple applications called widgets.

- **Dictionary** (Chapter 16) provides word definitions and synonyms and access to other reference materials.

- **DVD Player** (Chapter 15) enables you to play DVD-video on your Mac.

- **Facetime** (Chapter 29) lets you conduct live video conversations with others using a Mac, iPhone, or iPad.

- **Font Book** (Chapter 23) helps you manage your fonts.

continues on next page

- **Game Center** (Chapter 16), which is new in OS X Mountain Lion, enables you to set up and maintain a gaming network.

- **Image Capture** (Chapter 16) enables you to download image files from a digital camera or import images from a scanner and save them on disk.

- **iTunes** (Chapter 15) enables you to organize, purchase, and play audio and video content, including music, podcasts, movies, and TV shows.

- **Launchpad** (this chapter; page 140) makes it quick and easy to find and open any application installed on your computer.

- **Mail** (Chapter 29) is email client software for sending and receiving email messages.

- **Messages** (formerly iChat; Chapter 29) enables you to conduct live text, voice, or video chats.

- **Mission Control** (Chapter 18) helps you manage applications and documents as you work with them.

- **Notes** (Chapter 22), which is new in OS X Mountain Lion, lets you take notes that you can sync between multiple Macs and iOS devices.

- **Photo Booth** (Chapter 16) enables you to use your computer's built-in camera to take photos and apply special effects to them.

- **Preview** (Chapter 16) enables you to view images, PDF files, and a variety of other file types.

- **QuickTime Player** (Chapter 15) enables you to view, record, and share QuickTime-compatible movies and audio.

- **Reminders** (Chapter 22), which is new in OS X Mountain Lion, enables you to maintain a to-do list that you can sync among multiple Macs and iOS devices.

- **Safari** (Chapter 29) is web browser software, which you can use to view web pages and RSS feeds.

- **Stickies** (Chapter 16) enables you to place colorful notes on your computer screen.

- **System Preferences** (Chapters 32 through 36) enables you to customize your computer's operating system so it looks and works the way you want it to.

- **TextEdit** (Chapter 14) enables you to create, open, edit, and save text-based documents.

- **Time Machine** (Chapter 9) provides automated backup features, along with a method to restore lost or damaged files.

TIP This book does *not* include coverage of the iLife and iWork applications—iPhoto, iWeb, iMovie, iDVD, Pages, Numbers, and Keynote— because these applications are not part of a standard OS X installation, although they may come preinstalled on some new OS X computers. For more information about these applications, I recommend checking out other titles in Peachpit's *Visual QuickStart Guide* series.

The application menu always displays the name of the active application.

Multitasking & the Dock

OS X uses a form of *multitasking*, which makes it possible for more than one application to be open at the same time. One application that is always open is Finder, which is covered in detail in Parts I and II of this book. You can open other applications as you need to use them.

Only one application can be *active*. The active application is the one whose name appears at the top of the *application menu* Ⓐ (page 154) on the menu bar. You must make an application active to work with it—one of the easiest ways to do this is to click its icon in the Dock Ⓑ (page 34). Other open applications continue running in the background.

OS X uses *preemptive multitasking*, a type of multitasking in which the operating system can interrupt a currently running task to run another task, as needed.

OS X also features *protected memory*, a memory management system in which each program is prevented from modifying or corrupting the memory partition of another program. This means that if one application freezes up, your computer won't freeze up. You can continue using the other applications that are running.

Ⓑ The Dock offers a quick and easy way to switch from one open application to another.

Application Basics **135**

To learn which applications are running:

1. If necessary, enable the indicator lights for open applications feature in Dock preferences (page 501).

2. Look at the Dock.

   A tiny blue bubble appears beneath each application that is running **B**.

To switch from one open application to another:

Use one of the following techniques:

- In the Dock **B**, click the icon for the application you want to activate.

- Click any of the open windows for the application you want to activate.

- Hold down the Command key and press Tab to display a large icon for each open application **C**. Press Tab repeatedly to cycle though the icons until the one you want to activate is selected. Then release the keys.

The windows for the application you selected come to the front and the application name appears on the application menu **A**.

TIP You can also use Mission Control (page 253) and Exposé (page 255) to activate an application.

C Pressing Command-Tab displays a large icon onscreen for each of the active applications.

A The Applications folder is where you'll find most applications on your computer. This example shows the applications that come with OS X, as well as those that are part of the iLife suite of programs that may have come with your Mac.

B A generic document icon appears on documents for which the parent application is unknown or not installed.

Reservation Form

Using Applications & Creating Documents

You use an application by opening, or *launching*, it. It loads into the computer's memory. Its menu bar replaces the Finder's menu bar and offers commands that can be used only with that application. It may also display a document window and tools specific to that program.

Most applications create *documents*—files written in a format understood by the application. When you save documents, they remain on disk so you can open, edit, print, or just view them at a later date.

For example, you may use iWork's Pages application to write a letter. When you save the letter, it becomes a Pages document file that includes all the text and formatting you put into the letter, written in a format that Pages can understand.

Your computer keeps track of applications and documents. It automatically associates documents with the applications that created them. That's how your computer is able to open a document with the correct application when you open the document from the Finder.

OS X stores applications in the Applications folder **A** on your hard disk. Additional applications can be found in the Utilities folder within the Applications folder.

TIP You can launch an application by opening a document that it created.

TIP A document created by an application that is not installed on your computer is sometimes referred to as an *orphan* document since no parent application is available. An orphan document often has a generic document icon **B**.

To launch an application:

Use one of the following techniques:

- Double-click the application's icon.
- Select the application's icon and choose File > Open , or press Command-O.
- If an icon for the application is in the sidebar or Dock, click that icon once.

The application opens **E**.

TIP If the application you opened supports the Auto Save feature and you had open documents the last time you quit it, those documents should automatically reopen so you can continue working with them. This is part of OS X's Resume feature.

To open a document & launch the application that created it at the same time:

Use one of the following techniques:

- Double-click the icon for the document that you want to open.
- Select the icon for the document that you want to open **F** and choose File > Open **D**, or press Command-O.
- If an icon for the document is in the sidebar or Dock, click that icon once.

If the application that created the document is not already running, it launches. The document appears in an active window **G**.

C Select the icon for the application you want to open.

TextEdit

D Choose Open from the File menu.

E When you launch TextEdit by opening its application icon, it usually displays an empty document window.

F Select the icon for the document you want to open.

RTF

Letter to Cliff

G When you launch TextEdit by opening one of its documents, it displays the document.

H Drag the icon for the document you want to open onto the icon for the application you want to open it with.

I The Open With submenu lists installed applications that can open a selected document. The options that appear depend on what type of document is selected and what applications are installed on your computer.

To open a document with drag & drop:

1. Drag the icon for the document that you want to open onto the icon for the application with which you want to open it.

2. When the application icon becomes selected **H**, release the button. The application launches and displays the document **G**.

TIP In step 1, the application icon can be in a Finder window (or on the desktop), in the sidebar, or on the Dock.

TIP Drag and drop is a good way to open a document with an application other than the one that created it.

TIP Not all applications can read all documents. Dragging a document icon onto the icon for an application that can't open it either won't launch the application, will open the document but display only gibberish, or will display an error message.

To open a document with the Open With command:

1. Select the icon for the document that you want to open **F**.

2. Choose File > Open With to display the Open With Submenu **I** and choose the application you want to use to open the file.

   The application you chose opens and displays the document.

TIP The Open With submenu **I** will only list applications that are installed on your computer and are capable of opening the selected document.

Launchpad

Launchpad offers another way to open the applications on your computer. Simply click the Launchpad icon in the Dock. Open windows fade away, replaced with a full-screen view of icons for all the applications on your Mac .

You can scroll (or swipe) through multiple pages to see all installed applications. Just click an icon to launch its app. And when you decide you no longer want to use an app, you can use Launchpad to uninstall it.

TIP You can customize Launchpad to rearrange icons (page 471) or group them into folders (page 472).

To open an application with Launchpad:

1. Click the Launchpad icon in the Dock.

   The Launchpad interface appears on your desktop **A**.

2. If necessary, navigate through Launchpad's folders or screens to find the icon you want:

   ▸ To view the contents of a folder, click the folder's icon **B**.

   ▸ To return to the parent folder, click the folder's icon again.

   ▸ To view the icons on another Launchpad page, drag (or two-finger swipe on a Multi-Touch device) to the left or right.

3. Click the icon for the application you want to launch.

   Launchpad closes and the app opens.

TIP In Launchpad, a folder looks like a box with tiny icons representing the applications it contains **A** **B**.

A Launchpad displays icons for your installed applications.

B Clicking the icon for a folder displays the contents of that folder.

C As you type search characters, Launchpad displays results.

D Point to and press on the icon for the application you want to uninstall.

E When you click the X icon, a dialog pops up to ask whether you're sure you want to delete it.

To search for an app in Launchpad

In the Spotlight search box at the top of the Launchpad screen, type in all or part of the application name.

As you type, the screen's display changes to show only icons for the apps that match the characters you type **C**.

To close Launchpad without launching an application:

Do one of the following:

- Click anywhere on the Launchpad screen other than on an icon.

- Press the Esc key.

To uninstall an application:

1. Point to the icon for the application you want to uninstall.

2. Press the button down and hold it down.

3. When an X icon appears on the application and its icon begins to wiggle **D**, release the button.

4. Click the X icon for the application you want to delete.

5. Click Delete in the confirmation dialog that pops up **E**.

   The application is deleted from the Applications folder and its icon disappears from Launchpad.

TIP This technique does not work with all applications. In general, it works with applications you purchased and installed with the App Store (page 174).

TIP If you purchased and installed an application with the App Store (page 174), you can reinstall the application (page 175) at any time.

Full-Screen Apps

The full-screen apps feature helps reduce distractions while you work by clearing everything off the screen except the application you're working with . Even the menu bar slides off the screen and stays out of your way until you need it.

Once you've switched to full-screen view, you can switch from one app to another with a swipe. Press the Esc key at any time to exit full-screen view.

TIP Because this feature, which was introduced in OS X Lion, requires applications to be written to take advantage of it, it is not supported by all applications. Unsupported applications will appear in a normal screen view.

To enter full-screen view:

1. Open or switch to an application that supports the full-screen apps feature.

2. Click the Full-Screen button in the top-right corner of a document window **B**.

   The application switches to full-screen view **A**.

To display and use a menu in full-screen view:

Move the pointer to the top of the screen.

The menu bar slides back into view so you can access its menus and commands **C**.

A In full-screen view, all you see onscreen is the application window. This is Preview, viewing a PDF file.

Full-Screen button

B A small Full-Screen button appears in the upper-right corner of windows in applications that support the full-screen app feature.

C Point to where the menu bar should be and it appears, along with any toolbars that the application might display.

In this example, I'm using Multi-Touch gestures to swipe one application (Preview) aside to see another (iPhoto).

To switch from one app to another:

Use one of the following techniques:

- With a mouse or trackpad, point to the bottom of the screen to display the Dock and click the icon for the application you want to switch to.

- With a Multi-Touch device, use three fingers to swipe to the left or right **D**. The current app's screen moves aside to display the next app's. Repeat as necessary to display the app you want.

TIP Dashboard (Chapter 17) always appears in full-screen view and is always accessible by clicking or swiping as described above.

To exit full-screen view:

Use one of the following techniques:

- Press the Esc key.

- Display the menu bar **C** and click the tiny blue icon on the far right end.

The current application returns to normal screen view.

TIP If multiple applications are displayed in full-screen view, each one is returned to regular screen view independently.

Auto Save, Versions, Revert & Resume

Auto Save combines multiple features to create an automated solution for people who sometimes forget to save their documents as they work:

- **Auto Save** automatically saves changes to a document as you work on it. Not only does Auto Save save changes to documents that have already been manually saved (page 160) once, but it also saves changes to documents that have not yet been manually saved at all.

- **Versions** creates snapshots of a document each time it is saved. This makes it possible to go back to a previous version of a document, thus undoing many changes at once. You can even go back to a version that was saved before it was last manually saved—something the Undo command normally can't do.

- **Revert** enables you to revert to the last manually saved version of a document.

- **Resume** automatically reopens all document windows that were open when you last quit an application. This makes it easy to continue (or resume) working on the same documents after a computer restart or even days later.

Auto Save places a menu in the title bar of a document window, just to the right of the document name:

- If the document has not been edited since it was last manually saved, no indicator appears **Ⓐ**.

- If the document has been edited since it was last manually saved, the word *Edited* appears **Ⓑ**.

- If the document has been locked for editing, the word *Locked* appears **Ⓒ**.

ⒶⒷⒸ If the document has not been changed since last manually saved, no menu indicator appears (top); if it has been changed since last saved, *Edited* appears (middle); and if it is locked, *Locked* appears (bottom).

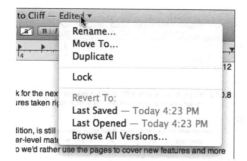

D The title bar menu has commands for working with the current file or reverting to a previous version.

Point to the indicator or just to the right of the document title to display a triangle; click it to display a menu with several options **D**, including various combinations of these:

- **Rename**, which is new in OS X Mountain Lion, enables you to rename the document from within the application, without the use of a Save dialog.

- **Move To**, which is also new in OS X Mountain Lion, lets you move the document to a different location on disk.

- **Duplicate** makes a copy of the document, leaving the original unchanged.

- **Lock** enables you to lock the document, thus preventing any changes to the document. This turns to an Unlock command when the document is locked.

- **Revert to Last Saved** or **Revert to Last Opened**, which is available only if the document has been edited since the last time it was opened or saved, restores the last saved or opened version of the document, thus removing all edits since that point.

- **Browse All Versions** uses an interface similar to that of Time Machine (page 115) to display all existing versions of the document so you can revert to a previous version.

This part of the chapter explains how you can use all of these features.

TIP These features work together to prevent data loss in the event of a computer problem and also help protect your work from errors you might make by making it possible to go back to an earlier version of the document.

TIP The Resume feature also works when you shut down or restart your computer (page 35) or log out of your account (page 123).

TIP Because these features require apps to be written to take advantage of them, they are not yet supported by all apps. Look for a menu in a document's title bar **D** to determine whether the app supports these features.

To rename a document:

1. Choose Rename from the menu in the title bar **D**.

   The document name become selected in the title bar **E**.

2. Type a new name for the document.

   The text you type replaces the selection.

3. Press Return or Enter.

   The document's name is changed **F**.

TIP Changing a document name within an application automatically changes its name in the Finder.

To move a document:

1. Choose Move To from the menu in the title bar **D**.

   A location dialog sheet appears **G**.

2. Choose a location from the Where pop-up menu **H**.

3. If the location you want does not appear in step 2, choose Other. Then use the dialog box that appears **I** to locate and select the location you want.

4. Click Move.

   The document is moved to the new location, where it can be found in the Finder from that point forward.

TIP You can learn how to use a dialog like the one in **I** starting on page 192.

E Choosing Rename from the title bar menu selects the document name in the title bar.

F When you press Return, the name changes in the title bar—and in the Finder.

G The Move To command displays a dialog with a pop-up menu of locations.

H Common locations in your Home folder appear in the Where pop-up menu.

I Choosing Other displays a dialog like this, which offers access to all disk locations.

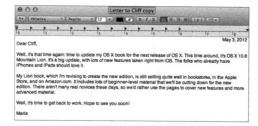

J Choosing Duplicate from the title bar menu makes a copy of the document.

K When you try to edit a locked document, a dialog like this appears.

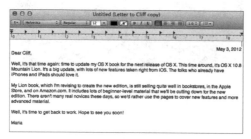

L Clicking the Duplicate button creates an unlocked copy of the document so you can edit it.

M To unlock a document, choose Unlock from the versions menu.

To duplicate a document:

1. Choose Duplicate from the menu in the title bar **D**.

   A copy of the document is created and appears with the original document. Its name is selected **J**.

2. Type a new name for the document and press Return or Enter.

   The document is saved with the name you entered in the same location as the original document.

To lock a document for editing:

Choose Lock from the menu in the title bar **D**.

The word *Locked* appears in the versions menu indicator **C**.

To work with a locked document:

1. Try to make any change to a locked document.

2. A dialog with three options appears **K**. Click a button:

   ▸ **Duplicate** creates an untitled copy of the document that is unlocked **L** so you can make and save changes to it. The original locked document remains open.

   ▸ **Cancel** cancels the changes without unlocking the document.

   ▸ **Unlock** unlocks the document so you can make and save changes.

To unlock a document:

Choose Unlock from the menu on the title bar **M**.

The word *Locked* disappears from the versions menu indicator.

To revert to the last saved version:

Use one of the following techniques:

- Choose an option from the Revert To submenu under the File menu .

- Choose an option from the bottom of the menu on the document's title bar **D**.

TIP Not all applications include a Revert command or submenu on the File menu.

TIP The Revert to Last Saved command is not available if the document has not been edited since the last time it was manually saved.

To browse versions & restore to a previous version

1. Choose Browse All Versions from the menu in the document's title bar **D**.

   The version browsing interface fills the screen, displaying the current version on the left and a series of older versions on the right **O**.

2. Use one of the following techniques to browse through the versions:

   - Click the timeline on the right side of the screen to go to a specific version.

   - Click the title bar of the window for the version you want to see.

3. Do one of the following:

   - To close the version browser without restoring to another version, click Done.

   - To restore the document to the version currently displayed on the right side of the version browser, click Restore.

   The version browser closes so you can continue working on the same or restored version of the document.

N The Revert To submenu in TextEdit includes commands for reverting to a previous version of a document.

O You can use the version browser to scroll backward through time and view previous versions of a document.

A The Share menu in Preview for an image file offers quite a few options.

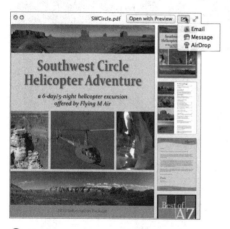

B The Share button appears in the upper-right corner of a Quick Look window.

C The Share menu is also available in a Finder window's toolbar.

Share Sheets

In OS X Mountain Lion, Apple introduced share sheets, a feature that makes it quick and easy to share documents with others. Instead of opening a separate application to share an open document, you can use the new share menu in the document window **A** to select a share destination, enter information into a share sheet window, and click a button to share it.

For example, suppose you're working with an image file in Preview and want to post it to Twitter. You could click the Share button in the document's toolbar, choose Twitter, enter information in the share sheet window that appears, and click Send. Your image is sent to Twitter—without leaving the Preview app.

The share sheets feature is supported by many apps, as well as in Quick Look **B**. It even works in the Finder for selected items; you can find the Share menu in the toolbar **C**.

This part of the chapter takes a look at the new share sheets feature in OS X.

TIP The services offered on the Share menu vary depending on the type of item and application you're working with. Apple plans to add support for additional services, including Facebook, which wasn't supported when this book went to press. So don't be surprised if the Share menu looks different on your computer than in the screenshots here.

To use a share sheet:

1. Do one of the following:

   ▸ Open the item you want to share in an application that supports share sheets.

   ▸ In a Finder window, select the icon for the item you want to share.

   ▸ Use Quick Look to display the contents of the item you want to share.

2. Click the Share menu button in the window to display a menu of sharing options Ⓐ Ⓑ Ⓒ.

3. Choose the share option you want.

   A share sheet appears Ⓓ Ⓔ.

4. Set options in the share sheet.

5. Click Send.

   The item is sent using the option you chose.

TIP The settings available in a share sheet Ⓓ Ⓔ vary depending on the sharing option you chose in step 2.

TIP If you have not yet configured an account for a sharing service, OS X tells you Ⓕ. Click the Add Account button to open the Mail, Contacts & Calendars preferences pane (page 546) and add the account.

Ⓓ This share sheet for Twitter offers a form for entering the text of your tweet and adding your location.

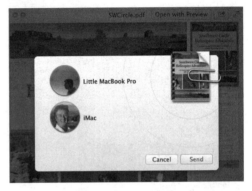

Ⓔ This share sheet for Air Drop automatically displays other nearby users with Air Drop open.

Ⓕ If an account isn't configured yet, OS X tells you so you can set it up.

About This Mac
Software Update...
App Store...

System Preferences...
Dock ▶

Recent Items ▶

Force Quit...　⌥⌘⏏

Sleep
Restart...
Shut Down...

Log Out Maria Langer...　⇧⌘Q

Ⓐ You can use the Force Quit command to force an unresponsive application to quit.

Force Quitting Applications

Occasionally, an application may freeze, lock up, or otherwise become unresponsive. When this happens, you can no longer work with that application or its documents.

The Force Quit command **Ⓐ** enables you to force an unresponsive application to quit. Then you can either restart it or continue working with other applications.

CAUTION When you use the Force Quit command to quit an application, any unsaved changes in that application's open documents may be lost. Use the Force Quit command only as a last resort, when the Quit command (page 156) cannot be used.

TIP OS X's protected memory (page 133) makes it possible for applications to continue running properly on your computer when one application locks up.

TIP If more than one application experiences problems during a work session, you might find it helpful to restart your computer. This clears out RAM and forces your computer to reload all applications and documents into memory.

To force quit an application:

1. Choose Apple > Force Quit , or press Option-Command-Esc.

2. In the Force Quit Applications window that appears **B**, select the application you want to force to quit.

3. Click Force Quit.

4. A confirmation dialog appears **C**.

   Click Force Quit.

   The application immediately quits.

TIP If you selected Finder in step 2, the button to click in step 3 is labeled Relaunch **D**. Finder must always be running in OS X.

B You can choose the application you want to force to quit and then click the Force Quit button.

C OS X confirms that you really do want to force the application to quit.

D If you select Finder in the Force Quit Applications window, the Force Quit button turns into a Relaunch button.

Standard
Application Menus

One of the great things about OS X is the level of standardization in basic interface elements such as menus. Apple user interface guidelines mandate that each application include a number of standard menus where specific commands can be found.

For example, every application will have a File menu and that menu will always include the application's Open, Close, New, and Print commands (if applicable). This makes it very easy to learn the basics of new software. After all, if every application's Open command is always on its File menu, you don't have to go looking for it each time you need to open a file in a different application.

This chapter covers the standard menus you'll find in just about all OS X applications and tells you a little about the commands you'll find there. It also provides some basic information about dialog boxes and their standard parts.

The Application Menu

The application menu takes the name of the currently active application—for example, the TextEdit application menu **A** or the iTunes application menu **B**. It includes commands for working with the entire application.

There are a number of commands that appear on most application menus:

- **About** provides information about the application.

- **Preferences** gives you access to application preference settings that you can use to customize the way the application works.

- **Services C** is a submenu full of commands you can use with the application or selected items within it.

- **Hide/Show** is a group of commands to hide or show applications.

- **Quit** closes the application when you're finished working with it.

Here's a closer look at what each of these commands does.

To learn about an application:

1. From the application menu, choose About *application name* **A B**.

2. A window with version and other information appears **D E**. Read the information it contains.

3. When you're finished reading about the application, click the window's close button.

A B The TextEdit application menu (left) and the iTunes application menu (right).

C Here's what the Services submenu looks like in TextEdit when some text is selected.

D E The About window for TextEdit (top) and iTunes (bottom) provide version number and copyright information.

F **G** The Preferences window for TextEdit (top) and the Preferences dialog for iTunes (bottom). Note that each one has individual panes of information.

To set application preferences:

1. From the application menu, choose Preferences **A** **B**.

2. The application's Preferences window **F** or dialog **G** appears. Set options as desired.

3. Do one of the following to save your changes and dismiss the window or dialog:

   ▸ Click the window's close button **F**.

   ▸ Click the dialog's OK **G** or Save button.

TIP Preference options vary greatly from one application to another. To learn more about an application's preferences, check its documentation or onscreen help.

TIP Preference windows **F** or dialogs **G** often include multiple *panes* of settings. You can switch from one pane to another by clicking a button that's usually near the top of the window or dialog.

TIP One of the first things I do to learn about a new application is explore the options in its preferences window or dialog. The settings help me get a good idea of the features the program offers.

To use application services:

1. From the application menu, select the Services option to display its submenu **C**.

2. Choose the command you want.

TIP The options on the Services submenu vary greatly by application, as well as what's currently selected in the application.

TIP You can customize the Services submenu by setting options in the Keyboard Shortcuts pane (page 528) of Keyboard preferences (page 526).

To hide an application:

From the application menu, choose Hide *application name* **Ⓐ Ⓑ**, or press Command-H.

All of the application's windows, as well as its menu bar, are hidden from view.

To hide all applications except the active one:

From the application menu, choose Hide Others **Ⓐ Ⓑ** or press Option-Command-H.

To hide the active application and display another application:

Hold down the Option key while switching to another application.

To display a hidden application:

Click the application's icon (or any of its minimized document icons) in the Dock.

To unhide all applications:

From the application menu, choose Show All **Ⓐ Ⓑ**.

To quit an application:

From the application menu, choose Quit *application name* **Ⓐ Ⓑ**, or press Command-Q.

The application automatically saves the status of any open windows, saves preferences (if applicable), and quits.

TIP Closing all of an application's open windows is not the same as quitting. An application normally remains running until you quit it.

TIP If an application is unresponsive and you cannot access its menus or commands, you can use the Force Quit command (page 151) to make it stop running.

A B C The File menu in TextEdit (top), Safari (middle), and Contacts (bottom).

The File Menu

The File menu **A B C** includes commands for working with files or documents. Most applications will include the following commands:

- **New** creates a new document or window.
- **Open** opens an existing document.
- **Close** closes the active document window.
- **Save/Save As** saves the active document.
- **Page Setup** enables you to set page options for the active document.
- **Print** lets you set print options and output the document to a printer or other output method.

This section discusses the New, Open, Close, Save, and Save As commands; the Page Setup and Print commands are discussed in detail in Chapter 24.

To create a new document or window:

Do one of the following:

- Choose File > New **A**.
- Choose File > New Window **B**.
- Press Command-N **A B C**.

A new untitled document or window appears.

TIP The exact wording of the command for creating a new document or window varies depending on the application and what the command does **A B C**. This command, however, is usually the first one on the File menu.

To open a file:

1. Choose File > Open **A** or press Command-O to display the Open dialog **D**.

2. Use standard Finder window techniques (Chapter 2) to navigate within the window in the dialog and locate the document you want to open. Here are some tips:

   ▸ Use the pop-up menu at the top of the dialog **E** to backtrack from the current location to an enclosing folders or to a recently accessed folder.

   ▸ Click sidebar buttons to quickly view a specific folder, volume, or other location.

   ▸ Click buttons near the top of the dialog to change the window view (Chapter 4).

   ▸ Enter all or part of the file's name or contents in the Spotlight search field (Chapter 7) to display a list of files that match **F**.

3. When the file you want to open appears, open it:

   ▸ Select the file and then click Open or press Return or Enter.

   ▸ Double-click the file.

TIP The exact wording of the Open command varies depending on the application and what you want to open. For example, the Open command on Safari's File menu **B** is Open File.

TIP The Open dialog **D** has many standard elements that appear in all Open dialogs.

TIP The Open Recent command, which is available on the File menu of some applications **A**, displays a submenu of recently opened items **G**. Choose the item you want to open it again.

D TextEdit's Open dialog includes all of the elements found in a standard Open dialog.

E The pop-up menu at the top of the Open dialog lets you backtrack from the currently displayed location to the folders in which it resides or a recently accessed folder.

F The Spotlight search feature works within the open dialog, too. In this example, I've searched for the phrase *letter to* on my entire computer.

G TextEdit's Open Recent submenu makes it easy to reopen a recently opened document.

H When you close a TextEdit document that has not yet been saved, a dialog like this appears.

To close a window:

1. Use one of the following techniques:

   ▸ Choose File > Close **A C** or File > Close Window **B**.

   ▸ Press Command-W.

   ▸ Click the window's close button.

2. If the window contains a document that has not yet been saved, a dialog sheet appears **H**.

   ▸ Click Don't Save to close the window without saving the document.

   ▸ Click Cancel or press Esc to keep the window open.

   ▸ Click Save or press Return or Enter to save the document.

TIP The exact appearance of the dialog sheet that appears when you close a document with unsaved changes **H** varies depending on the application. All versions of the dialog should offer the same three options, although they may be worded differently.

TIP OS X's Auto Save feature (page 144) automatically saves changes to existing documents periodically as you work and when you close them. If a document has been saved at least once, you will not be prompted to save changes when you close it.

To manually save a document for the first time:

1. Choose File > Save 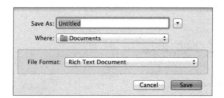, or press Command-S to display the Save dialog .

2. If necessary, click the disclosure triangle beside the Save As field 🅘 to expand the dialog 🅙.

3. Use standard Finder window techniques (Chapter 2) to navigate within the window in the dialog and select a location in which to save the document. Here are some tips:

    ▸ Use the pop-up menu at the top of the dialog 🅔 to backtrack from the current location to an enclosing folders or to a recently accessed folder.

    ▸ Click sidebar buttons to quickly view a specific folder, volume, or other location.

    ▸ Click buttons near the top of the dialog to change the window view (Chapter 4).

    ▸ Enter all or part of a folder or volume name in the Spotlight search field (Chapter 7) to display a list of matches.

    ▸ Click the New Folder button to create a new folder inside the currently selected folder. You can enter a name for the new folder in the New folder dialog that appears 🅚.

4. When the name of the folder in which you want to save the document appears on the pop-up menu above the file list area, enter a name for the document in the Save As box and click Save.

    The document is saved in the location you specified. The name of the file appears in the document window's title bar 🅛.

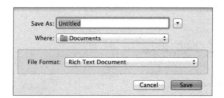

🅘 The Save As dialog might be collapsed, like this...

🅙 ...or expanded, like this.

🅚 Clicking the New Folder button displays the New Folder dialog, so you can name the new folder.

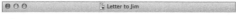

🅛 The name of the newly saved file appears in the window's title bar.

```
File
┌─────────────────────────────────┐
│ New Blank Document        ⌘N     │
│ New from Template...     ⇧⌘P     │
│ Open...                   ⌘O     │
│ Open URL...             ⇧⌘O     │
│ Open Recent                ▶    │
├─────────────────────────────────┤
│ Close                     ⌘W     │
│ Save                      ⌘S     │
│ Save As...              ⇧⌘S     │
│ Save as Web Page...              │
├─────────────────────────────────┤
│ Share                      ▶    │
├─────────────────────────────────┤
│ Web Page Preview                 │
├─────────────────────────────────┤
│ Restrict Permissions       ▶    │
├─────────────────────────────────┤
│ Reduce File Size...              │
├─────────────────────────────────┤
│ Page Setup...                    │
│ Print...                  ⌘P     │
├─────────────────────────────────┤
│ Properties...                    │
└─────────────────────────────────┘
```

Ⓜ Microsoft Word is an example of an application with both a Save and a Save As command.

TIP Not all applications enable you to save documents. iTunes, for example, does not include a Save command on its File menu.

TIP The Save dialog **ⒾⒿ** is also known as the Save Location dialog because it enables you to select a location in which to save a file.

TIP In step 1, you can also use the Save As command (if available **Ⓜ**). The first time you save a document, the Save and Save As commands do the same thing: display the Save dialog.

TIP Some applications automatically append a period and a three-character *extension* to a file's name when you save it. Extensions are used by OS X and Windows applications to identify the file type. You can toggle the display of file name extensions in Advanced Finder preferences (page 467).

To manually save changes to a document:

Choose File > Save **ⒸⓂ**, or press Command-S.

How the document is saved depends upon whether the application you are using supports OS X's versions feature (page 144):

- If the application supports versions (for example, TextEdit), a snapshot of the document is saved in the file as a version. It is possible to revert to an earlier version of the document, if necessary.

- If the application does not support versions (for example, Microsoft Word as of Summer 2012), the document is saved in the same location with the same name, thus overwriting the existing version of the document with the updated contents.

To save a document with a new name or in a new location:

Use one of the following techniques, depending on whether the application you are using supports the versions feature (page 144).

- If the application supports versions, choose File > Duplicate **G** and then save the duplicate document that is created, following the instructions in the section titled "To manually save a document for the first time" on page 160.

- If the application does not support versions, choose File > Save As **M** to display the Save As dialog sheet **I J**. Then follow steps 2 through 4 in the section titled "To manually save a document for the first time" on page 160.

TIP Saving a document with a new name or in a new location creates a copy of the existing document. Applications that support the versions feature create a second document window, so there is no confusion over which document is the copy.

TIP If you use the Save dialog to save a document with the same name as a document in the selected location, a warning dialog appears **N**. You can either click Cancel to return to the Save dialog and change the document's name or save location or click Replace to replace the document on disk with the current document.

N A dialog like this appears when you try to save a file with the same name as another file in a folder. This is what the dialog looks like in TextEdit.

Bullet in close button *Faded document icon*

O Two indications of unsaved changes in a document created by an application that does not support versions—in this example, Microsoft Word.

Edited indicator

P This TextEdit document has been edited since the last version was saved.

To identify unsaved documents:

How you identify a document with unsaved changes depends upon whether the document supports the OS X versions feature.

- In applications that do not support versions, one or more of the following indicators may appear:

  - A bullet or X character appears in the close button on the title bar of the window **O** for a document with unsaved changes.

  - The document icon appears faded on the title bar of the window **O** for a document with unsaved changes.

  - In some applications, a bullet character appears in the Window menu beside the name of the window for a document with unsaved changes.

- In applications that do support versions, an Edited indicator may appear on the far right end of the title bar **P**.

TIP The versions feature is relatively new, so not all applications support it. As support grows, you'll find more applications indicating unsaved changes in documents like TextEdit does **P**.

The Edit Menu

The Edit menu **Ⓐ Ⓑ** includes commands for modifying the contents of a document. Here's a quick list of the commands you're likely to find, along with their standard keyboard equivalents:

- **Undo** (Command-Z) reverses the last editing action you made.

- **Redo** (Shift-Command-Z) reverses the last undo.

- **Cut** (Command-X) removes a selection from the document and puts a copy of it in the Clipboard.

- **Copy** (Command-C) puts a copy of a selection in the Clipboard.

- **Paste** (Command-V) inserts the contents of the Clipboard into the document at the insertion point or replaces selected text in the document with the contents of the Clipboard.

- **Clear** or **Delete** removes a selection from the document. This is the same as pressing Delete when document contents are selected.

- **Select All** (Command-A) selects all text or objects in the document.

It's important to keep in mind that Edit menu commands usually work with selected text or graphic objects in a document. Not all Edit menu commands are available in all applications at all times; it really depends on what is selected and what you're doing.

Most Edit menu commands are discussed in detail in Chapter 14, which covers TextEdit.

Edit

Undo Typing	⌘Z
Redo Typing	⇧⌘Z
Cut	⌘X
Copy	⌘C
Paste	⌘V
Paste and Match Style	⌥⇧⌘V
Delete	
Complete	⌥⎋
Select All	⌘A
Insert	▶
Add Link...	⌘K
Find	▶
Spelling and Grammar	▶
Substitutions	▶
Transformations	▶
Speech	▶
Start Dictation	fn fn
Special Characters...	⌥⌘T

Edit

Undo Edit Person	⌘Z
Redo	⇧⌘Z
Cut	⌘X
Copy	⌘C
Paste	⌘V
Delete Card	
Remove From Group	
Select All	⌘A
Find	▶
Spotlight: "John Aabbott"	
Rename Group	
Edit Smart Group	
Edit Card	⌘L
Edit Distribution List...	
Start Dictation	fn fn
Special Characters...	⌥⌘T

Ⓐ Ⓑ The Edit menus for TextEdit (top) and Contacts (bottom).

A The Window menu in TextEdit (top) and iTunes (bottom).

B The Help menu in TextEdit (top), Preview (middle), and Microsoft Word (bottom).

The Window Menu

The Window menu **A** includes commands for working with open document windows as well as a list of the open windows. The commands you'll find most often are:

- **Minimize** (Command-M; page 27) shrinks a window down to the size of an icon and slips it into the Dock.

- **Zoom** (page 27) toggles a window's size between two custom sizes you create by dragging a window border.

- **Bring All to Front** (page 25) displays all of the application's open windows on top of open windows for other applications.

These commands are discussed as they relate to the Finder in Chapter 2; the page references above will take you right to each topic. Just as application windows have the same parts and controls as Finder windows, these commands work the same way in the Finder and other applications.

The Help Menu

The Help menu **B** includes commands for viewing onscreen help information specific to the application. Choosing the primary Help command opens the Help window with information and links.

Using onscreen help is discussed in detail in Chapter 5; refer to that chapter for more information about using standard Help features with OS X and its applications.

TIP The top option on the Help menu is a Spotlight search box you can use to search for help (page 73).

Dialogs

OS X applications use *dialog boxes* or *dialogs* to tell you things and get information from you. Think of a dialog as the way your computer has a conversation—or dialog—with you.

OS X has three main types of dialogs:

- **Modeless dialogs A** enable you to work with the dialog while interacting with document windows. These dialogs usually have their own window controls to close and move them.

- **Document modal dialogs B** appear as dialog sheets attached to a document window. You must address and dismiss these dialogs before you can continue working with the window, although you can switch to another window or application while the dialog is displayed.

- **Application modal dialogs C** appear as movable dialogs. These dialogs must be addressed and dismissed before you can continue working with the application, although you can switch to another application while the dialog is displayed.

Dialogs contain a variety of components to gather information and enable you to interact with them. This part of the chapter explains what these standard dialog parts are and how you can use them.

TIP You don't need to remember modeless vs. modal terminology. Just understand how dialogs differ and what the differences mean in terms of what you can do when they appear.

TIP Some standard dialogs covered in this chapter are very similar from one application to another, including Open (page 158), Save (page 160), and warning (page 162). Two more standard dialogs—Page Setup and Print—are covered in Chapter 24.

A The Spelling and Grammar dialog in TextEdit is an example of a modeless dialog—you can interact with the document while the dialog is displayed.

B This dialog sheet, which is attached to the TextEdit document window, is an example of a document modal dialog; you must address and dismiss it before you can continue working with the window it's attached to.

C An Open dialog, like this one in TextEdit, is an example of an application modal dialog; you must address and dismiss it before you can continue working with the application.

Pane   Pane buttons   Preview area

D The Screen Saver pane of Desktop & Screen Saver preferences.

Push buttons

Scrolling lists   Combination box

E The Fonts panel.

To use dialog parts:

- Click a *pane button* to view a *pane* full of related options **D**.

- Scroll to view the contents of *scrolling lists* **D E**. Click a list item once to select it or to enter it in a *combination box* **E**.

- Enter text or numbers into *entry fields* **F**, including those that are part of *combination boxes* **E**.

- Click a *pop-up menu* **F** to display its options; click an option to choose it.

- Click a *check box* **G** to toggle it on or off. (A check box is turned on when a check mark or X appears inside it.)

- Click a *radio button* **G** to choose its option. (A radio button is chosen when a bullet appears inside it.)

- Drag a slider control **G** to change a setting.

- Consult a preview area **D** to see the effects of your changes.

- Click a push button **D F** to activate it.

Here are a few additional things to keep in mind when using dialog parts:

- An entry field with a colored border around it is the active field **E F**. Typing automatically enters text in this field. You can advance from one entry field to the next by pressing the Tab key.

- If an entry field has a pair of arrows or triangles beside it you can click the triangles to increase or decrease a value already in the field.

- The default push button is the one that pulsates. You can always select a default button by pressing the Enter key and often by pressing the Return key.

continues on next page

- You can usually select a Cancel button **F** by pressing the Esc key.

- You can select as many check boxes **G** in a group as you like.

- One and only one radio button in a group can be selected **G**. If you try to select a second radio button, the first button becomes deselected.

- If you click the Cancel button in a dialog **F**, any options you set are lost.

- To select multiple items in a scrolling list, hold down the Command key while clicking each one. Be aware that not all dialogs support multiple selections in scrolling lists.

TIP There are other standard controls in OS X dialogs, but these are the ones you'll encounter most often.

Pop-up menu   *Entry fields*

F This is the dialog you'd use to create a new user account.   *Push buttons*

Check boxes *Slider control* *Radio buttons*

G The Dock preferences pane.

The App Store

Apple's App Store combines the convenience of an online shopping service with the ease of use of an OS X application. The result: a system that makes it easier than ever to find, buy, install, and update OS X applications on your computer.

The App Store, which works with your Apple ID, automatically maintains a list of the software you've purchased, so it's easy to download and reinstall if necessary. It also notifies you of updates to Apple software and other software you've purchased through the App Store so you can obtain and install those updates as soon as they become available.

This chapter will introduce the features of the App Store and help you get connected so you can shop for applications online. It'll also explain how you can download, install, and update the applications you buy.

In This Chapter:

Launching & Quitting App Store

Like any other application, you must launch App Store before you can use it. This loads it into your computer's memory so your computer can work with it.

To launch App Store:

Use one of the following techniques:

- Choose Apple > App Store.

- Open the App Store application icon in the Applications folder window (page 137).

- Click the App Store icon in Launchpad (page 140).

- Click the App Store icon in the Dock (page 34).

App Store launches and displays its Featured window **B**.

TIP The applications that appear in screenshots of App Store throughout this chapter will vary from what you see when you access App Store on your computer. New applications are constantly being added to the App Store, so you'll likely see much newer offerings than what's shown here.

To quit App Store:

Use one of the following techniques:

- Choose App Store > Quit App Store, or press Command-Q.

- Close the App store window.

App Store quits.

A The App Store application icon.

App Store

B The App Store's Featured window displays featured applications.

A Use this dialog to sign in to the App Store.

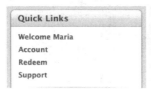

B When you're not signed in, you'll see a Sign In link in the Quick Links area.

C When you're signed in, you'll see a Welcome link in the Quick Links area.

Signing In & Out

To make the most of the App Store, you need to sign in with an Apple ID. Although you can browse the store to your heart's content without one, you need an account set up with Apple to make a purchase. If you've ever bought anything online from Apple or have used Apple's iCloud service (Chapter 19), you already have an Apple ID.

This part of the chapter explains how you can log in to and out of the App Store.

TIP If you're new to Apple products and don't have an Apple ID, you can easily create one. To get started, choose Store > Create Account. Then follow the onscreen prompts to enter account and payment information.

To sign in to the App Store:

1. Use one of the following techniques to display a Sign In dialog A:
   - Click the Sign In link in the Quick Links area B of any App Store screen.
   - Choose Store > Sign In.
2. Enter your Apple ID and password in the appropriate boxes and click Sign In.

   The dialog disappears and you are signed into the App Store.

TIP You can tell if you're signed in by looking at the Quick Links area on any App Store screen. If a Sign In link appears B, you're not logged in; if a Welcome link with your name appears C, you are logged in.

To sign out of the App Store:

Choose Store > Sign Out.

You are signed out of the App Store.

Browsing the App Store

The App Store is organized into five different screens, each of which is accessible from a button at the top of the window:

- **Featured** shows featured applications.

- **Top Charts** B shows the top-selling applications, organized by Top Paid, Top Free, and Top Grossing.

- **Categories** organizes applications by category C. You can click the name of a category to display a page full of applications in that category D.

- **Purchases** shows a list of software you've purchased. This list will be empty if you haven't purchased anything yet.

- **Updates** shows a list of updates to software you've purchased. This list will be empty if there aren't any updates or you haven't purchased anything yet.

You can also search the App Store using a Spotlight search box in the upper-right corner of any window.

A The Featured page shows featured apps. Be sure to scroll down to see them all.

B The Top Charts screen shows the top-selling apps, divided into three different groups.

C The Categories screen shows icons and titles for more than 20 categories.

D When you click a category icon **C**, you can see the apps listed within that category.

E When you click an app icon, you can see details about the app.

F Enter a search word in the search box at the top of the window.

G Apps that match the search word or phrase appear in the window.

To browse the App Store:

1. Click one of the first three buttons at the top of the App Store window: Featured, Top Charts, or Categories.

2. In the screen that appears, use any of the following techniques to browse available applications:

    ▶ Click a See All link **A** **B** **D** to see all the apps in a group.

    ▶ Click a category icon **C** to see all the apps in a category **D**.

    ▶ Click an application icon **A** **B** **D** to see details about that app **E**.

    ▶ Click the Back or Forward button at the top of the App Store window **A** **B** **C** **D** **E** to move backward or forward through screens you've already viewed.

TIP When shopping for an app, you might want to read the customer reviews before making a purchase decision—especially if the app isn't free. Be sure to scroll down in an app description **E** to see them. I've found that the more ratings an app has, the more realistic the overall rating will be.

To search the App Store:

1. Enter a search word or phrase in the search box at the top-right corner of the App Store window **F**.

2. Press Return.

    The App Store searches for the word you entered and displays search results in its window **G**.

TIP If there are many search results, you might consider sorting them. Use the Sort By pop-up menu near the top of the window to sort by Relevance, Most Popular, Release Date, or Customer Rating.

Buying & Installing Apps

When you see an app you want to buy, all you need do is click the price (or Free) button for it . That begins the process of purchasing, downloading, and installing the app on your computer.

To buy an app:

1. Click the price or Free button for the application you want to buy.

2. When the button turns into a Buy App or Install App button, click it.

3. If a Sign In dialog appears, enter your Apple ID and password and click Sign In.

   An icon for the app moves from the App Store window to the Launchpad icon in the Dock. If you open Launchpad, you'll see the app on one of Launchpad's screens. A message beneath the icon says "Downloading" and a progress bar appears in the icon .

4. When the download is complete, the app appears in Launchpad **D** where you can click it to open it and begin using it.

TIP If the app contains age-restricted material, a dialog may appear during the purchase process confirming that you are 17 or over. If you are, click OK.

TIP After installing an app, the Buy/Free button for the app turns into an Installed button **E** wherever the app appears in the App Store when you're signed in.

A Click the Buy or Free button to begin the purchase and installation process.

B Then click the Buy App or Install App button.

C An icon for the app appears in Launchpad as it downloads.

D When the download is complete, the app is ready to open.

E You don't have to worry about buying an app twice; the Buy/Free button turns into an Installed button once it has been purchased and installed.

The Purchases screen lists the apps you've purchased, including any that have not yet been installed.

 A progress bar appears in the Purchases screen while an app is being downloaded.

To review your purchases:

In the App Store window, click the Purchases button.

The Purchases screen displays a list of all your App Store purchases and indicates whether they have been installed .

To reinstall a purchased app:

1. In the App Store window, click the Purchases button to display a list of purchases .

2. Click the Install button beside any application that has not yet been installed.

3. If a Sign In dialog appears, enter your Apple ID and password and click Sign In.

   A download progress bar indicates that the app is being downloaded . When the progress bar disappears, the Install button is replaced with an Installed button and the app is ready to use.

TIP You can download and install your App Store purchases on any computer you own. In fact, the Purchases window will list apps purchased for any of the Macs on your Apple account.

TIP You can uninstall an app with Launchpad (page 141).

Updating Apps

If part of OS X or an application that you installed with the App Store is updated, the update will be available in the App Store's Updates screen . You'll know that an update is available because a badge will appear on the Update button **B** and in the Dock, indicating the number of updates that are available.

You can install the updates from within the App Store with just a click. Here's how.

TIP The software update feature of OS X now works directly with the App Store app to update all Apple software installed on your computer, even if it wasn't installed with the App Store. As a result, the Software Update app that was part of previous versions of OS X is no longer necessary—or available.

To update an app:

1. In the App Store window, click the Updates button to display a list of available updates **A**.

2. Beside each update you want to install, click the Update button.

3. If prompted for your password, enter it.

4. Wait while the software update is downloaded and installed.

   When installation is complete, the app is removed from the Updates list and the updated app is ready to use.

TIP If you're using a laptop and are not plugged in, a dialog will appear to confirm that you want to continue on battery power **C**. Click Continue to complete the update. Keep in mind that it's always best to update software while connected to a power source.

A Available updates appear in the Updates screen of App Store.

B A number on the Updates button indicates how many updates are available.

C If you're updating a laptop that isn't plugged in, you'll likely see this dialog.

TextEdit

TextEdit is a text editing application that comes with OS X. As its name implies, TextEdit lets you create, open, edit, and print text documents.

Over the years, TextEdit's feature set has been improved and expanded to offer many of the features found in more advanced word processing applications, such as iWorks' Pages and Microsoft Word. Indeed, TextEdit can open and edit documents created with either of those applications. You might even find that it meets most of your word processing needs.

This chapter explains how to use TextEdit to create, edit, and format documents. You'll find that many of the techniques you learn here for working with text and documents will be virtually the same in most other applications.

TIP If you're new to computers, don't skip this chapter. It not only explains how to use Text-Edit but provides instructions for basic text editing skills—such as text entry and the Copy, Cut, and Paste commands—that you'll use in all OS X applications.

Launching & Quitting TextEdit

Like any other application, you must launch TextEdit before you can use it. This loads it into your computer's memory so your computer can work with it.

To launch TextEdit:

Use one of the following techniques:

- Open the TextEdit application icon in the Applications folder window (page 132).

- Click the TextEdit icon in Launchpad (page 140).

TextEdit launches. Because TextEdit supports Auto Save (page 144), you'll see one of two things:

- If this is the first time you're using Text-Edit or if you closed all document windows the last time you used TextEdit, you'll see a blank, untitled document window .

- If you didn't close all document windows the last time you used TextEdit, those windows will reopen.

TIP The TextEdit document window has many of the same standard window parts found in Finder windows (page 23). They work the same way in TextEdit and other applications.

To quit TextEdit:

Choose TextEdit > Quit TextEdit, or press Command-Q.

TextEdit quits. Because TextEdit supports Auto Save, it automatically saves the current version of any open documents. Those documents will automatically reopen the next time you launch TextEdit.

A The TextEdit application icon can be found in the Applications folder.

TextEdit

B A blank, untitled TextEdit document window.

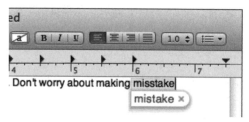

Ⓐ The text you type appears at the blinking insertion point.

Ⓑ If you have an iPhone or an iPad, the autocomplete/autocorrect feature in TextEdit should look familiar.

Entering & Editing Text

You enter text into a TextEdit document by typing it in. Don't worry about making mistakes; you can fix them as you type or when you're finished. This section explains how.

TIP The text entry and editing techniques covered in this section work exactly the same in most word processors, as well as many other OS X applications.

To enter text:

Type the text you want to enter. It appears at the blinking insertion point **Ⓐ**, which moves as you type.

Here are a few additional things to keep in mind:

- It is not necessary to press Return at the end of a line. When the text you type reaches the end of the line, it automatically begins a new line. This is called **word wrap** and is a feature of all word processors. By default, in TextEdit, word wrap is determined by the width of the document window.

- To correct an error as you type, press the Delete key. This key deletes the character to the left of the insertion point.

- TextEdit includes an autocomplete/autocorrect feature similar to the one on iOS devices such as the iPhone and iPad. You may see it in action as you type. To accept a suggested completion/correction **Ⓑ**, keep typing. To reject it, click the X button on the tag. This feature works with TextEdit's automatic spelling check feature (page 189).

To move the insertion point:

Use one of the following techniques:

- Press one of the arrow keys to move the insertion point left, right, up, or down one character or line at a time.

- Position the pointer, which looks like an I-beam, where you want the insertion point to appear **C** and click once. The insertion point appears at the pointer **D**.

TIP Since the text you type appears at the insertion point, it's a good idea to know where the insertion point is *before* you start typing.

TIP When moving the insertion point with the mouse or trackpad, you *must click* to complete the move. If you simply point with the I-beam pointer, the insertion point will stay where it is.

To insert text:

1. Position the insertion point where you want the text to appear **E**.

2. Type the text you want to insert.

   The text appears at the insertion point **F**.

TIP Word wrap changes automatically to accommodate inserted text.

C Position the I-beam pointer...

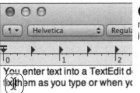

D ...and click to move the blinking insertion point.

E Position the insertion point where you want to insert text...

F ...and type the text you want to insert.

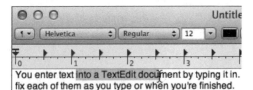

G Drag over text to select it.

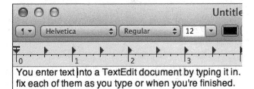

H Position the insertion point at the beginning of the text you want to select...

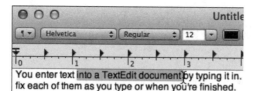

You enter text into a TextEdit document by typing it in.
fix each of them as you type or when you're finished.

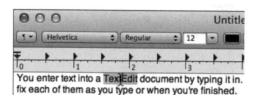

I ...and then hold down Shift while clicking at the end of the text you want to select.

You enter text into a TextEdit document by typing it in.
fix each of them as you type or when you're finished.

J Double-click a word to select it.

Edit	
Undo Typing	⌘Z
Redo	⇧⌘Z
Cut	⌘X
Copy	⌘C
Paste	⌘V
Paste and Match Style	⌥⇧⌘V
Delete	
Complete	⌥⎋
Select All	⌘A
Insert	▶
Add Link	⌘K

K To select all text in a document, choose Select All from the Edit menu.

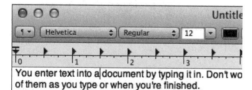

You enter text into a document by typing it in. Don't wo
of them as you type or when you're finished.

L Press Delete to remove selected text.

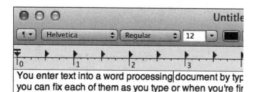

You enter text into a word processing document by typ
you can fix each of them as you type or when you're fir

M Type new text to replace selected text.

To select text by dragging:

Drag the I-beam pointer over the text you want to select **G**.

To select text with Shift-click:

1. Position the insertion point at the beginning of the text you want to select **H**.
2. Hold down the Shift key and click at the end of the text you want to select.

   All text between the insertion point and where you clicked becomes selected **I**.

TIP The Shift-click technique is a good way to select large blocks of text. After positioning the insertion point as instructed in step 1, scroll to the end of the text you want to select. Then Shift-click as instructed in step 2 to make the selection.

To select a single word:

Double-click the word **J**.

To select all document contents:

Choose Edit > Select All **K**, or press Command-A.

To delete text:

1. Select the text that you want to delete **J**.
2. Press the Delete key.

   The selected text disappears **L**.

To replace text:

1. Select the text that you want to replace **J**.
2. Type the new text.

   The selected text is replaced by what you type **M**.

Basic Text Formatting

TextEdit also offers formatting features that you can use to change the appearance of document text.

- **Font formatting** enables you to change the appearance of individual text characters. This includes the font typeface and family, character style, character size, and character color.

- **Text formatting** enables you to change the appearance of entire paragraphs of text. This includes alignment, line spacing, and ruler settings such as tabs and indentation.

This chapter introduces the most commonly used formatting options in TextEdit.

TIP TextEdit offers other formatting options that you can explore on your own. You'll find them all on the Format menu and its submenus.

TIP Some text formatting options are on the ruler. If the ruler is not showing, you can display it by choosing **Format > Text > Show Ruler** or by pressing **Command-R**.

A Select the text you want to format.

B The Font submenu under the Format menu.

C The Fonts window.

D You can see your changes immediately, as you make them.

ⓔ A check mark appears on the Font submenu beside the name of each style applied to selected text.

Font formatting buttons and menus

ⓕ You can use buttons and menus on the toolbar to apply font formatting to selected text.

TABLE 14.1 Shortcut Keys for TextEdit Font Formatting

Keystroke	Formatting Applied
Command-B	Bold
Command-I	Italic
Command-U	Underline
Command-+	Bigger (increase font size)
Command-–	Smaller (decrease font size)
Shift-Command-T	Make Plain Text (remove formatting)

To apply font formatting:

1. Select the text characters you want to apply font formatting to **ⓐ**.

2. Use any combination of the following techniques to apply font formatting:

   ▸ Choose Format > Font > Show Fonts **ⓑ**, or press Command-T, to display the Fonts window **ⓒ**, where you can set options as desired. You'll immediately see the results of your changes in the document window **ⓓ**; make changes if you don't like what you see. You can also select different text and format it without closing the Fonts window.

   ▸ Choose options from the Format menu's Font submenu **ⓑ** to apply formatting. You can choose any combination of options. A check mark appears beside the type of formatting applied to selected text **ⓔ**.

   ▸ Use TextEdit window toolbar buttons and menus **ⓕ** to set the font family, typeface, font size, text color, and style. You can point to a button or menu to see a Help Tag (page 68) that describes what it does.

   ▸ Press the shortcut key (**Table 14.1**) for the type of formatting you want to apply.

TIP To remove an applied style, choose it from the Font submenu or select its toolbar button or menu again.

TIP Fonts are covered in greater detail in Chapter 23.

To apply text formatting:

1. Select the paragraph(s) you want to format.

2. Use any combination of the following techniques to apply text formatting:

   ▸ Choose an option from the Format menu's Text submenu to apply formatting.

   ▸ Use TextEdit window toolbar buttons and menus to set the alignment, line spacing, paragraph spacing, and bullet or number formatting. You can point to a button or menu to see a Help Tag (page 68) that describes what it does.

   ▸ Press the shortcut key (**Table 14.2**) for the type of formatting you want to apply.

To set tab stops:

Add, remove, and modify tab stops on the ruler as follows:

- To remove a tab stop, drag it from the ruler into the document window . When you release the button, the tab is removed.

- To add a tab stop, click the ruler where you want to place it.

- To move a tab stop, drag it to a new position on the ruler .

- To change a tab type, right-click it to display a menu of options and choose the one you want.

TIP A tab stop is the position the insertion point moves to when you press the Tab key.

TIP Tab settings affect entire paragraphs. When you press Return to begin a new paragraph, the tab stops you set for the current paragraph are carried forward.

G Choose an option from the Text submenu under the Format menu.

Text formatting buttons and menus

H You can use these buttons and menus to apply text formatting to selected paragraphs.

TABLE 14.2 Shortcut Keys for TextEdit Text Formatting

Keystroke	Formatting Applied
Command-{	Align Left
Command-I	Center
Command-}	Align Right

I Drag the tab off the ruler. (The pointer disappears, so it's tough to illustrate.)

J Drag the tab to a new position on the ruler. (Again, invisible pointer!)

K Right-click to display a menu of tab types and choose the one you want.

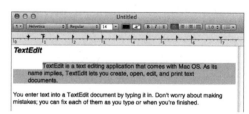

L If desired, type text at the beginning of the line.

M Press Tab and enter text at the first tab stop.

N The first line of a table created with tabs.

First Name	Last Name	Rate
Maria	Langer	23.95
John	Aabbott	14.75
Michael	Chillingerian	28.5
John	Doe	9.755
Jane	Doe	102.2

O A complete table using left and decimal tabs.

P Select the text you want to set indentation for.

First line indent
Left indent   Right indent

Q TextEdit Indent markers.

R In this example, all three indent markers were shifted to set indentation for this paragraph.

To use tab stops:

1. Add and remove tab stops as instructed in the section titled "To set tab stops" on page 184.

2. Position the insertion point at the beginning of the paragraph that tab stops are set for.

3. If desired, enter text at the beginning of the line **L**.

4. Press the Tab key.

5. Enter text at the tab stop **M**.

6. Repeat steps 4 and 5 until you have entered text as desired at all tab stops **N**.

7. Press the Return key to start a new paragraph.

8. Repeat steps 2 through 7 for each paragraph in which you want to use the tab stops **O**.

To set indentation:

1. Select the paragraph(s) for which you want to set indentation **P**.

2. Drag one of the icons on the end of the ruler **Q** to the left or right:

   ▸ To set the first line indentation for a paragraph, drag the horizontal rectangle icon.

   ▸ To set the left indent, drag the triangle on the left end of the ruler.

   ▸ To set the right indent, drag the triangle on the right end of the ruler.

   As you drag, a yellow box indicates the position of the indent. When you release a marker, the text shifts **R**.

Undoing & Redoing Actions

The Undo command **Ⓐ** enables you to reverse your last action, thus offering an easy way to fix errors immediately after you make them. The Redo command **Ⓐ**, which is available only when your last action was to use the Undo command, reverses the undo action.

TextEdit supports multiple levels of undo (and redo). That means you can undo (or redo) several actions, in the reverse order that they were performed (or undone).

TIP The Undo and Redo commands are available in most applications and can be found at the top of the Edit menu (page 164).

TIP The exact wording of the Undo (and Redo) command depends on what was last done (or undone). For example, if the last thing you did was to apply font formatting to selected text, the Undo command will be Undo Set Font **Ⓐ**.

To undo the last action:

Choose Edit > Undo **Ⓐ**, or press Command-Z.

The last thing you did is undone.

TIP To undo multiple actions, choose Edit > Undo repeatedly.

To redo an action:

After using the Undo command, choose Edit > Redo **Ⓐ**, or press Shift-Command-Z.

The last thing you undid is redone.

TIP To redo multiple actions, choose Edit > Redo repeatedly.

Edit	
Undo Center	⌘Z
Redo Set Font	⇧⌘Z
Cut	⌘X
Copy	⌘C
Paste	⌘V
Paste and Match Style	⌥⇧⌘V
Delete	
Complete	⌥⌤
Select All	⌘A
Insert	▶
Add Link...	⌘K
Find	▶
Spelling and Grammar	▶
Substitutions	▶
Transformations	▶
Speech	▶
Start Dictation	fn fn
Special Characters...	⌥⌘T

Ⓐ The Edit menu with Undo and Redo commands displayed. If one of these commands were not available, it would be gray.

Edit

Undo Typing	⌘Z
Redo	⇧⌘Z
Cut	⌘X
Copy	⌘C
Paste	⌘V
Paste and Match Style	⌥⇧⌘V
Delete	
Complete	⌥⎋
Select All	⌘A
Insert	▶
Add Link...	⌘K
Find	▶
Spelling and Grammar	▶
Substitutions	▶
Transformations	▶
Speech	▶
Start Dictation	fn fn
Special Characters...	⌥⌘T

Ⓐ You can find the Cut, Copy, and Paste commands on the Edit menu.

Quick Quiz: The Clipboard

Right *after* using the Paste command, what's in the Clipboard?

Answer: The same thing that was in it right *before* using the Paste command.

Using the Paste command pastes a *copy* of what's on the Clipboard. That content remains on the Clipboard to use again and again—until you use the Copy or Cut command to replace it with new content.

Copy, Cut & Paste

The Copy, Cut, and Paste commands **Ⓐ** enable you to duplicate or move document contents. Here's what each of these commands do:

- **Copy** copies selected content to the Clipboard. The selected text remains in the document.

- **Cut** copies selected content to the Clipboard and removes it from the document.

- **Paste** copies the contents of the Clipboard into the document at the insertion point.

Because the Clipboard is shared by all Mac OS applications, the Copy, Cut, and Paste commands work between applications. So, for example, you can copy text from a TextEdit document and then paste it into a Microsoft Word document.

TIP Almost all OS X-compatible applications include the Copy, Cut, and Paste commands on the Edit menu (page 164). These commands work very much the same in all applications.

TIP The Copy, Cut, and Paste commands also work with images and other content.

TIP TextEdit and many other OS X applications also support drag-and-drop text editing. Simply select the text you want to move and drag it to a new position in the document. Holding down the Option key while dragging copies the selection to the new location. Try it for yourself and see!

To copy text:

1. Select the text that you want to copy **B**.

2. Choose Edit > Copy **A**, or press Command-C.

   The text is copied to the Clipboard so it can be pasted elsewhere. The original text remains in the document.

To cut text:

1. Select the text that you want to cut **B**.

2. Choose Edit > Cut **A**, or press Command-X.

   The text is copied to the Clipboard so it can be pasted elsewhere. The original is removed from the document.

To paste Clipboard contents:

1. Position the insertion point where you want the Clipboard contents to appear **C**.

2. Choose Edit > Paste **A**, or press Command-V.

   The Clipboard's contents are pasted into the document **D**.

TIP The Clipboard contains only the last item that was copied or cut. Using the Paste command, therefore, pastes in the most recently cut or copied selection.

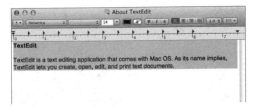

B Select the text you want to copy or cut.

C Position the insertion point where you want to paste the contents of the Clipboard.

D When you use the Paste command, the contents of the Clipboard are pasted at the insertion point.

A The default settings on Edit menu's Spelling and Grammar submenu in TextEdit.

Checking Spelling & Grammar

TextEdit includes a spelling checker and a grammar checker. These two features can be used either automatically, to check a document as you create it, or manually, to check a document that is fully or partially completed. Together, they can help you identify problems in your documents so you can correct them before sharing them with others.

TextEdit also has an automatic spelling correction feature similar to that on iOS devices such as the iPhone and iPad. This feature can automatically correct misspelled words as you type.

This part of the chapter takes a look at how you can set up and use TextEdit's spelling and grammar checking and correction features.

To check and correct spelling as you type:

1. Display the Spelling and Grammar submenu under the Edit menu **A** and choose the following options to place a check mark beside the ones you want:

   ▶ **Check Spelling While Typing** enables the automatic spelling check feature.

   ▶ **Check Grammar With Spelling** enables grammar checking.

   ▶ **Correct Spelling Automatically** enables the automatic spelling correction feature.

2. As you enter text in the document, TextEdit checks its spelling (and grammar, if enabled) and does one the following when it encounters a potential error:

continues on next page

Word of Advice: Don't Rely on Spelling and Grammar Checkers!

Don't depend solely on the spelling and grammar checkers in TextEdit (or any other application, for that matter) to make your documents perfect. Spelling checkers will not identify misspelled words that correctly spell other words—for example, *then* and *them*. Grammar checkers cannot identify all grammatical errors—and sometimes they inaccurately identify errors that aren't errors at all. These tools are no substitute for a good, old-fashioned proofreading!

- If automatic spelling correction is enabled and a possible correction is available, TextEdit may display an autocorrect tag **B**. To accept the correction, just keep typing; the incorrect spelling is automatically replaced. To reject the correction, click the X on the tag.

- If automatic spelling checking is enabled, TextEdit places a dashed red underline under each word that isn't in its dictionary **C**. You can either manually correct the error using standard text editing techniques (page 179) or right-click the error to display a menu of options **D** and choose the option you want.

- If automatic grammar checking is enabled, TextEdit places a green dashed underline under each word or phrase that could be a grammar error **C**. You can either manually correct the error using standard text editing techniques (page 179) or right-click the error to display a menu of options **E** and choose the option you want.

TIP Sometimes TextEdit's autocorrection feature will automatically correct a word's spelling without displaying a tag.

B TextEdit might display an autocorrect tag to offer to make a correction.

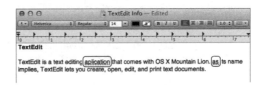

C TextEdit identifies potential errors with dashed underlines.

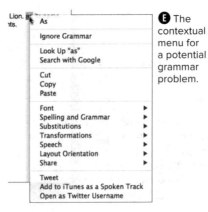

D The contextual menu for a potential spelling problem.

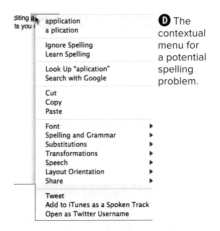

E The contextual menu for a potential grammar problem.

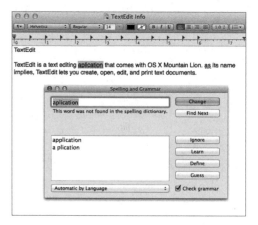

F Use the Spelling and Grammar window to resolve possible spelling and grammar errors.

To manually check spelling & grammar:

1. Choose Edit > Spelling and Grammar > Show Spelling and Grammar **A**, or press Command-: (colon), to display the Spelling and Grammar window.

    TextEdit selects and underlines the first possible misspelled word it finds. The word appears in a field in the Spelling and Grammar window and any suggested corrections appear in a list **F**.

2. You have several options:

    ▸ To replace the word with a listed word, select the replacement word and click Change.

    ▸ To enter a new spelling for the word, enter it in the box where the incorrect spelling appears and click Change.

    ▸ To ignore the word, click Ignore.

    ▸ To skip the word and continue checking, click Find Next.

    ▸ To add the word to OS X's dictionary, click Learn. TextEdit will never stop at that word again in any document.

3. Repeat step 2 for each word that TextEdit identifies as a possible misspelling or grammar error.

4. When you're finished checking spelling, click the Spelling and Grammar window's close button to dismiss it.

TIP To ensure that TextEdit uses the correct spelling dictionary, you can choose the language your document is written in from the pop-up menu at the bottom of the Spelling and Grammar window **F**.

TIP If you want to check grammar with spelling, make sure the Check Grammar check box is turned on in the Spelling and Grammar window **F**.

Using Dictation

OS X Mountain Lion's new dictation feature makes it possible to enter text by speaking it into your Mac. Simply enable the feature, speak clearly into your Mac's microphone, and click Done. OS X types what you said.

Dictation works by recording what you say and sending it to a speech recognition server, where it is transcribed and sent back to your Mac. Because of this, it requires an Internet connection.

Although dictation can transcribe words, it does not automatically punctuate. You can, however, add punctuation by including it in your dictation. For example, to type the previous sentence, you'd say: "You can comma however comma add punctuation by including it in your dictation period." Table 14.3 lists some of the punctuation and text commands that dictation recognizes.

This part of the chapter provides some basic information on how you can use dictation with TextEdit.

TIP The dictation feature is supported throughout OS X—not just within TextEdit. You can enable it with its keyboard shortcut to use it anywhere you can type.

TIP If you've ever used Dragon Dictate software, this feature should be very familiar to you. It works similarly, but processes dictation on your Mac using its own software. Dragon Dictate also supports a wide range of text editing commands, as well as commands for performing tasks on your Mac.

TIP You can set dictation options—including the language you will use to dictate text—in the Dictation & Speech preferences pane (page 585).

TABLE 14.3 Punctuation and Text Commands

To type this	Say this
.	Period
,	Comma
?	Question mark
!	Exclamation mark
begin a new line	New line
begin a new paragraph	New paragraph
Type a word in all capital letters	All caps

A The Start Dictation command can be found on TextEdit's Edit menu.

B The dictation icon appears at the insertion point.

C The text you dictated—or at least the text your Mac thinks you dictated—appears at the insertion point.

D You can click the About Dictation & Privacy button to learn more about how the speech recognition server works.

E Apple wants to make sure you don't mind sending them information.

To dictate text:

1. Start the dictation feature by using one of the following techniques:

   ▸ Choose Edit > Start Dictation **A**.

   ▸ Press the FN key twice.

   A microphone icon appears at the insertion point **B**.

2. Speak clearly into your Mac's microphone.

   The sound level of your voice is indicated in the microphone icon as you speak.

3. When you are finished dictating, click Done.

   After a moment, the text you dictated is typed at the insertion point and the dictation icon disappears **C**.

TIP In step 1, the first time you start the dictation feature, a pair of dialogs appear to confirm that you want to enable the feature **D E**. You must click OK in the first dialog **D** and Enable Dictation in the second dialog **E** to turn on this feature.

TIP If you decide not to dictate after starting the dictation feature, press Esc to dismiss the dictation icon.

TIP For best results, use dictation in a place with minimum background noise or use a headset microphone. Speak slowly and clearly at a normal speaking volume. To fine-tune the settings for your microphone, use the Sound preferences pane (page 540).

Saving Documents

When you're finished working with a TextEdit document, you may want to save it. You can then open it another time to review, edit, or print it or send it to someone else who might want to work with it.

TextEdit supports OS X's Auto Save feature (page 144), so it automatically saves all documents you create. It isn't until you close a document's window that TextEdit asks if you want to save it . If you don't save an unsaved document when closing it, TextEdit discards any information it may have automatically saved for it.

If you quit TextEdit, the next time you launch it, it automatically reopens all the document windows that were open when you quit—even if those documents were never saved. This is OS X's Resume feature in action.

Once you save a TextEdit document, it can be closed, reopened, or shared with someone else—just like any other document file. The Auto Save feature will also automatically save versions (page 144) of the file as you continue working on it. But you can manually save a version (page 161) any time you like. This makes it possible to restore a document to a previously saved version (page 148).

You use the Save command (page 157) and Save dialog to save a document for the first time (page 160) and to save subsequent changes to it (page 161).

A It isn't until you close a document window that TextEdit asks if you want to save it.

B You can use the File Format pop-up menu to save a TextEdit file in a specific format.

C To save a document as a plain text file, you must convert it to plain text first.

TextEdit supports the following file formats, which can be specified when you save the file for the first time, by choosing an option from the File Format pop-up menu in the Save dialog **B**:

- **Rich Text Document** (RTF) is supported by most word processing applications and enables you to include text formatting in the document file. This is TextEdit's default file format.

- **Rich Text Document with Attachments** is the same as Rich Text Document, but it enables you to include file attachments such as images in the file.

- **Web Page (.html)** and **Web Archive Document** are HTML format files that can be read by a Web browser such as Safari.

- **OpenDocument Text (.odt) Document** is a format that can be read by Open Office compatible word processing applications, such as Google Docs.

- **Word 2007 (.docx) Document**, **Word 2003 (.xml) Document**, and **Word 97 (.doc) Document** are three different Microsoft Word compatible formats.

TIP Remember that until you manually save a document, thus giving it a name and placing a copy of it on disk, that document is accessible through TextEdit only. Don't rely on the Auto Save feature—be sure to save all your important documents.

TIP You can also save a document as a plain text document if you convert it to plain text *before* saving it. To do this, choose Format > Make Plain Text **C**. This strips out all formatting in the document and displays different options in the File Format pop-up menu when you save the file.

Opening Documents

You can open any compatible text or word processing document with TextEdit. This includes documents in plain text, RTF, Word, and OpenDocument format.

You open a TextEdit document like any other document:

- Double-click its icon in the Finder (page 138).

- Drag its icon onto the TextEdit document icon (page 139).

- Select the icon and use the Open With command (page 139).

- Choose File > Open from within TextEdit and use the Open dialog that appears to locate, select, and open the file (page 158).

Because TextEdit supports OS X's Resume feature, when you open TextEdit, any document windows that were open the last time you quit it are automatically reopened.

Music & Video Applications

OS X comes with three applications that enable you to enjoy music and video on your Mac:

- **iTunes** lets you play audio and video files, as well as purchase or rent content to listen to or watch on your Mac.

- **QuickTime Player** enables you to view, record, edit, and share QuickTime-compatible media files.

- **DVD Player** allows you to play movies and other video stored on DVD media on your Mac.

This chapter introduces these three applications and explains how you can get started using them to play and share music and video on your Mac.

iTunes

iTunes is a digital media application that enables you to do a wide variety of things:

- Play digital audio files saved in a variety of common audio file formats.

- Encode music from audio CDs on your Macintosh in a variety of audio file formats.

- Organize music into playlists.

- Buy music, audio books, television shows, movies, and iOS apps from the iTunes Store.

- Subscribe to and listen to podcasts.

- Download free educational content from iTunes U.

- Save digital audio files in AAC and MP3 format.

- Create custom CDs of your favorite music.

- Listen to Internet-based radio stations.

- Share your iTunes library with other users on your local network.

- Play content via AppleTV.

- Sync content and apps with your iPod, iPhone, or iPad.

This part of the chapter explains how you can get started using iTunes to manage, buy, and play music and other media files.

TIP iTunes supports the following audio file formats: AAC, AIFF, Apple Lossless, MP3, MPEG-4, AAC (.m4a), and WAV.

TIP You can learn a lot more about all of iTunes' features at www.apple.com/itunes/features/.

A The iTunes application icon.

iTunes

B The iTunes window before you have stored any media files.

C iTunes includes access to a number of video tutorials that can help you learn more about it.

To launch iTunes:

1. Use one of the following techniques:
    *   Open the iTunes application icon **A** in the Applications folder window (page 137).
    *   Click the iTunes icon in Launchpad (page 140).
    *   Click the iTunes icon in the Dock (page 34).

2. If you are opening iTunes for the first time, a license agreement window appears. You must click Accept to use iTunes.

    If you are opening iTunes for the first time, the main iTunes window **B** displays some general information about iTunes, along with links to video tutorials to learn more. Once you have begun storing media files in iTunes, this window will display that media.

TIP You can access tutorial videos for using iTunes **C** by choosing Help > iTunes Tutorials. This window may open automatically the first time you open iTunes.

To quit iTunes:

Choose iTunes > Quit iTunes, or press Command-Q.

iTunes quits. Any changes you made to playlists or other settings are automatically saved.

To add songs from an audio CD to the iTunes Library:

1. Insert an audio CD in your CD drive.

   A few things may happen:

   ▸ If your computer has access to the Internet, it goes online to get CD song information.

   ▸ The CD's name appears in the source list and a list of its tracks appears in the song list **D**.

   ▸ A dialog offers to import the songs **E**.

2. Do one of the following:

   ▸ If the import dialog appeared **E**, click Yes to start the import.

   ▸ If the import dialog did not appear, in the song list, turn on the check box beside each song you want to add and click the Import CD button at the bottom of the window.

   iTunes begins importing the songs on the CD. The status area provides progress information **F**. The songs may play while they are imported. When iTunes is finished importing songs, it plays a sound.

3. Click the eject button beside the CD name in the source list **D** to eject the disc.

TIP Please observe copyright law and only import music you own into iTunes.

TIP You can specify an import format by setting iTunes preferences. Choose iTunes > Preferences, click the General button, and then click the Import Settings button to get started.

D iTunes displays the CD in the Devices list and a list of the songs it contains in the song list.

E iTunes displays a dialog asking if you want to import the CD.

F The status area at the top of the iTunes window reports import progress.

G Drag the icon for a music file from a Finder window into the iTunes window.

H The song you dragged is imported into iTunes.

I Here's an iTunes music library displayed in grid view with album artwork downloaded by iTunes.

To import music files on disk to the Library:

Drag the icon for the music file from the desktop or a Finder window to the iTunes window's Library list **G**.

After a moment, the song appears in the Library window **H**.

TIP You can use this technique to add several music files or folders full of music files at once. Simply select their icons and drag any one of them into the window.

TIP You can also import music with the Add to Library command on the iTunes File menu. Personally, I think the drag-and-drop technique is quicker and easier.

To get album art:

1. Choose Advanced > Get Album Artwork.

2. If a dialog prompts you to sign in to your iTunes Store account, click OK, choose Store > Sign In, and use the dialog that appears to sign in to the iTunes store. Then repeat step 1.

3. If a dialog ask if you're sure you want to get album artwork, click Get Album Artwork.

   iTunes goes online to search for and download missing album artwork for your iTunes library. When it's finished, it displays the artwork it's found with the album information in the song list **I**.

TIP You can use this feature to ensure you have artwork to take advantage of iTunes Cover Flow view.

To browse the source list:

Click one of the items in the source list on the left side of the iTunes window to display the contents of that source:

- **Library** is a list of all the content you have stored in your iTunes library. Categories within this area can include Music , Movies, TV Shows, Podcasts, iTunes U, Books, Apps, Tones, and Radio.

- **Store** displays iTunes Store related items, including the iTunes Store ⓚ, iTunes Match (if you're logged in to an iCloud account), Ping, and Downloads. You must have an Apple ID to use iTunes Store features.

- **Devices** displays iTunes-compatible devices connected to your computer, including inserted CDs ⓓ and iOS devices.

- **Shared** displays content available via network from a shared library.

- **Genius** displays playlists created for you by the Genius feature ⓛ, which creates playlists and mixes from your iTunes music library and suggests music you might like. You must have an Apple ID and turn on the Genius feature to use it; click Genius and follow the instructions that appear.

- **Playlists** displays the iTunes DJ feature, which automatically chooses songs to play from your iTunes music library, as well as any smart or regular playlists you may have created.

TIP Some features, such as the iTunes Store and Radio, require access to the internet to use.

ⓙ Your Music library includes all the music stored in iTunes. Here's what it looks like in Album list view.

ⓚ The iTunes Store is a great source of content for iTunes.

ⓛ The Genius feature can create playlists of similar songs. Here's what a custom Genius mix looks like in Cover Flow view.

Song list / Album list / Grid / Cover Flow

M The view buttons.

Back / Play / Stop / Forward / Volume

N Buttons at the top of the iTunes window let you control play and volume.

Create playlist / Shuffle / Repeat / Artwork

O Use buttons beneath the source list to add playlists, control play order and repeating, and display artwork or the movie viewer.

Authorize This Computer

This computer is not authorized to play "Valley Girl". Would you like to authorize it?

To play this song you must authorize this computer to play songs purchased using the account "mlanger@mac.com". You may authorize up to 5 computers for each account.

Apple ID

Password   Forgot?

Preview   Cancel   Authorize

P You'll need to authorize your computer to play protected songs purchased from the iTunes store. (Yes, I did buy "Valley Girl" by Frank Zappa. Gonna make somethin' of it?)

To change the window view:

Click one of the view icons at the top of the iTunes window **M** to change the view of items you are browsing:

- Song list view displays a list of songs.
- Album list view **J** displays a list of albums and, within each album group, the album's songs.
- Grid view **I** displays music by album cover.
- Cover Flow view **L** displays content in a split pane view, with artwork in the top pane and a list in the bottom pane.

To play content:

1. In the source list, select the source of the content you want to play.

   Individual items appear in the main part of the window **I** **J** **K** **L**.

2. Double-click the item you want to play.

   iTunes begins playing what you double-clicked.

TIP When you play music, iTunes automatically plays all music in the list that was displayed when you started playing.

TIP You can use buttons at the top of the iTunes window **N** to control play and volume.

TIP You can use buttons at the bottom of the source list **O** to work with the list and change the way music is played.

TIP To listen to protected songs purchased from the iTunes Store or accessible via shared library, you may have to authorize your computer. If so, a dialog will appear **P**; enter the account name and password for the owner of the music and click Authorize. You only need to do this once on your computer to listen to protected music. You can authorize up to five computers to play the protected songs you purchase.

To create a playlist:

1. Use one of following techniques:

   ▸ Click the New Playlist button beneath the source list .

   ▸ Choose File > New Playlist.

   ▸ Press Command-N.

   A new untitled playlist appears in the Playlists area of the source list **Q**.

2. Type a name for the playlist, and press Return to save it.

Q A new playlist appears at the bottom of the Playlists area in the source list.

To add songs to a playlist:

1. If necessary, select the source of the music you want to add to the playlist.

2. Drag a song from the song list to the playlist name in the source list **R**.

3. Repeat step 2 for each song you want to add to the playlist.

4. When you're finished adding songs, click the playlist name.

   The songs appear in the list.

R Drag a song from the song list to the playlist.

TIP In step 2, you can hold down the Command key while selecting songs to select more than one and then drag them to the playlist.

To remove a song from a playlist:

1. In the source list, select the playlist you want to modify.

2. In the song list, select the song you want to remove.

3. Press Delete.

4. If a confirmation dialog appears, click Remove.

   The song is removed from the playlist.

TIP Removing a song from a playlist does not remove it from the iTunes Library.

S The Smart Playlist dialog starts off like this.

T Here's an example of smart playlist settings with two criteria.

U Use this pop-up menu to specify how iTunes should select songs when you limit the selection.

V Here's the smart playlist showing the results of my criteria **T**.

To create a smart playlist:

1. Choose File > New Smart Playlist or press Option-Command-N to display the Smart Playlist dialog **S**.

2. Choose an option from the first pop-up menu, which includes all data fields that iTunes tracks for each item. Then set criteria using options on that line.

3. To add additional matching criteria, click the + button. The dialog expands to offer an additional line for criteria. Set criteria as desired in this line **T**. You can repeat this step to set all criteria.

4. If you set up multiple criteria in step 3, choose an option from the Match pop-up menu: **All** matches all criteria you set and **Any** matches any criteria.

5. To limit the size of the playlist, turn on the Limit to check box and choose an option from the pop-up menu: minutes, hours, MB, GB, or items. Then enter a value in the box beside it. You can also use the selected by pop-up menu **U** to specify how songs should be chosen.

6. To include only songs that are checked in the song list, turn on the Match only checked items check box.

7. To automatically update the playlist each time songs are added or removed from the Library, turn on the Live updating check box.

8. Click OK.

   A new smart playlist appears in the source list with a suggested name based on what you entered. When the list is selected, you can see the songs iTunes selected **V**.

To delete a playlist:

1. In the source window, select the playlist you want to delete.

2. Press the Delete key.

3. If a confirmation dialog appears, click Delete.

    The playlist is removed.

TIP Deleting a playlist does not delete the songs on the playlist from your music library.

To create a Genius playlist:

1. If the Genius feature has not already been enabled, choose Store > Turn on Genius. Then follow the instructions that appear onscreen to turn it on.

2. Select or play any song in your library.

3. Click the Start Genius button in the lower-right corner of the iTunes window.

    iTunes displays the Genius playlist, with a list of 25 songs it thinks are a good match for the one you selected **L**.

4. Play the playlist like any other playlist.

To save iTunes songs as audio files:

Drag the name of the song you want to export from the iTunes Library window to the desktop or a Finder window **W**.

After a moment, an audio file icon for the exported song appears in the Finder **X**.

TIP You can use this technique to export a bunch of audio files at once. Simply hold down the Command key while clicking each song you want to select. Then drag any one of them to the Finder window.

TIP Audio export format is determined by Import Settings in iTunes preferences. Choose iTunes > Preferences, click the General button, and then click Import Settings to get started.

W Drag the song file from the iTunes window into a Finder window.

X The song is exported as an audio file.

The Burn Settings dialog offers options for burning a CD from within iTunes.

To burn iTunes content to disc:

1. Create a playlist that contains the content you want to include on the disc.

2. Select the playlist.

3. Choose File > Burn Playlist to Disc.

4. In the Burn Settings dialog that appears ⓨ, set options as desired:

   ▸ **Preferred Speed** is the burn speed. Options vary depending on your CD/DVD writer.

   ▸ **Disc Format** enables you to choose from three formats: Audio CD, which will play in any CD player; MP3 CD, which will play in any CD player that supports MP3 CDs, including your computer; and Data CD or DVD, which stores the files as data. If you select Audio CD, you can set additional options.

5. Click Burn.

6. When prompted, insert a blank disc.

7. Wait while iTunes prepares and burns the disc.

   A progress indicator appears at the top of the iTunes window as it works. When iTunes is finished, it makes a sound and the disc icon appears on your desktop.

TIP Your computer must have a compatible CD-R drive or SuperDrive to burn audio CDs or data to CD or DVD. You can learn more about burning CDs and DVDs on page 109.

TIP If you are creating an audio CD and the playlist you have selected won't fit on a single disc, iTunes offers to split the songs over multiple CDs.

TIP You cannot burn an audio or MP3 CD containing protected audio files.

To share content with other network users:

1. Choose iTunes > Preferences.

2. Click the Sharing button to display Sharing preferences .

3. To share your iTunes content with other network users, turn on the Share my library on my local network check box. Then select one of the radio buttons:

   ▸ **Share entire library** shares all of your music.

   ▸ **Share selected playlists** enables you to toggle check boxes for individual playlists you want to share.

4. To require other network users to enter a password to listen to your music, turn on the Require password check box and enter a password in the box.

5. To allow devices sharing your music to update song play counts, turn on the Home Sharing computer and devices update play counts check box.

6. Click OK.

7. A dialog reminding you that sharing music is for personal use only may appear. Click OK.

TIP Once sharing is enabled, the Status area in the Sharing preferences dialog **Z** reports whether your music is being accessed by other users on the network.

TIP You can learn more about networking and sharing files with OS X in Part VI of this book.

Z Use the Sharing preferences window within iTunes to set music sharing options.

A The QuickTime Player icon.

QuickTime Player

QuickTime Player

QuickTime is a video and audio technology developed by Apple Inc. It is widely used for digital movies as well as for streaming audio and video available via the Internet.

QuickTime Player is an application you can use to:

- View QuickTime movies and streaming Internet content.
- Create your own audio, video, and screencast recordings.
- Share your QuickTime files on a variety of Internet services.

TIP To share content on Facebook, YouTube, Vimeo, or Flickr, you must have an account on the service you want to use.

TIP You can learn more about QuickTime technology on Apple's QuickTime Web site, www.apple.com/quicktime/.

To launch QuickTime Player:

Use one of the following techniques:

- Open the QuickTime Player application icon **A** in the Applications folder window (page 137).
- Click the QuickTime Player icon in Launchpad (page 140).
- Open a QuickTime-compatible audio or video file.

Because QuickTime Player supports OS X's Auto Save feature, the movie files that were open when you last quit QuickTime are automatically reopened. In addition, if you launched QuickTime Player by opening a QuickTime-compatible file, that file opens.

TIP QuickTime Player supports the full-screen apps feature of OS X (page 142).

To quit QuickTime Player:

Choose QuickTime Player > Quit Quick-Time Player, or press Command-Q.

QuickTime Player quits. Any changes to open files are automatically saved. The files that were open when you quit are automatically reopened the next time you launch QuickTime Player.

To open a QuickTime movie file:

Use one of the following techniques:

- Double-click a QuickTime movie file icon .

- Drag the icon for a QuickTime movie onto the QuickTime Player icon in the Applications folder window.

If QuickTime Player is not already running, it launches. The movie's first frame appears in a window **C**.

TIP You can also open a QuickTime movie by using the Open File command on QuickTime Player's File menu. You can learn more about opening documents from within applications on page 158.

TIP If you point to a QuickTime movie's document icon, a play button appears **D**. Clicking that button plays the movie in its icon using enhanced icon view (page 21). This technique also works in the Finder's column view (page 59) and in the Info window (page 88) for a QuickTime movie.

B A QuickTime-compatible movie file's icon normally displays a preview frame from its movie.

Wenatchee to Hillsboro.mov

C QuickTime's no-nonsense window hides all controls until you need them.

D Pointing to a QuickTime-compatible movie file's icon displays a play button you can click to play the movie right in its icon.

Wenatchee to Hillsboro.mov

E When you point to a movie window, a title bar and movie controls appear.

Volume · Fast rewind · Play / Pause · Fast Forward · Share

Timeline · Playhead

F QuickTime's movie controls.

Email
Message
AirDrop
Facebook
YouTube
Vimeo
Flickr

G Use the Share pop-up menu to share a movie with friends.

View	
Enter Full Screen	^⌘F
Float on Top	
Actual Size	⌘1
Fit to Screen	⌘3
Fill Screen	⌘4
Panoramic	⌘5
Increase Size	⌘+
Decrease Size	⌘—
Show Closed Captioning	⌥⌘T
Languages	▶
Subtitles	▶
Show Chapters	⌘R
Next Chapter	⇧⌘→
Previous Chapter	⇧⌘←
Show Clips	⌘E
Show Audio Track	⌘U
Loop	⌥⌘L

H The View menu offers options for changing the size of the movie window.

To control movie play:

When you point to a QuickTime Player window, a group of buttons and controls appears **E** **F**. Use them to control movie play:

- **Volume** changes movie volume; drag the slider left or right or click the volume icon to mute/unmute.

- **Fast rewind** plays the movie backward quickly, with sound.

- **Play** starts playing the movie. When the movie is playing, the Play button turns to a **Pause** button, which pauses movie play.

- **Fast Forward** plays the movie forward quickly, with sound.

- **Share** displays a menu you can use to copy the movie to iTunes or share it online with others **G**.

- **Timeline** tracks movie progress. By dragging the **Playhead**, you can quickly move or "scrub" to a specific scene in the movie.

TIP Each time you click the fast rewind or fast forward button, the speed is increased up to 8x normal speed. To play at normal speed, click the Play button.

TIP You can drag the play controls to another location within the QuickTime Player window.

To specify movie size:

Select a size option from the View menu **H**. The size of the movie's window changes accordingly.

To record a movie with QuickTime Player:

1. Choose File > New Movie Recording or press Option-Command-N.

    QuickTime Player displays a Movie Recording window , using the video input from your computer's built-in FaceTime camera or another compatible camera connected to your computer.

2. Click the red Record button to begin recording your movie.

    A timer appears on the bottom-left corner of the control area and the volume level bar shows how well QuickTime Player can "hear" you .

3. To stop recording, click the Stop button. (If the Stop button isn't showing, move the pointer to the window to display it.)

4. QuickTime Player saves the movie in your Movies folder. The movie remains open so you can play it.

TIP Clicking the Options button in the Movie Recording window displays a menu with options for fine-tuning movie settings **K**.

TIP You can use similar techniques to record audio or to make a movie of what appears on your computer screen as you work. Just start with commands under the File menu: New Audio Recording or New Screen Recording. The controls that appears are very similar to those that appear when you record a movie.

TIP When you close the movie, QuickTime displays a Save As dialog that you can use to save it to disk. Give the movie a name, specify a disk location, and choose one of the options on the Format pop-up menu. Then click Save to save it to disk.

I A Movie Recording window shows anything in front of the camera. (I have no idea why I'm smiling. I'm so far behind deadline that I fear my editor will soon kill me.)

J These are the controls in the Movie Recording window while a movie is being recorded. Note the movie length timer, sound level, and movie file size information that is displayed along the bottom of the controls.

K You can use this pop-up menu to set options for your movie.

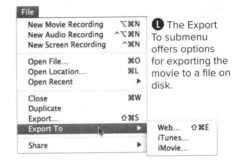

L The Export To submenu offers options for exporting the movie to a file on disk.

M The Share submenu offers options for sharing the movie with others via a number of methods.

N When exporting for the Web, check off the versions you want to create.

O When exporting to iTunes, you can specify which device will be used to view the movie.

To export or share movies:

1. If necessary, open the movie you want to export or share.

2. Choose an option from the Export To **L** or Share **M** submenu under the File menu or the Share menu **G** in the QuickTime Player window:

   ▸ **Web** saves the movie in a format optimized for delivery to cell phones, via Wi-Fi, or by broadband.

   ▸ **iTunes** adds the movie to your iTunes library. Once there, you can watch it in iTunes or an Apple TV or copy it to an iPad, iPod, or iPhone.

   ▸ **iMovie** saves the movie to an iMovie project. You must have iMovie installed to use this option.

   ▸ **Email** attaches the movie to an email message that you can send to others.

   ▸ **Message** attaches the movie to a new message in the Messages app.

   ▸ **AirDrop** opens an AirDrop share sheet so you can send it to another AirDrop user nearby.

   ▸ **Facebook**, **YouTube**, **Vimeo**, or **Flickr** saves the movie to your account on one of these services.

3. What happens next depends on which option you chose. QuickTime Player may prompt you to do any combination of the following things:

   ▸ **Specify a version N**. when exporting for the Web, you can indicate how the file will be transferred. This determines file size and quality.

   ▸ **Specify a device O**. When exporting to iTunes, you can specify which device it will be viewed on, thus determining its file size.

continues on next page

▸ **Sign in to your account** . If you're sharing your movie on an online service, you'll need to sign in so Quick-Time Player can upload it.

▸ **Provide descriptive information** **Q**. Some services will include a video name, description, category, and/or key words with your movie.

▸ **Enter or choose a recipient.** If sending via email, message, or AirDrop **R**, you'll need to provide destination information.

Follow the prompts that appear onscreen to set options and provide information.

4. When you're finished entering all required information, click the Export or Share button in the last dialog.

QuickTime Player exports the movie in a compatible format and, if necessary, uploads it to the service you are sending it to. This could take some time, depending on the speed of your computer and the size of the movie.

TIP Some online services have limits on the length or size of movies they will accept. QuickTime Player will warn you if your movie is longer or bigger than what is allowed on the service you selected.

TIP Please respect all copyrights and terms of service when exporting and sharing movies with friends and online.

P For some types of sharing, such as sharing on YouTube, QuickTime Player will prompt you for sign in information.

Q When sharing to social networking services, QuickTime Player will likely prompt you for descriptive information.

R When you send a file via AirDrop, you'll need to indicate a recipient computer.

A If DVD Player hasn't loaded a movie, it'll display a black player window with a floating Controller palette.

B What's more likely is that DVD Player will simply begin playing the movie. (Now *this* is a classic.)

C The DVD Player application icon.

DVD Player

DVD Player

DVD Player is a simple application that enables you to play DVD video discs on your Mac. All you need is an optical drive capable of reading DVD media, and DVD Player does the rest.

To launch DVD Player:

Insert a DVD video disc into your Mac.

DVD Player should launch and do one of two things:

- Display a black Viewer window with a floating Controller palette **A**.
- Immediately begin DVD play **B**.

If DVD Player does not launch at all, then use one of the following techniques to open it:

- Open the DVD Player application icon **C** in the Applications folder window (page 137).
- Click the DVD Player icon in Launchpad (page 140).

TIP If a Drive Region Code dialog appears the first time you play a DVD video, click the Set Drive Region button to set DVD Player's region to match that of the disc you inserted. Then click OK to dismiss the confirmation dialog that appears.

To quit DVD Player:

Choose DVD Player > Quit DVD Player (the menu appears, if necessary, when you point to it), or press Command-Q.

DVD Player quits.

To display the Controller:

Use one of the following techniques:

- Move the mouse or drag your finger across the trackpad while the DVD is playing.

- Choose Window > Show Controller (the menu appears, if necessary, when you point to it), or press Control-Command-C.

The Controller appears **D** **E**.

To show or hide additional DVD controls on the Controller **E**, double-click the pair of tiny lines on the right end of the Controller.

TIP While the movie is playing in full-screen view, the Controller looks different **F** but offers all of the same options.

To control DVD play:

Use one of the following techniques:

- Click buttons on the Controller **D** **E**.

- Choose a command from the Controls menu **G**.

TIP The Pause command on the Controls menu **G** changes into a Play command when a DVD is not playing.

To resize the Viewer window:

Choose an option from the View menu **H** or press the corresponding shortcut key.

D DVD Player's Controller.

E The Controller, expanded to show additional control buttons. Point to a button to learn its name.

F The Controller looks like this when the movie is playing in full-screen view.

Controls	
Pause	Space bar
Stop	⌘.
Slow Motion	⌥⇧→
Scan Forward	⇧⌘→
Scan Backwards	⇧⌘←
Scan Rate	▶
Slow Motion Rate	▶
Volume Up	⌘↑
Volume Down	⌘↓
Mute	⌥⌘↓
Timer	▶
New Bookmark...	⌘=
Use Current Frame as Jacket Picture	
Close Control Drawer	⌘]
Eject DVD	⌘E

G You can use the Controls menu to control DVD play.

View	
Half Size	⌘0
Actual Size	⌘1
Double Size	⌘2
Fit to Screen	⌘3
Enter Full Screen	⌘F
Deinterlace	▶
Viewer Above Other Apps	

H The View menu offers options for changing the size of the Viewer window.

16

Other OS X Applications

In addition to the applications discussed in detail in various places throughout this book, OS X includes a variety of more basic applications that you can use to perform tasks on your computer.

This chapter provides instructions for getting started with applications you can find in the Applications folder on your hard disk. Among these, you'll find applications for performing calculations, working with images and PDF files, looking up words, taking notes, and even challenging your computer to a nice game of chess.

As discussed in Chapter 11, you can launch any of these applications by opening its icon in the Applications folder window (page 138) or by clicking its icon in Launchpad (page 140). You quit an application by using the Quit command on its application menu (page 156).

You can find a complete list of the applications that are part of a standard OS X Mountain Lion installation—along with chapter references where you can learn more about each one—on page 133.

Calculator

Calculator displays a simple calculator that can perform addition, subtraction, multiplication, and division, as well as complex mathematical calculations and conversions.

> **TIP** If you use the Calculator application often, you might be interested in the Calculator widget (page 242), which is part of the OS X Dashboard (Chapter 17).

To perform basic calculations:

Use any combination of the following techniques:

- Use your mouse or trackpad to click buttons for numbers and operators.
- Press keyboard keys corresponding to numbers and operators.

The numbers you enter and the results of your calculations appear at the top of the Calculator window .

To keep track of your entries:

Choose Window > Show Paper Tape, or press Command-T.

The Paper Tape window appears. It displays your entries as you make them .

> **TIP** To hide the Paper Tape window, choose Window > Hide Paper Tape, press Command-T or click the Paper Tape window's close button.

> **TIP** To start with a fresh tape, click the Clear button.

> **TIP** You can use commands under the File menu to save or print the paper tape.

A Calculator's application icon.

Calculator

B Calculator looks and works like the calculator on your cell phone.

C The Paper Tape window makes it easy to keep track of your entries.

D The Scientific calculator.

E The Programmer calculator.

F The Basic calculator with Reverse Polish Notation turned on.

G In the dialog that appears, enter specifics about the units you want to convert from and to.

To use other kinds of calculators:

Choose a command from the View menu to choose the type of calculator you want to work with:

- **Basic** (Command-1) is the basic calculator **B**.

- **Scientific** (Command-2) is a calculator with scientific functions **D**.

- **Programmer** (Command-3) is a calculator with functions and features of interest to programmers **E**.

- **RPN Mode** (Command-R) enables Reverse Polish Notation for the currently displayed calculator. Note that the letters RPN appear on the calculator when this feature is enabled **F**.

TIP Reverse Polish Notation, or RPN, is an alternative format for entering calculations. It is commonly used on Hewlett-Packard brand calculators. (If you don't know what RPN is, you probably don't want to use it.)

To perform conversions:

1. Enter the value you want to convert.

2. Choose the conversion you want from the Convert menu.

3. In the dialog that appears **G**, set options for the conversion you want to perform.

4. Click Convert.

   The original value you entered is converted and appears at the top of the Calculator window.

TIP The Convert menu's Recent Conversions submenu makes it easy to repeat conversions you have done recently.

Chess

Chess is a computerized version of the classic strategy game of chess **B**. You can play against the computer or a friend. If you play against the computer, your pieces are white and you go first; the computer's pieces are black and it goes automatically after each of your moves.

A The Chess application icon.

TIP The first time you launch Chess, it prompts you to log into Game Center. To play chess with friends and save high scores, log in; otherwise, just click Cancel to play on your own. You can learn more about Game Center on page 223.

To move a chess piece:

Drag the piece onto any valid square on the playing board.

TIP If you attempt to make an invalid move, an alert sounds and the piece returns to where it was.

TIP If Speakable Items is enabled in the Accessibility preferences pane (page 590), you can use spoken commands to move chess pieces.

To start a new game:

1. Choose Game > New, or press Command-N.

   The Start a New Game dialog appears **C**.

2. Choose an option from the Players pop-up menu.

3. If desired, choose an option from the Variant pop-up menu.

4. If you're playing against the computer, use the slider to determine how long the computer "thinks" between each move.

5. Click Start.

B The Chess window displays a colorful, three-dimensional chess board.

C Set options in this dialog to begin a new game.

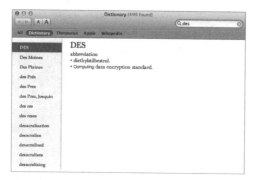

A The Dictionary application icon.

Dictionary

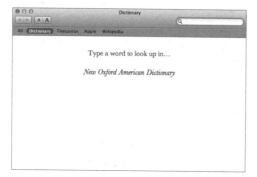

B The DIctionary application window, right after launching Dictionary.

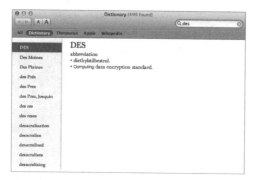

C Dictionary begins displaying search results immediately.

Dictionary

Dictionary **A** is like a reference library with all the features of a dictionary, thesaurus, and encyclopedia—but without all that paper. You can use it to get word definitions, pronunciations, and synonyms, as well as information from Wikipedia.

TIP If you use the Dictionary application often, you might be interested in the Dictionary widget (page 242), which is part of the OS X Dashboard (Chapter 17).

To look up a word or phrase:

1. Near the top of the Dictionary window **B**, click the button for the reference you want to search:

   ▸ **All** searches all references.

   ▸ **Dictionary** searches the *New Oxford American Dictionary*. Use this option to look up pronunciations and definitions.

   ▸ **Thesaurus** searches the *Oxford American Writer's Thesaurus*. Use this option to look up synonyms.

   ▸ **Apple** searches the *Apple Dictionary*. Use this option to look up Apple-related terms.

   ▸ **Wikipedia** searches the Wikipedia online encyclopedia. Use this option to look up more detailed information than what you'd find in a dictionary.

2. Enter the word or phrase you want to look up in the search box at the top of the Dictionary window.

   As you type, Dictionary begins displaying a list of matches **C**.

continues on next page

3. Double-click the word or phrase that interests you.

The window displays information for that entry from the reference you selected in step 1 **D** **E** **F**.

TIP To change the size of font characters in the Dictionary window, click one of the font size buttons in the window's toolbar.

TIP To print an entry, choose File > Print. You can learn more about printing in Chapter 24.

TIP You can click a word in an entry to look up that word, too.

D The definition of a selected word appears in Dictionary's window.

E Here are the synonym entries for the same word in Dictionary's Thesaurus.

F And here's the Wikipedia entry for the same word.

A The Game Center application icon.

Game Center

B The main Game Center window, before signing in.

C Game Center-compatible games may prompt you to sign in when you launch them.

D The first time you sign in to Game Center, you're prompted for some basic account information.

Game Center

Game Center **A**, which is new in OS X Mountain Lion, lets you create and maintain a gaming network. Keep track of your high scores, play multi-player games with friends online, and find new friends and games to play. All you need to get started is a Game Center compatible game, an Internet connection, and an Apple ID.

Game Center is primarily a tool for connecting with friends and monitoring game activity. Once you sign in and add friends to Game Center, compatible games will automatically be added to your account and your activity will be tracked. Many multi-player games can also use Game Center to help you find a person to play against—whether it's an existing friend or a random person interested in playing the game with someone new.

TIP Chess (page 220), which is part of OS X, works with Game Center.

To sign into Game Center:

1. Enter your Apple ID and password in the appropriate fields in Game Center's main window **B** or a Game Center sign in window that appears when you open a compatible game app **C**.

2. Click Sign In.

3. If this is the first time you're signing into Game Center, you'll be prompted to accept its Terms & Conditions. Turn on the check box and click Accept.

4. If you don't already have a Game Center nickname, a dialog prompts you for some basic account settings **D**. Provide the following information and click Continue:

continues on next page

- ▸ **Nickname** is a unique name to use within Game Center.

- ▸ **Public Profile** makes your profile information, including your name, visible to other Game Center players.

- ▸ **Use Contacts for Friend Suggestions** finds other Game Center players based on email addresses in your Contacts database.

Your account information appears in the Game Center window **E**.

> **TIP** If you don't already have an Apple ID, you can create one by clicking the **Create Apple ID** button **B C** and then following the prompts in the window that appears.

> **TIP** You can add or change a profile picture by clicking the **Change Photo** button in the **Me** pane of the Game Center window when you're signed in **E**. You can also add a brief status message by typing text into the **Status** box on the **Me** pane.

To sign out of Game Center:

1. In the Game Center window **D**, click your Account email address.

2. In the Game Center Account dialog that appears **F**, click Sign Out.

> **TIP** You can click the **View Account** button in the Game Center Account dialog **F** to display a dialog you can use to modify basic account settings.

> **TIP** When you're signed out of Game Center, your game activity is not tracked on the Game Center server.

E When you're signed into Game Center, your account information appears in its window.

F Use this dialog to sign out or to access and change account information.

G Use this dialog box to add friends to Game Center.

H The Friends pane lists your friends and provides details about their Game Center activity.

I Friend requests are listed in the Requests pane of the Game Center window.

To add friends:

1. In the Game Center window, click the Friends button.

2. Click Add Friends.

   The Friend Request dialog appears **G**.

3. In the To box, enter the email address or nickname for a friend and press Tab.

4. If desired, edit the message in the bottom half of the dialog to personalize it.

5. Click Send.

6. Wait until your friend accepts the request. This could be immediately, if your friend is online, or in a few hours or even days.

   When your request is approved, your friend's information appears in the Game Center Friends pane **H**.

TIP If you have Game Center configured to recommend friends, the Friends pane displays profile pictures for people in your Contacts database that also use Game Center **H**. Click the pictures to display a list of recommendations, click a person in the list, and then click Send Friend Request to add him or her.

TIP You can click buttons under a friend's name to see lists of his or her games **H**, points, and friends.

To respond to a friend request:

1. In the Game Center window, click the Requests button to see incoming requests.

2. Select the request you want to accept **I**.

3. Click Accept.

   The new friend is added to the Game Center Friends pane.

Image Capture

Image Capture **A** **B** is an application that performs three functions:

- Import image files from a digital camera to your computer's hard disk.

- Operate your scanner to scan and save images.

- Share images from a camera on a website or in a slide show.

In this part of the chapter, I explain how to import images from a digital camera and scan a document with Image Capture.

TIP Some devices require that driver software be installed in OS X before the camera or scanner can be used. Consult the documentation that came with your scanner or camera or check the device manufacturer's website for OS X compatibility and driver information.

TIP Not all devices are compatible with Image Capture. Generally speaking, if Image Capture does not "see" your camera or scanner when it is connected and turned on, the camera or scanner is probably not compatible.

TIP If you have Apple's iLife suite of products, you can also import images from a digital camera using iPhoto, which offers additional features for managing photos saved to disk.

TIP Image Capture may open automatically when you connect a scanner or camera or insert a media card in your computer or a connected card reader.

 A Image Capture's icon.

Image Capture

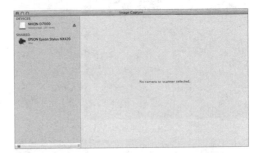

B The Image Capture window with one directly connected device and one shared device.

C Image Capture displays thumbnail images of the photos it finds on the device. In this example, I've attached an SD card reader from my camera to my Mac via USB.

D Use this pop-up menu to specify where you want to import images to.

To download images from a digital camera or media card:

1. Do one of the following:

   ▸ Attach your digital camera to your computer's USB or FireWire port, using the applicable cable. Then turn the camera on and, if necessary, set it to review mode.

   ▸ Insert your camera's media card into a USB card reader and plug the reader into one of your computer's USB ports.

   ▸ Insert your camera's SD card into your computer's SD card slot.

2. If necessary, select your camera or media card in the Devices list.

   Thumbnail images of the photos on the camera or card appear in the window **C**.

3. Use the Import To pop-up menu at the bottom of the window to select the location you want to import images to. There are four groups of options **D**:

   ▸ Folders that are commonly used for storing downloaded items or images.

   ▸ Applications that can open images.

   ▸ Tasks you can use to automate the creation of a webpage or PDF file of the imported images.

   ▸ Other enables you to choose a disk location or application for saving or opening the images.

   For this example, I chose the default option, which is the Pictures folder in the Home folder.

continues on next page

4. Do one of the following:

   ▸ To import all images, click the Import All button.

   ▸ To import some of the images on the camera, select the images you want to import and click the Import button. (You can hold down the Command key while clicking each image you want to add it to the selection.)

   A progress indicator appears while the photos are imported **E**. When it disappears, the import is complete; check marks appear beside each imported photo.

5. If necessary, click the Eject icon beside the camera or media card name in the Devices list before disconnecting or removing it.

TIP If iPhoto is installed on your computer, it may launch instead of Image Capture when you connect a digital camera. If so, you can quit iPhoto and launch Image Capture to use it.

TIP You can also use the thumbnail window **C** to delete images on the device. Select the images you want to delete, click the Delete button at the bottom of the window, and click Delete in the confirmation dialog that appears.

To scan a document:

1. Make sure your scanner is properly installed, connected, and turned on.

2. Place the document you want to scan on the scan bed.

3. Open Image Capture.

4. If necessary, select your scanner in the Devices list **F**.

E A progress indicator appears as images are copied to your computer.

F Select the scanner in the Devices list.

G Choose a Scan Size option.

H Use this pop-up menu to determine where images should be scanned to.

I In this example, I've scanned a photo to Preview. By double-clicking the name of the Scan in Image Capture's Scan Results window, I've opened it in Preview.

5. Choose an option from the Scan Size pop-up menu **G**:

    ▸ **Detect Separate Items** is for a document with individual images on it.

    ▸ **Detect Enclosing Box** is for a document with one item that does not occupy the entire scanner bed.

    ▸ **A4** and **US Letter** are two common paper sizes.

6. Choose the location you want to scan the document to from the Scan To pop-up menu **H**. There are three groups of options:

    ▸ Folders that are commonly used for storing scanned documents.

    ▸ Applications that can open scanned documents.

    ▸ Other enables you to choose a disk location or application for saving or opening the scanned document.

7. Click Scan.

8. Wait while the scanner scans the document. This could take a few moments and multiple scanner passes, depending on your scanner model. You may see an Overview image as it works.

    When it's finished, an image of the document you scanned appears in the Image Capture window and the document is saved to the location you selected in step 6 **I**.

TIP Clicking the Show Details button at the bottom of the Image Capture window **F** may offer additional options for scanning a document, including resolution, type of document, and size. The options vary depending on your scanner model and installed driver software.

Photo Booth

Photo Booth is an application that enables you to take snapshots with a FaceTime camera or digital video camera. You can take still photos **B** or short movies and can include special effects with the photos you take. Once you've made an image, you can email it to a friend or use it as a personal icon for your OS X account, iMessage, or Twitter.

TIP Photo Booth supports the full-screen apps (page 142) feature of OS X. If it opens in full-screen view, you can press Esc to use it in regular view as shown here.

To create a snapshot or movie:

1. Click one of the three buttons on the left side beneath the video preview:

   ▸ **Take four quick pictures** takes four still photos a second or so apart.

   ▸ **Take a still picture** takes a single still photo.

   ▸ **Take a movie clip** records a movie.

2. Click the Camera button.

   A countdown timer appears beneath the video preview **C**. When it reaches the end, one of three things happens:

   ▸ For four quick photos, four photos are snapped, one after the other. They appear in a single frame at the bottom of the window **D**.

   ▸ For still photos, the photo is snapped and appears as a thumbnail in the bottom of the window **D**.

   ▸ For a movie clip, the camera begins recording. Click the stop button to stop recording movie frames. A thumbnail of the movie appears at the bottom of the window **D**.

A The Photo Booth application icon.

Photo Booth

B Photo Booth's main window displays whatever your camera sees. (The deadline is *when*?)

C Photo Booth counts down before snapping photos.

D In this example, there are two single photos, one 4-shot photo, and one video.

E F G The first three screens of effects apply visual effects to the image.

To include special effects or a background image in a photo:

1. Choose View > Show Effects, or press Command-2.

2. Click the arrow buttons on either side of the Effects button to scroll through the five screens of effects **E F G H** until you find one you like.

3. Do one of the following:

   ▸ To apply a visual effect **E F G**, click to select it.

   ▸ To apply a backdrop **H**, click to select the backdrop you want. Then move out of the frame, as instructed until the background is detected.

4. Follow the steps on the previous page to create a snapshot or movie.

5. To return to photo view, choose View > Show Photo, or press Command-1.

TIP The fifth screen of effects (not shown) is for your own backdrop images. Drag the image you want to use to one of the blank spaces to add it to those available for use.

TIP To turn off an effect, choose Normal in any of the effects screens.

H Photo Booth comes with some fun backdrops, including ones suitable for video.

To use Photo Booth images:

1. At the bottom of the Photo Booth window, select the thumbnail for the image you want to use .

2. Click the Share menu to display options **I**.

3. Choose the command for the task you want to perform.

4. Follow the onscreen prompts that appear to complete the task.

To export a photo or movie:

Drag the thumbnail image for the photo or movie into a Finder window **J**.

When you release the thumbnail, an icon for the exported item appears where you dragged it. You can then work with it like any other image or movie file.

TIP You can also choose File > Export and use the dialog that appears to choose a disk location for the exported file.

To delete a Photo Booth image:

1. At the bottom of the Photo Booth window, select the thumbnail for the image you want to delete **D**.

2. Click the X button in the corner of the image thumbnail.

   The image is immediately deleted.

TIP Photo Booth images are stored in the Photo Booth Library file inside your Pictures folder. Opening the icon **K** launches Photo Booth.

I With an image selected, you can use options on the Share menu to share the image with others and perform other tasks.

J Exporting an item is as easy as dragging its thumbnail into a Finder window.

 K Photo Booth images are stored inside the Photo Booth Library file.

Photo Booth
Library

A The Preview application icon.

Preview

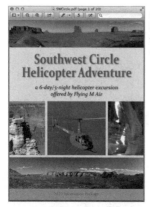

B Preview can open PDF files like this one...

C ...image files like this one, ...

D ... and even Microsoft Word files like this one.

Preview

Preview **A** is a program that enables you to open and view a variety of file types:

- **PDF**, or **Portable Document Format**, files **B** created with OS X's Print command, Adobe Acrobat software, or other software capable of creating PDFs.

- **Image files** **C**, including JPG (or JPEG), GIF, HDR, TIFF, PSD, PICT, PNG, BMP, RAW, and SGI.

- **Microsoft Office files**, including those created with Word **D** and Excel.

Preview also includes tools you can use to edit images and annotate images and PDFs.

This part of the chapter explores some of Preview's basic functionality.

TIP Preview supports the full-screen apps (page 142) and Auto Save (page 144) features of OS X.

TIP When you open PostScript (PS) or EPS format files, Preview automatically converts them to PDF files for viewing.

TIP Although you can open and view Microsoft Office files in Preview, you cannot edit them. You can, however, open and edit most Microsoft Word files in TextEdit (Chapter 14).

TIP You can also open PDF files with Adobe Reader software. You can learn more about Adobe Reader—and download a free copy of the software—on the Adobe Systems website, get.adobe.com/reader.

To open a file with Preview:

Use one of the following techniques:

- Drag the document file's icon onto the Preview icon in the Applications folder **E**.

- Right-click the file's icon and choose Preview from the Open With submenu on the contextual menu that appears **F**.

- Double-click the file icon for a Preview-compatible document. (This technique, however, might open the document in another compatible application installed on your computer.)

Preview launches and displays the file in its window **B C D**.

TIP You can also use Preview's Open command (page 158) to open any compatible file.

To change the view of a document:

Use a menu or buttons in Preview's toolbar to change the view of the document:

- **View** menu options **G** change the window's view to show or hide thumbnails **H**, a table of contents, highlights, and notes, as well as to set the number of pages and scrolling method.

- **Zoom** buttons reduce and increase the size of the image in the window.

TIP You can find additional view options on Preview's View menu.

E Drag the document onto the Preview application icon.

F Choose Preview from the Open With submenu on a contextual menu (or the File menu).

G The View menu on the toolbar offers most commonly used view options.

H If you open more than one image at a time in Preview, you can use thumbnails to move from one to another in the same window.

I You can search a PDF file for a specific word or phrase.

J Drag over text to select it.

To search for text in a PDF file:

1. Open the PDF file you want to search.

2. In the search box at the top-right corner of the window, enter a search word or phrase.

   As you type, Preview searches the document for the text you entered. It displays thumbnail images and excerpts of pages containing that text on the left side of the window. It also highlights the occurrences of the search text in the page that is displayed **I**.

3. To display a specific occurrence of the search text, click its page thumbnail. The search text is highlighted in yellow wherever it appears on that page **I**.

To select text in a PDF file:

1. If necessary, choose Tools > Text Selection to switch to the text selection tool.

2. Position the pointer over text in the document window.

   The pointer turns into an I-beam pointer.

3. Press the button down and drag to select text **J**.

TIP Once text is selected, you can use the Copy command (page 187) to copy it to the Clipboard and use it in another document.

TIP If a document is protected for copying or editing, you may not be able to select text.

To select part of a picture:

1. If necessary, choose Tools > Rectangular Selection to switch to the rectangular selection tool.

2. Position the pointer in the upper-left corner of the area you want to select.

3. Drag down and to the right.

   A selection box appears over the image, along with an indicator that shows the size of the selection in pixels.

4. Release the button to complete the selection .

TIP Once you have selected part of a picture, you can use the Copy command (page 187) to copy it to the Clipboard for use in another document.

K Release the button to complete the selection.

To crop an image:

1. Select the part of the image you want to keep **K**.

2. Choose Tools > Crop, or press Command-K.

   The image is trimmed to the selection **L**.

L The Crop command trims the image to your selection.

The Stickies application icon.

Stickies

Make a note of it!

Stickies lets you keep notes (like these) on your desktop. Use a Stickies note to jot down reminders, lists, or other information. You can also use notes to store frequently used text or graphics.

• To close this note, click the close button.

• To collapse this note, double click the title bar.

Your current notes appear when you open Stickies.

 When you first open Stickies, it displays two sticky notes with information about how to use it.

⊙ Start with a blank new note.

I don't use Stickies very often -- mostly because I have so many windows open on my Mac that I'd likely lose them in the digital clutter.

⊙ Type whatever you want to include in the note.

Stickies

Stickies **A** is an application that displays computerized "sticky notes" **B** that you can use to place reminders on your screen. Like any other application that supports Auto Save, when you open Stickies it automatically reopens any note that was open when you last quit it.

TIP If you use the Stickies application often, you might be interested in the Stickies widget (page 242), which is part of the OS X Dashboard (Chapter 17).

To create a new sticky note:

1. Choose File > New Note, or press Command-N to display a blank new note **⊙**.

2. Type the text that you want to include in the note **⊙**.

TIP You can use options under the Color and Font menus to change the appearance of notes or note text.

To print a sticky note:

1. Click the note to activate it.

2. Choose File > Print or press Command-P.

3. Use the Print dialog that appears (page 345) to set options for printing and click the Print button.

To close a sticky note:

1. Do one of the following:

   ▸ Click the sticky note's close box.

   ▸ Activate the sticky note and choose File > Close, or press Command-W.

2. In the confirmation dialog that appears **E**, click a button:

   ▸ **Don't Save** closes the note without saving its contents.

   ▸ **Cancel** leaves the note open.

   ▸ **Save** displays the Export dialog **F**, which you can use to save the note as plain or formatted text in a file on disk. Enter a name, select a disk location, choose a file format, and then click Save.

TIP Once a sticky note has been saved, it can be opened and edited with TextEdit or any other text editing application.

E A dialog like this appears when you close a note.

F Use the Export dialog to save the note's contents as plain or formatted text.

Dashboard

Dashboard is a feature of OS X that gives you instant access to simple applications called *widgets*. Widgets work with other applications such as iTunes, Calendar, and Contacts to provide you with quick access to the most commonly used features. They also work with the Internet to get up-to-date information such as stock quotes, weather, and business listings.

OS X comes with a bunch of widgets, all of which are accessible from the widget browser that you can display onscreen. Click a widget to open and use it. Leave it open so it's automatically available the next time you open Dashboard.

In this chapter, I explain how to use Dashboard and the new widget browser to display and organize widgets. I also tell you how to add, remove, and disable widgets. Finally, I provide a brief summary of the widgets that come with OS X Mountain Lion.

In This Chapter:

Opening & Closing Dashboard

The main purpose of Dashboard is to make widgets easily accessible without interfering with your work. Apple achieves this by making Dashboard quick and easy to open and close.

To open Dashboard:

Use one of the following techniques:

- Open the Dashboard icon in the Applications folder (page 137).

- Click the Dashboard icon in Launchpad (page 140).

- Press F12 or, on a laptop, press fn-F12.

- On a Multi-Touch device, use three fingers to swipe to the right until Dashboard appears.

Dashboard sweeps into view from the left, displaying the last widgets you used **B**.

TIP The keyboard shortcuts provided here assume your Mac has default settings in the Mission Control preferences pane (page 507).

TIP If you have an Apple Mouse, you can use the Mouse preferences pane (page 530) to configure one of its buttons to activate Dashboard.

To close Dashboard:

Use one of the following techniques:

- In the lower-right corner of the Dashboard screen, click the Return arrow.

- Press Esc, F12, or, on a laptop, fn-F12.

- On a Multi-Touch device, use three fingers to swipe to the left.

Dashboard sweeps away to the left.

A The Dashboard application icon.

Dashboard

B By default, these four widgets are open when you first launch Dashboard.

Ⓐ The widget browser takes the place of open Dashboard widgets onscreen.

Displaying the Widget Browser

The widget browser, which is new in OS X Mountain Lion, gives you access to all installed widgets and offers features to help you organize and find them.

To display the widget browser:

With Dashboard open, click the + button in the lower-left corner of your screen.

A few things happen **Ⓐ**:

- Any open widgets are hidden from view; icons for all installed widgets appear in their place.

- A Spotlight search box appears at the top of the Dashboard screen.

- Remove (–) and More Widgets buttons appear at the bottom of the Dashboard screen.

To hide the widget browser:

Click the + button near the lower-left corner of your screen again or press Esc.

The open Dashboard widgets reappear.

Using Widgets

To use a widget, you must open it. If you want a widget to appear automatically every time you open Dashboard, you can leave it open when you close Dashboard. Otherwise, you can close the widget.

Once a widget is open, you can work with the controls and options on its face to get the information you want. Widgets tend to be simple, so in most cases, you won't need help using them.

What isn't always obvious, however, is that most widgets offer the ability to set options on their reverse side. These can control the way the widget works.

This part of the chapter explains how to open, move, and close a widget, as well as how you can flip a widget over to access options normally hidden from view.

To open a widget:

1. Open Dashboard.

   If the widget you want to open is already displayed, you can skip the remaining steps; the widget is already open and ready to use.

2. If the widget you want to open is not already displayed or if you want to open a second copy of it, open the widget browser .

3. Click the icon for the widget you want to open.

   The widget browser disappears. The widget you clicked appears onscreen and is ready to use .

TIP Why would you want to open multiple copies of a widget? Well, suppose you want to see weather for Phoenix, AZ, and Wenatchee, WA. You can open the Weather widget twice and configure one for each city .

A To open a widget, start by displaying Dashboard and the widget browser.

B Clicking the Dictionary widget in the widget browser opens the widget in Dashboard.

C In this example, I've opened two copies of the Weather widget so I can see weather in two different cities. (Now you know why I go north for the summer.)

D To move a widget, just drag it.

E Pointing to the Weather widget displays its settings button in the lower-right corner.

F Here are the settings for the Weather widget.

G Clicking the – button displays close buttons for all open widgets.

H You can hold down the Option key while pointing to a widget to display its close button.

To move a widget:

Once a widget is displayed, you can drag it to move it to a new position onscreen **D**.

TIP Arrange the widgets you keep open so you know exactly where to look onscreen when you open Dashboard to access their features.

To set widget options:

1. Point to the widget.

   If settings are available, you should see a tiny *i* button, which normally—but not always—appears in the lower-right corner of the widget **E**.

2. Click the i button.

   The widget turns over so you can access settings on its reverse side **F**.

3. Set options as desired.

4. Click Done to save your settings and flip the widget back over.

To close a widget:

1. If necessary, display the widget's close button, which looks like an X:

   ▸ To display the close button for all open widgets **G**, click the – button in the bottom-left corner of the Dashboard.

   ▸ To display the close button for just one widget, hold down the Option key and point to the widget **H**.

2. Click the close button for the widget you want to close. The widget closes.

TIP Keep in mind that many widgets lose their settings when you close them. If you plan to use a widget with custom settings often, you may want to keep it open so you don't have to reset it each time you use it.

Managing Widgets

You can customize Dashboard by adding or removing widgets. You can also organize them into folders and use a Spotlight search field to find them.

TIP OS X stores the widgets you install in the Widgets folder inside the invisible Library folder in your Home folder (page 125). It stores the widgets that come with OS X in the Widgets folder inside the Library folder on your hard disk.

To install a widget:

1. Download or copy the widget file you want to install to your computer.

2. Double-click the widget file's icon **A**.

   A widget installer window appears **B**.

3. Click Install.

   Dashboard opens and the icon for the widget "jumps" into the widget browser **C**. Then Dashboard closes again. The widget is now ready to open and use.

TIP If you download a widget with Safari, the Widget Installer window **B** may open automatically when the download is complete. Follow step 3 to complete the installation.

TIP Additional widgets are available on Apple's Dashboard Widgets Web page, www.apple.com/downloads/dashboard/, which you can go to quickly by clicking the More Widgets button in the widget browser **C**. You can also find widgets on shareware distribution websites and on websites for third-party vendors.

Quotations of the
Day.wdgt

A Although some widgets have custom icons, this is what the default widget icon looks like.

B When you open a widget icon, an installer dialog like this appears.

C A newly installed widget's icon appears in the widget browser.

D Clicking the – button displays an X button beside any widget that can be deleted.

E Click the Delete button to delete the widget.

F Drag an icon into position.

G When you release it, it moves.

H Drag a widget on top of another widget ...

I ... to create a folder containing both widgets.

To remove a widget:

1. If necessary, open Dashboard and display the widget browser.

2. Click the – button in the lower-left corner of the screen.

   The widgets start to wiggle and an X button appears beside each widget that can be deleted **D**.

3. Click the X button for the widget you want to delete.

4. In the confirmation dialog that appears **E**, click Delete.

   The widget is removed from the widget browser and is no longer available for use.

TIP You cannot use the widget browser to delete the widgets that are installed as part of OS X. If you really must remove one of the OS X widgets, you can delete its widget file from the Widgets folder in the Library folder of your hard disk.

To rearrange & organize widgets in the widget browser:

- To move a widget, drag its icon into a new position **F**. Other icons shift accordingly to make room for it. When you release the icon, it moves into its new place **G**.

- To create a widget folder, drag the icon for a widget onto another icon you want to store it with. OS X creates a new folder and puts the other icon in it **H**. Release the icon to drop it in the folder **I**. (This feature works very much like the folder feature in Launchpad [page 140].)

OS X Widgets Overview

OS X Mountain Lion comes with 17 widgets that you might find useful as you work with your computer. Here's a quick summary of what each of them can do for you.

- **Calculator** , which is a lot like the Calculator application (page 218), puts simple calculations at your fingertips.

- **Calendar** Ⓑ (formerly iCal) gives you access to the events you manage with the Calendar application (Chapter 21).

- **Contacts** Ⓒ (formerly Address Book) works with the Contacts application (Chapter 20) to give you quick access to your contacts.

- **Dictionary** Ⓓ, which is a lot like the Dictionary application (page 221), offers a quick way to look up the definitions, pronunciations, and synonyms for a word. The Dictionary widget also includes Apple Inc. terminology.

- **ESPN** Ⓔ puts sports news links and scores on your Dashboard. You can configure it to show the sport that interests you most.

Ⓐ Calculator puts a simple calculator at your fingertips.

Ⓑ The Calendar widget displays events from Calendar.

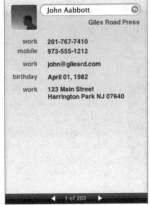

Ⓒ The Contacts widget offers a quick way to look up information stored in the Contacts application.

Ⓓ The Dictionary widget can help ensure that you use the right words.

Ⓔ ESPN offers up-to-date news and scores for current sports.

F Use Flight Tracker to see the status of a specific flight.

G The Movies widget helps you find out what's playing near you.

H Ski Report provides current conditions at the ski resort of your choice. (This works best in the winter.)

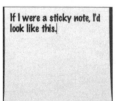

I The Stickies widget puts virtual sticky notes in Dashboard.

- **Flight Tracker G** can provide you with information about airline flights all over the world, including arrival and departure times, en route progress, and delays.

- **Movies G** can help you learn what's playing at nearby movie theaters.

- **Ski Report H** provides information of interest to skiers about ski resorts all over the world, including new snow, base depth, and trails open.

- **Stickies I**, which is a lot like the Stickies application (page 237), enables you to create reminder notes that look a lot like the sticky notes you might already have all over your workspace.

- **Stocks J** enables you to keep track of your favorite securities throughout the day.

- **Tile Game K** tests your puzzle-solving skills with a familiar—at least to old-timers like me—interface from your childhood.

continues on next page

J The Stocks widget helps you keep track of stock prices. (Good day on Wall Street!)

K Tile Game is a great digital version of the analog classic.

- **Translation** can translate text on the fly from one language to another.

- **Unit Converter** enables you to convert from one unit of measurement to another.

- **Weather** provides basic weather information for cities throughout the world.

- **Web Clip** is a do-it-yourself widget that works with the Safari Web browser (page 456) to capture information from the Web and display it in your Dashboard. As the source information changes, so does the information in the Web Clip widget.

- **World Clock** enables you to check the time in any major city in the world.

L Who needs a translator when there's one built into your Mac?

M Use Unit Converter to convert from one unit's measure to another's.

N The Weather widget puts a 7-day forecast in Dashboard.

O Use Web Clip to create custom widgets of content from the Web. This is a list of recently read posts on my blog that will be updated each time I open Dashboard.

P The World Clock widget lets you see the time of day anywhere in the world.

Desktop Management

OS X includes a number of desktop management tools that you might find helpful to work more efficiently and productively:

- **Stacks** puts expandable folders in the Dock. Clicking a folder displays its contents, making it quick and easy to open files you use often.

- **Mission Control** combines two OS X features:

  - **Exposé** helps you cope with screen clutter by arranging open windows so you can see their contents or your desktop with a press of a button.

  - **Spaces** enables you to organize windows into groups, thus helping you to manage projects or tasks.

- **Notification Center**, which is new in OS X Mountain Lion, organizes alerts and notifications for a variety of applications in one place, where they're easy to monitor.

This chapter explains how to use these features to keep your workspace organized while you work so you can be as productive as possible.

Stacks

Stacks displays the contents of any folder in the Dock as a fan **A**, grid **B**, or list **C**. Click the folder icon to display the stack. Then click the item in the stack to open it. This makes it easy to organize Dock items and access the applications, folders, and files you use most.

By default, OS X Mountain Lion is pre-configured with one stacks folder, Downloads **D**, which displays the contents of the Downloads folder inside your Home folder. You can add your own stacks to the Dock by simply adding folders.

TIP Whether a stack appears as a fan, grid, or list depends, in part, on settings for the stacks folder (page 470) or the number of items in the folder.

TIP If you upgraded to OS X Mountain Lion from a previous version of OS X, you may also have stacks folders for your Documents and/or Applications folders.

TIP A stack's Dock icon can appear as a pile (or stack) of icons with the most recently added item on top **D**. This helps give you an idea of the folder's contents.

To display a stack:

In the Dock, click the icon for the stack folder you want to display.

The contents of the folder appear in a fan **A**, grid **B**, or list **C**.

A You can display stacks as a fan, ...

B ...a grid, ...

C ...or a list.

D The Downloads stacks folder appears beside the Trash on the Dock.

To hide a stack:

Use one of the following techniques:

- Click anywhere other than a stack item.
- Click the stack folder again.

The stack collapses back into the stack icon in the Dock.

To open an item in a stack:

1. Display the stack containing the item you want to open **A B C**.
2. Click the item you want to open.

   The item opens.

To open a stack folder:

1. In the Dock, click the folder to open to display its stack **A B C**.
2. Click the appropriate button:

   ▸ For a fan **A**, click the Show in Finder or More in Finder button at the top of the fan. The wording of this command varies depending on whether all items are showing.

   ▸ For a grid **B**, click the Open in Finder button at the bottom of the grid. (You may have to scroll down in the grid to display this button.)

   ▸ For a list **C**, click the Open in Finder command at the bottom of the list.

The stacks folder opens in its own Finder window.

To navigate folders within a stack grid:

1. Display the stack grid you want to navigate **E** and, if necessary, scroll to display the folder you want to open.

2. Use any combination of the following techniques:

   ▸ To open a folder in the grid, click it. The grid displays the contents of the folder you clicked **F**. You can repeat this step as necessary to dig deeper into the folder hierarchy.

   ▸ To back out of a folder, click the Back arrow in the upper-left corner of the grid **F**.

To navigate folders within a stack list:

1. Display the stack list you want to navigate.

2. To open a folder in the list, point to it.

   The list turns into a hierarchical menu with the folder's contents displayed in a submenu **G**.

3. Repeat step 2 as necessary to open multiple submenus for deeply nested folders **H**.

TIP This is a great way to organize the files and folders you need to access using the Stacks feature.

E Here's a stack for my Documents folder, displayed as a grid.

F Click a folder to display its contents.

G Point to a folder in the list to display a submenu of items within that folder.

H You can display multiple levels of subfolders.

Mission Control

Mission Control Ⓐ combines the functionality of two OS X features—Exposé (page 255) and Spaces (page 257)—into one interface. These features work together to make it easier to stay organized and focused when working with multiple applications and documents on your Mac.

This part of the chapter introduces Mission Control's interface and explains how you can access it. The next two sections of this chapter go into detail on using the features of Exposé and Spaces within the Mission Control environment.

TIP The gestures and keystrokes discussed in this section are based on default OS X settings; if you changed them, the corresponding techniques may not work.

Dashboard   User-defined spaces   Full-screen app   Add Space button

Ⓐ Mission Control in action.   Dock (always visible)   Individual apps in currently displayed space (Desktop 1)

To open Mission Control:

Use one of the following techniques:

- Open the Mission Control icon in the Applications folder .

- Click the Mission Control icon in Launchpad.

- On a Multi-Touch device, swipe up with three fingers.

- Press the Mission Control key (normally F3, if present on your keyboard) or Control-Up Arrow.

Mission Control opens Ⓐ.

TIP The Control-Up Arrow keystroke replaces the F9 keystroke associated with Exposé (page 255) in previous versions of OS X.

To switch to a specific space with Mission Control:

1. Open Mission Control Ⓐ.

2. Along the top of the top of the screen, click the space you want to switch to.

   Mission Control closes and the screen displays just those applications and windows in the space you clicked Ⓒ.

To close Mission Control:

Use one of the following techniques:

- Press the Esc key.

- On a Multi-Touch device, swipe down with three fingers.

- Press the Mission Control key (normally F3, if present on your keyboard) or Control-Up Arrow.

TIP The gesture and keystroke here are based on default OS X settings; if you changed either, the corresponding technique may not work. Learn more about customizing Mission Control settings on page 507.

Ⓑ You can find the Mission Control icon in the Applications folder.

Mission Control

Ⓒ Clicking the Desktop 2 icon in Ⓐ displays the application windows open in that Space.

A Pressing Control-Down Arrow opens the Application Windows view of Exposé.

B Pressing F11 (or FN-F11 on a laptop) opens the Show Desktop view of Exposé, which can be handy if you keep a lot of icons on your desktop. (You know who you are.)

TABLE 18.1 Exposé Keyboard Shortcuts

Key	Description
Control-Down Arrow	Displays all open windows for the current application.
F11 or FN-F11 on a laptop	Displays the desktop for the current space.

Exposé

If you're like most OS X users, you probably have multiple applications and windows open at the same time while you work. The result can be a cluttered screen, with many layers of windows hiding other windows and the desktop.

Exposé helps solve the problem of screen clutter by making it easy to see all open windows in a single application A or the entire desktop B at once. Simply press one of Exposé's keyboard shortcuts (**Table 18.1**) to see what you need to see.

Exposé's features have been worked into Mission Control (page 253) and combined with Spaces (page 257), to create a unified interface for accessing spaces, applications, and application windows.

TIP You can customize Exposé's keyboard shortcuts or add additional Exposé triggers in the Mission Control preferences pane (page 507).

To see all open windows in the active application:

Press Control-Down Arrow.

All open windows in the active application resize and arrange themselves into a grid while other windows simply disappear A.

To switch to a specific application window:

1. Press Control-Down Arrow.

   Exposé displays all of the open windows for one application .

2. Press the Tab key.

   Exposé displays all open windows for the next application .

3. Repeat step 2 until the application you want to work with is displayed.

4. Use one of the following techniques to activate a specific window in the displayed application:

   ▸ Press the Right Arrow or Left Arrow key to move a blue border from one window to the next . Press Return when the blue border is around the window you want to activate.

   ▸ Click the window you want to activate.

   Three things happen :

   ▸ Exposé closes.

   ▸ If your Mac is set up with multiple spaces, it switches to the space the window you clicked is part of.

   ▸ The window you clicked becomes active.

To see the desktop:

Press F11, or, on a laptop, press FN-F11.

All open windows shift to the edges of the screen so you can see the desktop **B**.

To close Exposé:

Press the Esc key.

C Pressing the Tab key while Exposé is activated switches to the next application.

D When you point to a window, a blue border appears around it.

E Clicking a window in Exposé activates it in its space.

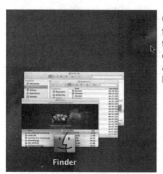

A Spaces appear at the top of the Mission Control screen.

B Point to the corner of the screen to display and click an Add Space button.

C An empty space is added to the top of the Mission Control screen.

Spaces

OS X's Spaces feature enables you to organize groups of windows into multiple spaces. Then, when you work in a space, only the windows that are part of that space appear onscreen.

For example, while working on a chapter of this book, I might have a space that includes my InDesign chapter document, Photoshop (which I use to edit screen-shots), and the three Finder windows that I use for the chapter's documents. I might also have another space set up with Mail, Messages, and Safari. I can then quickly switch from my work space to my commu-nication space when I need to check email or track down someone for a chat. When I want to return to work without distractions from those other applications, I can quickly switch back to my work space.

Spaces is part of the Mission Control fea-ture (page 253). This part of the chapter explains how to set up and remove spaces, assign applications to specific spaces, and switch from one space to another.

TIP By default, OS X creates separate spaces for Dashboard (Chapter 17) and for each full-screen app (page 142).

To add a space:

1. Press Control-Up Arrow to open Mis-sion Control **A**.

2. Move the pointer to the top-right corner of the screen and click the Add Space button that appears **B**.

   An icon for a new empty space appears at the top of the screen **C**.

To remove a space:

1. Open Mission Control **C**.

2. Point to the space you want to remove.

3. Click the black delete button that appears **D**.

   The space is removed. All of its windows appear in the previous space.

To switch from one space to another:

Use one of the following techniques:

- Open Mission Control **C** and click the icon at the top of the screen for the space you want to switch to.

- On a Multi-Touch device, use three fingers to swipe to the left or right until the space you want to switch to appears.

   If Mission Control was open, it closes. Your Mac switches to the space you clicked **E**.

To add windows to a space:

1. Activate the window you want to move to another space.

2. Drag the window to the edge of the screen and pause **F**.

   After a moment, the current space slides away to the side, displaying the next space.

3. Repeat this process as necessary until the space you want to move the window to is displayed.

4. Release the window **G**.

   The window moves to the currently displayed space.

TIP In case you're wondering, it is possible to display different windows for the same application in different spaces.

D When you point to a space and pause, a delete button appears.

E A new, empty space.

F Drag the window you want to move to the edge of the screen and pause.

G Release the window in the space you want to place it.

H The contextual menu in the Dock for an application that is running.

I The Options submenu includes commands for assigning the application to a specific space.

To assign a specific application to a specific space:

1. Switch to the space you want to assign the application to.

2. In the Dock, right-click the icon for the application you want to assign to that space.

   A contextual menu appears for that application **H**.

3. Point to the Options menu to display a submenu **I**.

4. Choose This Desktop.

   The application's windows move to the current space. From that point forward, every time you open that application, it will open in the same space.

To open an application in all spaces:

1. In the Dock, right-click the icon for the application you want to open in all spaces.

   A contextual menu appears **H**.

2. Point to the Options menu **I**.

3. Choose All Desktops.

   From that point forward, every time you open that application, it will open in all spaces.

To remove an application's space assignment:

1. In the Dock, right-click the icon for the application you want to remove the space assignment from.

   A contextual menu appears **H**.

2. Point to the Options menu **I**.

3. Choose None.

   From that point forward, the application can open in whatever space is active.

Notification Center

Notification Center, which is new in OS X Mountain Lion, displays notification banners and alerts for events, incoming email, tweets, and other activity you need to know about. You configure it for the applications that support it and it works in the background, displaying notifications when necessary in the upper-right corner of your screen as you work **A**. If you miss a notification or want to view recent activity, you can open Notification Center with just a click to see a list **B**. Click a list item to view its details.

This part of the chapter explains how to display and hide Notification Center, as well as how to send tweets to Twitter right from the Notification Center window.

TIP You can learn how to configure Notification Center for each application that supports it on page 517.

TIP Notifications are automatically disabled when you use Keynote, so you don't have to worry about them interrupting your presentations. A discussion of Keynote, which is part of the iWork suite of products, is beyond the scope of this book.

To display Notification Center:

Click the Notification Center button in the upper-right corner of the screen.

The screen's contents shift to the left and Notification Center's window appears on the right side of the screen **B**.

To hide Notification Center:

Click the Notification Center button again.

The screen's contents slide back to the right to hide Notification Center's window.

A A notification banner is an onscreen reminder that's part of Notification Center.

B Clicking the Notification Center button in the top-right corner of the screen displays current and recent notifications.

C When you click the Click to Tweet button, a Twitter share sheet appears at the top of the Notification Center.

D Enter the text of your tweet in the share sheet and click Send.

To send a tweet from Notification Center:

1. Click the Notification Center button to display the Notification Center window **B**.

2. At the top of the Notification Center window, click the Click to Tweet button.

   The window slides down to display a Tweet share sheet **C**.

3. Enter the text of your tweet in the share sheet **D**.

4. To include your location in the tweet, click the Add Location button.

   OS X attempts to determine your location; if it is successful, it displays this information where the Add Location button appeared.

5. Click Send.

   Your tweet is sent to Twitter and the share sheet closes.

TIP You must have a Twitter account set up within OS X to send tweets and receive tweet notifications from Twitter. Learn how to set up OS X for use with Twitter on page 546.

TIP If you have included your location in previous tweets, the Add Location button may already display your location.

TIP If your location is displayed and you don't want to include it in the tweet, click the location to clear it.

iCloud-Savvy Applications

In This Part

19

Working with iCloud

iCloud is the latest version of Apple's online file storage and syncing service. It offers the following features:

- Store iWork documents so they can be accessed by any other OS X computer or iOS device on your account.

- Synchronize Contacts records, Calendar events, Reminders, Notes, Mail accounts, and Safari bookmarks.

- Use Photo Stream to automatically share photos with devices on your account.

- Back up iOS devices and restore from those backups when necessary.

- Use Find My Mac, iPhone, iPad, and iPod touch to locate a lost or stolen computer or iOS device.

- Use Find My Friends to locate friends and family members.

- Get access to iTunes Store purchases, including apps and ebooks, on all devices associated with your account.

This chapter explains how to set up iCloud and begin using some of its features on your Mac.

Setting Up iCloud

Setting up iCloud is easy. Simply enter your Apple ID in the iCloud preferences pane to log in, set a few options, and you're good to go.

TIP To use iCloud, you must have an Apple ID. If you don't already have one, you can create one on the fly as you set up iCloud.

TIP In addition to using your Apple ID for iCloud, you use it to make purchases from Apple's App Store and the iTunes Store.

To sign in to iCloud for the first time:

1. Choose Apple > System Preferences, or click the System Preferences icon in the Dock to open System Preferences.

2. Click the iCloud icon under Internet & Wireless.

   The iCloud Sign In screen appears **A**.

3. Enter your Apple ID and password in the appropriate boxes.

4. Click Sign In.

5. In the settings screen that appears next **B**, toggle check boxes to enable features:

   ▸ **Use iCloud for contacts, calendars, reminders, notes, and Safari** automatically stores data on iCloud so it can be accessed by other OS X computers and iOS devices on your account.

   ▸ **Use Find My Mac** enables you to find your computer if it's lost or stolen and, if necessary, lock or erase it.

6. Click Next.

A The iCloud preferences pane looks like this before you've signed in.

B Toggle check boxes to enable or disable iCloud features.

C If your Calendar events include attachments, you might see a dialog like this.

D OS X asks permission to use the location of your Mac for Find My Mac.

E Once signed in, the iCloud preferences pane looks like this.

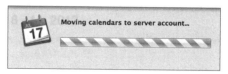

F Your Mac moves data onto its servers when you enable certain features.

G H With iCloud features enabled, iCloud appears in Contacts and Calendars as the data location.

7. You may see a dialog warning you that iCloud does not support event attachments **C**. If you want to use iCloud with Calendars, click Turn on Calendars.

8. If you enabled the Use Find My Mac option in step 5, a dialog asks permission to share the location of your Mac **D**. Click Allow.

   The iCloud preferences pane displays a list of the applications and features that are currently enabled for your account **E**.

TIP In step 3, if you do not yet have an Apple ID, click the Create an Apple ID link in the sign In screen **A**. Then follow the instructions that appear onscreen to create your account.

TIP If Calendar (Chapter 21) is open when you enable iCloud's calendar features, you may see a progress dialog telling you that your calendars are being moved to the server account **F**.

TIP When iCloud has been enabled for Contacts and Calendars, iCloud appears as the location in the Groups list **G** and Calendars list **H**.

TIP You can learn more about setting iCloud options on page 544.

To set up an iCloud email address:

1. If the Mail check box in the iCloud preferences pane **E** is not toggled on, turn on the check box.

2. In the dialog that appears **I**, enter a name for your email account and click OK.

3. In the confirmation dialog that appears **J**, click Create.

4. Wait while your Mac checks the availability of the name you entered. One of two things happens:

   ▸ If the name is not available, a message tells you **K**. Enter a new name in the Email box or choose one of the suggested emails and click OK. Then repeat steps 3 and 4.

   ▸ If the name is available, it's assigned to your Apple ID. Both iCloud and Mail are configured with the account information. You're done.

> **TIP** iCloud email addresses are free and optional—you don't have to use one if you use iCloud.

> **TIP** Your iCloud email address is the name you entered followed by @me.com—for example, j.aabbott@me.com.

> **TIP** You can learn more about using Mail to send and receive email messages in Chapter 29.

I Use this dialog to enter a name for your iCloud email address.

J You can't change your mind later, so OS X asks if you're sure about the name.

K If the name already exists, your Mac tells you and offers suggestions.

A When you're signed into the iCloud website, its Home page should look like this.

Using the iCloud Website

The iCloud website lets you access the data you have stored in iCloud, as well as use the Find My Mac feature. It also offers ways to change account settings and buy more storage space.

The iCloud website's interface is simple: it offers five buttons for accessing features **A**:

- **Mail** lets you access your iCloud email account.

- **Contacts** lets you access the contacts database you manage with Contacts on your Mac or iOS device.

- **Calendar** lets you access the event database you manage with Calendar on your Mac or iOS device.

- **Find My iPhone** lets you locate any Mac or iOS device for which you have enabled location tracking on your account.

- **iWork** gives you access to the Keynote, Pages, and Numbers documents you've created on your Mac or iOS device and stored on iCloud.

This part of the chapter explains how to sign in to the iCloud website and use some of the tools and options you'll find there.

TIP You can sign in to iCloud from any computer—not just the one you configured for your iCloud account.

To sign in to the iCloud website:

1. Use a Web browser such as Safari (page 456) to visit **www.icloud.com**.

2. If a Sign In message appears, click Sign In. Then enter your Apple ID and password in the fields that appear **B** and click the right arrow button.

3. The first time you connect, you'll be prompted for some information **C**. Enter it as follows and click Done:

   ▸ To change the profile picture, click it to display a pop-out dialog **D**. Click Choose and use an Open dialog to choose an image file. When the image has been uploaded, use the slider to resize it. Click Done.

   ▸ To change the language, click it to display a pop-out dialog **E**. Click the language you want.

   ▸ To change the time zone, click it to display a pop-out map **F**. Click the map near your location, click the button beneath the map, and choose a city closest to you in your time zone.

When you're signed in, your name and profile picture appear near the top of the window **A**.

B Enter your Apple ID and password in the appropriate boxes.

C The first time you log in, you're prompted for some basic account information.

D Click the image to display a pop-up window with tools for changing it.

E To change the language, choose one from this menu.

F You can click your location on the map to begin the process of setting your time zone.

G You can use iCloud to access your iCloud email account, ...

H ...contacts database, ...

I ... and calendar events and reminders.

To access Mail, Contacts & Calendar data on iCloud:

1. Sign in to the iCloud website as discussed on the previous page.

2. On the iCloud Home page **A**, click the button for the feature you want: Mail, Contacts, or Calendar.

   The interface for the feature you selected fills the browser window **G H I**.

3. Use options in the window to browse, edit, add, and remove data.

TIP The interfaces for these features are very similar to their OS X counterparts: Mail (page 434), Contacts (Chapter 20), Calendar (Chapter 21), and Reminders (Chapter 22).

TIP If you have multiple Macs or iOS devices, you should love iCloud. If you enable each device for use with iCloud, your contacts, calendar events, and reminder items are automatically synced between them. This means that any change you make on one device—or the iCloud website—is automatically copied to the others. That gives you up-to-date data everywhere with no additional effort.

To change account settings:

1. While signed into the iCloud website, click your name near the top of the window.

2. In the account window that appears , set options as desired. (Step 3 in the section titled "To sign in to the iCloud website" on page 270 explains how.)

3. Click Done.

To remove all Photo Stream photos from iCloud:

1. While signed into the iCloud website, click your name near the top of the window.

2. In the Account dialog that appears , click Advanced.

3. In the Advanced dialog , click Reset Photo Stream.

4. In the confirmation dialog that appears, click Reset.

5. If prompted, enter your account password and click OK.

6. A dialog confirms that Photo Stream has been reset. Click OK.

7. Click the button with your Apple ID to go back to the Account dialog .

8. Click Done to dismiss the account dialog.

TIP Any photo in Photo Stream is automatically shared with any OS X computer or iOS device associated with your account.

TIP When you reset Photo Stream, photos are removed from iCloud. They should still remain on the devices where they originated. For example, when you reset Photo Stream, any photos you took with your iPhone remain in the camera roll of your iPhone.

You can change settings for your account in the Account dialog.

Click the Reset Photo Stream button to remove all photos from Photo Stream.

A The documents you store on iCloud are organized by app and appear as preview icons. In this example, I have two Pages documents stored on iCloud.

B The same two documents appear in Pages on my iPad.

Using iCloud with iWork

You can use iCloud to store documents you create with iWork applications—Pages **A**, Numbers, and Keynote—on your Mac or iOS devices. Then, when you change the contents of a document, the modified document is available to all of your OS X and iOS devices.

When you enable iWork applications for iCloud on your iOS devices, all documents you create are automatically saved to iCloud **B**. If you have multiple iOS devices, they all have access to the same group of documents.

To make iWork documents you create on your Mac accessible to your iOS devices, you can upload them to iCloud. Then, if you make changes to a document with an iWork app on your iOS device, those changes are automatically saved to iCloud. You can download a modified document to work with it on your Mac. If you have multiple Macs, iCloud is also a convenient place to store documents you want to share among them.

This part of the chapter explains how to access iWork documents stored on iCloud from OS X.

TIP As this book went to press, Apple was still developing iCloud and working on ways to link it to iWork applications on OS X. As iCloud and iWork evolve, Apple will likely introduce additional ways to share documents with these tools.

To access iWork documents stored on iCloud:

1. Sign in to the iCloud website.

2. On the iCloud Home page **C**, click the iWork button.

3. At the top of the page, click the button for the type of document you want to access: Keynote, Pages, or Numbers.

   One of two things happens:

   ▸ If documents for that application have not yet been saved to iCloud, the browser window will be empty, with buttons to learn more or get the iOS version of the app **D**.

   ▸ If documents for that application have been saved to iCloud, the browser window will display preview icons for each document **A**.

To upload an iWork document to iCloud:

1. Navigate to the page on iCloud.com for the application you're working with: Keynote, Pages, or Numbers.

2. Drag the icon for the document you want to store on iCloud from a Finder window to the Web browser window **E**.

3. Release the button.

   The file is uploaded to iCloud **F** and, after a moment, its preview icon appears in the browser window **G**. It's now accessible to any computer with access to your iCloud account, as well as any iOS devices connected to your iCloud account **H**.

> **TIP** Uploading a file to iCloud does not remove the copy on your computer. Instead, you'll have two copies of the file: the original on your computer and the copy on iCloud.

C The iCloud Home page, once you've signed in.

D If there are no documents for an app, its page should look something like this.

E To upload a document, drag it into the Web browser window from a Finder window.

F The file is uploaded to iCloud.

G A preview icon for the uploaded file appears on the application's page on the iCloud website.

H The document is also available in any iOS application that is linked to your iCloud account—in this example, an iPad.

I When you click the icon for a document, a Download button appears on it.

J Choose the option you want from the menu that appears.

To download an iWork document from iCloud:

1. Navigate to the page on iCloud.com for the application that created the document: Keynote, Pages, or Numbers.

2. Click the preview icon for the document you want.

   A download button appears on the icon **I**.

3. Click the Download button to display a menu of options **J**.

4. Choose the one you want.

5. Wait while the document is prepared and downloaded. When it's finished, it opens in the appropriate application.

TIP iWorks files are downloaded to your Downloads folder.

TIP Downloading a file from iCloud does not remove the copy on iCloud. Instead, you'll have two copies of the file: the one on iCloud and the copy on your computer. If you make changes to the copy you downloaded and save those changes, the copy on iCloud is not automatically updated.

To enable an iWork app on an iOS device for use with iCloud:

1. On your iOS device, tap Settings.

2. In the Settings column, tap iCloud to view its settings .

3. If necessary, tap Documents & Data and set the option to On. Then click iCloud to return to the main Settings screen.

4. In the Settings column, scroll down to the iWork app you want to enable for use with iCloud and tap its name to display its options .

5. Set Use iCloud to On .

   If you already have documents stored for that app on your device, they're copied to iCloud. From that point forward, your device will remain in sync with iCloud for that app.

TIP In step 2, if your iOS device isn't already set up for iCloud, you'll need to enter your Apple ID and password to view settings.

TIP The first time you use an iOS version of an iWork app, a screen offers to turn on iCloud for you **M**. Click Use iCloud to store all documents for that app on iCloud.

TIP To store all iOS documents for an app on your device instead of iCloud, set the Use iCloud option **L** to Off.

K Turn on Documents & Data in iCloud settings

L You can then turn on the Use iCloud option for the app.

M The first time you open an iOS app, it offers to turn on iCloud access for you.

Ⓐ The iCloud Home page, once you've signed in.

Ⓑ Enter your password in this box and click OK.

Ⓒ Select an item to see its location.

Using Find My Mac

Find My Mac works with iCloud and an iOS device or Apple's iCloud website. If enabled on your computer, it tracks the location of your computer and records it on Apple's server. If your computer is lost or stolen, you can use Find My Mac to locate it, display a message on it, or erase its contents.

TIP To use Find My Mac, it must be enabled in iCloud settings on your computer (page 544).

TIP If you have an iOS device, you can use the Find iPhone app to perform the same tasks without using a Web browser to access the iCloud website.

To find your Mac or iOS device:

1. Sign in to the iCloud website.

2. On the iCloud Home page **Ⓐ**, click Find My iPhone.

3. Enter your Apple ID password in the dialog that appears **Ⓑ** and click OK.

   After a moment, a list of all devices registered with the Find My iPhone feature appears in the window. When you select a device, its location appears on a map **Ⓒ**.

To work with a found device:

1. Follow the instructions on the previous page to find your devices and select the one you want to work with **C**.

2. Click the i button for the device's label on the map to display device options **D**.

3. Click the button for the option you want:

   ▸ **Play Sound or Send Message** displays a window you can use to enter a message and turn an alert sound on or off **E**. When you click Send, the message appears onscreen on the selected device **F**.

   ▸ **Remote Lock** displays a window you can use to set a 4-digit passcode to lock the computer **G**. You might find this useful if you can't get your hands on the computer but are concerned that someone else can. When you click Lock, the computer's contents cannot be accessed until the passcode is entered correctly.

   ▸ **Remote Wipe** displays a window similar to **G** that you can use to set a 4-digit passcode to lock the computer. When you click Wipe, it displays a window similar to **E** that you can use to enter a message to the person who has the computer. Clicking Wipe in that window erases all of your personal data from the computer, leaving just the operating system and apps, which are locked down. If you later recover the computer, you can enter the passcode to regain access. Your data, however, is permanently removed. (You do back up regularly, don't you?)

D Clicking the Info button displays options for working with the selected device.

E Use this window to type in a message to display on the device.

F The message you send looks like this on the found computer.

G Enter a passcode that must be entered to unlock the computer.

A The iCloud preferences pane offers options for managing iCloud storage.

B The Manage Storage dialog shows how much space each app is using and enables you to delete individual documents.

C You can use the Buy More Storage dialog to select one of the storage plans Apple offers for a fee.

Managing iCloud Storage

iCloud comes with 5 GB of free storage space. You can use this space to store your iWork documents, mail, and iOS devices backed up to iCloud. iTunes Store and App Store purchases are not counted when calculating storage space used.

You can see how much iCloud space you're using in the iCloud preferences pane. That's also where you can buy more storage space if you need it.

TIP You can learn more about the iCloud preferences pane on page 544.

To manage iCloud storage space:

1. Choose Apple > System Preferences, or click the System Preferences icon in the Dock.

2. In the System Preferences window, click iCloud to display iCloud preferences.

3. To see how much storage space is used for your iCloud account, consult the bar at the bottom of the preferences pane **A**.

4. To get details on how the storage space is used, click the Manage button. A list of apps and the amount of space each one is using appears. You can click an app to get more details **B**. You can also click an item on the right side of the window and click Delete to remove it.

5. To buy more storage space, click the Buy More Storage button to display options **C**. Click the button for the option you want and follow the onscreen prompts to complete the transaction. The space is added to your account immediately.

Disabling iCloud

If you decide you no longer want to use iCloud's features on your Mac, you can disable it by simply signing out.

To sign out of iCloud:

1. Choose Apple > System Preferences, or click the System Preferences icon in the Dock.

2. In the System Preferences window, click iCloud to display iCloud preferences **A**.

3. Click the Sign Out button.

4. You'll be presented with a series of dialogs explaining what will happen for each of the iCloud services you use **B C D E F**. Read the information in each dialog carefully and click the appropriate button to proceed. Note that in most instances, you will not be able to keep iCloud data on your Mac.

   OS X removes iCloud data from your Mac and signs out.

TIP The data you stored on iCloud remains there and is still accessible from the iCloud website, other OS X computers and iOS devices associated with your Apple ID, and iWorks applications.

TIP If you sign back into iCloud, data for the services you enable are copied back to your Mac.

A The iCloud preferences pane.

B C D E F When you sign out of iCloud, your Mac displays a series of dialogs like these to tell you what will happen. In most cases, data will be deleted from your Mac, although it will remain on iCloud.

Contacts

Contacts is a contact management application that enables you to keep track of the names, addresses, phone numbers, email addresses, Web URLs, and similar information for people and businesses that you know. Data you enter into Contacts can be grouped, sorted, searched, and printed. When you search your Mac using the Spotlight search menu (page 94), search results can include Contacts records.

The information you store in Contacts can be used by Mail (page 434) to send email messages, Messages (page 443) to send instant messages, FaceTime (page 451) to initiate video calls, Calendar (Chapter 21) to invite people to events, and Reminders (Chapter 22) to set locations for tasks.

Contacts records can be shared with others through the use of compatible servers, such as CardDAV and Exchange. They can also be synchronized with online services such as Google and mobile devices such as iPad and iPhone.

This chapter provides enough information to get you started using Contacts for your contact management needs.

Getting Started with Contacts

Like any other application, you must launch Contacts before you can use it. This loads it into your computer's memory so your computer can work with it. You can then use its familiar interface to work with contact records.

To launch Contacts:

Use one of the following techniques:

- Open the Contacts application icon in the Applications folder window (page 137).

- Click the Contacts icon in Launchpad (page 140).

- Click the Contacts icon in the Dock (page 34).

Contacts launches **B**.

TIP If the Contacts window displays just a single contact card **C**, you can click the book button in its lower-left corner to expand the view and display it as a book with a list of records on the left and details about the selected record on the right **B**.

TIP You can resize the Contacts window by dragging any of its edges (page 26). You can move the Contacts window to a new location on screen by dragging it from any location except an edge, button, or data.

A The Contacts application icon.

Contacts

B When you first open Contacts, it only has two records: one for Apple and one for you.

C The Contacts window can also be displayed as a single contact card.

D Here's what the List and Card view of Contacts might look like with a bunch of contacts entered.

E This example shows all three columns: Groups, List, and Card.

Group

List and Card

Card Only

F Use these buttons to change the display mode.

View	
✓ Groups	⌘1
List and Card	⌘2
Card Only	⌘3
Hide Last Import	⌥⌘L

G Use View menu commands or their keyboard shortcuts to quickly switch view.

To navigate the Contacts Interface:

Contacts appears as a book with a list on the left and details for a selected list item on the right **B D**. If you have organized your contacts into groups, you can display a list of Groups in an additional column on the left **E**.

Here are some tips for navigating the Contacts interface; you'll use this information throughout this chapter and whenever you work with Contacts:

- To view the items in a list, scroll through the list using standard scrolling techniques (page 28).

- To switch from one display mode to another, click the appropriate button at the bottom of the window **F**, use commands under the View menu **G**, or use the corresponding keyboard shortcut.

- To view all the contacts in a group, in Group display mode, click the name of the group **E**.

- To view all contacts, click the All Contacts group.

- To view contact details, select the contact name. Details appear on the right side of the window **B D E**.

To quit Contacts:

Choose Contacts > Quit Contacts, or press Command-Q.

Contacts quits. Any changes you made to contact records are automatically saved.

Working with Contact Cards

As you work with Contacts, you'll be adding, removing, and editing *contact cards*. A contact card is a collection of information about a specific person or business. Information is entered into predefined fields to keep data entry consistent throughout the Contacts database.

To add a new card:

1. Use one of the following techniques:

   ▸ Click the Create a new card button (+) at the bottom of the Contacts window.

   ▸ Choose File > New Card, or press Command-N.

   A few things happen :

   ▸ A *No Name* record is created in the list of contacts on the left.

   ▸ A blank address card appears on the right, with the First field selected.

   ▸ Contacts switches to edit mode.

2. Enter information about the contact into appropriate fields:

   ▸ When a field is active, text appears within it to prompt you for information . Type to replace selected text.

   ▸ Press Tab or click a field to move from field to field.

   ▸ Additional fields appear automatically when you enter data into all available fields of a specific type. For example, if you enter information into both phone number fields, another phone number field appears .

A Contacts creates a new blank contact card and selects the first field for data entry.

B Contacts automatically adds fields when you use up all fields of an available type.

C You can use a pop-up menu to change a field's label.

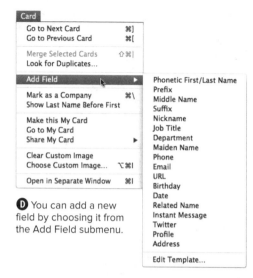

Card	
Go to Next Card	⌘]
Go to Previous Card	⌘[
Merge Selected Cards	⇧⌘|
Look for Duplicates...	
Add Field	▶
Mark as a Company	⌘\
Show Last Name Before First	
Make this My Card	
Go to My Card	
Share My Card	▶
Clear Custom Image	
Choose Custom Image...	⌥⌘I
Open in Separate Window	⌘I

Phonetic First/Last Name
Prefix
Middle Name
Suffix
Nickname
Job Title
Department
Maiden Name
Phone
Email
URL
Birthday
Date
Related Name
Instant Message
Twitter
Profile
Address

Edit Template...

D You can add a new field by choosing it from the Add Field submenu.

3. To change the label that appears beside a field, click the label to display a menu **C**, and then choose the label you prefer.

4. To add another field, choose the field you want from the Add Field submenu under the Card menu **D**.

5. To remove a field, click the red minus button beside it. The field is removed. (Empty fields that do not have a red minus button **B** will not appear on completed contact record.)

6. When you are finished entering contact information, click the Done button to view the completed card **E**.

E A completed contact card shows only the fields that contain data.

F To list a record by company name, turn on the Company check box.

TIP You can enter information into any combination of fields; if you do not have information for a specific field, skip it and it will not appear in the completed card.

TIP To list an entry by company name rather than the person's name **E**, turn on the Company check box beneath the Company field **F**. A contact that does not include a person's name is automatically listed by the company name.

To delete a contact record:

1. On the left side of the Contacts window, select the contact you want to delete.

2. Press the Delete key.

3. In the confirmation dialog that appears, click Delete or press Return.

   The contact disappears.

To edit a contact card:

1. On the left side of the Contacts window, select the contact you want to edit **E**.

2. Click the Edit button at the bottom of the window to switch to edit mode **G**.

3. Make changes as desired in the record's address card.

4. Click Done to save your changes and view the modified card.

To add an image to a contact card:

1. On the left side of the Contacts window, select the contact that you want to add a picture or logo to.

2. If necessary, click the Edit button to switch to edit mode **G**.

3. Drag the icon for the file containing the photo or logo you want to add from a Finder window to the image well in the address card window **H**.

4. When you release the button, the image appears in a pop-up window **I**.

5. Drag the slider at the bottom of the dialog to resize the image. You can then drag the image around in the frame to determine the resized image's edges.

6. Click Done.

   The image appears in the contact card **J**.

TIP Another way to add an image to a card is to choose Card > Choose Custom Image to display the image pop-up window **J**. Then either drag the image into that window or click one of the buttons on the left to use one of the default images, use a recent image, or create a new image with your computer's camera.

TIP To remove an image from a contact record, select the contact and choose Card > Clear Custom Image or click the image while the record is in edit mode and press Delete.

G When you click the Edit button, you can make changes to the currently displayed contact card.

H Drag the image file's icon to the image area in the contact card.

I The image appears in a pop-up window.

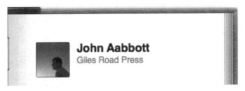

J An Image in a contact card.

A A vCard file icon, as it appears in OS X. Note the custom image; this card file includes the contact's photo.

Chuck Joiner.vcf

B One way to add a vCard's information to Contacts is to drag the icon into the list of contacts.

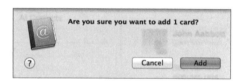

C A dialog confirms that you want to add the card to Contacts.

D The card appears in Contacts with all of the information it contains.

Importing & Creating vCards

vCard, or *virtual address card*, files are commonly used to share contact information electronically. A vCard file, which normally has a .vcf filename extension **A**, can contain all of the contact information for an individual or organization. Because the file uses a standard format, it is readable by most contact management software.

If you receive a vCard file, you can import it into Contacts to quickly add that contact's record to your Contacts file. Similarly, you can create a vCard file for anyone in Contacts and share it with someone else so they can add it to their contact management application.

To import a vCard:

1. Use one of the following techniques:
   ▸ Double-click a vCard file icon **A**.
   ▸ Drag a vCard file icon from a Finder window to the left side of the Contacts window **B**.

   A dialog appears, asking if you're sure you want to add the card **C**.

2. Click Add.

   A Contacts contact card is created based on the vCard contents **D**.

TIP If a vCard contains more than one record, all records are imported.

TIP If you already have a record for that contact in Contacts, Contacts offers to update it or let you keep the original.

To save contact information as a vCard:

Drag the name of a contact from the right side of the Contacts window to the desktop or a Finder window **E**.

The vCard file's icon appears where you dragged it **F**.

TIP You can save multiple vCards in one file. Just hold down the Command key and click to select multiple contacts. Then drag any of them to a Finder window as discussed above.

To share a contact's card with someone else:

1. In the left side of the Contacts window, select the card you want to share **D**.

2. In the bottom of the Contacts windows, click the Share button **D**.

3. From the menu that appears **G**, choose a method to share the card.

4. What you do next depends on what you chose in step 3:

   ▸ If you chose Email Card, OS X opens your email application, creates a new message, and attaches a vCard to it. Address the message and click Send.

   ▸ If you chose Message Card, OS X opens a Messages share sheet with a vCard attached **H**. Address the message and click Send.

   ▸ If you chose AirDrop Card, OS X opens an AirDrop share sheet with a vCard attached. Choose the Mac you want to send it to and click Send.

TIP You can send your vCard to anyone you like. This makes it easy for people to add your contact information to their contact database.

TIP You can learn more about the Share button and share sheets on page 149.

E Drag the name of a contact from Contacts to a Finder window.

F The icon for the contact's vCard file appears where you dragged the name.

G Click the share menu to display sharing options.

H This example shows a Messages share sheet with the vCard attached.

A Contacts's General preferences window offers options for changing the display and sort order of contacts.

B Contacts offers two options for sorting its contacts list.

C You can sort contacts by first name.

Organizing Contact Cards

Once Contacts has more than just a few contact cards, it's important to be able to locate the ones you want quickly, when you want them. Contacts includes a number of features you might find helpful for keeping contacts organized:

- Sort cards based on first or last name.
- Search for cards based on any field of information.
- Organize cards into groups.
- Create smart groups to keep cards organized automatically based on criteria you specify.

This part of the chapter takes a look at all of these features.

TIP The Last Import group is automatically created (or modified) by Contacts when you import one or more contacts.

To sort contact cards:

1. Choose Contacts > Preferences, or press Command-, (comma) to open the Contacts Preferences window.

2. If necessary, click the General button at the top of the window to display General preferences **A**.

3. Choose an option from the Sort By pop-up menu **B**.

    The contacts are immediately sorted by the option you chose **C**.

4. Click the General preferences window's close button to dismiss it.

TIP By default, contact cards are sorted by last name.

To search for a contact card:

1. Begin entering a search word or phrase in the Search box at the top of the Contacts window.

   Contacts immediately displays all records that match what you've typed .

2. Continue typing to narrow down the list of contacts that match the search word or phrase.

   Each character you type reduces the list of matches **E**.

TIP You can search by any text that might appear in a contact's record. For example, if you're trying to find a person who works at a certain company but can't remember the person's name, you can enter the company name to display a list of all contacts at that company.

TIP If you have set up multiple groups (as discussed next), make sure you select either the All Contacts group or the group you expect to find the contact before beginning your search. If the contact you're looking for is not in the group you're searching, you won't find him.

D In this example, searching for the characters *jo* instantly displays a bunch of matches.

E Adding another character narrows down the search results.

F An untitled group appears in the group list.

G When you type in a new name and press Return the untitled group is named.

H Drag a name from the contact list to the group.

I Select a group name to see the contact cards within it.

To organize contact cards into groups:

1. Choose File > New Group, or press Shift-Command-N.

   A new entry appears in Groups view with its name, *untitled group*, selected **F**.

2. Enter a name for the group and press Return to save it **G**.

3. In the list of groups, select All Contacts.

4. In the contact list, locate a contact you want to add to the new group.

5. Drag the contact's name from the list of contacts onto the name of the group you want to add him to **H**.

   When you release the button, the contact is added to the list.

6. Repeat steps 4 and 5 to add as many contacts as you like to the group.

TIP To see which contact cards are in a group, click the name of the group on the left side of the window. The names of the contacts in the group appear in the list to the right **I**.

TIP You can create as many groups as you need to organize your contacts.

TIP A contact can be included in more than one group.

To remove a contact from a group:

1. In Group view, select the group you want to remove the contact from .

2. In the list of contacts on the right side of the window, select the contact you want to remove.

3. Press the Delete key.

4. Click the appropriate button in the confirmation dialog that appears ❶:

   ▸ **Cancel** does not delete the contact.

   ▸ **Delete** deletes the contact from the Contacts database and any groups it might be part of.

   ▸ **Remove from Group** removes the contact from the group. The contact remains in the Contacts database and any other groups it might be part of.

TIP Deleting a contact from the All Contacts group completely removes it from Contacts.

To delete a group:

1. In Group view, select the group you want to remove .

2. Press the Delete key.

3. In the confirmation dialog that appears ❶, click Delete.

   The group is removed but all contacts that were in it remain in Contacts.

TIP You cannot remove the All Contacts group.

❶ A dialog like this appears when you try to delete a contact from a specific group.

❷ Use this dialog to confirm that you want to delete the selected group.

L A dialog like this appears when you use the New Smart Group command.

M Set criteria by choosing options and entering match text.

N You can add lines for additional criteria if necessary.

O In this example, I used a smart group to automatically group contacts based in three different states.

To create a smart group:

1. Choose File > New Smart Group, or press Option-Command-N.

   A smart group settings dialog appears **L**.

2. Enter a name for the group in the Smart Group Name box.

3. Use options in the middle of the dialog to set criteria for matching contacts **M**.

4. To add more matching criteria, click the + button at the far right end of the line of criteria you already set. The dialog expands to offer an additional line and a pop-up menu for matching options **N**. Set options as desired.

5. Repeat step 4 as necessary to add more matching criteria.

6. If you have set more than one line of criteria, choose a matching option from the pop-up menu beneath the smart group name field.

7. Click OK.

   The smart group is created and populated with contacts that match the criteria you specified **O**.

TIP To create a smart group from search results, perform a search and then choose File > New Smart Group from Current Search.

TIP You can delete a smart group the same way you delete a regular group (page 292).

TIP You cannot manually remove a contact from a smart group. The only way a contact can be removed from a smart group is if it no longer matches the criteria you specified when you set up the smart group.

TIP To edit a smart group's criteria, select the group and choose Edit > Edit Smart Group. Then use the dialog that appears to modify settings and click OK.

Printing Contact Cards

Contacts makes it possible to print individual contact cards, selected contact cards, or groups of contact cards in a number of formats. Start by selecting the cards you want to print and then using the Print dialog to set printing options and send the print job to your printer.

Although printing in OS X is discussed in detail in Chapter 24, here's a quick overview of how you can print your contacts.

TIP Before you can print, you must have a printer set up to use with your computer. You can learn more about printing in Chapter 24.

To print contact cards:

1. Select the card(s) you want to print:
   - To print just one card, in Group or List and Card view, select the card.
   - To print multiple cards, in Group or List and Card view, select the cards. (You can hold down the Command key to select multiple cards at once.)
   - To print all the cards in a group, in Group view, select the group.

2. Choose File > Print, or press Command-P.

   The Print dialog appears **A B C D**.

3. Choose the name of the printer you want to use from the Printer pop-up menu.

4. Choose an option from the Style pop-up menu:
   - **Mailing Labels** **A** prints mailing labels on a variety of widely available label sheets.
   - **Envelopes** **B** prints envelopes on common envelope sizes.

A Some of the Mailing Labels options in the Print dialog.

B Some of the Envelopes options in the Print dialog.

C Lists options in the Print dialog.

Pocket Contacts options in the Print dialog.

▸ **Lists** ● prints contact lists that include the database fields you specify.

▸ **Pocket Contacts** ● prints pocket-sized address books.

5. Set options as desired in the dialog:

▸ For mailing labels ●, click the Layout button and set label layout options. Then click the Label button and set options for label content, sort order, color, and font.

▸ For envelopes ●, click the Layout button and set envelope layout options. Then click the Label button and set options for envelope content, print order, color, and font. Finally, click the Orientation button and select an envelope print orientation.

▸ For lists ●, set Paper Size, Orientation, and Font Size options. Then turn on check boxes in the Attributes area to specify what information you want to print for each record.

▸ For pocket address books ●, set Orientation, Flip Style, and Font options. Then turn on check boxes in the Attributes area to specify what information you want to print for each record.

Note the changes in the dialog's preview area as you change settings.

6. Click Print.

Contacts sends the information to your printer, and it prints.

TIP After step 3, if the Print dialog that appears is small and does not offer many options, click the Show Details button at the bottom of the dialog to expand it.

Calendar

Calendar, which was known as iCal in previous versions of OS X, is a personal calendar application that enables you to keep track of appointments and other events. With Calendar, you can:

- Create multiple color-coded calendars for different categories of events—for example, home, business, or school.

- View calendars individually or together.

- View calendars by day, week, or month.

- Send email invitations for events to people in your OS X Contacts database.

- Get notification of upcoming events on screen or by email.

- Share calendars on the Web with family, friends, and business associates.

Although previous versions of this application also included features for tracking to-do list items, that functionality has been spun off into the Reminders application (Chapter 22).

This chapter provides basic instructions for setting up and using Calendar.

Launching & Quitting Calendar

Like any other application, you must launch Calendar before you can use it. This loads it into your computer's memory so your computer can work with it.

To launch Calendar:

Use one of the following techniques:

- Open the Calendar application icon **A** in the Applications folder window (page 137).

- Click the Calendar icon in Launchpad (page 140).

- Click the Calendar icon in the Dock (page 34).

Calendar launches and displays its main calendar window **B**.

TIP The appearance of the Calendar window varies depending on which calendar view is displayed.

TIP Calendar supports OS X's full-screen apps feature (page 142).

To quit Calendar:

Choose Calendar > Quit Calendar, or press Command-Q.

Calendar quits. Any changes you made to events are automatically saved.

A The Calendar application icon.

Calendar

B The main calendar window for Calendar, shown in Week view.

A Use the View menu to show or hide Calendar window elements a number of ways.

Working with the Calendar Window

Calendar's main calendar window can be displayed in a number of different views. Once you've chosen a view you like, you can view any date in the year.

Here's a quick rundown of how you can change the calendar view and see specific dates.

To change the calendar view:

Choose an option from the top of the View menu **A**, press one of the corresponding keyboard shortcuts, or click one of the view buttons at the top of the calendar window **B C D**.

- **By Day** shows a day at a glance, along with an agenda of upcoming events **B**.
- **By Week** shows a week at a glance **C**.
- **By Month** shows a month at a glance **D**.
- **By Year** shows a year at a glance, with colored squares indicating dates with events scheduled.

B The Calendar window in Day view.

C The Calendar window in Week view.

D The Calendar window in Month View.

To scroll through calendar dates:

1. Switch to the calendar view you prefer (page 299).

2. Click the Back or Forward buttons near the top-right corner of the window **E** to scroll backward or forward through calendar pages. For example, in Week view, the calendar will scroll a week at a time; in month view, it will scroll a month at a time.

TIP You can use standard window scrolling techniques (page 28) to scroll the contents of the Calendar window whenever necessary.

To view a specific day, week, or month:

1. Choose View > Go to Date **A**, or press Shift-Command-T.

2. Enter the date you want to go to in the tiny dialog sheet that appears **F**.

3. Click Show.

   The calendar page changes (if necessary) to display that date.

To view today's date:

Use one of the following techniques:

- Click the Today button near the top-right corner of the window **E**.

- Choose View > Go to Today **A**.

- Press Command-T.

The Calendar page changes (if necessary) to display the current date.

Back   *Forward*

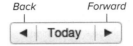

E Use these buttons to scroll backward or forward through calendar pages.

F Use this dialog to enter the date you want to view.

A One way to create an event is to drag in the calendar window.

B An untitled event box appears in the calendar.

C Enter a new name and press Return to save it.

Working with Events

An event is a date-based activity that you might include on your calendar. Meetings and appointments are examples of events. Events can be one-time or recurring. They can also be scheduled for a specific time of day or last all day.

This part of the chapter explains how to create events, add and modify event details, and delete events.

To add an event by clicking or dragging in the calendar window:

1. Display the date you want to add the event to.

2. Use one of the following techniques:

   ▸ In Day or Week view, drag from the event's start time to end time **A**.

   ▸ in Month or Year view, double-click inside the event's date box.

   A box for the event appears in the calendar window with its default name (*New Event*) selected **B**.

3. Enter a new name for the event, and press Return **C**.

4. Continue following instructions in the section titled "To set event details" on the next page.

TIP Double-clicking a calendar date number switches to Day view for that date.

To add an event with the Quick Event feature:

1. Use one of the following techniques:

   ▸ Click the + button near the top-left of the Calendar window.

   ▸ Choose File > New Event.

   ▸ Press Command-N.

   A Create Quick Event pop-up window with sample event text appears beneath the + button **D**.

2. Type some descriptive text for the event that includes the date and time **E** and press Return.

   Calendar switches to the day of the event, creates a box at the specified time, and opens the inspector so you can enter more event details **F**.

3. Continue following instructions in the section titled "To set event details" in the next section.

TIP Whether Calendar properly schedules the event depends on how you enter its descriptive text. Practice with this feature to see how you can get the best results.

To set event details:

1. If necessary, in the calendar window, double-click the event you want to set details for to open the event's detail window **G**.

2. If necessary, click the Edit button to switch to edit mode **F** **H**.

3. To modify the event name, click the existing name to display an edit box and edit the contents of the box **G** **H**.

D The Quick Event pop-up window appears with sample event text.

E Type some descriptive text for your event.

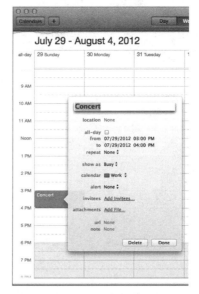

F When you press Return, Calendar creates the event and opens its detail window in edit mode.

G Double-clicking an event box displays its details.

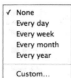

H You must click the Edit button to enter edit mode and make changes.

I You can click a date in a calendar pop-up menu to quickly enter it.

J Turning on the all-day check box hides the time fields.

| ✓ None |
| Every day |
| Every week |
| Every month |
| Every year |
| Custom... |

K Use this pop-up menu to choose a repeating option.

Frequency: Weekly

Every 1 week(s) on:

S M T W T F S

Cancel | OK

L This pop-up dialog enables you to set custom repeating options for an event.

repeat Custom... ⬍
Every 2 weeks
end On date ⬍ 12/20/2013

M A repeating event with an end date.

4. To specify a location for the event, click to the right of the location label and type what you want to appear.

5. Set the beginning and ending dates for the event as follows:

   ▸ Click a date field and then click the date you want in the pop-up calendar that appears **I**.

   ▸ Click numbers in the date fields and type new values.

6. Set the event times as follows:

   ▸ To indicate that the event lasts all day (or multiple days), turn on the all-day check box. The time fields disappear **J**.

   ▸ To specify starting and ending times for the event, make sure the all-day check box is turned off and then enter the starting and ending times in the two time areas.

7. To set the event to repeat on a regular basis, choose an option from the repeat pop-up menu **K**. If none of the standard options apply, you can choose Custom and use the dialog that appears **L** to set a custom repeating schedule. Then, if necessary, set an ending option in the end field that appears **M**.

8. To specify how the event time should appear on a shared calendar, choose an option from the Show as pop-up menu. Your options are Free or Busy.

9. To specify the calendar to add the event to, choose a calendar from the calendar pop-up menu. The menu lists all calendars you have created.

continues on next page

10. To be reminded about the event, choose an option from the alarm pop-up menu . Then set other alarm options as necessary 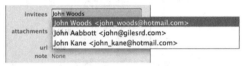. You can repeat this process to set multiple alarms.

11. To invite others to the event, click the Add Invitees link. Then enter contact names or email addresses in the box that appears. As you type, Calendar attempts to match names to those in Contacts with an email address recorded ; select the name you want to add. You can repeat this step to invite multiple people.

12. To attach a file to the event, click the Add File link. Then use the standard Open dialog that appears to locate, select, and open the file you want to attach. When you click Open, the file is added to the event details . You can repeat this step to attach multiple files.

13. To associate a webpage with the event, click to the right of the url label and type a URL in the box that appears.

14. To add notes about the event, click to the right of the note label and type what you want to appear **R**.

15. When you're finished entering event details, click Done. The details are saved with the event; some details appear in the main calendar window **S**.

N If you choose an option from the alarm pop-up menu...

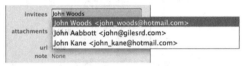

O ...you can set options for one or more event reminders.

P As you enter a name in the invitees field, Calendar attempts to match it to a Contacts contact with an email address.

Q An event can include one or more file attachments.

note | This box expands as you type text into it so you can make your note as long or as short as you like.

R You can enter a note about the event.

S Some of the event's details appear in the Calendar window.

T Clicking an invitee name displays a menu of options like this one.

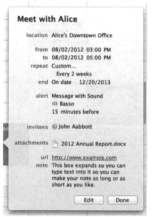

U If you change a repeating event, a dialog like this one asks if you want to change all of the events or just one.

V Here's an example of a completed event's details.

TIP You can follow these steps to add details for a new event or make changes to an existing event.

TIP The all-day event check box is handy for entering information about vacations and other events that span multiple days.

TIP In steps 5 and 6, the ending time or date must be *after* the starting time or date. It may be necessary to change AM to PM before entering the second time.

TIP A quick way to change an event's time is to drag its top or bottom border in Day or Week view of the main calendar window. This automatically changes the time information in the event details dialog.

TIP A quick way to change an event's date is to drag its event box from one date to another in the main calendar window. This automatically changes the date information in the event details dialog.

TIP You can click an invitee's name to access a menu of options for that invitee and the invitee field **T**.

TIP If an event has invitees who have not yet been invited to the event, the Done button appears as a Send button at the bottom of the event details dialog. Clicking Send sends email invitations to invitees.

TIP You can enter multiple invitees for an event by separating each name with a comma.

TIP If you set an event to repeat, any time you change that event's details, a dialog appears **U**. Click the appropriate button for the change.

To view event details:

In any view of the main calendar window, double-click the event.

Details appear in a pop-up window **V**.

To delete an event:

1. In the calendar window, select the event you want to delete.

2. Press the Delete key.

   What happens next depends on the settings for the event.

   ▸ If the event has no special settings, it simply disappears.

   ▸ If the event has an attachment, a dialog appears to warn you . You must click Continue to delete the event.

   ▸ If the event is a recurring event, a dialog appears with three options 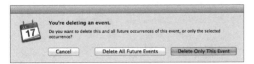: **Cancel** does not delete the event, **Delete All Future Events** deletes just the events in the future, and **Delete Only This Event** deletes only the event for the date and time that you've selected.

   ▸ If the event has invitees, a dialog appears with three options : **Cancel** does not delete the event, **Delete and Don't Notify** deletes the event but does not notify invitees that it has been canceled, and **Delete and Notify** deletes the event and notifies the attendees that it has been canceled.

W A dialog like this appears to warn you that deleting an event with an attachment can't be undone.

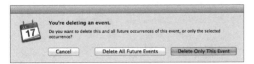

X Use this dialog to determine which repeating event(s) should be deleted.

Y Use this dialog to determine whether invitees should be notified when an event is cancelled.

A The Calendar list appears on the left side of the window, beneath the Calendars button.

B A new untitled calendar appears in the calendar list.

C Enter a new name for the calendar and press Return to save it.

Creating & Deleting Calendars

Calendar comes preconfigured with two calendars: Home and Work. But you can create additional calendars if necessary to better organize your calendar items. You can also display any combination of calendars at once, making it possible to focus on one aspect of your schedule or see the whole thing.

This part of the chapter explains how to create, display, and delete calendars.

To display the Calendar list:

Use one of the following techniques:

- Choose View > Show Calendar List.
- Click the Calendars button in the upper-left corner of the Calendar window.

The Calendar list appears on the left side of the calendar window **A**.

To add a calendar:

1. Choose File > New Calendar, or press Option-Command-N.

   An untitled calendar appears on the Calendar list with its default name (*Untitled*) selected **B**.

2. Enter a name for the calendar, and press Return to save it **C**.

TIP You can use the New Calendar Group command on the File menu to add calendar groups. You can then organize your calendars by dragging them into groups on the Calendar list.

To rename a calendar:

1. If necessary, display the Calendar list .

2. Click the name of the calendar you want to rename.

   A selection box appears around it and its name becomes selected **B**.

3. Enter a new name for the calendar and press Return to save it **C**.

To display events from only certain calendars:

1. If necessary, display the Calendar list **A C**.

2. Click to toggle the check boxes beside the calendars you want to show or hide.

   The calendars with check marks beside them will appear in the Calendar window.

To delete a calendar:

1. If necessary, display the Calendar list **A C**.

2. Select the calendar you want to delete.

3. Choose Edit > Delete, or press Command-Delete.

4. If a confirmation dialog appears **D**, click Delete.

   The calendar and all of its events are removed.

D You'll need to click Delete in this dialog to delete a calendar with events.

A Select the calendar you want to publish.

B You can make your calendar public...

C ...or share it with the people you specify.

Sharing Calendars

You can use Calendar to share your calendars with others on iCloud or publish them to a compatible WebDAV server. You can then give others the URL they need to access your calendar on the Web or subscribe to it with their calendar software.

Likewise, you can subscribe to a calendar published by someone else. All you need is the calendar's URL to add it to Calendar.

This part of the chapter explains how you can share your calendars on iCloud and subscribe to someone else's.

TIP Calendar also supports calendars shared via CalDAV, Exchange, Google, Yahoo!, and other popular formats. A discussion of these advanced features is beyond the scope of this book; consult Calendar help for more information.

TIP You must have a connection to the Internet to share or subscribe to a calendar.

To share a calendar on iCloud:

1. If necessary, display the Calendar list.

2. Select the calendar you want to share **A**.

3. Choose Edit > Share Calendar to display the share calendar dialog **B C**.

4. In the Share calendar as edit box, enter the name of the calendar as it will appear when accessed by others.

5. Select one of the two Share with options:

   ▸ **Everyone B** creates an online calendar that anyone can read but no one can modify. All changes must be done by you via Calendar. If you select this option, skip ahead to step 11.

continues on next page

- ▶ **Only the people you invite ⓒ** creates an online calendar that only the
  people you specify can read or read
  and write to. When you select this
  option, the dialog expands to offer
  more options.

6. If you're sharing an invitation-only calendar, click the + button beneath the list
   box. An empty line appears **ⓓ**.

7. Begin typing the name of a person in
   your Contacts database who you want
   to invite. As you type, a list of matches
   appears **ⓔ**.

8. Select the name of the person you want
   to invite from the list.

9. Choose an option from the Privilege
   pop-up menu for that line to specify
   whether that person has Read & Write
   or just Read access **ⓕ**.

10. Repeat steps 6 through 9 for each per-
    son you want to invite.

11. Click Share.

12. Wait while your computer updates the
    sharing information on the iCloud server
    for your calendar. When it's finished, a
    broadcast icon appears in the Calendar
    list beside the calendar you shared **ⓖ**.

TIP Your Mac must be configured to use
iCloud's Calendar & Reminders service to
share a calendar on iCloud. You can learn
more about setting up your computer for use
with iCloud in Chapter 19 and on page 544.

TIP When you share a calendar with specific people, each person receives an email
invitation with a button to click to access your
calendar **ⓗ**.

TIP To change settings for a shared calendar,
in the Calendar list, select the calendar you
want to change and choose Edit > Sharing
Settings. Then set options in the dialog that
appears **ⓑ ⓒ** and click Update.

ⓓ When you click the + button an empty line
appears in the list.

ⓔ Start typing a name and a list of matches
appears.

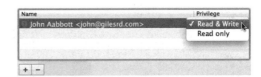

ⓕ Set the privileges for the invitee.

ⓖ A broadcast
icon appears
beside the name of
a calendar that has
been shared.

ⓗ Calendar invitees get an email message like
this one.

I Calendar can generate an email message with information about accessing the calendar online.

J Use this dialog to indicate who invitations should be re-sent to.

K Calendar confirms that you want to stop sharing a calendar.

To share a link to a calendar:

1. In the Calendar list, select the calendar you want to share a link to.

2. Choose Edit > Resend Sharing Invitations.

One of two things happens:

▸ If the calendar is shared with everyone, Calendar opens Mail and generates an email message containing a link to the calendar **I**. Address the message and send it.

▸ If the calendar is shared with just the people you invite, a dialog with a list of the people you invited appears **J**. Toggle check boxes to specify who should get another invitation and click OK. Calendar sends new email invitations **H** to the people you specified.

TIP To generate a link to a calendar shared with everyone, select the calendar in the Calendar list and choose Edit > Resend Sharing Invitations. Calendar creates an email message with a link to the selected calendar.

To stop sharing a calendar:

1. In the Calendar list, select the calendar you want to stop sharing.

2. Choose Calendar > Stop Sharing.

3. In the confirmation dialog that appears **K**, click Stop Sharing.

The calendar's events are no longer available to others.

To subscribe to a calendar:

1. Choose File > New Calendar Subscription, or press Option-Command-S.

2. In the dialog that appears **L**, type (or paste) in the URL for the calendar you want to subscribe to and click Subscribe.

3. Calendar displays a dialog you can use to set subscription options **M**:

   ▸ **Name** is the name of the calendar as it should appear in your Calendar list.

   ▸ **Subscribed to** is the URL of the calendar on the Web.

   ▸ **Location** is where the calendar data is stored.

   ▸ **Remove** enables you to toggle check boxes to remove or disable alerts and attachments for the calendar.

   ▸ **Last updated**, which cannot be changed, indicates the date and time the calendar was last refreshed.

   ▸ **Auto-refresh** lets you set a frequency for Calendar to automatically update the calendar. Choose an option based on how often you expect the calendar to change. Choosing No disables automatic refreshing.

4. Click OK.

   The calendar's events appear in the Calendar window and the calendar name appears under Subscriptions in the Calendar list **N**.

TIP You cannot add, modify, or delete events on a calendar that you subscribe to.

TIP To manually update the contents of calendars you have subscribed to, choose View > Refresh Calendars, or press Command-R.

TIP To unsubscribe from a calendar, delete it from the Subscriptions list (page 308).

L Enter the URL for the calendar you want to subscribe to in a dialog like this.

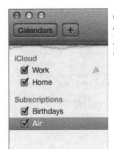

M Calendar lets you set options for the calendars you subscribe to.

N The calendars you subscribe to also appear on the Calendar list.

O Here's an example of an invitation to a shared iCloud calendar.

P The calendar is added to iCloud...

Q ...and to the Calendar app on your Mac.

To join a shared calendar:

In the invitation email **O**, click Join Calendar.

A few things happen:

- Your Web browser application opens and goes to iCloud.com.

- If you're not already signed in, you'll have to enter your Apple ID and password in the appropriate boxes.

- Your browser displays the Calendar page for iCloud with the calendar added in the Calendar list **P**.

- In the Calendar app, you'll see the calendar added as a shared calendar **Q**.

TIP Depending on how privileges have been set for your email address, you may or may not be able to modify a shared calendar's events.

TIP If Calendar is open when you join a calendar, you may have to choose View > Refresh Calendars to get the newly added calendar to appear in the list **Q**.

TIP To remove a shared calendar you have joined, delete it from the Shared list (page 308).

Reminders
& Notes

As part of Apple's efforts to enhance inter-activity between Macs running OS X and iOS devices such as iPhones and iPads, it created OS X versions of two apps already available on iOS: Reminders and Notes.

Reminders functionality already existed in iCal (now Calendar, covered in Chapter 21), but it lacked the ability to sync to-do items between your Mac and your iPhone or iPad. Similarly, Mail had notes functionality, but access to notes was limited to Mail. By spinning off these features into stand-alone apps with the same feature set as iOS apps already familiar to many iPhone and iPad users, Apple made it easier for Mac users to share up-to-date reminder and note data with their iOS devices.

This chapter introduces the Reminders and Notes applications on OS X and explains how you can get started using them.

Reminders

The Reminders app offers a simple interface 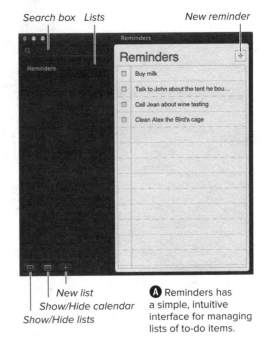 for creating and organizing to-do list items. Reminders can include any combination of the following fields of information:

- **Name**, which is required, is a brief description of the reminder.

- **Date and time** is the time your computer should remind you to perform the task. If you set this option, you can also specify whether the reminder should repeat on a schedule you specify.

- **Location** is the place you should be near to trigger a location-based reminder. This option relies on the location services feature of OS X to work. If you set this option, you can indicate whether you should be leaving or arriving at the location you specify.

- **Priority** is the importance of the reminder.

- **Note** is a field you can use to include notes about the reminder.

This part of the chapter explains how to display, create, set options for, remove, and group to-do list items in Reminders.

TIP Reminders works with Notification Center (page 260); set options in the Notifications preferences pane (page 517) to specify how reminders should appear onscreen.

TIP If you have an iOS device such as an iPhone or an iPad, you can use iCloud to synchronize reminder items. This not only puts the reminders from your Mac on your iOS device, but it also enables you to modify and create new reminders on your device and have them appear automatically on your Mac. You can learn more about syncing Reminders with iCloud on page 545.

Search box   Lists   New reminder

New list
Show/Hide calendar
Show/Hide lists

A Reminders has a simple, intuitive interface for managing lists of to-do items.

B The Reminders application icon.

Reminders

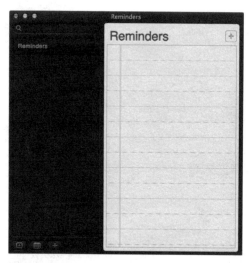

C The Reminders list starts off empty.

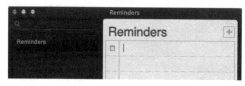

D You can click on the first empty line to create a new item.

E Type the name of the item to add it to the list.

To open Reminders:

Use one of the following techniques:

- Open the Reminders icon **B** in the Applications folder.
- Click the Reminders icon in LaunchPad.
- Click the Reminders icon in the Dock.

The Reminders window appears **A C**.

TIP The first time you use Reminders, the Reminders list should be empty **C**.

To add a reminder:

1. Use one of the following techniques:
   - ▸ Choose File > New Reminder, or press Command-N.
   - ▸ Click the + button at the top of the Reminders list.
   - ▸ Click in the first empty line at the bottom of the Reminders list.

   An empty line with a check box is added to the list with the blinking insertion point beside it **D**.

2. Enter a name for the reminder **E**.

3. To create another reminder, press Return to create another new line and then repeat step 2.

TIP A reminder's name can be as long or as short as it needs to be. If it's too long to fit in the window, it will be truncated in the list **A**.

To set reminder details:

1. In the Reminders list, use one of the following techniques to open the options dialog for the item you want to modify:

   ▸ Double-click the item.

   ▸ Point to the item and then click the *i* icon that appears on its far-right end **E**.

   Details about the item appear in a pop-up dialog **F**.

2. To modify the item name, use standard editing techniques to edit it.

3. To set a reminder date and time, turn on the On a Day check box to expand the pop-up dialog **G**. You can then click the date and use the calendar that appears **H** to set the date and edit the time to set the time.

4. To set a reminder location, turn on the At a Location check box to expand the pop-up dialog **I**. You can then enter an address or contact name in the drop-down list to specify a location. Be sure to select the correct option to specify whether you should be reminded when you leave that location—for example, when you leave work—or when you arrive there—for example, when you arrive at the supermarket.

5. To set up the reminder so that it repeats periodically, make sure you set a date and time as instructed in step 3 and then choose an option from the repeat pop-up menu **J**. You can then specify an end date if desired.

6. To set a priority for the item, choose an option from the priority pop-up menu **K**.

7. To add notes about the item, click to the right of the note label and type your notes **L**.

F Double-clicking an item displays its details in a pop-up dialog.

G When you turn on the On a Day check box, the dialog expands to offer date, time, and repeat options.

H Clicking the calendar displays a pop-up calendar you can use to quickly enter a date.

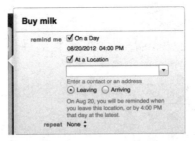

I Turning on the At a Location check box expands the dialog to offer location-related options.

J You can choose an option from the repeat pop-up menu.

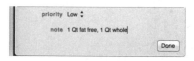

K The priority pop-up menu offers four options.

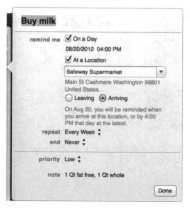

L You can enter a note to provide additional details about the task.

M A finished reminder using all the available options might look like this.

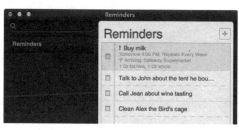

N The details appear in the Reminders list.

8. When you're finished entering information **M**, click Done.

   The dialog closes and the details are added to the Reminders list **N**.

To mark a reminder as done:

Click the check box to the left of a reminder item. Several things happen:

- As you might expect, a check mark is placed in the box.

- If a Completed list is not already showing on the left side of the window, one appears **O P**.

- The completed item is moved from its list into the Completed list. You can select the Completed list to see it **P**.

- If the item was set to repeat, a new copy of the item appears in the original list with its next reminder date **O**.

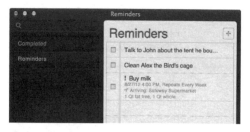

O A Completed list appears on the right side of the window and a new reminder is created for a completed repeating item.

P You can select the Completed list to see the items you've marked as done.

To delete a reminder:

1. In the Reminders list, select the item you want to delete.

2. Press the Delete key.

   The item disappears.

To add a list:

1. Use one of the following techniques:

   ▸ Choose File > New List, or press Command-L.

   ▸ Click the New List button at the bottom of the Reminders window **Ⓐ**.

   A new, untitled list appears on the left side of the window and is selected **Ⓠ**.

2. Type a new name for the list and press Return.

   The list is renamed **Ⓡ**.

To add reminders to a specific list:

Do one of the following:

- Select the list you want to add the reminder item to before adding the reminder. The reminder is automatically added to that list.

- Point to a reminder item, press and hold the button down, and drag the item to the list you want it to appear in **Ⓢ**. When you release the button, the reminder is moved.

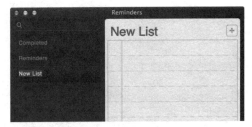

Ⓠ You can add a new list to help organize reminder items.

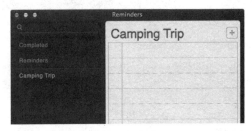

Ⓡ Give your list a name that makes sense for the tasks grouped within it.

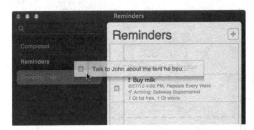

Ⓢ You can drag an existing reminder item from one list to another.

New   Hide folder list   Share note
note   Show folder list   Delete note

A Use the Notes application to store free-form notes about anything you like.

B The Notes application icon.

C Notes might look something like this the first time you open it or when you create your first note.

Notes

The Notes application **A** **B** offers an easy way to jot down free-form notes and store them on your Mac. Each note is time-stamped and notes are searchable so it's easy to find one no matter how many you've stored away. And a handy Share button lets you share your notes with others via email or message.

This part of the chapter explains how to create, modify, and delete notes with the Notes app.

TIP If you have an iOS device such as an iPhone or an iPad, you can use iCloud to synchronize your notes. This not only puts the notes from your Mac on your iOS device, but it also enables you to modify and create new notes on your device and have them appear automatically on your Mac. You can learn more about syncing Notes with iCloud on page 545.

To open Notes:

Use one of the following techniques:

- Open the Notes icon **B** in the Applications folder.
- Click the Notes icon in LaunchPad.
- Click the Notes icon in the Dock.

The Notes window appears **A** **C**.

TIP The first time you use Notes, the Note list may display just one note: the one it created when you opened the app **C**.

To add a note:

1. Click the New Note button at the bottom of the window **A**.

    A new, untitled note appears **C**.

2. Enter the text of your note on the right side of the window.

    The first line of your note becomes the title for the note and appears in the notes list on the left side of the window **D**.

TIP The right side of the Notes window works like any text editor. You can type, delete, select, copy, cut, and paste text as needed. You can learn more about text editing in Chapter 14, which covers the TextEdit application.

TIP You can use commands under the Format menu's submenus **E** to apply formatting to selected text.

TIP To edit a note, select it in the left side of the window and make changes on the right side of the window.

TIP Double-clicking a note opens it in its own window.

To delete a note:

1. In the left side of the window, select the note you want to delete.

2. Do one of the following:

    ▸ Click the Delete button at the bottom of the window.

    ▸ Press Delete.

3. Click Delete Note in the confirmation dialog that appears **F**.

    The note disappears.

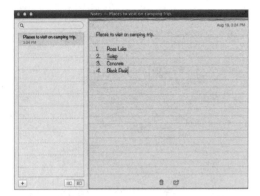

D The first line of your note is the note title; the note itself appears on the left side of the window.

E Use commands under the Format menu and its submenus, like this one, to format selected note text.

F You must click Delete Note in this dialog to delete a note.

Mac OS Utilities

In This Part

23

Fonts

Fonts are typefaces that appear onscreen and in printed documents. When they're properly installed, they appear on all Font menus and in font lists.

OS X, which has long been a favorite operating system among design professionals who work extensively with fonts, has several tools for managing fonts and using them in documents:

- **Font Book** is an application that enables you to install, preview, search, activate, and deactivate fonts with an easy-to-use interface.

- The **Fonts panel** enables you to apply and manage fonts within documents.

- The **Character Viewer** makes it easy to insert special characters in your documents.

This chapter tells you more about fonts and explains how to use all of these OS X font features.

In This Chapter:

Font Formats

OS X supports several types of fonts in both OS X and Windows specific formats:

- **PostScript Type 1 fonts** are used primarily for printing. These fonts must be accompanied by corresponding screen font files. PostScript font technology was developed by Adobe Systems, Inc.

- **TrueType font** (.ttf) and **TrueType font collections** (.ttc) can display high-quality output onscreen and in print.

- **Multiple Master** is a special PostScript format that enables you to create custom styles, called instances, by setting font weight, width, and other variables. OS X supports Multiple Master instances.

- **System or Data fork suitcase format** (.dfont) stores all information in the data fork of the file, including resources used by OS X drawing routines.

- **OpenType font format** (.otf), which can contain 65,000 different glyphs or characters, are popular for non-Roman languages. OpenType format fonts come in two versions: PostScript-based fonts from Adobe and TrueType-based fonts from Microsoft.

Do you need to know all this to install and use fonts with your Mac? Not really. Just make sure the fonts you buy are OS X compatible and you shouldn't have any trouble with them.

Ⓐ Font Book is an application that makes it easy to manage your fonts.

Font Book

Font Book **Ⓐ** is an OS X application that enables you to install, uninstall, organize, preview, search, activate, deactivate and troubleshoot fonts.

Font Book organizes all fonts into collections and libraries listed in its first column:

- Installation-based collections are groups of fonts organized by where they are installed (**Table 23.1**).

- User Libraries are user-defined groups of fonts stored anywhere on your computer—not just in a Fonts folder.

- Language-based collections and smart collections are collections defined for a specific language or criteria. Smart collections are new in OS X Mountain Lion.

- Other collections are predefined groups of fonts organized by purpose or user-defined font collections.

Within each library or collection is one or more *font families*, each of which may contain one or more *typefaces*. Each typeface is a slightly different version of the font—for example, bold, italic, or condensed.

Font Book makes it possible to turn fonts on or off. This helps keep your applications' font menus and lists neat by letting you display only those fonts that you want to display.

TABLE 23.1 Font Collections

Collection Name	Installation Location	Purpose
All Fonts	Various	All fonts available for use.
Computer	Hard Disk/Library/Fonts	Fonts available to all user accounts on your computer. This collection only appears on the list if one of the next two collections appears.
User	~/Library/Fonts	Fonts available only for your user account.
Network	Network Hard Disk/Network/Library/Fonts	Fonts available only when connected to the network computer on which the fonts are installed.

To launch Font Book:

Use one of the following techniques:

- Double-click the Font Book icon in the Applications folder .

- Double-click a font file . This also displays the font's characters in a preview window **D**.

- Choose Manage Fonts from the action pop-up menu in the Fonts Panel **E**.

Font Book's main window opens **A**.

TIP The Fonts Panel can be displayed in a variety of applications, including TextEdit (Chapter 14) and Mail (Chapter 29).

To quit Font Book:

When you are finished using Font Book, choose Font Book > Quit Font Book.

To install a font from the Finder:

1. Double-click the font file **C**.

   The font opens in Font Book's preview window **D**.

2. Click Install Font.

   The font is added to the default install location.

TIP The default installation location for adding fonts is the User collection. You can change this option in Font Book Preferences. Choose Font Book > Preferences to get started.

B You can find the Font Book application icon in the Applications folder.

Font Book

C Here's an example of a font file icon.

ITC Zapf Dingbats

D Double-clicking the file icon for a font that has not yet been installed opens a preview window like this in Font Book.

E Another way to open Font Book is to choose Manage Fonts from the action pop-up menu in the Fonts panel.

F Font Book's
File menu.

G Use an Open dialog to locate, select, and open
the font you want to install.

To install a font from within Font Book:

1. In the Collection list, select the collection or library you want to add the font to.

2. Choose File > Add Fonts **F**, or press Command-O.

3. Use the Open dialog that appears **G** to locate and select the font you want to install.

4. Click Open.

   One of two things happens:

   ▸ If you selected a collection in the Collection list, the font's files are installed by copying them to the collection's location on disk.

   ▸ If you selected a library in the Collection list, the font's files are *not* copied. Instead, Font Book installs them by creating a reference to them within Font Book.

   Either way, the font's files are installed and ready to use.

TIP You can also install a font by dragging the font's file icon(s) onto a library or collection name in the main Font Book window.

To uninstall a font:

1. Select the name of the font in the Font list of the main Font Book window Ⓐ.

2. Press the Delete key.

3. In the confirmation dialog that appears ⒽⒾ, click Remove.

   One of two things happens:

   ▸ If you selected a font installed in a collection Ⓗ, the font's files are moved to the Trash. Emptying the Trash permanently removes them from your computer.

   ▸ If you selected a font installed in a library Ⓘ, Font Book removes its reference to the font's files.

   Either way, the font's files are uninstalled and no longer available to use.

TIP You may find it more convenient to disable a font than to delete it. You can learn how on page 334.

TIP Font Book won't let you uninstall a font needed by the System for operation Ⓙ.

To view fonts by library or collection:

In the Collection list of the main Font Book window, select the name of the library or collection you want to view.

The fonts in that library appear in the Font list Ⓐ.

TIP A font can be in more than one library or collection.

TIP You can copy a font from one collection to another by dragging it from the Font list to the name of another collection.

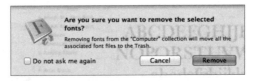

Ⓗ A dialog like this appears when you remove a font from a collection.

Ⓘ This dialog appears when you remove a font from a library.

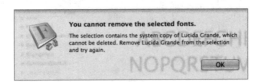

Ⓙ You can't remove a System font.

Ⓚ To view a typeface within a font family, select its name.

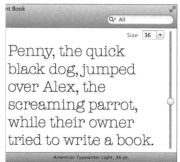

L You can change the size of the sample text.

M Choose an option from the Preview menu.

N You can display a repertoire of all characters in a selected font or typeface.

O You can also display sample text. (Having a home office is not always what it's cracked up to be.)

To preview font or typeface characters:

1. In the Collection list of the main Font Book window, select All Fonts or the name of a library or collection that the font is part of **A**.

2. In the Font list, select the name of the font family you want to preview.

   The characters for the regular typeface of the font appear on the right side of the window **A**.

3. To see a specific typeface in the font family, click the disclosure triangle to the left of the font name to display all typefaces **A**. Then click the name of the typeface you want to see.

   The typeface characters appear on the right side of the window **K**.

TIP To change the size of characters in the preview part of the window, enter a value in the Size box, choose a value from the Size drop-down list, or drag the slider on the far right side of the window. The size changes accordingly **L**.

To change the preview text:

Choose one of the first three options on the Preview menu **M**:

- **Sample** (Command-1) displays the characters shown throughout this chapter.

- **Repertoire** (Command-2) displays all characters in ASCII order **N**.

- **Custom** (Command-3) enables you to specify your own sample text **O**.

The text changes accordingly.

To add a collection or library

1. Do one of the following:

   ▸ To add a collection, choose File > New Collection **F**, or press Command-N.

   ▸ To add a library, choose File > New Library **F**, or press Option-Command-N.

   An unnamed collection or library appears in the Collection list with its name selected **P**.

2. Enter a new name and press Return.

3. To add fonts to the collection or library, follow instructions in the section titled "To install a font from within Font Book" on page 329 and make sure the collection or library is selected in step 1.

TIP You can also add fonts to a collection by dragging them from another collection. This does not duplicate font files.

To add a smart collection:

1. Choose File > New Smart Collection **F**.

   An unnamed collection appears in the Collection list and a dialog appears **Q**.

2. In the Collection name box, type a name for the collection.

3. Set options in the dialog to specify matching criteria for the fonts to be included. You can click + buttons to add additional lines of criteria if necessary **R**.

4. Click OK.

   The collection automatically fills with fonts that match your criteria **S**.

TIP Like Finder smart folders (page 99), Font Book smart collections are automatically updated whenever you install or delete fonts that match the criteria you specify.

P In this example, I've created a new collection, which appears in the bottom area of the Collection column.

Q When you create a smart collection, you're prompted for a name and matching criteria.

R In this example, I want the collection to include sans serif fonts with English characters.

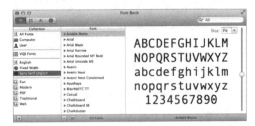

S Here's the resulting smart collection.

T Click Remove in this dialog to remove the selected collection or library.

To edit a smart collection:

1. In the Collection list, select the smart collection you want to edit.

2. Choose File > Edit Smart Collection **F**.

3. In the smart collection settings dialog that appears **R**, change settings as desired.

4. Click OK.

    The fonts in the collection change accordingly.

To remove a collection or library:

1. In the Collection list, select the library or collection you want to remove.

2. Use one of the following techniques:

    ▸ Press the Delete key.

    ▸ Choose File > Delete "*Collection Name.*"

    ▸ Choose File > Delete "*Library Name.*"

3. Click Remove in the confirmation dialog that appears **T**.

    The collection or library is removed.

TIP Removing a library or a collection does not delete font files from disk.

TIP When you remove a library, its fonts are no longer available for use in applications. When you remove a collection, the collection name no longer appears in the Fonts panel, but the fonts it contains are still available for use in applications.

TIP You may find it more convenient to disable a library or collection than to delete it. Learn how on page 334.

TIP You cannot remove the collections that appear at the top of the Collection list.

To disable a collection, library, or font:

1. In Font Book, select the name of the collection, library, font family, or typeface you want to disable.

2. Do one of the following:

   ▸ To disable a collection or library, choose Edit > Disable "*Collection Name*" , choose Edit > Disable "*Library Name*" , or press Shift-Command-E.

   ▸ To disable a font family or typeface, choose Edit > Disable "*Font Name*" Family , choose Edit > Disable "*Typeface Name*" , press Shift-Command-D, or click the check box at the bottom of the Font list.

3. If a confirmation dialog appears, click Disable.

   What happens depends on what you disabled :

   ▸ If you disabled a collection or library, its name appears in gray in the Collection list.

   ▸ If you disabled a font family or typeface, its name appears in gray with the word *Off* in the Font list.

TIP When you disable a library, you disable all of its fonts.

TIP A disabled library or collection will not appear in the Fonts panel.

TIP If a font appears in one collection and that collection is disabled, the font is disabled.

TIP When you disable a font in a collection, that font will not appear in the Font panel when the collection is selected. When you disable a font in a library, that font is not available for use in any application.

TIP You cannot disable a System font.

U The Edit menu when a font family and a user-defined collection are selected.

V The Edit menu when a typeface and a library are selected.

W In this example, I've disabled several collections, font families, and typefaces.

X The Edit menu with a disabled collection and font family selected.

Y A yellow warning icon appears beside any font families or typefaces with problems.

Z Font Book resolves the conflict by simply disabling one of the typefaces.

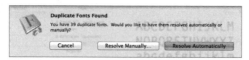

AA Font Book can resolve all font conflicts at once.

To enable a library, collection, font, or font family:

1. In Font Book, select the name of the disabled collection, library, font family, or typeface that you want to enable.

2. Do one of the following:

   ▸ Choose Edit > Enable "*Collection Name*" **X**, choose Edit > Enable "*Library Name*," or press Shift-Command-E.

   ▸ Choose Edit > Enable "*Font Name*" Family **X**, choose Edit > Enable "*Typeface Name*," press Shift-Command-D, or click the check box at the bottom of the Font list.

   The selected collection, library, font family, or typeface is enabled.

To resolve font conflicts:

1. In the Font list, locate and select a font family with a yellow warning icon to the right of its name **Y**.

2. If necessary, click the triangle to the left of the font name to display its typefaces. At least one of them should have a yellow warning icon beside its name.

3. Click the Resolve Automatically button at the bottom of the preview area **W**.

   Font Book disables one of the conflicting typefaces **Z**.

TIP Font conflicts are often caused when multiple copies of a font family or typeface are installed in the same computer but in different places. Disabling one of the copies stops the conflict.

TIP You can resolve all conflicts on your computer at once. Choose Edit > Look for Enabled Duplicates **U V X**, or press Command-L. In the dialog that appears **AA**, click Resolve Automatically.

To validate a font:

1. In the Font list, select the font or font family you want to validate.

2. Choose File > Validate Font .

   Font Book checks the font and displays results in the Font Validation window **BB**.

3. Consult the results summary at the bottom of the Font Validation window.

4. To get detail about a minor or serious problem, click the disclosure triangle beside a problem to see details **BB**.

5. To remove problem fonts, turn on the Select all fonts check box and click Remove Checked. Then click Remove in the Confirmation dialog that appears.

TIP It's a good idea to uninstall any fonts with font errors.

TIP In step 1, you can select multiple fonts by holding down the Command key and clicking each font you want to select.

TIP By default, Font Book automatically validates each font you install with it.

TIP The File menu's Validate File command **F** displays an Open dialog you can use to validate a font file that is not installed on your computer.

BB The Font Validation window displays font error details and enables you to remove the bad fonts.

A The Fonts panel closely resembles the layout of Font Book.

B Choose Show Fonts from the Font submenu under TextEdit's Format menu.

C You can access other features with the action pop-up menu.

D The Preview pane can help you see what your font settings look like applied to text.

The Fonts Panel

The Fonts panel **A** offers a standard interface for formatting font characters in a document. This OS X feature is fully integrated with Font Book, so the time you spend organizing your fonts there will help you be more productive when working with the Fonts panel.

The Fonts panel is *not* a dialog box (page 166). That means you can leave it open and switch back and forth between your documents and the Fonts panel's formatting options. Changes are applied immediately; there's no need to click an Apply or OK button. You can even leave the Fonts panel open all the time when you work with an application.

In this part of the chapter, I explain how to use the Fonts panel to format text.

TIP This chapter looks at the Fonts panel as it appears in TextEdit, the text editor that comes with OS X. You can learn more about using TextEdit in Chapter 14.

To open TextEdit's Fonts panel:

In TextEdit, choose Format > Font > Show Fonts **B**, or press Command-T.

TIP The command to open the Fonts panel in other applications that support it is similar.

TIP You can open Font Book from within the Fonts panel by choosing Manage Fonts from the action pop-up menu **C**.

TIP To display a preview of font formatting in the Fonts panel, choose Show Preview from the shortcut menu **C**. A pane appears at the top of the Fonts panel with a preview of the selected font settings **D**.

To apply basic font formatting:

1. Select the text you want to apply font formatting to or position the insertion point where you want the formatting change to begin.

2. If necessary, open the Fonts panel .

3. Select a collection from the Collection list.

4. Select a font family from the Family list.

5. Select a style from the Typeface list **E**.

6. Set the font size by entering a value in the Size box, selecting a size from the Size list, or dragging the Size slider up or down **F**.

   The changes you make are applied to the selected text or text typed at the insertion point.

TIP The styles that appear in the Typeface list vary depending on the font selected in the Family list. Some font families offer more styles than others.

TIP Oblique is similar to italic. Light, regular, medium, bold, and black refer to font weights or boldness.

E In this example, I've used the Fonts panel to change the formatting of some selected text.

F The Fonts panel offers three different ways to set the font size.

Text Underline | Text Strikethrough | Text Color | Document Color

G Use these menus and buttons to apply additional font formatting options.

H Use the Colors panel to choose a color to apply.

To apply font effects:

Use the effects controls at the top of the Fonts panel window **G** to apply other font formatting options to selected text or start formatting at the insertion point:

- **Text Underline** offers four underline options: None, Single, Double, and Color. If you choose Color, you can use the Colors panel **H** to set the underline color.

- **Text Strikethrough** offers four strikethrough options: None, Single, Double, and Color. If you choose Color, you can use the Colors panel **H** to set the strikethrough color.

- **Text Color** enables you to set the color of text. When you click this button, the Colors panel appears **H** so you can choose a color for text.

- **Document Color** enables you to set the color of the document background. When you click this button, the Colors panel appears **H** so you can choose a color for the entire document's background.

TIP The Colors panel is covered in more detail on page 496.

The Character Viewer

The Character Viewer enables you to insert any character in any installed font in a document. It is especially useful for typing special characters, like mathematical symbols, arrows, and dingbats characters.

TIP The Character Viewer is available within some OS X applications, including TextEdit.

To display the Character Viewer:

Use one of the following techniques:

- In TextEdit, choose Edit > Special Characters **B**, or press Option-Command-T.

- In the Fonts panel, choose Characters from the action pop-up menu **C**.

TIP You can also display the Character Viewer by choosing Show Character Viewer from the Input menu (page 526).

To insert a character with the Character Viewer:

1. In a document window, position the insertion point where you want the character to appear.

2. Display the Character Viewer **A**.

3. Select a character group in the left column.

4. Select one of the characters or groups in the middle part of the window.

5. In the middle or Font Variation pane of the window, double-click the character you want to insert.

   The character appears at the insertion point in your document.

A The Character Viewer offers a visual way to insert special characters.

B In TextEdit, you can choose Special Characters from the Edit menu.

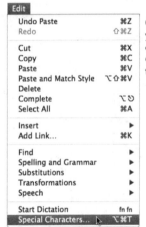

C Choose Characters from the action pop-up menu.

Printing

In OS X, printing is handled by the operating system rather than individual applications. You choose the Print command in the application that created the document you want to print. OS X steps in, displaying the Print dialog and telling the application how to send information to the printer.

There are two main benefits to this:

- If you can print documents created with one application, you can probably print documents created with any application.

- The Page Setup and Print dialogs look very much the same in most applications.

This chapter covers most aspects of printing documents on a computer running OS X. It also explains how you can use the Print dialog to create and email PDF files and fax documents right from your computer.

Printing: An Overview

To print on your Mac, you need to complete three basic steps, two of which you may only have to do once. Here's a quick overview of the process.

1. If necessary, add your printer to the Printers list in the Print & Scan preferences pane. You only need to do this once for each printer you use. You can find complete instructions starting on page 535.

2. If necessary, in the document you want to print, open the Page Setup dialog, set options, and save them. In most cases, the default or last-used options will be fine for your document, so you won't need to change them. You can learn more about the Page Setup dialog in this chapter, on page 344.

3. Open the Print dialog, set options, and click Print. This is the one step you'll need to do with most of the documents you print. You can learn about using the Print dialog in this chapter, starting on page 345.

There are a few additional things you might want to keep in mind about printing. I'll discuss them briefly here.

Printer Drivers

A *printer driver* is software that OS X uses to communicate with a specific kind of printer. It contains information about the printer and instructions for using it. You can't open and read a printer driver, but your computer can.

A standard installation of OS X installs printer drivers for the printers it detects during installation. If you have an Internet connection, OS X checks to make sure you have the most up-to-date version of the

Do You Really Need to Print It?

Let's face it: these days, most documents don't need to be printed at all.

Before you click that Print button, take a moment and think about it. Do you really need hard copy? What will you do with it? Is it just a quick printout for proofreading? Will it wind up in the wastepaper basket or shredder when you're done? Can't you just work with it onscreen?

If you need to share a document with someone else, consider creating a PDF file of the document instead. It's quick and easy to email it, right from within the Print dialog. Or you could put it on a network server or file sharing service such as Dropbox or your iDisk. Not only is this a much quicker and cost-effective way to share a document, but it prevents the waste of paper, ink, or toner.

And look at it this way: The less you print, the longer your printer will last. My primary document printer is nearly 15 years old—can you say the same about yours?

So think about it—and don't print when you don't have to.

installed printer drivers. It can also install printer drivers on the fly when you set up a new printer.

When you buy a printer, it should come with a CD or access to a website that includes OS X-compatible printer driver software; if your computer does not recognize your printer, you'll need to install this software to use it.

Sharing Printers

If your Mac is connected to a network, you may be able to access printers that are shared or otherwise available on the network. This means you can print without having a printer directly connected to your Mac.

You can also share a printer that is directly connected to your Mac with other users on your network. As long as your computer is turned on and connected to the network, other network users can use it to print.

If you have access to multiple printers, you can create a *printer pool*, or group of shared printers. When you or another user prints to a printer pool, the document prints on the first available printer in the pool. This is especially helpful on a busy network when many users have access to just a handful of printers.

You can set up printer sharing features using various System Preferences panes:

- Use the Sharing preferences pane (page 553) to enable printer sharing for your printers.

- Use the Print & Scan preferences pane (page 534) to add network printers to your computer and create a printer pool.

The Page Setup Dialog

The Page Setup dialog lets you set page options prior to printing, including the printer the document should be formatted for, paper size, orientation, and scale.

TIP Not all applications offer access to the Page Setup dialog. If Page Setup does not appear on the File menu for the application you're printing from, this dialog is not available in that application.

To set Page Attributes:

1. In the application you plan to print from, choose File > Page Setup **B** to display the Page Setup dialog.

2. If necessary, choose Page Attributes from the Settings pop-up menu to display Page Attributes options **A**.

3. Set options as desired:
   ▸ To format the document for a specific printer, choose the printer's name from the Format For pop-up menu **C**. This menu includes all of the printers listed in the Print & Scan preferences pane (page 534).
   ▸ To change the paper size, choose an option from the Paper Size pop-up menu **D**. This menu lists common paper sizes or, if you chose a specific printer, all the paper sizes supported by that printer.
   ▸ To change the page orientation, click the Orientation option you want.
   ▸ To change the print scale, enter a scaling percentage in the Scale box.

4. Click OK to save your settings and dismiss the Page Setup dialog.

TIP Default printer and paper size are set in the Print & Scan preferences pane (page 534).

A The Page Setup dialog, as it appears for a TextEdit document.

B Choose Page Setup from the File menu. Here's what it looks like in TextEdit.

C To format for a specific printer, choose the printer from this menu.

D Choose a paper size from the Paper Size pop-up menu.

A The Print dialog can appear with few options...

B ...or be expanded to show many options.

C Choose Print from the File menu. Here's what it looks like in TextEdit.

Setting Options in the Print Dialog

The Print dialog **A** **B** enables you to set printing options and output the document to a printer, fax modem, or PDF file.

Like the Page Setup dialog, the Print dialog is a standard dialog, but two things can cause its appearance and options to vary:

- Print options vary depending on the selected printer.

- Additional options may be offered by specific applications.

The Print dialog offers two modes: a simple view with few options **A** and a detailed view with all options **B**. Simply click a Show Details or Hide Details button to toggle from one view to the other.

This section explains how to set Print options available for most printers and applications.

TIP If your Print dialog includes options that are not covered here, consult the documentation that came with your printer.

TIP For information about using Print options specific to an application, consult the documentation that came with the application.

To open the Print dialog:

1. Choose File > Print **C**, or press Command-P.

   The Print dialog appears **A** **B**.

2. If necessary, click the Show Details button at the bottom of the dialog to expand it and show all of its options **B**.

To set basic printing options:

On the top-right corner of the Print dialog **B**, set options as desired:

- **Printer** **D** is the printer you want to print to. This menu includes all of the printers listed in the Print & Scan preferences pane (page 534).

- **Presets** **E** is a set of predefined options. I explain how to use this feature later in this section.

- **Copies** is the number of copies to print.

- **Pages** enables you to enter a range of pages to print:

  - **All** prints all pages in the document.

  - **From** enables you to enter values in the From and to boxes to set a range of pages to print.

- **Paper Size** **F** is the size of paper you want to print to. This menu includes all the paper sizes supported by the selected printer.

- **Orientation** is the paper orientation for printing: portrait or landscape.

TIP Choosing Add Printer from the Printer pop-up menu **D** opens the Add Print dialog, which you can use to add a printer to the Print & Scan preferences pane (page 534).

D The Printer menu includes all printers in the Print & Scan preferences pane.

E The Presets menu enables you to save or select predefined options

F Use this pop-up menu to select the paper size you want to print to.

G Use this pop-up menu to select the type of option you want to edit. This menu varies depending on the printer you're printing to.

H **I** Application-specific settings vary from one application to another. These are the settings for TextEdit (top) and Preview (bottom).

To set other options:

1. In the lower-right corner of the Print dialog, choose an option from the pop-up menu at the divider line **G**. Here are some of the possible options:

   - *Application name* **H I** displays application-specific options.

   - **Layout** **J** enables you to set the number of pages per sheet, layout direction, border, two-sided printing, and reverse page orientation, which prints the pages in reverse order.

   - **Color Matching** **K** enables you to set color-matching options.

   - **Paper Handling** **L** enables you to specify which pages to print (all, even, or odd), set scaling options, and set the page order (normal or reverse).

   - **Paper Feed** **M** enables you to specify whether paper will be fed automatically or manually.

   - **Cover Page** **N** enables you to set options for a cover page that can be printed before or after the document.

   - Print Settings **O**, Color Options **P**, Color/Quality Options **Q**, Printer Features **R**, Finishing **S**, and Supply Levels **T**, all of which are illustrated on the next page, are examples of printer-specific options you might see for your printers.

2. Set options as desired in the bottom half of the Print dialog.

3. Repeat steps 1 and 2 for each group of options you want to set.

TIP Many of the options that appear in the lower half of the print dialog customized for specific printers, so what you see may vary from what is shown in this book.

J Layout options control pages per sheet and related settings.

K Color Matching options enable you to select a color matching method.

L Paper Handling options control collation, page selection and order, and print scaling.

M Paper Feed options control how paper is fed into the printer.

N Cover page options enable you to print a cover page for the print job.

To save settings as a preset:

1. Follow the instructions on the previous two pages to set options as desired in the Print dialog **B**.

2. Choose Save Current Settings as Preset from the Presets pop-up menu **E**.

    The Save Preset As dialog appears **U**.

3. Enter a name for the settings in the Preset Name box.

4. Choose a Preset Available For option to specify whether it should be available for just the current printer or all printers.

5. Click OK.

    The name you entered is added to the Presets menu and chosen **V**.

TIP It's a good idea to save settings if you often have to change the Print dialog's settings. This can save time when you need to print.

TIP To save changes to a preset, follow these steps and save the preset with the same name.

To use preset settings:

In the Print dialog **B**, choose the name of the preset settings you want to use from the Presets pop-up menu **V**.

All Print dialog settings are set according to the saved settings.

O P Q R S T Examples of printer-specific settings in the Print dialog for various printers.

U Use this dialog to name and save a preset.

V The preset you created appears on the Presets menu.

W You can view, duplicate, or delete settings for each preset in a dialog like this.

To view preset settings:

1. In the Print dialog **B**, choose Show Presets from the Presets menu **V**.

2. In the Presets dialog that appears, select the preset you want to view **W**.

3. If necessary, click disclosure triangles on the right side of the dialog to display setting information.

4. Repeat steps 2 and 3 for each preset you want to view.

5. When you are finished viewing presets, click OK to dismiss the dialog.

TIP You can click the Duplicate button in the Presets dialog **W** to make a copy of a selected preset. You can then make changes to the original or copy to create a different preset.

To delete a preset setting:

1. In the Print dialog **B**, choose Show Presets from the Presets menu **V**.

2. In the Presets dialog that appears, select the preset you want to delete **W**.

3. Click the Delete button.

   The preset setting is deleted.

Previewing Documents

The Print dialog includes a preview area that you can use to get a large thumbnail preview of each page of the document. This is a good way to see how a document will print before actually printing it.

TIP You can also use the Print dialog's Open PDF in Preview command, which I discuss on page 351, to create a PDF of the document and open it in Preview (page 233). This gives you a full-sized version of the document to examine before printing.

Ⓐ The left side of the Print dialog shows a preview of the document as it will print.

To preview a document in the Print dialog:

1. Follow the instructions on pages 346 and 347 to set options as desired in the Print dialog's panes.

2. Look at the Preview area on the left side of the Print dialog to see what the first page looks like **Ⓐ**.

3. If the document has multiple pages, use the controls beneath the preview to scroll through the document.

TIP Some applications include a Print Preview command. This displays a preview of the document from within the application and does not open the Print dialog.

A Use options on this menu to create and distribute PDF files.

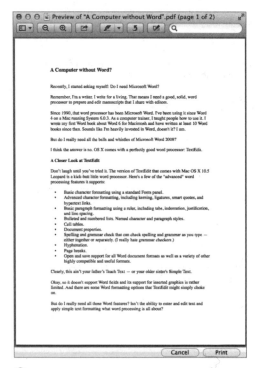

B Opening a document as a PDF in Preview is a good way to see what the document will look like before printing. You can then print right from Preview.

TIP I tell you about OS X automation tools like AppleScript and Automator on page 392.

Saving Documents as PDF Files

PDF, which stands for *Portable Document Format*, is a standard file format that can be opened and read by Preview, Adobe Reader, and some other applications. PDF is a good format for distributing a formatted document when you're not sure what software the document's recipient has. Most computer users have some kind of PDF reader software; if they don't, they can download Adobe Reader for free.

The PDF menu in the Print dialog offers several options for saving a document as a PDF file **A**:

- **Open PDF in Preview** opens the document as a PDF file in Preview **B**.

- **Save as PDF** saves the document as a PDF file in the location you specify.

- **Save as PostScript** saves the document in PostScript format. The file can then be sent to a PostScript output device.

- **Fax PDF** uses a fax modem to fax the document as a PDF. This command only appears if your Mac is configured with a fax modem.

- **Add PDF to iTunes** adds the file to iTunes as a PDF. Once there, it can be copied to an iOS device.

- **Mail PDF** attaches a PDF file of the document to an email message form.

- **Save PDF to Web Receipts Folder** saves the document as a PDF file in the Web Receipts folder in your Documents folder.

- **Edit Menu** displays a dialog you can use to add or remove PDF workflows created with AppleScript or Automator.

To save a document as a PDF file:

1. Follow the instructions on pages 346 and 347 to set options as desired in the Print dialog's panes.

2. Choose Save as PDF from the PDF menu **A**.

3. A Save dialog (page 160) appears. If necessary, click the disclosure triangle beside the Save As field to expand it to show all options **C**.

4. Enter a name and select a disk location for the PDF file.

5. If desired, provide additional information about the file in the Title, Author, Subject, and Keywords boxes in the bottom part of the dialog.

6. To secure the document against unauthorized access or use, click the Security Options button. Then set options in the PDF Security Options dialog that appears **D** and click OK.

7. Click Save.

   The file is saved as a PDF file in the location you specified.

TIP You can use the PDF Security Options dialog **D** to require separate passwords to open the document or copy and print its content.

C Use this Save dialog to name and choose a destination for the PDF file.

D Use the PDF Security Options dialog to secure your PDF from unauthorized access or to restrict copying or printing.

E You can choose your fax modem from the Printer pop-up menu.

F Use the form in the bottom-right of the window to fill in fax recipient and cover sheet information.

G If you choose Fax Modem from the pop-up menu near the bottom of the dialog, you can set options for your fax modem.

To fax a document:

1. Set options as desired in the Print dialog's panes.

2. Do one of the following:
   ▸ Choose Fax PDF from the PDF menu **A**.
   ▸ Choose a fax modem from the Printer pop-up menu **E**.

   The bottom half of the Print dialog changes to offer options for faxing the document **F**.

3. Enter the fax phone number you are faxing the document to in the To box.

4. If you need to dial a number to get a dial tone (like in an office or hotel) or a 1 for long distance, enter these numbers in the Dialing Prefix box.

5. To include a fax cover page, turn on the Use cover page check box, type a subject in the Subject box, and type a message in the Message box.

6. Click Fax.

   A Print status dialog appears briefly as the document is spooled to the fax modem's queue. A moment later, the computer dials and sends the fax.

TIP You must add a fax modem to the Print & Scan preferences pane before you can fax a document. Learn more on page 534.

TIP The header on each page of the faxes you send includes the date, time, and page number.

TIP You can set options for a fax modem from within the Print dialog. While a fax modem is chosen from the Printer menu, choose Fax Modem from the pop-up menu on the divider line in the bottom half of the Print dialog **G**. Then set options for dialing, sound, and dial tone.

Printing Documents

As you've probably figured out, the Print dialog also enables you to send a document to a printer to be printed.

To print a document:

1. Follow the instructions on pages 346 and 347 to set options as desired in the Print dialog's panes.

2. Click Print.

   The print job is sent to the print queue, where it waits for its turn to be printed.

A A quick way to print a document is to drag its icon on top of a desktop printer.

Desktop Printers

OS X's desktop printers feature lets you create an icon for a printer you use frequently. Then, when you want to print a document on that printer, simply drag the document icon onto the printer icon.

TIP You can learn how to set up a desktop printer on page 539.

To print with a desktop printer:

1. Drag the icon for the document you want to print onto the printer icon **A**.

2. When you release the button, the document is sent to the printer's print queue and prints.

   The Print dialog does not appear.

TIP You can drag any number of document icons onto the printer icon. They will all be spooled to the printer.

A One way to open a print queue is to select the printer in the Print & Scan preferences pane and then click Open Print Queue.

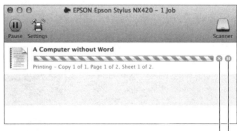

B You can also open a print queue by double-clicking the printer's icon if it appears in the Dock.

C If you've created a desktop printer icon for a printer, you can double-click it to open its print queue.

EPSON Epson
Stylus NX420

	EPSON Epson Stylus NX420 – 1 Job	
Pause Settings		Scanner

A Computer without Word

Printing - Copy 1 of 1, Page 1 of 2, Sheet 1 of 2.

D A typical print queue with one job queued and printing.

Delete
Pause

Print Queues

A print queue is a list of documents or print jobs waiting to be printed. When you click the Print button to send a document to a printer, you're really sending it to the printer's queue, where it waits its turn to be printed.

You can open a printer's queue window to check the progress of print jobs that are printing; to stop printing; and to hold, resume, or cancel a specific print job.

TIP Although this section discusses printer queues, a fax modem also has a queue that works exactly the same way.

To open a printer's queue window:

Use one of the following techniques:

- Open the Print & Scan preferences pane **A** (page 534), select the name of the printer you want to open the print queue for, and click Open Print Queue.

- If the printer has at least one print job spooled, click the printer's icon in the Dock **B**.

- Double-click the desktop printer icon for a printer **C**.

The printer's queue window opens **D**.

TIP Clicking the tiny button to the left of a document's status in the print queue displays a preview of the document.

To control printing:

In the print queue window **D**, use any of the following techniques:

- To pause all printing, click the Pause button. Any printing stops and the Pause button turns into a Resume button.

- To restart print jobs, click the Resume button in the print queue window. The next print job starts printing.

- To hold a specific print job, click the Pause button for that job. *Paused* appears beneath the job name in the print queue window. If the job was printing, it stops and another queued job prints.

- To resume a specific print job, click the Resume button for that job. *Paused* disappears from beneath the job name in the print queue window. If no other jobs are printing, the job begins to print.

- To cancel a specific print job, click the Delete button for that job. The job is removed from the print queue. If it was printing, printing stops.

TIP You can use commands under the Printer **E** and Jobs **F** menus to access print queue options. The commands that are available vary depending on the printer and how your computer is connected to it.

Printer	
Pause	
Make Default	⌘D
Settings	⌘S
Supply Levels...	
Print Test Page	
Network Diagnostics	
Error Log	
Print & Scan Preferences	⌘L

E Use this menu to access options for your printer.

Jobs	
Delete Job	⌘⌫
Resume Job	
Resume Job On Page...	
Hold Job	
Quick Look "A Computer without Word"	⌘Y
Show Everyone's Jobs	

F This menu offers options for working with a selected print job.

File
New Finder Window   ⌘N
New Folder   ⇧⌘N
New Folder with Selection   ^⌘N
New Smart Folder   ⌥⌘N
New Burn Folder
Open   ⌘O
Open With   ▶
Print   ⌘P
Close Window   ⌘W
Get Info   ⌘I
Compress "TextEdit Info"
Duplicate   ⌘D
Make Alias   ⌘L
Quick Look "TextEdit Info"   ⌘Y
Show Original   ⌘R
Add to Sidebar   ⌘T
Move to Trash   ⌘⌫
Eject   ⌘E
Burn "TextEdit Info" to Disc...
Find   ⌘F
Label:
☒ ⬤ ⬤ ⬤ ⬤ ⬤ ⬤ ⬤

A You can use the Finder's Print command to send selected documents to the default printer.

The Finder's Print Command

The Finder's File menu also includes a Print command **A**. This is a quick-and-dirty command for sending a selected document to the default printer, without even displaying the Print dialog.

TIP The Finder's Print command works very much like the Print One command available in some applications.

To use the Finder's Print command:

1. In a Finder window, select the document(s) you want to print.

2. Choose File > Print **A**, or press Command-P.

   If necessary, the application that created the document opens. The document is sent to the default printer and prints. The application that opened it remains open.

25

Disk Utility

Disk Utility is a utility application for working with disks and volumes. As discussed in Chapter 8, a *disk* is a storage device and a *volume* is a part of a disk formatted for storing files.

Disk Utility can:

- Provide general information about a disk or volume.
- Verify and repair a disk or volume.
- Erase a selected disk or volume.
- Divide a disk into several volumes or partitions.
- Create disk images.
- Mount a disk image as a disk.
- Burn a disk image to CD or DVD.
- Set up a RAID disk.
- Restore a disk from a backup image.

This chapter explains how to use Disk Utility's most commonly used features.

In This Chapter:

Launching & Quitting Disk Utility

Like any other OS X application, you need to launch Disk Utility to use it. You can find Disk Utility's application icon **A** in the Utilities folder inside the Applications folder on your hard disk.

TIP Certain features of disk utility cannot be used on the startup disk. If you need to repair or format your startup disk, you must start your Mac with another startup disk or DVD or your computer's recovery partition (page 119).

To open Disk Utility:

Use one of the following techniques:

- Open the Disk Utility icon in the Utilities folder in your Applications folder **A**.

- Click the Disk Utility icon in the Other folder in Launchpad (page 140).

Disk Utility's main window appears **B**. It lists mounted disks with their volumes, as well as recently opened or created disk image files on the left side of the window.

To quit Disk Utility:

Use one of the following techniques:

- Choose Disk Utility > Quit Disk Utility, or press Command-Q.

- Close Disk Utility's window **B**.

A Disk Utility's application icon.

Disk Utility

B The main Disk Utility window with the First Aid button selected.

A Some information about a selected disk appears at the bottom of the Disk Utility window.

B Information about a selected disk...

C ...and for a selected volume.

Learning More about a Disk or Volume

Disk Utility can provide additional information about a mounted disk or volume that can't be found in the Info window (page 88). You might find this information useful for troubleshooting problems.

To get information about a disk or volume:

1. On the left side of the Disk Utility window, select the disk or volume you want information about.

   Some information about the item appears at the bottom of the window A.

2. Use one of the following techniques:

   ▸ Click the Info button on the toolbar.

   ▸ Choose File > Get Info, or press Command-I.

   A window with additional information appears B C.

3. When you are finished reviewing the information in the window, click its close button to dismiss it.

Verifying & Repairing Disks

One of the main components of Disk Utility is Disk First Aid, which can be used to verify and repair permissions and disks that can get damaged during regular use, unexpected power outages, or by disconnecting an external disk before it has been properly unmounted.

OS X automatically checks the startup disk when you start your Mac and can repair any minor directory problems it finds. You may, however, want to run Disk First Aid to verify or repair disk permissions and disks occasionally as a general maintenance routine.

TIP Permissions (page 415) determine how users can access files. If permissions are incorrectly set for a file, it may not be accessible by the users who should be able to use it. If permissions are really messed up, your computer might not work correctly.

TIP Disk Utility's First Aid feature cannot repair all disk problems. For severely damaged disks, you may need to acquire third-party utilities.

A In this example, I've selected the startup volume. I can verify or repair disk permissions or verify the disk, but I can't repair the disk.

B As shown here, Disk Utility found and repaired quite a few permissions problems on my startup volume.

C While verifying my startup volume, Disk Utility did not find any problems.

To verify or repair a disk or volume or its permissions:

1. In the Disk Utility window, click the First Aid button.

2. In the left side of the window, select the disk or volume you want to verify or repair **A**.

3. Click the button for the action you want to perform:

   ▸ **Verify Disk Permissions** verifies file permissions on an OS X startup volume.

   ▸ **Repair Disk Permissions** repairs file permissions on an OS X startup volume.

   ▸ **Verify Disk** verifies the directory structure and file integrity of a disk or volume.

   ▸ **Repair Disk** repairs damage to the directory structure of any disk or volume other than the startup disk, as long as it is not write-protected.

4. If you are verifying the startup volume, a dialog may appear to warn you that your computer may be slow or unresponsive while the startup disk is being verified. Click Verify Disk to continue.

5. Wait while your computer checks and/ or repairs the selected disk or volume and its permissions.

   When it's done, it reports its results on the right side of the window **B C**.

TIP To repair your startup volume, start your computer from its recovery partition (page 119). After specifying a language, click the Disk Utility option in the OS X Utilities window that appears. Then follow these steps.

TIP To select more than one disk or volume in step 2, hold down the Command key while clicking each item.

Erasing & Partitioning Disks

You can use Disk Utility to erase and partition disks.

When you *erase* a disk, you remove all files and directories on that disk. This prepares the disk to accept new data.

An erased disk has a single *volume* or *partition*, which is what appears in the Finder. You store files on the volume. If you want to, you can split a disk into multiple partitions so that multiple volumes appear in the Finder. Each partition is treated by OS X as a separate disk.

To erase a disk or volume:

1. In the Disk Utility window, click the Erase button.

2. In the column on the left side of the window, select the disk or volume you want to erase .

3. Set options for the volume:
   - **Format** ⑧ is the format applied to the volume.
   - **Name** is the name of the volume.

4. To specify how disk space occupied by deleted files should be erased, click the Erase Free Space button. (This option is only available if you have selected a volume to erase.) Then select an option in the Erase Free Space Options dialog ⑨ and click Erase Free Space.

5. To increase security and prevent the disk from being unerased, click the Security Options button. Then select an option in the Secure Erase Options dialog ⑩ and click OK.

6. Click Erase.

   A confirmation dialog appears ⑪.

ⓐ In this example, I've selected a USB storage device and set options to erase and rename it.

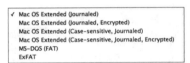

ⓑ There are several Format options, depending on the type of media you are erasing.

ⓒ You can use the slider in this dialog to determine how quickly or securely you want to erase free space on a volume.

D Use the slider in this dialog to determine how quickly or securely a disk is erased.

E Disk Utility asks one more time if you're sure you want to erase the disk.

F The newly erased disk appears in the Finder.

CAUTION Erasing a disk or volume permanently removes all data. Do not erase a disk if you think you will need any of the data it contains.

7. If you're sure you want to continue, click Erase.

8. Wait while your computer erases the disk or volume. A progress dialog appears as it works.

   When it's finished, an icon for the erased disk or volume reappears in Disk Utility and in the Finder **F**.

TIP You cannot erase the startup disk. (And that's a good thing.) If you want to erase your computer's startup disk, you must start your computer with another disk.

TIP When you erase a disk, you replace all volumes on the disk with one blank volume. When you erase a volume, you replace that volume with a blank volume.

TIP If you're not sure which volume format to choose in step 3, choose OS X Extended (Journaled). If you wanted one of the other formats, you'd know it.

TIP In steps 4 and 5, dragging the slider to different settings displays the corresponding explanation for that setting. This should be enough information to help you decide which option is right for you.

TIP Using the security options in steps 4 and 5 can considerably lengthen the amount of time it takes to erase the disk, especially for high-capacity disks.

TIP After erasing a disk or volume, a dialog may appear, asking if you want to use that volume to back up with Time Machine (page 115). Click the appropriate button for your situation.

TIP If you're concerned about unauthorized persons recovering data from files you erase, be sure to check out the Secure Empty Trash feature (page 50).

To partition a disk:

1. Select the disk you want to partition.

2. In the Disk Utility window, click the Partition tab **G**.

3. Choose an option from the Partition Layout pop-up menu **H**.

   The area beneath the pop-up menu changes accordingly **I**.

4. In the Partition Layout area, select a volume. Then set options in the Partition Information area as desired **J**:

   ▸ **Name** is the name of the volume.

   ▸ **Format** **K** is the format applied to the volume.

   ▸ **Size** is the amount of disk space allocated to that partition.

5. Repeat step 4 for each partition.

6. Click Apply.

   A confirmation dialog appears **L**.

   CAUTION Partitioning a disk permanently removes all data. Do not partition a disk if you think you will need any of the data on an existing partition.

7. If you're sure you want to continue, click Partition.

8. Wait while your computer creates the new partitions.

   When it's finished, icons for each partition appear in Disk Utility beneath the disk name **M** as well as in the Finder **N**.

   TIP You can also change the partition size in step 4 by dragging the divider between partitions in the Partition Layout area **O**.

   TIP If you select Free Space as the format for any partition in step 4, that partition cannot be used to store files.

G Choose the disk you want to partition and then click the Partition button.

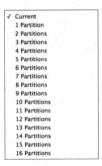

H Use the Partition Layout pop-up menu to choose how many partitions you want.

I In this example, I chose 2 partitions.

J Select a partition and set options for it.

K Partition Format options.

L Disk Utility confirms that you really do want to repartition the disk.

M The partitions appear under the disk in Disk Utility.

N The partitions also appear as individual volumes in the Finder.

TIP If you're not sure what volume format to choose in step 4, choose OS X Extended (Journaled). If you needed one of the other formats, you'd know it.

TIP If you are partitioning removable media that may be used as a startup disk for a Macintosh or a Windows PC, before step 6, click the Options button in the Partition pane. Select the appropriate option in the dialog that appears **P** and click OK.

O You can drag the border between two partitions to resize them.

P If necessary, set options in a dialog like this to create a bootable disk partition.

Working with Disk Image Files

A *disk image* is a single file that contains everything on a disk. You can mount a disk image on your desktop just like any other disk .

Disk images are often used to distribute software on the Internet. They usually have a .dmg filename extension.

Disk Utility enables you to create disk image files, store data on them, mount them as disks, and burn them to CD or DVD.

To create a blank disk image file:

1. On the left side of the Disk Utility window, click beneath the list of disks and volumes so that none of them are selected.

2. Click the New Image button in Disk Utility's toolbar.

3. At the top of the dialog that appears , enter a file name and specify a disk location to save the disk image file. (You can click the disclosure triangle beside the Save As field to display additional location options if necessary.)

4. Set options in the bottom part of the dialog:

   ▶ **Name** is the name of the volume within the Disk Image file. This is the name that will appear on the disk's icon in the Finder when the disk image is mounted.

   ▶ **Size** is the size of the volume. Choose an option from the pop-up menu . If you choose Custom, use a dialog sheet to set the size.

A The icon for a disk image file looks like this.

Example Disk.dmg

B When you open a disk image file, a mounted disk appears in the Finder. You can use this like any other disk.

C Set options for a new disk image file in this dialog.

D The size of the disk determines the size of the disk image file.

✓ Mac OS Extended (Journaled)
  Mac OS Extended
  Mac OS Extended (Case-sensitive, Journaled)
  Mac OS Extended (Case-sensitive)
  MS-DOS (FAT)
  ExFAT

E Disk images can be formatted the same as any other disk.

✓ none

  128-bit AES encryption (recommended)
  256-bit AES encryption (more secure, but slower)

F You can encrypt a disk image file.

  Hard disk
  CD/DVD
✓ No partition map
  Single partition – Apple Partition Map
  Single partition – Master Boot Record Partition Map
  Single partition – GUID Partition Map
  Single partition – CD/DVD
  Single partition – CD/DVD with ISO data

G You can also set custom partition options for a disk image.

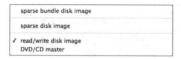

  sparse bundle disk image

  sparse disk image

✓ read/write disk image
  DVD/CD master

H In most cases, you'll want to create a read/write disk image.

I Once you've created a disk image, it's mounted on your computer and appears in Disk Utility's window.

- ▸ **Format E** enables you to select the format of the volume.

- ▸ **Encryption F** offers file encryption options for the disk image file.

- ▸ **Partitions G** enables you to set a partition map for the disk image file.

- ▸ **Image Format H** refers to the type of disk image. In most cases, you'll want to select read/write disk image.

5. Click Create.

   Disk Utility creates a disk image file to your specifications, adds it to the list in Disk Utility **I**, and mounts it **B**.

TIP The size of a disk image file is determined by the size specified in step 4.

TIP If you're not sure what to choose for options in step 4, leave them set to the default values.

TIP Once you have created and mounted a blank disk image, you can copy items to it as if it were a regular disk (page 46). The items you copy to the disk are automatically copied into the disk image file.

To create a disk image file from a folder or disk:

1. In Disk Utility, do one of the following:

   ▸ To create a disk image file from a folder, choose File > New > Disk Image from Folder ⓙ, or press Shift-Command-N.

   ▸ To create a disk image file from a disk, select the disk on the left side of Disk Utility's window and then choose File > New > Disk Image from "*Disk Name*" ⓙ.

2. If you are creating a disk image from a folder, use the Select Folder to Image dialog ⓚ to locate and select the folder you want to create a disk image of and then click Image.

3. In the top part of the dialog that appears ⓛ, enter a name and choose a disk location for the image file.

4. In the bottom part of the dialog, set options as desired:

   ▸ **Image Format** ⓜⓝ refers to the type of disk image.

   ▸ **Encryption** ⓞ offers file encryption options for the disk image file.

5. Click Save.

   Disk Utility creates a disk image file containing the contents of the folder or disk, adds it to the list in Disk Utility's window, and saves it in the location you specified.

> **TIP** The size of a disk image file is determined by the amount of data in the folder or disk and the Image Format option you chose in step 4.

> **TIP** If you choose read/write from the Image Format pop-up menu in step 4, you can add files to the mounted disk image disk. Otherwise, you cannot.

ⓙ Use the New menu to create a disk image from a folder or a disk.

ⓚ If you're creating a disk image from a folder, you need to tell Disk Utility which folder.

ⓛ Set options for the new disk image file in a dialog like this.

ⓜⓝ The Image Format menu for a disk image created from a folder (top) and a disk (bottom).

O Use this dialog to locate, select, and open a disk image file.

P In this example, the selected volume is not mounted. I can click the Mount button to mount it.

Q Select the volume you want to unmount and click the Unmount button.

To mount a disk image:

Use one of the following techniques:

- Double-click the disk image file's icon in the Finder **A**.

- On the left side of the Disk Utility window, select the name of the disk image you want to mount **I** and click the Open button in the toolbar.

- In Disk Utility, choose File > Open Disk Image, or press Option-Command-O. Then use the Select Image to Attach dialog that appears **O** to locate, select, and open the disk image file.

The disk image file's disk icon appears in the Finder and, if Disk Utility is open, in the list of disks and volumes.

TIP To mount an unmounted disk or partition, select it in the list on the left side of Disk Utility's main window **P** and click the Mount button in the toolbar.

To unmount a disk image:

Use one of the following techniques:

- In the Finder, drag the icon for the mounted disk to the Trash.

- In a Finder window's sidebar, click the Eject button beside the name of the mounted disk.

- In the Disk Utility main window, select the disk image volume you want to unmount **Q** and click the Unmount button in the toolbar.

Although the icon disappears from the desktop, all of its contents remain in the disk image file.

To burn a disc from a disk image:

1. In the Disk Utility window, select the disk image you want to burn to CD or DVD 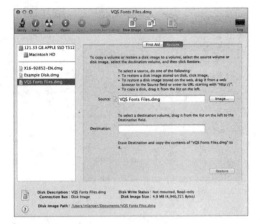.

2. Click the Burn button in the toolbar.

   A burn disc dialog appears **S**.

3. Insert a writable CD or DVD disc in your drive.

4. Click Burn.

5. Wait while Disk Utility writes to the disc. A progress dialog appears as it works.

   When the disc is finished, Disk Utility ejects the disc and displays a dialog **T**.

6. Click OK.

   The disc appears mounted in Disk Utility as well as in the Finder.

TIP You must have a Combo Drive, Super-Drive, or compatible disc writer to burn CD or DVD discs.

TIP If a disk image file you want to burn to disc does not appear in the Disk Utility window, mount it as instructed in the section titled "To mount a disk image" on page 371 and then follow these instructions.

TIP If you click the disclosure triangle in the burn disc dialog **S**, the dialog expands to offer additional options **U**.

TIP Burning content to CD or DVD disc in the Finder is covered in detail starting on page 109.

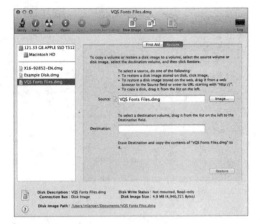

R Select the disk image you want to burn to disc.

S When you click the Burn button on the toolbar, a dialog like this prompts you to insert a disc.

T This dialog confirms a successful disc burn.

U Clicking the disclosure triangle in the burn disc dialog **S** displays more options.

26

OS X Utility Applications

OS X includes utility applications that you can use to work with your computer and its files.

This chapter provides instructions for getting started with a number of utilities, most of which you find in the Utilities folder inside the Applications folder on your hard disk. Among these, you'll find applications for monitoring system activity, installing Windows on your Mac, entering Unix commands using a command-line interface, creating screen shots, and automating repetitive tasks.

This chapter does not cover utilities that are discussed elsewhere in this book: AirPort Utility (page 398), Bluetooth File Exchange (page 408), Disk Utility (Chapter 25), or Network Utility (page 425). A discussion of Audio MIDI Setup, Java Preferences, Podcast Capture, Podcast Publisher, RAID Utility, and X11 is beyond the scope of this book.

In This Chapter:

Activity Monitor

Activity Monitor enables you to get information about the various processes running on your computer. It also displays, in graphical format, CPU activity, memory usage, and disk and network statistics. You may find this information helpful if you are a programmer or network administrator or you are trying to troubleshoot a computer problem.

TIP A *process* is a running program that performs a task.

To monitor computer activity:

1. Open the Activity Monitor icon in the Utilities folder **A**.

   The Activity Monitor window appears **B**.

2. To view only specific types of processes, choose an option from the pop-up menu at the top of the window **C**.

   The list of processes in the top half of the window changes accordingly.

3. Click a button at the bottom of the window to view other information:

   ▸ **CPU B** displays CPU activity.

   ▸ **System Memory D** displays RAM usage.

   ▸ **Disk Activity E** displays disk access activity.

   ▸ **Disk Usage F** displays free and utilized disk space. Use the pop-up menu to choose other available disks.

   ▸ **Network G** displays network activity.

TIP To sort processes in the Activity Monitor window, click the column you want to sort by. You can reverse the sort order by clicking the same column again.

A Activity Monitor can be found in the Utilities folder.

Activity Monitor

B The main Activity Monitor window lists active processes.

C Use this menu to specify which processes you want to show.

D E F G The bottom of the Activity Monitor window can show System Memory, Disk Activity, Disk Usage, or Network info.

H Use options under the Window menu and its Floating CPU Window submenu to display various Activity Monitor windows.

I The CPU Usage window displays activity for your computer's CPU(s).

J The CPU History window displays CPU usage over time for your computer's CPU(s).

K The tiny Floating CPU window displays CPU activity anywhere you like onscreen.

L The Activity Monitor Dock icon offers menu commands for displaying various windows.

To display other monitor windows:

Choose an option from the Window menu or its Floating CPU Window submenu **H**:

- **Activity Monitor** displays the Activity Monitor window **B**.

- **CPU Usage I** displays a graphical representation of current CPU usage.

- **CPU History J** displays a window with a chart of CPU usage over time.

- **Floating CPU Window** submenu commands display a horizontal **K** or vertical bar with a graphical representation of current CPU usage.

TIP You can also use the contextual menu that appears when you right-click the Activity Monitor's Dock icon **L** to show various windows.

TIP You can use the Update Frequency submenu under the Monitor menu to change how often monitor windows are updated.

TIP If your computer has multiple processors, it will display a separate graph for each one **I J**.

Boot Camp Assistant

Boot Camp is an Apple technology that makes it possible to run Microsoft Windows on your Intel-based Macintosh computer. Once installed and configured, you can boot, or start, your Macintosh in either OS X or Windows and use the software you have installed for the system you've booted.

Boot Camp Assistant is a utility application that installs the software you need to use Boot Camp. You run it once, install Boot Camp and Windows, and shouldn't have to run it again.

Boot Camp has some very specific requirements:

- OS X 10.7 Lion or later.
- A USB keyboard and mouse or a built-in keyboard and trackpad.
- A built-in or compatible external optical disc drive.
- Windows 7 Home Premium, Professional, or Ultimate. Boot Camp does not include Windows; it must be purchased separately.

Although this chapter doesn't provide step-by-step instructions for installing and using Boot Camp, Apple's got you covered. To print a 13-page guide for installing and setting up Windows on your Mac using Boot Camp, open the Boot Camp Assistant application icon **A** in the Utilities folder, click the Print Installation Guide button in the Introduction window that appears **B**, and follow the instructions onscreen. This guide will tell you everything you need to know to install Windows on your Mac.

A Book Camp Assistant helps you install Windows on your Mac.

Boot Camp Assistant

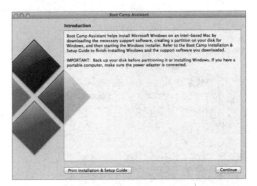

B The Introduction window tells you a little about the installation process and offers a button you can click to print complete instructions.

A The ColorSync Utility icon.

ColorSync Utility

B The main Profile First Aid window provides information about what this feature does.

C The results of verifying (or repairing) profiles appear in the Profile First Aid window.

ColorSync Utility

ColorSync is an industry-standard technology that helps designers match the colors they see onscreen to those in devices such as scanners, printers, and imagesetters. For the average user, color matching may not be very important, but for a designer who works with color, correct reproduction makes it possible to complete complex projects on time and within budget.

In this section, I explain how to use the ColorSync utility to check ColorSync profiles and view profiles and devices.

TIP A complete discussion of ColorSync is far beyond the scope of this book. To learn more about ColorSync features and settings, visit developer.apple.com/library/mac/#technotes/tn2035/_index.html.

To verify or repair ColorSync profiles:

1. Open the ColorSync Utility icon in the Utilities folder **A**.

2. In the window that appears, click the Profile First-Aid icon **B**.

3. Click one of the buttons at the bottom of the window:

   ▸ **Verify** checks all installed profiles for errors.

   ▸ **Repair** repair any errors in installed profiles.

   ColorSync Utility checks or repairs installed profiles. When it's finished, it displays results in its window **C**.

TIP You can use this feature to check or fix ColorSync Profiles if you notice a difference between what you see on your monitor and what you see on printed documents.

To view lists of installed profiles, registered devices & available filters:

1. Open the ColorSync Utility icon in the Utilities folder **A**.

2. In the ColorSync Utility window, click an icon in the toolbar:

   ▸ **Profiles D** displays a list of installed ColorSync profiles.

   ▸ **Devices E** displays a list of registered ColorSync devices.

   ▸ **Filters F** displays a list of available ColorSync filters.

3. If necessary, click triangles beside a folder pathname to view a list of the items in the folder **D E** or settings for the item **F**.

TIP A *registered device* is one that is recognized by the system software and has a ColorSync profile assigned to it.

TIP Clicking the name of a profile or device displays information about it in the right side of the window **D E**.

TIP You can change a device's profile by choosing an option from the **Current Profile** pop-up menu when the item is displayed **E**.

TIP The filters that are installed with OS X are locked and cannot be changed.

D The Profiles pane displays a list of all installed profiles. Click a profile to learn more about it.

E The Devices pane displays a list of registered devices. Click a device to learn more about it.

F The Filters pane lists all available filters and enables you to create or customize them.

G This example shows a conversion from the RGB Color LCD profile to a generic CMYK profile.

H Clicking the magnifying glass icon enables you to use a magnified cursor to select a single pixel onscreen.

To convert color values:

1. Open the ColorSync Utility icon in the Utilities folder **A**.

2. In the ColorSync Utility window, click the Calculator icon **G**.

3. On the left side of the window, use the pop-up menus to set the color space or profile you are converting from.

4. Use the sliders on the left side of the window to enter color values.

5. On the right side of the window, use the pop-up menus to set the color space or profile you are converting to.

   The converted color values appear on the right side of the window **G**.

TIP To find the color value for a pixel on your screen, click the magnifying glass icon to change the mouse pointer into a magnified cross-hairs pointer **H**. Click the pixel you want to get the color values for to insert the values on the left side of the screen. This feature is similar in functionality to DigitalColor Meter, which I discuss a little later in this chapter.

Console

The Console application enables you to read messages from OS X system software and applications. You might find this useful if you handle text support or are troubleshooting a problem. (If not, you'll probably think it looks like a bunch of gibberish.)

To view system messages:

1. Open the Console icon in the Utilities folder 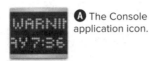 to display Console's main window.

2. On the left side of the window, select the log or report you want to read. You can click a disclosure triangle to view lists of individual reports.

3. Read the messages in the right side of the window 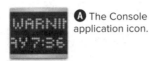.

TIP You can click the Clear Display button in the Console window 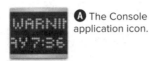 to erase the contents of the window and start a fresh log.

To save a copy of the log:

1. Choose File > Save a Copy As, or press Shift-Command-S.

2. Use the standard Save As window that appears to save the contents of the currently displayed window as a plain text file.

TIP Following these steps makes it possible to send a copy of a log file to someone helping you to troubleshoot a problem on your Mac.

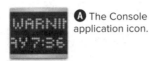

A The Console application icon.

Console

B In this example, Console is displaying all messages recorded by the system.

A The DigitalColor Meter icon.

DigitalColor Meter

B Point to a color onscreen, and Digital-Color Meter displays measurements for it.

 C Use a pop-up menu to choose a different measuring system.

D If you change the measuring system, the values change accordingly.

E Use the View menu to work with the sample image.

F Changing the Aperture Size averages the colors within the selection area.

DigitalColor Meter

DigitalColor Meter enables you to measure colors that appear on your display as a variety of standard values. This makes it possible to precisely record or duplicate colors that appear onscreen.

TIP A discussion of color technology is far beyond the scope of this book. To learn more about how your Mac can work with colors, visit the ColorSync page on Apple's developer website, developer.apple.com/library/mac/#technotes/tn2035/_index.html.

To measure color values:

1. Open the DigitalColor Meter icon in the Utilities folder **A** to display the Digital-Color Meter window **B**.

2. Point to the color onscreen that you want to measure.

   Its values appear in the right side of the DigitalColor Meter window **B**.

3. If desired, choose a different option from the pop-up menu above the measurements **C**.

   The value display changes to convert values to that measuring system **D**.

TIP You can use commands under the View menu and its Display Values submenu **E** to work with the color sample image.

TIP You can change the amount of color that is sampled by dragging the Aperture Size slider to the right or left. A large aperture size will average the colors within it **F**.

Grab

Grab is an application that can capture screen shots of OS X and its applications. You tell Grab to capture what appears on your screen, and it creates a TIFF file. You can then view the TIFF file with Preview or any application capable of opening TIFFs.

TIP You might find screen shots useful for documenting software—or for writing books like this one.

TIP Although Grab is a handy screen shot utility, it isn't the best available for OS X. Snapz Pro X, a shareware program from Ambrosia Software, is far better. If you take a lot of screen shots, be sure to check it out at www.ambrosiasw.com.

To create a screen shot:

1. Set up the screen so it shows what you want to capture.

2. Do one of the following:

   ▸ If Grab is not already running, open the Grab icon in the Utilities folder **A**.

   ▸ If Grab is already running, click its icon on the Dock to make it active.

3. Choose an option from the Capture menu **B** or press its corresponding shortcut key:

   ▸ **Selection** (Shift-Command-A) enables you to capture a portion of the screen. When you choose this option, the Selection Grab dialog **C** appears. Use the mouse pointer to drag a box around the portion of the screen you want to capture **D**. Release the mouse button to capture the screen.

   ▸ **Window** (Shift-Command-W) enables you to capture a window. When you choose this option, the Window Grab dialog **E** appears. Click the Choose

A The Grab application icon.

B Use the Capture menu to specify what you want to capture.

C The Selection Grab dialog provides instructions for capturing a portion of the screen.

D Drag a selection box around the portion of the screen you want to capture.

E The Window Grab dialog.

F The Screen Grab dialog assures you that it won't be included in your screen shot.

G You can start a timer in the Timed Screen Grab dialog.

H The screen shot appears in a Grab window.

Window button, then click the window you want to capture.

▸ **Screen** (Command-Z) enables you to capture the entire screen. When you choose this option, the Screen Grab dialog **F** appears. Click outside the dialog to capture the screen.

▸ **Timed Screen** (Shift-Command-Z) enables you to capture the entire screen after a ten-second delay. When you choose this option, the Timed Screen Grab dialog **G** appears. Click the Start Timer button, then activate the program you want to capture and arrange onscreen elements as desired. In ten seconds, the screen is captured.

4. Grab makes a camera shutter sound as it captures the screen. The image appears in an untitled document window **H**.

5. Do one of the following:

▸ If you are satisfied with the screen shot, choose File > Save or press Command-S and use the Save As dialog that appears to save it as a file on disk.

▸ If you are not satisfied with the screen shot, choose File > Close or press Command-W to close the window. In the Close dialog, click Don't Save.

TIP You can create screen shots without Grab. Press Shift-Command-3 or Shift-Command-4 to capture the entire screen or a portion of the screen that you select. The screen shot is automatically saved on the desktop as a PNG image file.

Grapher

Grapher is a charting tool that can create static and dynamic 2D and 3D graphs based on formulas.

To graph a formula:

1. Open the Grapher icon in the Utilities folder .

2. If necessary, choose File > New or press Command-N to display the New Graph dialog **B**.

3. Click a button near the top of the dialog to list either 2D or 3D document types.

4. In the list on the left side of the dialog, select the type of graph you want.

   A preview appears in the right side of the dialog **B**.

5. Click Choose.

   An untitled window with an empty graph appears **C**.

6. Type the formula you want to chart in the box at the top of the window.

7. Press Return.

   The formula's graph appears in the window and the formula is added to the Definitions list **D**.

8. If desired, click the + button at the bottom of the formula list and repeat steps 6 and 7 to add other formulas to the graph.

TIP Grapher's Equation Palette makes it a bit easier to enter complex formulas. To display it, choose Window > Show Equation Palette or press Shift-Command-E.

TIP Once you've created a graph, you can save or print it using commands under the File menu.

A The Grapher icon.

Grapher

B Set basic options in the New Graph dialog.

C A graph begins with a frame like this.

D Here's an example of a 3D graph for a simple formula.

A Keychain Access is an application for working with keychain items.

Keychain Access

The Wi-Fi network "MyPad" requires a WPA2 password.

Password: ••••••••

☐ Show password
☑ Remember this network

?   Cancel   Join

Enter your name and password for the server "iMac".

Connect as: ○ Guest
                ● Registered User
                ○ Using an Apple ID

Name: mlanger

Password: ••••••••

☑ Remember this password in my keychain

Change Password...   Cancel   Connect

B C Two examples of login dialogs you may encounter. The top one is an example of a Wi-Fi network login dialog; the bottom one is an example of a server login dialog. In both examples, you use a check box to remember the network or password.

D Here are the two keychain items created based on the examples in **B** and **C**.

Keychain Access

OS X's keychain feature offers users a way to store passwords for accessing password-protected applications, servers, and Internet locations.

OS X automatically creates a keychain for each user. This is the default, or *login*, keychain. Each user's keychain is automatically unlocked when he logs in, so the passwords it contains are available when needed to access secured files and sites.

Keychain Access **A** gives you direct access to the keychain items stored for your account. You can use it to manually add, modify, or remove keychain items.

TIP The keychain feature only works with applications that are keychain-aware.

TIP Your keychain is automatically maintained by OS X as you access various websites, servers, and applications. You might never need to open Keychain Access.

To add a keychain item when accessing a secure application, server, or Internet location:

1. Follow your normal procedure for accessing the secure item.

2. Enter your password when prompted.

3. Use a check box or other control to indicate that your Mac should remember the site or your password. The way this appears varies based on what you're accessing; **B** and **C** show two examples.

4. Finish accessing the secure item.

   Later, if you open Keychain Access **D**, you'll see that a keychain item has been created for accessing that item.

To view or modify your keychain:

1. Open the Keychain Access icon in the Utilities folder Ⓐ.

   A list of items in your keychain appears Ⓓ.

2. Do one of the following:

   ▸ To view a keychain item's information, select it and consult the information at the top of the window Ⓓ.

   ▸ To modify a keychain item, select it and choose File > Get Info or press Command-I. Then make changes in the dialog that appears Ⓔ and click Save Changes.

   ▸ To manually add a keychain item, click the + button at the bottom of the window. In the dialog that appears Ⓕ, enter details about the keychain item and click Add.

   ▸ To delete a keychain item, select it and press the Delete key. In the confirmation dialog that appears Ⓖ, click Delete.

3. When you are finished making changes, choose Keychain Access > Quit Keychain Access, or press Command-Q to quit. Your changes are saved automatically.

TIP As you work with Keychain items, you may be prompted to authenticate by entering an administrator user name and password. If you cannot do so, you will not be able to proceed.

TIP Removing a keychain item does not prevent you from accessing an item. It just prevents you from accessing it without entering a password.

Ⓔ You can make changes to a keychain item in a dialog like this.

Ⓕ It's possible to manually add a keychain item using a dialog like this one.

Ⓖ Keychain Access asks if you're sure you want to delete the keychain item.

Migration Assistant

 A The Migration Assistant icon.

B The first screen of Migration Assistant asks whether you want to transfer data from or to another computer.

C If you indicate that you want to transfer data from another computer or backup, Migration Assistant prompts you for more information.

Migration Assistant

Migration Assistant enables you to copy user accounts, applications, computer settings, and files between Macs or from a PC to a Mac. This makes it possible to transfer your information from an old Mac to a new one, restore user information with Time Machine, or add user accounts from or to another Mac.

When you first start Migration Assistant **A**, it offers two options:

- **From a Mac, PC, Time Machine backup, or other disk** enables you to transfer user information from another computer or backup to the computer you're working on **B**. If you choose this option, you'll be able to specify whether you want to transfer from another computer or from a backup **C**.

- **To a Mac** enables you to transfer user information from the Mac you're working on to another Mac.

The Migration Assistant is very easy to use. It provides clear instructions for completing every step and walks you through the process of copying user information. Simply double-click its icon to get started and follow the prompts.

TIP The OS X Setup Assistant (page 9) may automatically perform the same tasks as the Migration Assistant, depending on your answers to questions during setup.

TIP The Migration Assistant requires that you provide an Administrator user name and password to use it. This prevents unauthorized users from adding accounts to the computer.

TIP Most users will never need to use the Migration Assistant after completing the setup process for a Mac.

System Information

The System Information application provides information about your computer's hardware, software, network, and logs. This information can come in handy when you are troubleshooting problems or just need to know more about the hardware and software installed on your computer.

A The System Information icon.

System Information

To view system information:

1. Open the System Information icon in the Utilities folder **A** to display the System Information window for your computer.

2. In the list on the left side of the window, click the type of information you want to view **B C D**.

3. The information appears in the window **B C D**.

> **TIP** Clicking an item in the top-right portion of a System Information window displays details about that item **C D**.

> **TIP** You can use the File menu's Save and Print commands to save or print the information that appears in System Information. You might find this handy if you need to document your system's current configuration for troubleshooting or backup purposes.

B C D Three examples of the kind of information you can get from the System Information application: general hardware information, general network information, and a complete list of applications.

Ⓐ The Terminal icon.

Terminal

Ⓑ When you open Terminal, it displays the current date and a shell prompt.

Ⓒ In this example, I used the ls command to get a list of the items in my home folder. (Aren't you glad you don't have to deal with this on a regular basis?)

About the Shell Prompt

The shell prompt shown in **Ⓑ** and **Ⓒ** (MacBook-Air: ~mlanger$) includes the following components:

- *Computer name* is the name of the computer you're logged in to.
- *Directory* is the current directory.
- ~ (the tilde character) is Unix shorthand for your home directory.
- *User name* is your user name, which, in this example, is mlanger.
- $ is the end of the prompt.

Terminal

Terminal is an application that enables you to enter command line instructions into your Mac. These instructions are interpreted by Unix, the operating system beneath OS X. This makes it possible to modify your Mac's internal settings with Unix and run Unix applications.

CAUTION Don't know anything about Unix? Then you'd probably want to steer clear of Terminal. Typing an incorrect command into Terminal can render your Mac useless.

TIP A discussion of Unix is beyond the scope of this book.

To use Terminal:

1. Double-click the Terminal icon in the Utilities folder **Ⓐ**.

   A Terminal window with a shell prompt appears **Ⓑ**.

2. Use your keyboard to enter commands into Terminal. Be sure to press Return to send each command to Unix.

   The results of your commands appear in the Terminal window **Ⓒ**.

VoiceOver Utility

VoiceOver is a built-in screen reader that helps visually impaired people use their computers. Once configured, VoiceOver enables you to hear descriptions of everything onscreen, move around the screen, select items, and read and manipulate text.

A complete discussion of VoiceOver is beyond the scope of this book. This section, however, provides enough information to get started with the VoiceOver Utility, the application you use to configure VoiceOver.

TIP VoiceOver can be enabled or disabled in the Accessibility preferences pane, which is discussed on page 590.

TIP To learn more about configuring and using VoiceOver, open VoiceOver Utility and choose Help > VoiceOver Help. Then follow the links to get the information you need.

To configure VoiceOver:

1. Open the VoiceOver Utility icon in the Utilities folder **A**.

2. The VoiceOver Utility window appears. Click buttons to set options in each of ten categories:

   ▸ **General B** lets you set the greeting and how portable preferences are used.

   ▸ **Verbosity C** includes four panes of settings that control how much speaking VoiceOver does.

   ▸ **Speech D** enables you to select the default voice and voices for various types of spoken text.

A The VoiceOver Utility icon.

VoiceOver Utility

B C D Examples of settings screens in VoiceOver Utility: General, Verbosity Announcements, and Speech Pronunciation.

- ▸ **Navigation** controls how VoiceOver moves and tracks the cursor and text selections.

- ▸ **Web** ⓕ controls how VoiceOver works with your Web browser.

- ▸ **Sound** enables you to set sound-related preferences.

- ▸ **Visuals** ⓖ enables you to set the size of the VoiceOver cursor and menu magnification, as well as configure the Caption Panel.

- ▸ **Commanders** ⓗ enables you to map commands to the trackpad, numeric keypad, or keyboard.

- ▸ **Braille** ⓘ lets you set the way Braille display works.

- ▸ **Activities** lets you create custom settings groups that you can use with the applications you specify.

3. Choose VoiceOver Utility > Quit Voice-Over Utility, or press Command-Q, to save your settings.

ⓔⓕⓖⓗ Examples of settings in VoiceOver Utility: Navigation, Web Navigation, Visuals VoiceOver Cursor, and Commanders Trackpad.

ⓘ Braille Layout settings in VoiceOver Utility.

Automation Tools

Computers are supposed to make our lives easier, right? They can—if we "teach" them to perform repetitive tasks automatically.

For example, when I begin work in the morning, I start my computer and launch the applications I use every day: Mail, Calendar, iTunes, InDesign, and Photoshop. I check my email, delete junk mail, and start playing one of my iTunes playlists. Then I open book chapter files and folders. When I'm done with a chapter, I save it as a PDF file, create an archive of the chapter's folder, and upload it all to my publisher's FTP site. There are many repetitive tasks here—tasks my computer has been trained to do automatically at my request. This saves time; my Mac can do things a lot faster than I can.

OS X includes two tools for automating repetitive tasks:

- Automator enables you to build workflows that automate tasks in multiple applications—all without knowing a single line of programming code. You can find Automator in the Applications folder on your hard disk.

- AppleScript is a scripting language that enables you to automate tasks and extend the functionality of OS X. You use AppleScript Editor to create and edit scripts and save them in a variety of formats—including formats that work with Automator. You can find AppleScript Editor in the Utilities folder on your hard disk.

A discussion of these two automation tools is beyond the scope of this book. But once you've mastered the basics of OS X, why not give them a try?

A You can find the Automator application icon in the Applications folder.

Automator

B This example Automator workflow retrieves movie trailers from Apple's website and displays them in Safari.

C AppleScript Editor can be found inside the Utilities folder.

AppleScript Editor

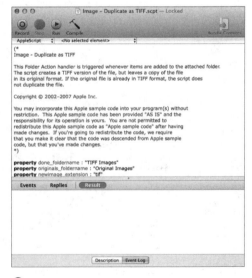

D This sample AppleScript duplicates an image and saves it as a TIFF file.

Network & Internet Connectivity

In This Part

Networking

Networking uses wired or wireless connections and network protocols to link your computer to others on a *network*. Once connected, you can share files, access email, and run special network applications on server computers.

This chapter looks at peer-to-peer networking, which uses the built-in features of OS X to connect to other computers for sharing. It explains how to configure an AirPort base station for use as a networking tool. It also covers some of the advanced network configuration applications available as OS X utilities.

This chapter touches only briefly on using networks to connect to the Internet. Connecting to the Internet is discussed in detail in Chapter 28. A discussion of OS X Server, which is designed to meet the demands of large workgroups and corporate intranets, is beyond the scope of this book.

In This Chapter:

Network Interfaces

OS X computers support the following types of network interfaces:

- **Wi-Fi** is a wireless networking technology. Through the use of *AirPort* (page 398), Apple's Wi-Fi connectivity device, your Mac can join wireless networks using the 802.11a, b, g, or n specifications.

- **Bluetooth** (page 408) is a wireless technology designed for short-range (less than 30 feet) connections between devices. Although Bluetooth is commonly used to connect to input devices such as a keyboard or mouse, it's also a viable connection method between computers or handheld computing devices such as smart phones.

- **Ethernet** (page 408) is a network connection method that uses Ethernet cables to connect computers, network printers, routers, and hubs. Ethernet was a common method of networking until a few years ago, when the benefits of wireless networking—no wires!—started providing a real alternative.

- **FireWire** (page 414), which is also known as *IEEE 1394*, is an Apple technology for extremely fast data connections. Although it's commonly used for data transfer between computers and hard disks or video devices, it can also be used to attach two computers for networking using IP over FireWire.

- **Modem** can establish a connection between two computers over a phone line. This older technology is used primarily for Internet connections when faster alternatives are not available.

You can check the status of a network interface or add additional interfaces in the Network preferences pane **Ⓐ**.

Ⓐ You can check network status for any connection to your computer in the Network preferences pane.

TIP Other network technologies supported by OS X Mountain Lion include VPN, PPPoE, and 6 to 4. A discussion of these technologies is beyond the scope of this book.

TIP Network hardware configuration details involving hubs and routers are far beyond the scope of this book. If you need help setting up a complex network, refer to a detailed networking reference or contact a network consultant.

TIP Not all Macs support all network interfaces. For example, my MacBook Air does not have Ethernet or FireWire ports, so without special adapters, it would not support either of these network interfaces.

To check network status:

1. Use one of the following techniques to open System Preferences:

   ▸ Choose Apple > System Preferences.

   ▸ Click the System Preferences icon in the Dock.

   The System Preferences window opens.

2. Choose View > Network or click the Network icon to display Network preferences **A**.

3. To get details about the status and settings for a specific connection, select it in the list on the left side of the window.

   Details appear in the right side of the window **A**.

TIP You can set advanced options for a selected interface by clicking the Advanced button near the bottom of the Network preferences window. You can learn more about the Network preferences pane starting on page 548.

AirPort

AirPort is Apple's version of the Wi-Fi local area network technology. It enables your computer to connect to a network or the Internet via radio waves instead of wires. All new Macintosh computers come with AirPort functionality pre-installed.

In addition to a Mac's AirPort capabilities, Apple offers three different AirPort devices:

- **AirPort Extreme Base Station** is an external device that works as a router to share an incoming Internet connection, printer, and external hard disk with other computers.

- **Time Capsule** is an AirPort Extreme Base Station with a built-in hard disk. It's designed for use with the Time Machine feature for automated backup, but it can be used for a centralized storage space for network users.

- **AirPort Express Base Station** is an external device that can connect to a network via Ethernet or can extend an existing AirPort network. It also supports AirPlay, which makes it possible to receive data from iTunes to play music on compatible stereo speakers.

OS X includes AirPort Utility, which enables you to configure an AirPort device for networking. This part of the chapter explains how to configure two kinds of AirPort base stations: a Time Capsule and an AirPort Express. It explains how to get started with AirPort base station manual settings. And finally, it tells you how to connect to an AirPort network with a Mac.

TIP An AirPort network can include multiple base stations and computers.

TIP You can learn more about AirPort devices and networking on Apple's Website at www.apple.com/wifi/.

TIP It's not possible to show every single combination of configuration options. Instead, I've done my best to show the configuration options you're most likely to use for your setup.

TIP If you're not sure how to set an option in an AirPort Utility configuration screen, consult your ISP.

TIP If a firmware update for your base station is available, a dialog or notification in the AirPort Utility window may appear to tell you. Follow onscreen instructions to install any updates that are available.

TIP The base station and network passwords you're prompted for when setting up a base station are for different things. The base station password controls access to the device's configuration. The network password controls access to the network by wireless users.

TIP If you are the only user of your AirPort network, it's OK to have the same password for the network as the base station. But if multiple users will be using the network, you should assign a different password to the base station to prevent other users from changing base station settings.

A The AirPort Utility application icon can be found in the Utilities folder.

AirPort Utility

B In this example, AirPort utility found three devices: an AirPort Express, an old AirPort Extreme, and a Time Capsule (selected). (Yes, I admit that I never throw any computer equipment away.)

C Set Time Capsule name and security options.

To launch AirPort Utility:

Use one of the following techniques:

- Open the AirPort Utility icon **A** in the Utilities folder inside the Applications folder.

- In LaunchPad (page 140), click Other and then click AirPort Utility.

AirPort opens, scans for AirPort base stations within range, and displays what it finds **B**.

To create a Time Capsule network:

1. In AirPort Utility's main window, select the Time Capsule you want to configure **B** and click Continue.

2. If a dialog asking if you want to switch networks appears, click Switch.

3. AirPort Utility scans the Time Capsule for current settings and displays its first screen **C**. Set options.

   ▸ **Time Capsule Name** is the name you want to assign to the Time Capsule.

   ▸ **Time Capsule Password** and **Verify Password** is the same password for the Time Capsule, entered twice. You'll need this password to make changes to the Time Capsule configuration in the future.

   ▸ **Remember this password in my keychain** automatically creates a keychain item for the Time Capsule password.

   ▸ **Use a different password to secure disks** enables you to specify a different password to protect the data on disks inside and connected to the Time Capsule.

4. Click Continue.

continues on next page

5. The next screen 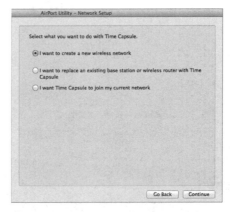 asks what you want to do:

- ▶ **I want to create a new wireless network** uses the Time Capsule to create a wireless network. Choose this option to continue following instructions here.

- ▶ **I want to replace an existing base station or wireless router with Time Capsule** enables you to swap out another wireless router with the Time Capsule.

- ▶ **I want Time Capsule to join my current network** adds the Time Capsule to an existing network, thus extending the network's reach and adding the devices connected to Time Capsule to the network.

6. Click Continue.

7. The next screen enables you to set network name and security options:

- ▶ **Wireless Network Name** is the name of the network. If you have multiple networks, you may want to give it a name related to its location or use.

- ▶ You have two security options: **WPA2 Personal** password-protects your network so no one can join it without a password. If you choose this option, enter a password of 8 to 63 characters in both boxes. **No security** leaves your network open so anyone can join it without a password.

8. Click Continue.

9. A screen offering to create a guest network appears next . This allows other people to use your Internet connection without being able to access the computers on the network. To enable this feature, turn on the check box, enter a name for the guest network, choose a

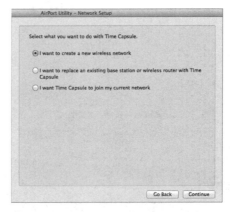

D Choose an option to proceed.

E Set network name and security options.

F You can set up a guest network.

G Indicate whether you use DHCP.

H If you want to set up Time Machine, say so.

security option, and if necessary, enter the same password in each Password box.

10. Click Continue.

11. In the next screen **G**, indicate whether you use DHCP.

- ▸ **I connect to the Internet with a DSL or cable modem using DHCP** uses the DHCP information you receive from your Internet connection to set IP addresses for the computers on your network.

- ▸ **I do not use DHCP** disables IP address sharing on your network.

12. Click Continue.

13. Next, you're asked if you want to set up Time Machine (page 115) to back up your computer **H**. If you choose yes, you'll be prompted as part of the setup to configure Time Machine (page 115).

14. Click Continue.

15. A summary of your settings appears **I**. Click Update.

16. A dialog warns you that the network will be temporarily unavailable. Click Continue.

The Time Capsule restarts. It may take a while. When it's finished, it appears in AirPort Utility's list of base stations with a green bullet beside it and the name you specified.

17. Click Quit.

I At the end of the process, AirPort Utility displays a summary of settings.

To create an AirPort Express network:

1. In AirPort Utility's main window, select the AirPort Express you want to configure and click Continue.

2. If a dialog asking if you want to switch networks appears, click Switch.

3. AirPort Utility scans the AirPort Express for current settings and displays its first settings screen ⓚ. Set options.

   ▸ **AirPort Express Name** is the name you want to assign to the AirPort Express.

   ▸ **AirPort Express Password** and **Verify Password** is the same password for the AirPort Express, entered twice. You'll need this password to make future changes to the configuration.

   ▸ **Remember this password in my keychain** automatically creates a keychain item (page 385) for the AirPort Express password.

4. Click Continue:

5. Next, select an option to proceed ⓛ:

   ▸ **I want to create a new wireless network** uses the AirPort Express to create a wireless network. Choose this option to continue following instructions here.

   ▸ **I want to replace an existing base station or wireless router with AirPort Express** enables you to swap out another wireless router with the AirPort Express.

   ▸ **I want AirPort Express to join my current network** adds the AirPort Express to an existing network, thus extending the network's reach and adding the devices connected to AirPort Express to the network.

ⓙ Select the AirPort Express you want to configure. In this example, the selected base station has never been configured.

ⓚ Use this screen to name your AirPort Express.

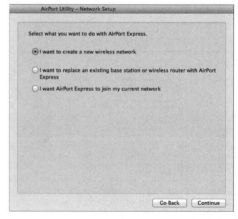

ⓛ Choose an option for setup.

M Enter a network name and set security options.

N Indicate DHCP use.

O AirPort Utility summarizes settings.

6. Click Continue.

7. Next, enter a name and set security options for the network **M**. There are three security options:

   ▸ **WPA2 Personal** is a security method that works with computers that support WPA2. Enter a password of 8 to 63 characters in both Password boxes.

   ▸ **128-bit WEP** is an older and less secure but more compatible security method. Enter a password of exactly 13 characters in both Password boxes.

   ▸ **No security** does not secure the network at all. Anyone within range can connect.

8. Click Continue.

9. In the next screen **N**, indicate how you use DHCP.

   ▸ **I connect to the Internet with a DSL or cable modem using DHCP** uses the DHCP information you receive from your Internet connection to set IP addresses for the computers on your network.

   ▸ **I do not use DHCP** disables IP address sharing on your network.

10. Click Continue.

11. A summary of your settings appears **O**. Click Update.

12. A dialog warns you that the network will be temporarily unavailable. Click Continue.

    The base station restarts. This might take a while. When it's finished, it appears in AirPort Utility's list of base stations with a green bullet beside it and the name you specified.

13. Click Quit.

To manually set AirPort base station options:

1. In AirPort Utility's main window, select the AirPort base station you want to configure **P** and click Manual Setup.

2. If necessary, enter the base station password when prompted.

3. The manual configurations window appears. It offers several categories of options, depending on the base station model you selected in Step 1 and the peripherals attached to it. Click a button in the toolbar at the top of the window to display and set options in a variety of panels:

   ▸ **AirPort** includes basic AirPort options, which include Summary **Q**, Time Capsule, Wireless, Guest Network, and Access Control.

   ▸ **Internet** displays Internet configuration options, which include Internet Connection **R**, TCP/IP, DHCP, and NAT.

   ▸ **Music** (not shown) displays options for enabling and configuring AirPlay.

   ▸ **Printers** **S** shows printers connected to the base station.

   ▸ **Disks** shows disks connected to the base station **T** and enables you to set file sharing options for AirPort Disks.

   ▸ **Advanced** includes a number of advanced networking options, such as Logging & Statistics **U**, Port Mapping, MobileMe, and IPv6.

4. Repeat step 3 for each screen of options you want to change.

5. Click update to save your changes to the base station and restart it.

P In this example, I've selected a Time Capsule.

Q The Summary pane of AirPort settings.

R The Internet Connection pane of Internet settings.

TIP The manual configuration options offered by AirPort Utility are advanced and powerful. Do not make changes to these options unless you know what you're doing, or you may inadvertently disable your network.

TIP Want more advanced information about setting up an AirPort network? Consult the Apple documentation that can be downloaded from support.apple.com/manuals/airport/.

S The Printers settings.

T The Disks pane of Disks settings.

U The Logging & Statistics pane of Advanced settings.

Using the Wi-Fi Status Menu

The Wi-Fi Status menu can be displayed at the right end of the menu bar. it indicates the status of your Wi-Fi connection:

- If the icon has one or more black arcs, you are connected to a network **A**.

- If the icon has gray arcs, Wi-Fi is turned on but you are not connected to a network.

- If the icon looks like an empty fan **B**, Wi-Fi is turned off.

The menu also has options for enabling or disabling your computer's AirPort connectivity, connecting to Wi-Fi networks, creating your own Wi-Fi network, and accessing networking preferences options.

This part of the chapter explores the options you'll likely use most.

TIP To use the Wi-Fi Status menu (A), it must be enabled. You can enable it in the Network preferences pane (page 548) when your AirPort interface is selected (page 397).

To enable or disable your computer's AirPort connectivity:

Do one of the following:

- To enable AirPort, choose Turn Wi-Fi On from the Wi-Fi Status menu **B**.

- To disable AirPort, choose Turn Wi-Fi Off from the Wi-Fi Status menu **A**.

TIP When your computer's AirPort connectivity is enabled, the command reads *Turn Wi-Fi Off* (A). When it is turned off, the command reads *Turn Wi-Fi On* (B).

A You can use the Wi-Fi Status menu to connect to a wireless network or perform other tasks.

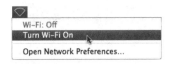

B If Wi-Fi is disabled, you can use the Turn Wi-Fi On command to enable it.

C Use this dialog to enter a password, if one is necessary to join the network.

D You can use a dialog like this one to connect to an unlisted network, provided you know its name and security settings.

To connect to a Wi-Fi network:

1. Choose the name of the network you want to connect to from the Wi-Fi Status menu **A**.

2. If the network requires a password, a dialog appears **C**. Enter the password and set other options as desired:

   ▸ **Password** is the network password. You must enter the correct password for the Join button to work.

   ▸ **Show password** displays the password as plain text characters instead of bullets so you can see what you're typing.

   ▸ **Remember this network** adds the network to the Network preferences pane so your computer can automatically connect to it in the future. It also adds the password to your keychain so you don't have to type it in every time you connect.

3. Click Join.

   The Wi-Fi menu's indicator displays black arcs to indicate you are connected to a network.

TIP An available network's signal strength and password requirement are indicated in the menu with black arcs to indicate signal strength and a padlock icon to indicate password is required **A**.

TIP If the network you want to join is not listed on the Wi-Fi Status menu, you can use the Join Other Network command to connect. Just enter the network name and security information in the dialog that appears when you choose this command **D** and click Join.

TIP If the base station has a dial-up connection to the Internet, a Connect command will also appear on this menu. Use this command to connect to the Internet.

Bluetooth

Bluetooth is a very short-range—30 feet or less—wireless networking technology. It enables you to connect Bluetooth-enabled computers, smart phones, and other mobile devices to each other. It also lets you connect Bluetooth-enabled input devices, such as a mouse or keyboard, to your Mac.

OS X includes two tools for working with Bluetooth:

- **Bluetooth preferences pane** (page 550) allows you to configure Bluetooth and pair Bluetooth devices with your computer.

- **Bluetooth File Exchange** enables you to send files from one Bluetooth device to another or browse files on another Bluetooth-enabled computer.

This part of the chapter explains how to configure and use Bluetooth to exchange files between two computers.

TIP You can learn more about Bluetooth technology at www.bluetooth.com.

TIP Don't confuse Bluetooth with AirPort (page 398). AirPort makes it possible for an AirPort-enabled computer to connect to and exchange information on an AirPort network. Bluetooth enables your computer to exchange information with a single Bluetooth-enabled device.

TIP Before you can use a Bluetooth connection to another device, your computer and the other device must be paired. You can learn how to pair devices on page 552.

A Bluetooth File Exchange makes it possible to send files from one computer to another via Bluetooth.

Bluetooth File Exchange

B The Bluetooth Status menu offers options for working with Bluetooth devices.

C Use this dialog to locate and select the file you want to send.

D Choose the receiving device from the list in this dialog.

To transfer a file from one computer to another via Bluetooth:

1. If necessary, do all the following:

   ▸ Enable Bluetooth (page 550).

   ▸ Enable Bluetooth sharing on the receiving computer (page 558).

   ▸ Set up Bluetooth pairing between your computer and the receiving computer (page 552).

2. Use one of the following techniques to open Bluetooth File Exchange:

   ▸ Double-click the Bluetooth File Exchange icon **A** in the Utilities folder inside the Applications folder.

   ▸ In LaunchPad (page 140), click Utilities and then click AirPort Utility.

   ▸ Choose Send File from the Bluetooth Status menu **B**.

3. Use the Select File to Send dialog that appears **C** to locate and select the file you want to send.

4. Click Send.

5. In the Bluetooth Devices list of the Send File dialog that appears **D**, select the computer you want to send the file to.

continues on next page

6. Click Send.

A dialog appears while your computer waits for the receiving computer to accept the file **E**.

7. On the receiving computer, click Accept in the Incoming File Transfer dialog **F**.

8. Wait while the file is transferred.

You'll see a progress dialog on the sending Mac **G**; one will also appear on the receiving computer.

When the file has been transferred, the receiving computer displays a dialog with information about it **H**.

TIP In step 3, you can select multiple files by holding down the Command key while clicking each one.

TIP In step 7, you can turn on the Accept all check box **F** to receive all files without giving you an opportunity to accept or decline.

TIP You can click the magnifying glass button in the Incoming File Transfer window **H** to open the folder where the file has been saved.

E Your Mac waits for the receiving device to accept the file.

F On the receiving device, click Accept.

G A progress bar appears to indicate transfer progress.

H On the receiving device, a dialog indicates that the file has been received.

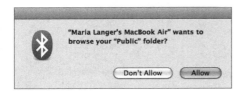

① Click Allow in this dialog to allow another computer to browse via Bluetooth.

① The contents of the device's Public folder appear in a window.

To browse another device via Bluetooth:

1. If necessary, do all the following:

   ▸ Enable Bluetooth (page 550).

   ▸ Enable Bluetooth sharing on the receiving computer (page 558).

   ▸ Set up Bluetooth pairing between your computer and the computer you want to browse (page 552).

2. Do one of the following:

   ▸ In Bluetooth File Exchange, choose File > Browse Device or press Shift-Command-O.

   ▸ Choose Browse Device from the Bluetooth Status menu **B**.

3. In the Browse Device dialog (which looks a lot like the Send File dialog **D**), select the computer you want to browse.

4. Click Browse.

   On your computer, an empty window named for the device appears.

5. On the computer you want to browse, a dialog asks if your computer can browse its Public folder **①**. Click Allow.

   On your computer, the device window fills with the contents of the other computer's Public folder **①**.

6. Use standard Finder techniques to navigate and copy files between your computer and the other computer.

7. When you are finished working with the device window, click its close button to dismiss it and stop browsing.

To use the Bluetooth Status menu:

Choose commands on the Bluetooth Status menu to perform the following tasks:

- **Turn Bluetooth Off** disables Bluetooth on your computer.

- **Send File** launches Bluetooth File Exchange so you can send a file to a Bluetooth device, as explained on page 409.

- **Browse Device** launches Bluetooth File Exchange so you can add another Bluetooth device, as discussed on page 411.

- *Device Name* displays a submenu for the device with options that are appropriate for the device **K**.

- **Set up Bluetooth Device** launches the Bluetooth Setup Assistant, so you can set up a Bluetooth device (page 552).

- **Open Bluetooth Preferences** opens the Bluetooth preferences pane (page 550).

TIP The Bluetooth Status menu can be displayed from within the Bluetooth preferences pane (page 550).

K The Bluetooth Status menu offers options for each Bluetooth device paired with your Mac.

A In this example, the Ethernet connection consists of a cable connected from one Mac to another.

Ethernet

Despite the rush to connect without wires, Ethernet is still a familiar and widely used networking option, especially in business environments and in places where network administrators see Wi-Fi as a security challenge.

A simple Ethernet connection involves stringing an Ethernet cable between the Ethernet port—which looks like a big fat telephone port—on two computers **A**. A more complex setup involves hubs and routers.

Once a Mac is connected to an Ethernet network, it knows it and takes advantage of all that network has to offer, including Internet sharing (page 557) and printer sharing (page 556), if available. So, for example, if you have access to the Internet via Wi-Fi on one computer but not the other, you can connect the two computers with an Ethernet cable and share the Internet connection over that cable.

TIP Not all Macs have an Ethernet port. If your computer doesn't have an Ethernet port and you need one, you can buy an Apple USB Ethernet Adapter from the Apple Store.

TIP Apple's AirPort Extreme and Time Capsule base stations, which are discussed on page 398, offer three Ethernet ports for connecting computers and other devices that do not have wireless capabilities.

TIP A discussion of Ethernet hubs and routers is far beyond the scope of this book.

FireWire

Although FireWire can be used to connect two computers for networking, it isn't often used that way. Instead, it's more often used to exchange information between two Macs when transferring configuration information as part of an OS X installation or to use one computer's hard disk in target disk mode. And, of course, it's most often used to connect peripheral devices, including hard disks and digital video cameras.

There's not much to say about connecting two computers for networking via FireWire. It's pretty straightforward. Just connect a FireWire cable to each computer's FireWire port. Your Mac will use the FireWire cable to make a connection **Ⓐ**.

TIP Not all Macs have FireWire ports.

TIP If you want to share an Internet connection over FireWire, be sure to set up Internet sharing (page 557).

TIP Using a FireWire connection to transfer configuration information or to set up a disk in target disk mode is beyond the scope of this book. If you need to use either of these features, you can learn more on Apple's website.

Ⓐ In this example, I've connected two computers with a FireWire cable.

Users, Groups & Privileges

Network file sharing access is determined by the users and groups set up for the computer, as well as the privileges settings for each file or its enclosing folder.

Before you start setting up file sharing on your computer, it's a good idea to know a little bit about how this works.

TIP The concept of users, groups, and privileges is also referred to as *permissions*.

Users & Groups

Each person who connects to a computer (other than with Guest access) is considered a *user*. Each user has his own user name or ID and a password.

User names are set up by the computer's system administrator, using the Users & Groups preferences pane (page 560). The password is also assigned by the system administrator, but in most cases, it can be changed by the user in the Users & Groups preferences pane when logged in to his account. This enhances security.

Each user can belong to one or more *groups*. A group is one or more users who have the same privileges. Some groups are set up automatically by OS X when you install it. A system administrator can also add groups with the Users & Groups preferences pane.

Privileges

Each file or folder can be assigned a set of privileges. Privileges determine who has access to a file and how it can be accessed.

There are four possible privileges settings:

- **Read & Write** privileges allow the user to open and save files.

- **Read only** privileges allow the user to open files but not save files.

- **Write only** (Drop Box) privileges allow the user to save files but not open them.

- **No Access** means the user can neither open nor save files.

Privileges can be set for three categories of users:

- **Owner** is the user or group who can access and set access privileges for the item. In OS X, the owner can be you (if it's your computer and you set it up), system, or admin.

- **Group** is a group that has access to the item.

- **Everyone** is everyone else on the network, including users logged in as Guest.

TIP You can check or set an item's privileges in the Sharing & Permissions area of the Info window for the item **A** **B** **C**.

A **B** **C** Privileges settings in the Info window for the Applications folder (top), Public folder (middle), and a document (bottom).

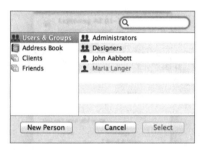

D You may have to enter an administrator's name and password in a dialog like this to make changes to an item's permissions.

E Use this dialog to add a specific user or group to the Permissions list.

F Choose an option from the pop-up menu beside the user or group.

G You can use the action pop-up menu to apply your changes to all items within a folder.

To set an item's permissions:

1. Select the icon for the item you want to change permissions for.

2. Choose File > Get Info or press Command-I to display the Info window.

3. If necessary, click the triangle beside Sharing & Permissions to display permissions information **A** **B** **C**.

4. If the padlock icon at the bottom of the window indicates that settings are locked, click it. Then enter an administrator name and password in the dialog that appears **D** and click OK.

5. To add specific user or group privileges, click the + button under the Name column. Then use the dialog that appears **E** to select an existing account from Users & Groups or your Contacts database. Or click the New Person button to add a new user account on the fly. When you click Select, the additional user is added to the Name list.

6. To set permissions for a user or group, choose an option from the pop-up menu that appears beside its name **F**.

7. If the item is a folder, you can choose Apply to enclosed items from the Action pop-up menu at the bottom of the window **G** to apply the settings to all folders within it.

8. Close the window to save your changes.

TIP You cannot change privileges for an item if you are not the owner **A** unless you have an administrator password.

TIP The Write only (Drop Box) privilege is only available for folders and disks.

Connecting for File Sharing

Once your computer is connected to a network, as discussed earlier in this chapter, and set up for file sharing, as discussed on page 555, you can connect to another computer and access its files. OS X offers two ways to do this:

- The Go menu's Connect to Server command **A** prompts you to enter the address of the server you want to connect to. You enter a user name and password to connect, choose the volume you want to access, and display its contents in Finder windows.

- The network browser enables you to browse the computers on the network—from the Finder **B** and from within Open and Save dialogs. You open an alias for another computer and you're prompted for a user name and password. Enter login information, choose a volume, and work with the files just as if they were on your computer.

The main difference between these two methods is that the Connect to Server command makes it possible to connect to servers that are not listed in the network browser.

The next few pages provide instructions for connecting to other computers using both methods, along with some tips for speeding up the process in the future.

TIP OS X's networking features refer to network-accessible computers as *servers*.

TIP To mount a server volume, you must have access as a user or guest (page 415).

A The Go menu.

B In this example, the Network Browser "sees" a Windows PC, an iMac, a MacBook Pro, and a remote Time Capsule.

Click to log in with a user account

C When you connect to a server as a guest, you have limited access to files.

D To connect to the server as a registered user, provide a user name and password.

E Once you connect as a registered user, you have access to whatever files and folders that user account can access.

To use the network browser:

1. Choose Go > Network **A**, or press Shift-Command-K.

   The Network window opens, displaying the servers you have access to **B**.

2. Do one of the following:

   ▶ To connect to a server as a guest, double-click its icon or click its name in the sidebar. Folders that guests have access to appear in the server's window **C**. Use these folders as you would any other Finder item. Skip the remaining steps.

   ▶ To connect to a server with a registered user account, select the server's name in the sidebar. Then click Connect As in the connection bar near the top of the window **C**.

3. In the Login dialog that appears **D**, select Registered User, enter a user name and password that is recognized by the server, and click Connect.

4. Folder icons for the available volumes appear in the window **E**. Use these folders as you would any other Finder item.

TIP If guest access is disabled, you will not be able to connect as a guest, or, if you can connect, you will not have access to any items.

TIP When you are connected to a server using a registered user account and have accessed a volume, an eject button appears beside the server name in the sidebar **E**. Click the button to disconnect from the server.

TIP In step 3, turning on the Remember this password in my keychain check box enables you to connect in the future without entering your password.

To use the Connect to Server command:

1. In the Finder, choose Go > Connect to Server **A**, or press Command-K.

2. In the Connect to Server dialog that appears **F**, enter the network address of the server you want to connect to and click Connect.

3. In the Login dialog that appears **D**, select Registered User, enter a user name and password that is recognized by the server, and click Connect.

4. In the dialog that appears **G**, select the volume(s) you want to mount and click OK.

   The name of the server appears in the Shared area of the sidebar with an eject button beside it. You can open the volume you selected like any other disk to work with its contents.

TIP You can specify a server address by IP or server name. This information appears in the Sharing preferences pane (page 553) when File Sharing is enabled and selected.

TIP After step 2, you can click the + button to add the server address to the Favorite Servers list in the Connect to Server dialog **F**. You can then access a favorite server by double-clicking its address in the list.

TIP In step 2, to open a recently opened server, choose its address from the Recent Servers pop-up menu **H**.

F Enter the server address in this dialog and click Connect.

G Choose the volume you want to open.

H Your Mac remembers recently opened servers.

I Use this dialog to change your password on the server.

To change your password on the server:

1. Follow the steps on page 419 or 420 to display a login window **D**.

2. Select the Registered User option and enter your user name in the Name box.

3. Click the Change Password button.

4. In the password dialog that appears **I**, enter your current password in the Old Password box and your new password in the New Password and Verify boxes.

5. Click Change Password.

    Your password is changed and you are connected to the server.

TIP It's a good idea to change all of your passwords occasionally, just to enhance security.

AirDrop

AirDrop is a feature of OS X that makes it easy to share files with other OS X Lion and Mountain Lion users. There's no complex configurations, no pairing devices or logging in to servers. Just start AirDrop, identify the icon of the computer you want to share with, and drag the file you want to share onto it. When the recipient accepts the file, it's transferred.

TIP AirDrop works within Wi-Fi range—that is, the range your computer can pick up a Wi-Fi connection.

To open AirDrop:

In the Finder, use one of the following techniques:

- In the sidebar, click AirDrop **A**.

- Choose Go > AirDrop **B**, or press Shift-Command-R.

Three things happen:

- The AirDrop icon in the sidebar changes from a parachute to a sweeping radar scope **A** to indicate that it's working.

- Your computer begins broadcasting that it is available to share files via AirDrop.

- Your computer looks for other computers with AirDrop open and displays their icons in the AirDrop window **C**.

TIP If AirDrop does not appear in the sidebar, you can add it. I explain how on page 466.

AirDrop icon

A Starting AirDrop is as easy as opening its Finder window. In this example, John has opened AirDrop on his MacBook Air.

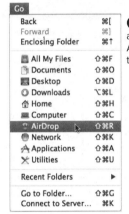

B You could also choose AirDrop from the Go menu.

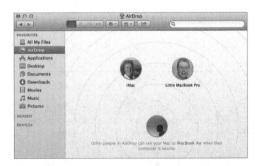

C AirDrop displays icons for the AirDrop computers it finds. In this example, AirDrop has found my iMac and Miraz's Little MacBook Pro.

D Drag a file from a Finder window onto the icon for the computer you want to send it to. In this example, John is using AirDrop to send me a file.

E A pop-up dialog confirms that you really do want to send the file. In this example, it's asking John if he really wants to send me the file.

F On the recipient's computer a pop-up dialog asks whether the file should be received. In this example, I can see that the file is coming from John and click a button to determine what to do with it.

To share a file with AirDrop:

1. With AirDrop open **C**, identify the icon of the computer you want to share a file with.

2. Drag a file from a Finder window onto the icon of the computer you want to share with **D**.

3. A pop-up dialog asks if you're sure you want to send the file **E**. Click Send.

4. On the recipient's computer a pop-up dialog announces that your computer wants to send a file **F**. Click one of three buttons:
   ▸ **Save and Open** accepts the file and immediately opens it.
   ▸ **Decline** refuses to accept the file.
   ▸ **Save** accepts the file and saves it to the Downloads folder without opening it.

5. If the recipient accepts the file, it is transferred from your computer to his.

TIP This shouldn't need saying, but just in case: don't accept files from people you don't know.

TIP I think one of my favorite fun features of OS X is AirDrop's animation of a file being saved to the Downloads folder.

To close AirDrop:

Do one of the following:

- Close the AirDrop window.
- Select any other item in the sidebar.

AirDrop stops broadcasting and makes your computer invisible to other AirDrop users.

Using a Remote Disc

If your Mac doesn't have an optical drive—for example, a MacBook Air—you can use DVD or CD Sharing (page 520) to utilize the optical drive on another computer on your network.

To access an optical disc on another computer:

1. In the Finder, use one of the following techniques:

   ▸ Select Remote Disc in the sidebar **A**.

   ▸ Choose Go > Computer, or press Shift-Command-C. In the computer window that appears **B**, double-click Remote Disc.

   Computers configured to share their optical drives appear in the window.

2. Double-click the icon for the computer with the optical drive you want to access.

3. If the other computer is set up to require permission before access, click the Ask to use button in the network browser window **C**. A dialog on the other computer appears, asking for permission **D**. Click Accept.

4. If a disc is inserted in the other computer's optical drive, it appears in the window **E**. Access it as if it were attached directly to your computer.

TIP DVD or CD Sharing must be enabled and configured in the Sharing preferences pane (page 553) of the computer with the optical drive for this to work.

A The Remote Disc window displays computers set up to share their optical drive.

B You can open the Remote Disc window from the Computer window.

Click to ask permission

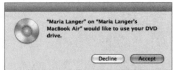

C You may have to ask permission to access another computer's optical drive.

D This dialog appears on the other computer.

E The inserted CD or DVD appears in the window.

A You can find Network Utility in the Utilities folder inside your Applications folder.

Network Utility

B Use the Info pane to get information about a network interface.

C Use the Netstat pane to get network performance statistics.

D Use the Ping pane to "ping" another computer on the network or Internet.

Network Utility

Network Utility **A**, which can be found in the Utilities folder in your Applications folder, is an information-gathering tool to help you learn more about and trouble-shoot a network. Its features are available in eight screens:

- **Info B** provides general information about the network interfaces.

- **Netstat C** enables you to review network performance statistics.

- **Ping D** tests your computer's access to specific domains or IP addresses.

- **Lookup E** uses a domain name server to convert between IP addresses and domain names.

- **Traceroute F** traces the route from your computer to another IP address or domain.

- **Whois G** uses a whois server to get information about the owner and IP address of a specific domain name.

- **Finger H** gets information about a person based on his email address.

- **Port Scan I** scans a specific IP address for active ports.

TIP The tools within Network Utility are used primarily for troubleshooting network problems and getting information about specific users or systems.

TIP Many of these utilities are designed to work with the Internet and require Internet access.

TIP In this day and age of increased privacy and security, you'll find that Finger **H** and Port Scan **I** are seldom successful in getting information about a person or server.

To use Network Utility:

1. Use one of the following techniques to open Network Utility:

   ▸ Open the Network Utility icon **A** in the Utilities folder inside the Applications folder.

   ▸ In LaunchPad (page 140), click Utilities and then click Network Utility.

2. Click the button for the utility you want to use **B** **C** **D** **E** **F** **G** **H** **I**.

3. Enter the domain name, IP address, or email address you want to check.

4. Click the button to start the scan process. (The name of the button varies from one utility to another.)

   The results appear at the bottom of the Network Utility window.

G Use the Whois pane to look up information about a domain name.

I Use the Port Scan pane to check for active ports on an IP address or domain.

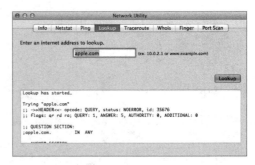

E Use the Lookup pane to get the IP address for a specific domain name.

F Use the Traceroute pane to trace the routing between your computer and another IP address.

H You can try to use Finger to look up information about a person based on his email address.

Connecting to the Internet

The Internet is a vast, worldwide network of computers that offers information, communication, online shopping, and entertainment for the whole family.

Although accessing the Internet was once just a small part of what your computer could do, these days it's pretty much assumed that your computer has access to the Internet. Indeed, when you use the OS X Setup Assistant (page 9) after installing OS X Mountain Lion or buying a new computer, one of the first things you're prompted for is your Internet connection method. Not only does OS X use your connection to check for software updates (page 583), but it also uses the Internet to provide expanded help information (page 69), update your system clock (page 579), and enable you to shop for applications (Chapter 13).

This chapter provides some basic information about the Internet and explains how you can use the Network Setup Assistant and Network Diagnostic tools to set up and troubleshoot a connection.

In This Chapter:

Internet Connection Methods

Internet connections are provided by *Internet Service Providers*, or *ISPs*, for a fee. It works much like the phone company—in fact, your ISP might even be the local phone company.

Your computer uses *TCP/IP* to connect to the Internet. TCP/IP is a standard Internet protocol, or set of rules, for exchanging information.

There are two main ways to connect. Each method uses one of your computer's network interfaces (page 396). Each has its own pros and cons.

Direct, or Network, Connection

In a *direct*, or *network*, connection, your computer has a live, high-speed broadband connection to the Internet all the time. This is common for workplace computers on companywide networks. At home, cable modems and DSL offer direct connections.

The connection is made possible by physical cables that connect your home or office to the ISP's servers. In some cases, an Ethernet cable directly connects your computer to the ISP's equipment. In other cases, there's a router between the ISP's equipment and your computer. That router could connect multiple computers at your location via Ethernet cables or Wi-Fi network.

These days direct connections are most popular, primarily because they're fast, convenient, and affordable.

Modem, or Dial-up, Connection

In a *modem* (page 396), or *dial-up*, connection, your computer uses a modem to dial in to a server, which gives it access to the Internet. This functionality is also available to some cell phone users utilizing *tethering* or *dial-up networking* (*DUN*). Mobile Wi-Fi *hotspots* created with a smartphone connection to an ISP make it seem, to the computer, as if it's accessing any other Wi-Fi network.

Although once the *only* way for an average user to connect to the Internet, modem connections are rare these days. That's a good thing because they're generally slow, require a phone line, and are not very convenient. Modems, which were standard equipment in many Macintosh models for years, are increasingly difficult to find.

Mobile hotspots, however, are gaining popularity among laptop users who need to be assured of an Internet connection when they're on the go. This service is available for many smartphone models—including iOS devices such as iPhones and iPads—as well as stand-alone mobile hotspot devices such as a Novatel MiFi. To your computer, a mobile hotspot connection looks like any other Wi-Fi hotspot.

No matter how your dial-up connection to the Internet works, access speed will generally be slower than direct connections. These connections must be established or enabled to be used.

TIP You can check or change settings for your Internet connection in the Network preferences pane (page 548).

TIP Mobile Wi-Fi hotspot and DUN service and setup vary based on wireless carrier and service offered. A complete discussion of mobile hotspots and DUN is beyond the scope of this book.

Network Setup
& Diagnostics

OS X includes two tools to help you set up network connections and diagnose problems with existing connections:

- The **Network Setup Assistant** steps you through the process of setting up an Internet connection using a Wi-Fi network, telephone modem, DSL modem, cable modem, or local area network with Ethernet connection. It automatically sets options in the Network preferences pane (page 548) for your connection.

- **Network Diagnostics** checks each part of your Internet connection to determine where a problem might be. It then provides you with tips for resolving the problem.

This part of the chapter introduces the Network Setup Assistant and Network Diagnostics so you can use them to set up or troubleshoot your Internet connection.

TIP If you set up your Internet connection when you configured your computer for OS X (page 9), your computer should be ready to connect to the Internet and you can skip this part of the chapter. But if you didn't set up your connection or if your Internet connection method has changed since setup, the Network Setup Assistant is a good way to configure your computer to connect to the Internet.

TIP The Network Setup Assistant groups all settings for a connection as a *location* . If your computer has more than one way to connect to the Internet, you can create a location for each method.

To use the Network Setup Assistant:

1. Choose Apple > System Preferences or click the System Preferences icon in the Dock.

2. In the System Preferences window that appears, click the Network icon.

   Network preferences appears, displaying network status and connection information for one of your network interfaces .

3. Click the Assist me button at the bottom of the window.

4. In the dialog that appears **B**, click the Assistant button.

   The Introduction screen of the Network Setup Assistant appears **C**.

5. Enter a name for the connection in the Location Name box and click Continue.

6. In the How Do You Connect to the Internet? screen that appears next **D**, select the method you use and click Continue.

7. Follow the remaining prompts to enter information about your connection.

8. At the last screen, click Done.

TIP Before you use the Network Setup Assistant to configure your computer for an Internet connection, make sure you have all the information you need to properly configure the options. You can get all of the information you need from your ISP or network administrator.

TIP In step 6, only the connections that are available for your computer can be selected. The others will be gray.

A The Network preferences pane.

B Click Assistant in this dialog.

C Start by entering a name for the configuration.

D Select the way you connect.

E F Two examples of Network Diagnostics in action. The top image shows a perfectly functioning Internet connection while the bottom one shows a connection with some problems.

To use Network Diagnostics:

1. Choose Apple > System Preferences or click the System Preferences icon in the Dock.

2. In the System Preferences window that appears, click the Network icon.

   Network preferences appears, displaying network status and connection information for one of your network interfaces **A**.

3. Click the Assist me button at the bottom of the window.

4. In the dialog that appears **B**, click the Diagnostics button.

   The Network Diagnostics window appears. Your Mac checks the selected configuration and reports its status in the left side of the window **E F**.

5. If you have more than one configuration set up, select the name of the location in the list.

6. Click Continue.

7. Follow the instructions that appear in the window to troubleshoot and repair any problems found.

TIP In many cases, you can fix an Internet connection problem by restarting your computer or shutting down and then powering up your router. In fact, that's one of the suggestions Network Diagnostics often makes.

Using Wi-Fi Hotspots

When you're on the go with your laptop, you'll likely rely on Wi-Fi hotspots available in hotels, airports, and coffee shops to connect to the Internet. You connect to these hotspots by choosing the one you want from the Wi-Fi menu on the menu bar **Ⓐ**, as discussed on page 406.

Here are a few things to keep in mind when connecting to public Wi-Fi networks.

- Networks with padlock icons beside their names are password protected. You'll need a password to connect.

- It's possible to connect to a network and still be required to provide a password or agree to some terms of service. In most cases, a window will appear to prompt you for information **Ⓑ**.

- The fan icon beside each network name indicates signal strength. Whenever possible, try to connect to a network with at least two black curved bars.

- Some public networks require that you pay a fee to access them. Before entering any credit card information into a form on a public network, make sure the form is legitimate and secure.

For safety's sake, remember the following:

- Many public networks are not secure. When you connect to an unsecured network, you run the risk of your data being accessed by others.

- It's important to disable or limit guest network access for file sharing before joining a public network.

- Networks listed under Devices are not regular Wi-Fi networks. Instead, they might connect you directly to someone else's computer, possibly for reasons not in your best interest.

Ⓐ Choose a network from the Wi-Fi menu.

Ⓑ Some networks allow you to connect but then prompt you for login information or credit card information to pay for access.

Internet Applications

OS X includes four applications for interacting with the Internet:

- **Mail** enables you to exchange email messages, create to-do lists, and subscribe to RSS feeds.

- **Messages** (formerly iChat) enables you to exchange instant messages and conduct audio or video conferences with OS X, iOS, AIM, Google Talk, Jabber, and Yahoo! users.

- **FaceTime** enables you to conduct video phone calls with OS X Lion and Mountain Lion users, as well as some iPhone and iPad users.

- **Safari** enables you to browse websites, download files from FTP sites, and save Web pages to read later.

This chapter provides brief instructions for using these tools—just enough to get you started. You can explore the other features on your own.

Mail

A Mail's application icon.

Mail **A** is an email client application. It enables you to send and receive email messages using Internet email accounts.

Here's how it works. Imagine having a mailbox at the post office. As mail comes in, the postmaster sorts it into the boxes—including yours. To get your mail, you need to go to the post office to pick it up. While you're there, you're likely to drop off any letters you need to send.

Email works the same way. Your email is delivered to your email server—like the post office where your mailbox is. The server software (like the postmaster) sorts the mail into mailboxes. When your email client software (Mail, in this case) connects to the server via the Internet, it picks up your incoming mail and sends any outgoing messages it has to send.

If you provided an Apple ID with an iCloud email address when you set up OS X or if you used the Mail, Contacts & Calendars preferences pane (page 546) to set up other email accounts, that information is automatically stored in Mail so it's ready to use. Just open Mail and it automatically makes that virtual trip to the post office to get and send messages.

In this part of the chapter, I explain how to set up an email account with Mail. I also explain how to compose, send, read, and retrieve email messages.

TIP Mail's interface is remarkably similar to the Mail app in iOS devices. It also supports OS X's Full-Screen apps feature (page 142).

B The Welcome to Mail window appears if you do not have any email accounts set up.

C Mail's Message Viewer window lists messages on the left and the contents of a selected message on the right.

D The first screen of the Add Account window looks a lot like the Welcome to Mail window **B**.

To open Mail:

Use one of the following techniques:

- Open the Mail application icon **A** in the Applications folder.

- Click the Mail icon in the Dock.

- Click the Mail icon in Launchpad.

One of two things happens:

- If Mail has not yet been set up with at least one email account, the Welcome window appears **B**.

- If Mail has already been set up with at least one email account, the Message Viewer window opens **C** and Mail checks for new mail (if your computer is connected to the Internet).

To set up an email account:

1. If necessary, choose File > Add Account to display the first screen of the Add Account window **D**.

2. Enter basic information for the account:

   ▸ **Full Name** is your full name.

   ▸ **Email Address** is your email address.

   ▸ **Password** is your email account password.

3. Click Continue.

4. Your next step depends on the kind of account you're creating:

   ▸ If you're creating an iCloud, Google, or Yahoo! account, skip ahead to step 6.

   ▸ If you're creating an account with a different ISP, continue following the remaining steps.

continues on next page

5. In the Incoming Mail Server dialog ,
enter information for your incoming mail
server and click Continue.

- ▶ **Account Type** is the type of account.
  Your options are POP, IMAP,
  Exchange, and Exchange IMAP.

- ▶ **Description** is an optional description
  for the account.

- ▶ **Incoming Mail Server** is the domain
  name or IP address of your incoming
  mail server.

- ▶ **User Name** is your user ID on the
  mail server.

- ▶ **Password** is your password on the
  mail server.

6. In the Outgoing Mail Server dialog ,
enter information for your outgoing mail
server and click Continue.

- ▶ **Description** is an optional description
  for the server.

- ▶ **Outgoing Mail Server** is the domain
  name or IP address of your outgoing
  mail server. You can choose a server
  from the drop-down list or enter information for a different server. If you
  turn on the Use only this server check
  box, the server you enter or select is
  the only one that can be used with
  the account.

- ▶ **Use Authentication** tells Mail to send
  your user name and password when
  sending mail. This is required by most
  mail servers. If you turn on this check
  box, be sure to enter your account
  user name and password in the boxes
  below it.

7. When Mail has verified all information
you entered, it displays the results in an
Account Summary window: **G H**:

Ⓔ Enter incoming mail server settings in this
window.

Ⓕ Enter information about your outgoing server in
this window.

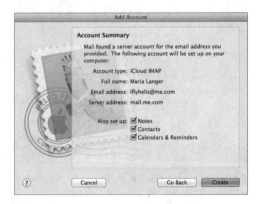

Ⓖ For some types of email accounts, such as
iCloud accounts, all Mail needs is the email
address and password.

H Mail summarizes the information you entered.

I If Mail can't verify your server, it displays a dialog like this.

▸ If you're creating an iCloud **G**, Gmail, or Yahoo! account, toggle check boxes to specify whether you also want to set up Notes (page XX), Contacts (Chapter 20), Calendars (Chapter 21), and Reminders (page XX).

▸ If you're creating an account for another ISP **H**, check the accuracy of the information in the dialog.

8. Make sure the Take account online check box is turned on.

9. Click Create.

The new account is added to Mail's Accounts list, Mail switches to that account's inbox, and Mail checks for and displays mail for that account.

TIP You can also set up an email account by adding an account to the Mail, Contacts & Calendars preferences pane (page 546).

TIP Your ISP or network administrator can provide all of the important information you need to set up an email account, including the account name, password, and mail servers.

TIP In step 5, additional options might appear for Exchange and Exchange IMAP accounts; click the Help button in the dialog to learn more about these options.

TIP If Mail can't verify the identity of a mail server, it may display a dialog **I**. You have several choices to proceed: Show Certificate displays the certificate and additional information for the server. Cancel aborts the attempt to connect with the server. Connect connects with the server despite the problem.

TIP You cannot use the outgoing mail server for a MobileMe account to send email messages for an account with another ISP. The MobileMe outgoing mail server only works with MobileMe accounts. Outgoing or SMTP server information should be provided by your ISP.

To create & send a message:

1. Use one of the following techniques to open a New Message window :

   ▸ Click the Compose New Message button at the top of the Message Viewer window **C**.

   ▸ Choose File > New Message, or press Command-N.

2. Use one of the following techniques to enter the recipient's address in the To box:

   ▸ Type the recipient's email address.

   ▸ If the recipient is someone in your Contacts database (Chapter 20) or someone you have received an email message from in the past, enter the person's name. As you type, Mail attempts to match the name **K**. Click the correct entry.

3. Repeat step 2 to add additional names. When you are finished, press the Tab key twice.

4. Enter a subject for the message in the Subject field, and press Tab.

5. If you have more than one email address, choose the address you want to use to send the message from the From pop-up menu. For some types of accounts, you may also have to select an outgoing mail server from a menu that appears beside it.

6. Type your message in the large box at the bottom of the window **L**.

7. Use one of the following techniques to close the window and send the message:

   ▸ Click the Send Message button in the top-left corner of the window.

   ▸ Choose Message > Send, or press Shift-Command-D.

J A New Message window.

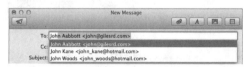

K When you start typing the name of someone in Contacts, Mail guesses which one you want.

L A very simple message might look like this.

M Use this dialog to locate and select a document to attach to the email message.

A multiple-page PDF attached to a message.

The Format bar has buttons you can use to format selected text in a message.

If you have iPhoto installed, you can use the Photo Browser to attach images to a message.

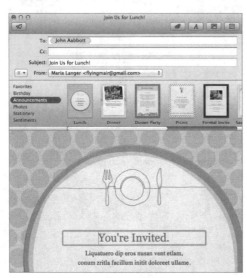

The Stationery Pane in action.

To enhance an outgoing message:

1. Follow steps 1 through 5 on the previous page to prepare a new mail message.

2. Click the toolbar button ⓙ for the task you want to perform:

   ▸ **Attach a Document to This Message** displays a standard Open dialog ⓜ. Locate and select a file you want to attach and then click Choose File. The file is attached ⓝ.

   ▸ **Show Format Bar** displays an additional row of buttons ⓞ that you can use to format selected text in the body of the message.

   ▸ **Show or Hide the Photo Browser** toggles the display of the Photo Browser window ⓟ, which you can use to select and attach iPhoto images to the message.

   ▸ **Show or Hide the Stationery Pane** toggles the display of stationery templates above the message form. Select a category in the left column and then click to select the stationery you want to use. The stationery's formatting fills the message body area ⓠ. Replace sample text and/ or images with your own content to complete the message.

   TIP Attached images and one-page PDFs appear as images in mail messages. Other types of files appear as icons ⓝ.

   TIP You can also attach a file by simply dragging its icon into the message window.

To retrieve email messages:

Click the Get New Messages in All Accounts button at the top of the Message Viewer window .

Mail accesses the Internet, connects to your email server, and downloads messages that are waiting for you. Incoming messages appear in the first column of the window with any Inbox selected .

TIP A blue bullet character appears beside each unread email message.

TIP Messages that Mail thinks are junk mail are colored brown. To set junk mail preferences, choose Mail > Preferences and click the Junk Mail button.

TIP Mail automatically creates a separate inbox for each email account. You can view a specific inbox by choosing its name from the Inbox menu in the Message Viewer window's toolbar .

To read a message:

1. On the left side of the Message Viewer window, click the message that you want to read.

   The message contents appear in the right side of the window .

2. Read the message.

TIP You can double-click a message to display it in its own message window .

TIP Mail's conversations feature displays multiple messages on the right side of the window when you select a conversation . To read an entire message, click the See More link at the bottom of the message.

TIP To save attachments, click the Details link at the top-right of the message to display additional information , including a Save menu for attachments. Choose a command from the menu to save one or all attachments.

R You can use this menu to view a specific inbox or click the Inbox button to view them all together.

S Double-clicking a message displays it in its own window.

T Mail's conversations feature displays all the messages with the same subject line.

U Click the Details link to display additional message header information and buttons for saving attachments and using Quick Look.

V You can use the Save menu to save all or just one of a message's attached files.

W In this example, I created a reply with just some of the original text quoted.

X In this example, I'm forwarding an entire message.

To reply to a message:

1. To quote only part of the message's original text in the reply, select the text you want to quote.

2. Click one of the Reply buttons at the top of the window:

   ▸ **Reply to Sender of Selected Message** addresses the reply to the person who sent you the message.

   ▸ **Reply to All Recipients of the Selected Message** addresses the reply to the person who sent you the message as well as everyone else who received it.

   A pre-addressed message window opens **W**. It includes the selected text or the entire message as a quote.

3. Type the text of your reply in the message body.

4. Click the Send Message button.

TIP Don't reply to all recipients of a message unless you really believe they all want or need to see your reply.

To forward a message:

1. To forward only part of the message's original text, select the text you want to forward.

2. Click the Forward Selected Messages button at the top of the window.

   A copy of the selected text or the entire message appears in a new message form **X**.

3. Enter the email address of the person you want to forward the message to in the To box.

4. If desired, enter a message at the top of the message body.

5. Click the Send Message button.

To add a message's sender to Contacts:

1. Select or open a message sent by the sender you want to add.

2. Click the From name at the top of the message window to display a menu of options .

3. Choose Add to Contacts.

   Mail adds the person's name and email address to your Contacts database.

4. If desired, open Contacts (Chapter 20) and add additional information for the record.

TIP As shown in , the menu offers other options you might find useful while working with email.

To create a Calendar event from an email message:

1. Display the email message with date or time information for the event you want to create.

2. Point to the date or time.

   A pop-up menu outline appears around the information 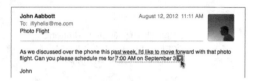.

3. Click the triangle to display the event as a Calendar item .

4. Click Add to Calendar to add the event to your Calendar database.

5. If necessary, open Calendar (Chapter 21) and modify the information to include the correct name, duration, calendar, and other settings.

TIP Creating an event like this automatically links it to the email message where you created it. You can click the Show in Mail link in the event's details in Calendar to quickly open the linked email message.

Clicking a sender's email address displays a handy menu.

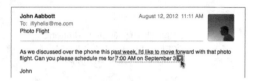

Point to a date or time (or date and time as shown here) to display the outline of a menu.

Click the menu button to see the event that Mail can create.

An event created from a Mail message is automatically linked to the message.

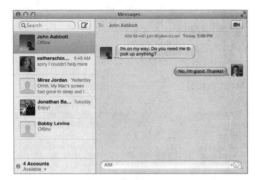

A Messages combines text messaging with iOS devices and chat with AIM, Yahoo!, Google Talk, and Jabber accounts.

TIP Messages replaces iChat, which offered much of the same functionality in previous versions of OS X.

TIP Messages is compatible with Notification Center (page 260). If notifications are set up for Messages, you'll be notified of incoming messages even if the Messages app isn't running on your Mac.

TIP To use Messages, you must have an Apple ID, AIM, Yahoo!, Google Talk, or Jabber account. To use the audio or video features, you must have a microphone (for audio only) or compatible video camera (for audio and video) and a fast Internet connection.

Messages

The Messages application **A** works as a centralized place for sending and receiving several types of instant messages:

- Use iMessage to exchange text messages with other OS X Mountain Lion and iOS 5 (or later) users using the Messages app.

- Participate in chats with other AIM, Yahoo!, Google Talk, and Jabber users.

To get started, configure Messages with your account information and the information for your buddies who use compatible chat networks. Then, while you're connected to the Internet with Messages running, Messages does three things:

- It listens for incoming iMessages from your friends and displays them in the Messages window.

- It tells the network(s) that you're available to receive instant messages and participate in chats.

- It tells you when your buddies are online and available to chat.

At any time, you can use Messages to send an iMessage to another OS X or iOS user. You can even start a conversation on your Mac and finish it later on your iPhone. In addition, when a chat buddy is available, you can send him an instant message to start a chat.

Messages includes audio and video conferencing features, including FaceTime integration for communicating with OS X and iOS users.

In this part of the chapter, I explain how to configure Messages for your account(s), set up a Messages Buddies window, and participate in chats.

To open Messages:

Use one of the following techniques:

- Open the Messages application icon in the Applications folder.

- Click the Messages icon in Launchpad.

- Click the Messages icon in the Dock.

One of two things happens:

- If your Apple ID has not yet been entered into OS X or Messages, the iMessage Setup window appears **C**. Follow the instructions in the section titled "To set up Messages for iMessages," which is next.

- If Messages has already been set up, the Messages window opens **A** and Messages checks to see which of your buddies is online.

To set up Messages for iMessages:

1. Open Messages.

2. In the iMessage Setup window **C**, enter your Apple ID and password in the appropriate boxes. Then click Sign In.

   Messages sends your Apple ID to Apple's iMessage server to identify you as a Messages user. The Messages window appears with a blank New Message form selected **D**.

> **TIP** In step 2, if you don't have an Apple ID, you can click the Create Apple ID button to create one.

> **TIP** In step 2, if you prefer not to use your Apple ID with Messages, you can click the Not Now button and then click Skip in the dialog that appears. You'll then be prompted to add an account with a compatible chat service. Consult the section titled "To add a chat account" on the next page for more information.

B The Messages application icon.

Messages

C If your Apple ID has not already been entered, the iMessage Setup window appears when you open Messages.

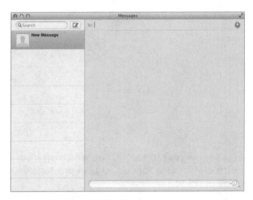

D When you set up messages with your Apple ID, it displays the Messages window with a blank New Message form, all ready for you to send someone a message.

E Accounts preferences lists all of your accounts, lets you set options for each one, and enables you to add new ones.

F Use this dialog to provide information for your chat account.

G If you're setting up a Jabber account, you can click the triangle beside Server Options to set additional options.

To add a chat account:

1. Choose Messages > Preferences, or press Command-, (comma) to display the Preferences window.

2. Click the Accounts button to display a list of your accounts **E**.

3. Click the + button at the bottom of the account list.

4. In the Account Setup dialog that appears **F**, enter account information into each field:

   ▸ **Account Type** is the type of account. Your options are AIM, Jabber, Google Talk, and Yahoo!

   ▸ **Username** or **Account Name** is your user name on that service.

   ▸ **Password** is your password on that service.

5. If you're setting up a Jabber account, you can click the disclosure triangle beside Server Options to display and set additional options for your account **G**. Consult your system administrator if you need assistance with these settings.

6. Click Done. The new account is added to the list of accounts **H**.

H A new chat account is added to the list.

To send an iMessage:

1. If the Messages window is not showing, choose Window > Messages, or press Command-0 (zero).

2. If a New Message item is not displayed, click the Compose New Message button beside the Search box on the upper-left side of the window.

3. Select the New Message item. The insertion point should appear in the To field on the right side of the window **D**.

4. Type the name of someone in your Contacts database who uses iMessage.

   As you begin to type, Messages matches the contact information and offers options **I**.

5. Select the name and contact method you want to send the message to.

   The name and contact info appears in the To box.

6. Type the text of your message in the box at the bottom of the window **J**.

7. Press Return.

   The message is sent and a chat transcript begins in the Messages window **K**.

8. Wait for your friend to reply.

   When your friend starts typing, an ellipsis appears in the chat window **L**. When the reply arrives, it appears in the chat transcript beneath your message **M**.

9. Repeat steps 6 through 8 to conduct your conversation.

TIP A chat transcript from a conversation with a friend is saved until you delete it—even if conducted over a period of days, weeks, or months.

I In this example, John wants to send an iMessage to me; his Contacts database tells him that there are all these valid ways to contact me.

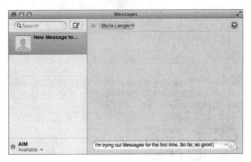

J Type a message at the bottom of the window.

K When you press Return, your message is sent.

L When your friend begins to type a reply, an ellipsis appears in the window.

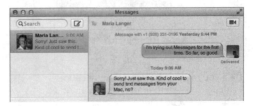

M The response appears in the window.

N The Buddies window lists all of your buddies and indicates whether they're online.

O Choose Add Buddy from this menu.

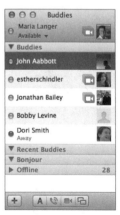

P Use this dialog to enter details about your buddy's chat account.

Q My new buddy, John, appears in my Buddies window.

To display the Buddies window:

Choose Window > Buddies, or press Command-1.

The Buddies window appears **N**.

> **TIP** A buddy's online status and audio or video capabilities is indicated in the Buddies window with a color-coded bullet and phone or camera icons **N**.

To add a buddy:

1. Choose Add Buddy from the + button menu at the bottom of the Buddies window **O**.

2. In the New Buddy dialog **P**, fill in the form with information about your buddy's account.

3. Click Add.

   The buddy is added to the Buddies window **Q**.

> **TIP** The Buddies window automatically includes contacts for which you have provided AIM information in Contacts, as well as buddies you may have added while using any previous version of Messages (or iChat).

> **TIP** Google Talk and Jabber buddies must authorize you as a buddy before their status appears in the Buddies window **N**.

To remove a buddy:

1. Select the name of the buddy you want to remove.

2. Press the Delete key.

3. Click Remove in the confirmation dialog that appears.

To conduct a text chat:

1. In the Buddies window **Q**, select the name of a buddy who is available for chatting.

2. Click the Start a Text Chat button at the bottom of the Buddies window **Q**.

   A new chat is added to the Messages window **R**.

3. Enter your message in the box at the bottom of the window.

4. Press Return.

   The message appears on the right side of the window **S**.

5. Wait for your friend to reply.

   When your friend starts typing, an ellipsis appears in the chat window. When the reply arrives, it appears in the chat transcript beneath your message **T**.

6. Repeat steps 3 through 5 to conduct your conversation.

TIP A chat transcript from a conversation with a friend is saved until you delete it—even if conducted over a period of days, weeks, or months.

To read & respond to a message:

1. When another iMessages user or chat buddy sends you a message, a blue bullet appears in the Messages window beside his name **U**. Click his name to view his message in the chat transcript.

2. Enter your response in the box at the bottom of the window.

3. Press Return.

   The message appears in the chat transcript on the right side of the window.

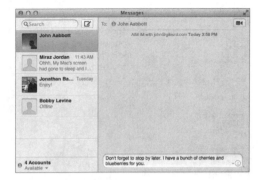

R With the name of the person you're chatting with selected, enter the text of your message in the box at the bottom of the Messages window.

S When you press return, the message is sent to your buddy.

T When your buddy replies, his message appears beneath yours in the Messages window.

U A blue bullet appears beside the name of any iMessage user or chat buddy who has sent you a message you haven't read yet.

V While waiting for your buddy to answer your call, the video chat window shows a preview of what your buddy will see.

W When the chat begins, you can see your buddy in the window with your image inset in a smaller box. (Coffee is king!)

To conduct a video chat:

1. In the Buddies window, select the name of a buddy who is available for video chatting.

2. Click the Start a Video Chat button at the bottom of the Buddies window.

   A video chat window appears **V**.

3. Wait until your buddy responds.

   When he accepts the chat, the window changes to show his live image, with yours in a small box **W**.

4. Talk!

TIP Audio chats work a lot like video chats—but without the picture.

TIP To conduct a video chat, both you and your buddy must have video capabilities. Look for a camera icon beside a buddy's name **N**.

TIP Video chats require sufficient bandwidth to work. If your connection—or your buddy's—to the Internet is too slow, an error message will appear.

TIP If the inset picture is blocking your view, you can move it to another position in the window. Just drag it.

TIP You can use the Effects button at the bottom of the window to apply a special effect like those in Photo Booth (page 230) to your image.

To respond to a video chat invitation:

1. When another Messages user invites you to a video chat, an invitation window appears and Messages makes a phone ringing sound. Click the window to display a Video Chat window .

2. Do one of the following:

   ▸ To accept the invitation, click Accept or press Return. Messages establishes a connection with the caller and the window changes to show his live image, with yours in a small box ❼. Start talking!

   ▸ To decline the invitation, click the Decline button or click the window's close button. The Video Chat window disappears.

   ▸ To respond with a text message, click Text Reply. Then use the Messages window to conduct a text chat with your buddy ❶.

❌ A video chat invitation looks like this.

❗ When you click it, the window expands to show a preview of what your buddy will see when you answer.

❼ Clicking Accept begins the video chat.

FaceTime

FaceTime is a video communications application that makes it possible to make video calls to OS X Lion and Mountain Lion users, as well as some iOS users.

What's cool about FaceTime is that it makes it possible to see, in real time, the person you're contacting. But this goes beyond simple video conversations. You can share whatever is within sight of your FaceTime camera and the person you're connecting to can do the same. So, for example, if you're having a FaceTime conversation with a friend who wants to show you his new car or a coworker who wants to show you a problem with a job out in the field, you can see and discuss it live.

To use FaceTime, you need the following:

- **Apple ID.** This is the same ID you might already use for iCloud, the App Store, or the iTunes Store. If you don't have an Apple ID, you can create one from within FaceTime.

- **Internet connection.** For best results, it should be fast.

- **Camera.** This can include a FaceTime camera built into your Mac, a video camera connected via FireWire, or a UVC-compliant video camera connected by USB.

- **Microphone.** This can include the microphone built into your computer, an external microphone connected to the audio input port, or a Bluetooth or USB headset.

- **Contacts.** FaceTime uses the Contacts database as its contact list.

This part of the chapter explains how to set up FaceTime, make a FaceTime call, and answer a FaceTime call.

To open FaceTime:

Use one of the following techniques:

- Open the FaceTime application icon in the Applications folder.

- Click the FaceTime icon in the Dock.

- Click the FaceTime icon in Launchpad.

FaceTime opens and displays its main screen. What appears on the right side of the screen depends on whether you are logged in to FaceTime and it is turned on:

- If you are not logged in to FaceTime, the Enter Apple ID pane appears **B**.

- If you are logged in to FaceTime but it has not been enabled, the Preferences pane appears with the slider set to Off **C**.

- If FaceTime has been enabled, either the Preferences pane appears with the slider set to On **D** or the Contacts pane appears **E**.

A The FaceTime application icon.

FaceTime

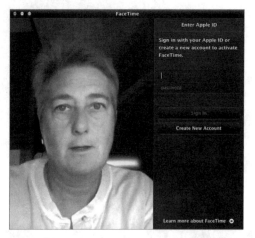

B When you start FaceTime for the first time, it may ask you to enter your Apple ID and password.

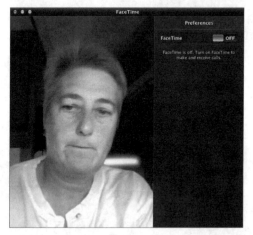

C The FaceTime window with FaceTime turned off.

D In this example, FaceTime is turned on and the Preferences pane is displayed.

E Here's the FaceTime window showing people in my Contacts database.

F If necessary, enter your preferred email address.

To log in and enable FaceTime:

1. If FaceTime's main window displays the login screen **B**, enter your Apple ID and password and click Sign In.

2. You may be asked which email address you want to use for people to call you **F**. If necessary, enter your preferred email address in the Address field and click Next.

3. FaceTime verifies your account, turns on, and displays the Contacts pane **E**.

TIP If FaceTime's main window displays the Preferences pane with the slider set to Off **C**, click the slider to turn it on and then click Done.

TIP If FaceTime's main window displays the Preferences pane with the slider set to On **D**, just click Done.

To make a FaceTime call:

1. If necessary, click the Contacts button at the bottom of the FaceTime window to display your contacts **E**.

2. Click the name of the contact you want to call to display his record details **G**.

3. Click the contact number or email address you want to call.

   FaceTime initiates the call. The window shrinks to show just a preview of what the contact will see, along with a status message at the top of the window **H**. When the contact answers the call, his face appears in the window and yours appears in an inset at the bottom of the window **I**.

4. Talk.

G Clicking a contact name displays his record details so you can choose the contact number or email address you want to use to place your FaceTime call.

H Wait while the call connects. (I don't look too uncertain here, do I?)

I When it connects, start talking!

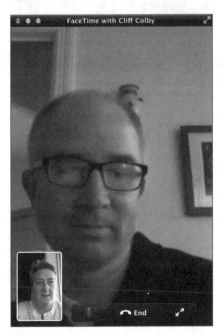

J An incoming FaceTime call looks like this.

K When you answer, the conversation can begin.

To answer a FaceTime call:

1. When another FaceTime user calls you, an invitation window appears **J** and FaceTime makes a phone ringing sound. Click the window to activate it.

2. Do one of the following:

   ▸ To accept the invitation, click Accept. FaceTime establishes a connection with the caller and the window changes to show his live image, with yours in a small box **K**. Start talking!

   ▸ To decline the invitation, click the Decline button or click the window's close button. The FaceTime window disappears.

To turn off FaceTime:

If you don't want to be bothered by incoming FaceTime calls, choose FaceTime > Turn FaceTime Off, or press Command-K.

FaceTime is disabled and the Preferences pane appears with the slider set to Off **C**.

Safari

Safari is a Web browser application. It enables you to view, or browse, pages on the World Wide Web.

A Web page is a window full of formatted text and graphics **A** **B**. You move from page to page by clicking text or graphic links or by opening *URLs* (*uniform resource locators*) for specific Web pages. These two methods of navigating the World Wide Web can open a whole universe of useful or interesting information.

To open Safari:

Use one of the following techniques:

- Open the Safari application icon **C** in the Applications folder.

- Click the Safari icon in the Dock.

- Click the Safari icon in Launchpad.

- Click a Web link in any email message, chat window, or document.

Safari opens. If you opened it by clicking a link, it displays the Web page for that link. Otherwise, it displays the default home page **A** or the page that was open when you last quit Safari.

TIP You can change the default home page by specifying a different page's URL in Safari's preferences. Choose Safari > Preferences and click the General button to get started.

To follow a link:

1. Position the mouse pointer on a text or graphic link. The mouse pointer turns into a pointing finger **A**.

2. Click.

   Safari loads and displays the location for the link you clicked **B**.

A The default home page is Apple's Start page.

B Clicking a link displays the page it links to.

C The Safari application icon.

D As you type a URL, Safari tries to match it with a page you've visited in the past.

E You can type a search word or phrase right into the address bar to conduct a search.

F Search results fill the window.

To view a specific URL:

1. Type the URL into the address box.

   As you type, Safari tries to match the URL with pages you have visited in the past. It displays results in a menu **D**.

2. Do one of the following:

   ▸ If the page you want to view appears on the menu beneath the address box **D**, click it.

   ▸ If the page you want to view is not listed, keep typing to finish entering the URL and then press Return.

   Safari loads and displays the page.

To conduct a search:

1. Enter a search word or phrase in the address bar at the top of the window.

   As you type, Safari displays a menu of guesses for what you might be looking for **E**.

2. Do one of the following:

   ▸ If the search topic appears on the menu **E**, click it.

   ▸ If the search topic does not appear on the menu, keep typing to finish entering it and then press Return.

   The search results appear almost immediately **F**. You can click a link in the results to browse pages that might have the information you're looking for.

TIP By default, Safari uses Google's search engine for searching the Web. If you want to use a different search engine, you can change it in Safari's preferences. Choose Safari > Preferences to get started.

To bookmark a page:

1. Display the Web page that you want to create a bookmark for.

2. Do one of the following:

   ▸ Click the Share button to the left of the address bar to display the Share menu 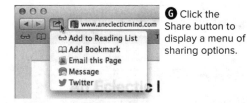 and choose Add Bookmark.

   ▸ Choose Bookmarks > Add bookmark, or press Command-D.

   The Add Bookmark dialog appears 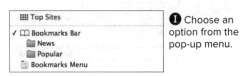.

3. Choose one of the options on the pop-up menu to specify where the bookmark should be added.

4. Enter or edit a page name in the edit box as desired.

5. Click Add.

   The bookmark is added to the location you specified **J**.

To view a bookmarked page:

Do one of the following:

- If the bookmark is on the bookmarks bar **J**, click it.

- If the bookmark is in one of the book-marks bar folders, click the folder name on the bookmark bar to display a menu of bookmarks **K** and click the book-mark you want to open.

- If the bookmark is on the Bookmarks menu, click the menu to display it **L** and then click the bookmark you want to open.

TIP You can use commands under the Book-marks menu **L** to review and organize your bookmarks.

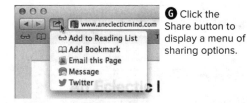

G Click the Share button to display a menu of sharing options.

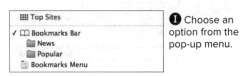

H Enter or edit a name for the bookmark.

I Choose an option from the pop-up menu.

J The bookmark appears in the location you added it—in this case, on the bookmarks bar.

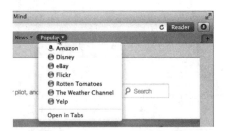

K Folders on the bookmark bar appear as menus.

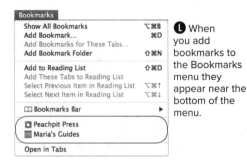

L When you add bookmarks to the Bookmarks menu they appear near the bottom of the menu.

M The Reading List feature makes it easy to save pages to read later.

N If you prefer a distraction-free version of the page, click the Reader button in the address bar.

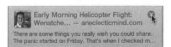

O To remove a page from your Reading List, click the X button.

TIP You can remove all items from your reading list by clicking the Clear All button at the top of the Reading List pane **M**.

To save a page to read later:

1. Display the Web page that you want to read later.

2. Do one of the following:

   ▸ Click the Share button to the left of the address bar to display the Share menu **G** and choose Add to Reading List.

   ▸ Choose Bookmarks > Add to Reading List, or press Shift-Command-D.

   An animation shows the page moving into the eyeglasses icon on the bookmarks bar.

To read pages on your Reading List:

1. Click the eyeglasses button on the bookmarks bar.

   A sidebar displays large buttons for your reading list items.

2. Click the button for the page you want to read.

   The page you clicked appears in the main part of the window **M**.

TIP To list only unread items, click the Unread button at the top of the Reading List pane **M**.

TIP To remove distractions from the page such as images and advertisements, click the Reader button in the Address bar **N**. This feature may not be available for all pages.

TIP To hide the Reading List, click the eyeglasses icon in the bookmarks bar again.

To remove an item from your Reading List:

1. Point to the item you want to remove.

2. Click the X button that appears in the item's upper-right corner **O**.

   The item is removed from the list.

To display a grid of your top sites:

Choose History > Show Top Sites or press Option-Command-1.

A page with thumbnail images of your most frequently visited Web pages appears . Click a thumbnail to go to that page.

TIP You can manually add a site to the Top Sites grid. Follow the instructions in the section titled "To bookmark a page" on page 458, but choose Top Sites in step 3.

TIP Clicking the History button at the top of the Top Sites grid **P** displays thumbnail images of recently visited pages.

To share a page:

1. Display the Web page that you want to share.

2. Click the Share button to the left of the address bar to display the Share menu **G** and choose the method you want to use to share the page.

3. Use the share sheet that appears to specify options for the method you selected **Q**.

4. Click Send.

P The Top Sites grid displays the pages you visit most.

Q When you choose Message from the Share menu, a window like this appears so you can address the message and enter comments to go with it.

Customizing
Your Mac

In This Part

Customizing the Finder

One of the great things about OS X is its user interface flexibility. Although the OS X Finder looks the same on every computer when first installed, it is highly customizable, making it possible for every Mac user to set up his or her computer so it looks and works just right.

This chapter covers the following ways to customize the Finder:

- Finder preferences enable you to set general Finder options, as well as text for labels, sidebar contents, and advanced options.

- Dock icons can be added, removed, and rearranged to include the items you want in the order you want them to appear.

- Launchpad icons can be rearranged and grouped into folders.

- Menu bar icons can be added, rearranged, and removed to better suit your needs.

In This Chapter:

Setting Finder Preferences

Finder preferences enable you to customize several aspects of the desktop and Finder to change the way they look and work.

The Finder Preferences window is organized into four different panes of options:

- **General** lets you set basic options for the desktop and Finder windows.

- **Labels** enables you to set label names for the Finder's label feature.

- **Sidebar** lets you set options for the sidebar.

- **Advanced** enables you to set options for the display of file extensions and the Trash warning.

To set Finder preferences, open the preferences pane you need to change, make changes, and close the window. Your changes are automatically saved.

To open Finder Preferences:

Choose Finder > Preferences or press Command-, (comma).

The Finder Preferences window opens, displaying the last pane of options you accessed.

Ⓐ Choose Preferences from the Finder menu.

Ⓑ The default Finder General preferences settings.

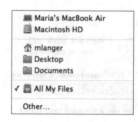

Ⓒ Use this pop-up menu to choose what you want to appear in new Finder windows.

D E The top-level hard disk (top) and Home folder (bottom) are two of the options for a new Finder window.

F Use a dialog like this to choose a different folder to open in a new Finder window.

To set General Finder Preferences:

1. In the Finder Preferences window, click the General button to display General options **B**.

2. To specify what items should appear on the desktop (page 12), toggle check boxes under Show these items on the desktop:

   ▶ **Hard disks** displays icons for internal hard disks.

   ▶ **External disks** displays icons for external hard disks and thumb drives.

   ▶ **CDs, DVDs, and iPods** displays icons for removable media, including CDs and DVDs, as well as iPods.

   ▶ **Connected servers** displays icons for mounted server volumes.

3. To specify what should appear in a new Finder window (page 24), choose an option from the New Finder windows show pop-up menu **C**:

   ▶ *Computer name* displays icons for the computer and mounted volumes.

   ▶ *Hard Disk name* displays the root level of your hard disk **D**.

   ▶ *Your account name* displays the contents of your Home folder **E**.

   ▶ **Desktop** displays the contents of your Desktop folder.

   ▶ **Documents** displays the contents of your Documents folder.

   ▶ **All My Files** displays the All My Files smart folder (page 99).

   ▶ **Other** displays a dialog that you can use to select a different folder **F**.

continues on next page

4. To set other options, toggle check boxes in the bottom half of the window:

▸ **Always open folders in a new window** opens a new window to display the contents of the folders you open.

▸ **Spring-loaded folders and windows** enables the spring-loaded folders feature (page 78). Use the slider to set the delay time for this feature.

To customize labels:

1. In the Finder Preferences window, click the Labels button **G**.

2. To change the name of a label, select the text for the label you want to change and enter new text **H**.

3. Repeat step 2 for each label you want to change.

TIP Assigning labels to icons is covered on page 81.

TIP The names of labels appear on the File menu and contextual menus when you point to a label and in a list view window when the Label column is displayed **I**, as discussed on page 480.

To set Sidebar preferences:

1. In the Finder Preferences window, click the Sidebar button **J**.

2. Toggle check boxes to specify what items should appear in each area of the sidebar (page 31). The options are self-explanatory.

TIP Customizing the sidebar to add, remove, and rearrange items is covered on page 485.

G Labels preferences let you change the text assigned to colored labels.

H Changing label text is easy: just type in the new text.

I Labels can appear in list view windows.

J Toggle check boxes to specify which items should appear in the sidebar.

K Default settings for Advanced Finder preferences.

L This dialog warns you of the consequences of changing a file name extension.

To set Advanced preferences:

1. In the Finder Preferences window, click the Advanced button **K**.

2. Toggle check boxes to set options:

   ▸ **Show all filename extensions** displays file extensions in Finder windows. This option turns off the Hide extension check box in the Name & Extension area of the Info window (page 88) for all files from then on.

   ▸ **Show warning before changing an extension** displays a warning dialog when you change a file name extension **L** (page 43).

   ▸ **Show warning before emptying the Trash** displays a confirmation dialog **M** when you Use the Finder's Empty Trash or Secure Empty Trash command (page 50).

   ▸ **Empty Trash securely** enables the secure empty Trash feature (page 50) each time you empty the Trash.

3. Choose an option from the When performing a search pop-up menu **N** to set how OS X's search feature (Chapter 7) should work.

M You can use Advanced Finder preferences to prevent this dialog from appearing when you empty the Trash.

N Choose a default search location from this pop-up menu.

Customizing the Dock

The contents of the Dock (page 34) can be customized a number of ways:

- Include icons for items that you use often. This makes them quick and easy to open any time you need them.

- Remove icons for items you seldom use. This reduces Dock clutter.

- Rearrange Dock icons to better suit your needs. This can make you more productive.

- Customize the appearance and functionality of stacks folders so they work the way you want them to.

This part of the chapter covers all of these customization options.

TIP You can also set Dock preferences to control how the Dock looks and works; learn more on page 501.

To add an item to the Dock:

1. Open the window containing the item you want to add to the Dock.

2. Drag the item from the window to the Dock.

   Items on the Dock shift to make room for the new item **A**.

3. Release the button.

   The icon appears where you released it **B**.

TIP Dragging an item to the Dock does not remove it from its original location.

TIP Add applications to the left of the Dock's divider and documents, folders, websites, and servers to the right of the divider.

A Drag an icon from a Finder window to the Dock.

B The icon appears on the Dock, right where you dropped it.

C Drag an item off the Dock.

D The item is removed from the Dock.

E Drag an icon from one position to another on the Dock.

F When you release it, it moves.

To remove an item from the Dock:

1. Drag the item from the Dock to the desktop.

   As you drag away from the Dock, the space occupied by the item closes up and a cloud appears on the icon **C**.

2. Release the button.

   The item disappears **D** in a puff of digital smoke.

TIP You cannot remove the Finder or Trash from the Dock.

TIP Removing an item from the Dock does not delete it from disk.

TIP If you remove an icon for an application that is running, the icon will not disappear from the Dock until you quit.

To rearrange Dock items:

1. Drag the item you want to move from its current place on the Dock to a new place.

   As you drag, icons shift to close up empty space and open up new space **E**.

2. Release the button.

   The item moves to its new position **F**.

To customize the display of a stacks folder:

1. In the Dock, point to the folder you want to set options for.

2. Use one of the following techniques to display a menu of options :

   ▸ Hold down the Control key and click.

   ▸ Right-click or, on a Multi-Touch device, click with two fingers.

   ▸ If the stack is set to display as a list, click to display the list and then choose Options to display the Options submenu **H**.

3. To change the sort order of items in the stack, choose a Sort by option.

4. To set the appearance for the stack's icon on the Dock **I**, choose a Display as option:

   ▸ **Folder** displays the stack's icon using the same icon as its source folder.

   ▸ **Stack** displays the stack's icon as a stack of icons.

5. To set the appearance for the folder's open stack, choose a View content as option:

   ▸ **Fan** always displays the stack as a fan.

   ▸ **Grid** always displays the stack as a grid.

   ▸ List always displays the stack as a list.

   ▸ **Automatic** displays the stack as a fan unless there are too many items in the folder to fit—then it displays them as a grid.

TIP You can see examples of stack appearance in Chapter 18, where using the stacks feature is discussed in detail.

G You can view stacks options in a contextual menu like this...

H ...or in a submenu like this.

I Stacks can be displayed as folders (left and center) or stacks of icons (right).

A To move an icon, just drag it to a new position in the grid.

B The icon appears in its new position.

Organizing Launchpad

Launchpad is similar to stacks in that it displays icons in a way that makes them easy to find and click. But Launchpad automatically identifies and displays only applications, making it a useful tool for opening an application quickly.

But what happens when you have many applications installed on your Mac? Launchpad can get messy and extend into multiple windows, making applications a little less easy to find. Fortunately, there are two ways you can customize Launchpad to make the applications you use most easily accessible:

- Rearrange Launchpad icons to put them in a more convenient order.
- Organize applications into Launchpad folders to group them logically.

This part of the chapter covers both of these techniques.

TIP Some applications may already be stored in folders—for example, a standard OS X installation gathers a bunch of applications in the Other folder.

TIP Do you have an iOS device such as an iPhone or an iPad? If so, Launchpad should look familiar—it's a lot like the home screen in iOS.

To rearrange Launchpad icons:

1. In Launchpad, drag the icon you want to move from its current position to a new position in Launchpad's grid.

    As you drag, icons shift to close up empty space and open up new space **A**.

2. Release the button.

    The icon moves **B**.

To organize Launchpad icons by folder:

1. In Launchpad, drag the icon for one item you want to group into a folder onto the icon for another item you want to group in the same folder **C**.

   The destination icon turns into a dark colored square and then a folder menu containing the destination icon opens beneath it **D**.

2. Release the button to drop the icon into the folder **E**.

3. Click the folder icon to go back to Launchpad's main screen.

   A square icon representing the new folder is in the grid position formerly occupied by the destination icon **F**.

4. Drag another icon onto the new folder icon and release it.

5. Repeat step 4 for every application you want to include in that folder.

TIP Each item you add to a Launchpad folder is represented by a tiny icon on the folder icon **G**.

C In this example, I'm dragging the Preview icon on top of the Photo Booth icon.

D Launchpad displays a menu for a folder that it automatically created and named *Entertainment*.

E When I release the button, the icon I'm dragging drops into the new Launchpad folder.

F The new folder icon appears where the destination icon was in the main Launchpad screen.

G I can tell by looking at this icon that it contains four items.

H Click a folder to display a menu of its contents.

I Click the folder name to select it.

J Type a new name and press Return to save it.

K Drag the icon out of the menu.

To rename a Launchpad folder:

1. In Launchpad, click the folder you want to rename to display a menu of its contents H.

2. Click the name of the folder in the upper-left corner of the menu.

   The name becomes selected I.

3. Type a new name for the folder and press Return to save it.

   The folder is renamed J.

To remove an item from a Launchpad folder:

1. In Launchpad, click the name of the folder you want to remove the item from to display a menu of its contents H.

2. Drag the item you want to remove from the folder up and out of the menu K.

   The menu closes to reveal the main Launchpad screen L.

3. Drag the item into the grid position where you want it to appear.

4. Release the button.

   The item moves into its new position.

L The menu closes to reveal the main Launchpad screen.

Rearranging Menu Bar Icons

The right end of the OS X menu bar at the top of the screen may display any combination of icons . In many instances, these icons are menus that offer access to System or application features.

In addition to showing or hiding these icons with various System Preferences options (as discussed in Chapters 33 through 36), you can also rearrange many of these icons to suit your needs.

TIP Note that you cannot move the Spotlight or Notifications icon or move other any icon to their right.

To move a menu bar icon:

1. Hold down the Command key and drag an icon to a new position on the end of the menu bar.

   As you drag, icons shift to close up empty space and open up new space **B**.

2. Release the button.

   The icon moves into its new position **C**.

TIP Dragging a menu bar icon off the menu is a quick way to remove it without opening System Preferences or the application that put it there.

A A typical collection of menu bar icons includes Time Machine, Bluetooth, Wi-Fi, Sound, Battery Level, Date & Time, User Name, Spotlight, and Notifications.

B Hold down the Command key while dragging the icon you want to move.

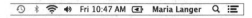

C When you release the button, the icon moves into its new position.

Customizing Finder Windows

OS X makes it possible to customize the appearance and functionality of windows and the desktop a number of different ways:

- Set view options to control icon size, grid spacing, sort order, text size, background, and other options for individual windows and, on a limited basis, the desktop.

- Customize the toolbar to add, remove, and reorganize buttons and other options.

- Customize the sidebar to add, remove, and reorganize folders and other items.

Making changes like these helps you set up your computer so it works best for your particular needs.

This chapter takes a look at the things you can do to customize Finder windows and the desktop.

In This Chapter:

Setting View Options

You can customize Finder window and desktop views a number of ways:

- Change the settings for the default view for icon, list, column, and Cover Flow views.

- Change the settings for an individual window's view.

- Change the view for the desktop.

You do all this with the view options window for the active window or desktop.

The settings offered in the view options window vary depending on the window's current view settings. Here are some examples:

- **Icon view** settings include icon size, grid spacing, label text size and position, display options, arrangement, and background.

- **List view** settings include icon size, text size, columns, date format, and item size calculation.

- **Column view** settings include text size, icon appearance, and preview column.

- **Cover Flow** view options include icon size, text size, columns, date format, and item size calculation.

- **Desktop view** settings include icon size, label text size and position, display options, and arrangement.

OS X remembers a window's view settings and uses them whenever you display the window. Any change you make in the view options window is automatically saved for use in the future.

TIP Chapter 4 discusses window views and how to switch from one view to another. That's also where you can find details about sorting window contents.

A Open the window you want to set options for. In this example, the Applications folder window is open and displayed in icon view.

B Choose Show View Options from the Finder's View menu.

C Here's the view options window for a window displayed in icon view.

D The Arrange By options for the Applications folder window. Options on this menu vary depending on what window is open.

E In this example, I've arranged the icons by Application Category and then sorted them by Date Last Opened.

To set view options:

1. Open the window you want to set view options for **A**.

2. If necessary, switch to the view you want to customize.

3. Choose View > Show View Options **B**, or press Command-J.

   The view options window for that view appears **C**.

4. Set options as desired.

5. Click the window's close button or choose View > Hide View Options to dismiss the view options window.

TIP To open the view options window for the desktop, make sure no window is active before choosing View > Show View Options.

TIP The options in the view options window will change if you make a different window active. The view options window always displays options and settings for the currently active window.

To set icon view options:

In the view options window **C** for the icon view window you want to customize **A**, set options as desired:

- **Always open in icon view** sets the window so it always opens in icon view.

- **Browse in icon view** also displays the contents of a window's folders in icon view when they are opened. This option is only available when the Always open in icon view option above it is enabled.

- **Arrange By ⓓ** sorts and groups icons by the option you specify **E**.

continues on next page

- **Sort By** 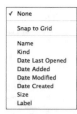 sorts icons by the option you specify. In some instances, when the Arrange By option is set to something other than None, the Sort By option is not available.

- **Icon size** enables you to use a slider to change the size of icons in the window , from 16 x 16 pixels to 512 x 512 pixels.

- **Grid spacing** enables you to use a slider to change the amount of space between each icon **①**.

- **Text size** lets you change the size of text characters in the icon label **①**. Options range from 10 to 16 points.

- **Label position ①** enables you to set the position of an icon's label at the bottom (the default option) or to the right of the icon.

- **Show item info ①** displays information about the item beneath its name.

- **Show icon preview** displays a document's preview, if available, in place of its standard icon.

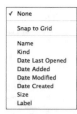

F The options on the Sort By menu—and the availability of the menu itself—vary depending on what is selected in the Arrange By menu; in this case, it's None.

G The icons in Ⓐ are 64 pixels; here's the same window with the icons sized 148 pixels.

H In this example, the icons are the same size as they are in Ⓐ, but the grid spacing is much tighter.

I Changing the text size also changes the grid spacing.

J This example from my Documents folder shows label position to the right and item info displayed. Like the other illustrations here, the icon preview option is enabled, too.

K When you select Color, a color well appears in the view options window.

L Clicking the color well displays the Colors panel.

M Drag a picture file into the image well.

N The picture appears as the background for the window.

- **Background** enables you to set the window's background:

  ▸ **White** makes the background white, which is the default setting.

  ▸ **Color** enables you to select a background color for the window. If you select this option, click the color well that appears beside it **K** and use the Colors panel **L** (page 496) to select a color.

  ▸ **Picture** enables you to set a background picture for the window. If you select this option, you can drag an image file into the image well that appears beside it **M** to use that picture as a background image **N**. (You can change the picture by dragging a different picture into the image well; you can remove the picture by selecting one of the other two options.)

TIP Another way to resize the icons in a window is to drag the Icon size slider in the status bar (if displayed) left or right.

TIP A window's background cannot be customized if the window's contents are arranged.

To set list or Cover Flow view options:

In the view options window for the list view ⓟ or Cover Flow view window you want to customize, set options as desired:

- **Always open in list view** or **Always open in Cover Flow** sets the window so it always opens in list view or Cover Flow view.

- **Browse in list view** or **Browse in Cover Flow** also displays the contents of a window's folders in list view or Cover Flow view when they are opened. This option is only available when the option above it is enabled.

- **Arrange By** ⓓ sorts and groups icons by the option you specify ⓠ.

- **Sort By** ⓡ sorts icons by the option you specify ⓠ. In some instances, depending on the Arrange By setting, the Sort By option is not available.

- **Icon size** enables you to select from two different icon size options.

- **Text size** lets you change the size of text characters in the icon label. Options range from 10 to 16 points.

- **Show Columns** lets you toggle check boxes to specify which columns should appear.

- **Use relative dates** displays the date in relative terms (that is, using the words *today* and *yesterday*).

- **Calculate all sizes** displays the disk space occupied by items and the contents of folders in the list.

- **Show icon preview** shows a document preview for the icon, if available.

TIP Turning on the Calculate all sizes check box ⓞ makes it possible to sort a list by size—even if it includes folders.

ⓞ The view options window for a window in list view. These options are virtually identical for a window in Cover Flow view.

ⓟ The Applications window in list view.

ⓠ In this example, I arranged by Application Category and then sorted by name.

✓ Name
Kind
Date Last Opened
Date Added
Date Modified
Date Created
Size
Label

R The Sort By menu for list and Cover Flow views is slightly different from the one for icon view.

S The view options for a window in column view.

T A window in column view with default settings.

U In this example, I've arranged by Date Last Opened. The Sort By menu turns gray and can't be used.

To set column view options:

In the view options window **S** for the column view **T** window you want to customize, set options as desired:

- **Always open in column view** sets the window so it always opens in column view.

- **Browse in column view** also displays the contents of a window's folders in column view when they are opened. This option is only available when the option above it is enabled.

- **Arrange By** **D** sorts and groups icons by the option you specify **U**.

- **Sort By** **R** sorts icons by the option you specify. In some instances, depending on the Arrange By setting, the Sort By option is not available.

- **Show icons** shows file icons.

- **Show icon preview** shows a document preview for the icon, if available.

- **Show preview column** shows a preview for a selected item in the far right column **S** **U**.

To set desktop view options:

In the view options window **V** for the desktop, set options as desired:

- **Icon size** enables you to use a slider to change the size of icons in the window **G**, from 16 x 16 pixels to 512 x 512 pixels.

- **Grid spacing** enables you to use a slider to change the amount of space between each icon.

- **Text size** lets you change the size of text characters in the icon label. Options range from 10 to 16 points.

- **Label position** enables you to set the position of an icon's label at the bottom (the default option) or to the right of the icon.

- **Show item info** displays information about the item beneath its name.

- **Show icon preview** displays a document's preview, if available, in place of its standard icon.

- **Sort By** **F** sorts icons by the option you specify.

TIP As you can see, these options are nearly identical to those for an icon view window **C**.

TIP You can set the desktop color or picture in the Desktop & Screen Saver preferences pane (page 497).

V You can also use the view options window to set options for the desktop.

To set view options as the default for all windows in icon or list view:

1. Use the view options window **C O** to set options for an icon or list view window.

2. Click the Use as Defaults button.

   The current options are set as defaults for that view.

A Choose Customize Toolbar from the View menu.

B The Customize Toolbar dialog.

C Drag a button from the Customize Toolbar dialog onto the toolbar.

D The button appears where you dragged it.

E Drag a button off the toolbar.

Customizing the Toolbar

The toolbar, which is discussed on page 29, can be customized to include buttons and icons for a variety of commands and items. You can also rearrange toolbar items to display them in any order you like.

TIP When you customize the toolbar, your changes affect the toolbar in all windows in which the toolbar is displayed.

TIP You must display the toolbar to customize it. To display the toolbar, choose View > Show Toolbar, or press Option-Command-T.

To customize the toolbar:

1. With any Finder window open and the toolbar displayed, choose View > Customize Toolbar **A**.

   The Customize Toolbar dialog appears **B**.

2. Make changes to the toolbar as follows:

   ▸ To add an item to the toolbar, drag it from the dialog to the position you want it to occupy on the toolbar **C**. When you release the item, it appears on the toolbar **D**.

   ▸ To remove an item from the toolbar, drag it off the toolbar **E**. When you release the item, it disappears in a puff of digital smoke and is removed from the toolbar **F**.

   continues on next page

F When you release the button, it disappears.

▸ To rearrange the order of items on the toolbar, drag an item into the desired position **G**. When you release the item, it moves **H**.

3. To specify how items should appear on the toolbar, choose an option from the Show pop-up menu at the bottom of the window:

   ▸ **Icon & Text** displays both the icon and the icon's name **I**.

   ▸ **Icon Only** displays only the icon. This is the default setting.

   ▸ **Text Only** displays only the name of the icon **J**.

4. When you are finished making changes, click Done.

TIP You don't have to use the Customize Toolbar dialog to rearrange or remove toolbar items. Just hold down the Command key and drag the item you want to move to a new position or drag the item you want to remove off the toolbar.

TIP The toolbar includes spacers that you can move or remove like buttons. They appear on the toolbar as light gray boxes.

To restore the toolbar to its default settings:

1. With any Finder window displaying the toolbar open, choose View > Customize Toolbar **A**.

   The Customize Toolbar dialog appears **B**.

2. Drag the group of items in the box near the bottom of the window to the toolbar **K**.

   When you release it, the toolbar is reset to its default configuration **L**.

3. Click Done.

G To rearrange items, drag them into a new position on the toolbar.

H When you release an item, it moves.

I You can set the toolbar so it shows icons and text labels...

J ...or just text labels.

K To restore the toolbar to its default settings, drag the collection of tools at the bottom of the dialog onto the toolbar.

L When you release them, the toolbar is restored.

A When you position the pointer on the dividing line between the sidebar and the rest of the window, it turns into a line with two arrows.

B Drag the border of the sidebar to change its width.

Customizing the Sidebar

In addition to using Finder preferences (page 466) to specify what standard items should appear in the sidebar (page 31) you can customize the sidebar a number of other ways:

- Change the width of the sidebar to better display long item names.

- Add or remove folders, files, and other items in the bottom half of the sidebar.

TIP The sidebar only appears if the toolbar (page 29) is displayed.

To change the sidebar width:

1. Position the pointer on the divider between the sidebar and the rest of the Finder window.

   The pointer turns into a line with two arrows **A**.

2. Press the button down and drag.

   As you drag, the sidebar's width changes **B**.

3. When the sidebar is the desired width, release the button.

TIP Making the sidebar wider does not make the entire window wider. Instead, it just shifts the dividing point between the sidebar and the rest of the window.

To add a sidebar item:

Drag the icon for the item you want to add to the sidebar's Favorites area.

A blue line indicates where it will appear **C**. When you release the item, it appears on the sidebar **D**.

TIP The icon you drag can be the one that appears in the item's title bar.

TIP Adding an item to the sidebar does not move it from where it resides on disk. Instead, it creates a pointer to the original item and adds it to the sidebar.

TIP Be careful when adding an icon to the sidebar. If you drag the icon on top of a folder or disk icon on the sidebar, the icon will move into that folder or disk.

To remove a sidebar item:

Hold down the Command key and drag the item off the sidebar **E**.

When you release the item, it disappears in a puff of digital smoke and is removed from the sidebar.

TIP Removing an item from the sidebar does not delete it from disk. Instead, it removes the pointer to the original item from the sidebar.

TIP If you remove all the items under a sidebar heading, the heading disappears. It reappears if you add an item that belongs under that heading.

To rearrange sidebar items:

Drag the item you want to move into a new position on the sidebar.

Other items on the sidebar will shift to make room for it **F**. When you release the item, it moves.

C Drag an item's icon into the Favorites area of the sidebar.

D When you release the item, it appears where you dragged it.

E To remove an item from the sidebar, hold down Command and drag it off.

F To rearrange items, drag an item into a new position on the sidebar.

System Preferences Basics

One of the great things about OS X is the way it can be customized to look and work the way you want it to.

Many customization options can be set with the System Preferences application. That's where you'll find a variety of preferences panes, each containing settings for a part of OS X.

System Preferences panes are discussed in detail in the following chapters. This chapter provides an overview of System Preferences, with information about how they're organized and how you can access them. It also explains how you can lock preferences to prevent accidental or unauthorized changes to settings.

Getting Started with System Preferences

System Preferences panes are organized into five categories, four of which are included on a standard installation of OS X :

- **Personal** preferences panes (Chapter 33) enable you to set options to customize various OS X appearance and operation options for personal tastes. These preferences panes include:
  - ▸ General
  - ▸ Desktop & Screen Saver
  - ▸ Dock
  - ▸ Mission Control
  - ▸ Language & Text
  - ▸ Security & Privacy
  - ▸ Spotlight
  - ▸ Notifications
- **Hardware** preferences panes (Chapter 34) control settings for various hardware devices. These preferences panes include:
  - ▸ CDs & DVDs
  - ▸ Displays
  - ▸ Energy Saver
  - ▸ Keyboard
  - ▸ Mouse
  - ▸ Trackpad
  - ▸ Print & Scan
  - ▸ Sound
- **Internet & Wireless** preferences panes (Chapter 35) enable you to set options related to Internet and network connections. These preferences panes include:

The System Preferences window for a standard installation of OS X on a MacBook Air.

  - ▸ iCloud
  - ▸ Mail, Contacts & Calendars
  - ▸ Network
  - ▸ Bluetooth
  - ▸ Sharing
- **System** preferences panes (Chapter 36) control various aspects of your computer's operation. These preferences panes include:
  - ▸ Users & Groups
  - ▸ Parental Controls
  - ▸ Date & Time
  - ▸ Software Update
  - ▸ Dictation & Speech
  - ▸ Time Machine
  - ▸ Accessibility
  - ▸ Startup Disk
- **Other** preferences panes may be installed on your computer when you install various third-party software. They would appear in a fifth group at the bottom of the main System Preferences window and are not covered in this book.

B Choose System Preferences from the Apple menu.

C The System Preferences application icon.

System Preferences

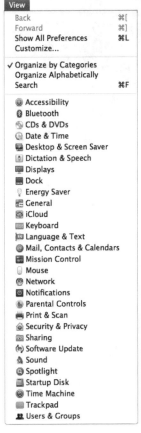

D System Preferences' View menu gives you access to all preferences panes.

To open System Preferences:

Use one of the following techniques:

- Choose Apple > System Preferences **B**.
- Open the System Preferences application icon **C** in the Applications folder window (page 137).
- Click the System Preferences icon in Launchpad (page 140).
- Click the System Preferences icon in the Dock (page 34).

The System Preferences window opens. It either displays all System Preferences pane icons **A** or the preferences pane you last used.

To open a specific preferences pane:

Use one of the following techniques:

- If all System Preferences pane icons are showing **A**, click the icon for the pane you want to display.
- Choose the name of the pane you want to display from the View menu **D**.

To show all preferences pane icons:

Use one of the following techniques:

- Choose View > Show All Preferences **D**, or press Command-L.
- Click the Show All button in the toolbar of the System Preferences window **A**.

To reorganize preferences panes:

Choose a command from the View menu:

- Organize by Categories displays all icons organized by category **A**.
- Organize Alphabetically displays all icons organized alphabetically by name **B**.

To find a preferences pane by task or topic:

1. Enter a search word or phrase in the search box in the upper-right corner of the System Preferences window.

   Three things happen **F**:

   - The window gets dark.
   - Icons for related preferences panes are highlighted.
   - A menu of possible topics appears.

2. Do one of the following:

   - Select a topic from the menu.
   - Click a highlighted icon.

   The appropriate preferences pane opens.

To quit System Preferences:

Use one of the following techniques:

- Choose System Preferences > Quit System Preferences.
- Press Command-Q.
- Click the System Preferences window's close button.

TIP System Preferences is one of the OS X applications that automatically quits when all of its windows are closed.

B If you prefer, you can view preferences panes in alphabetical order.

F You can search System Preferences to find the preferences pane you need to perform a task.

A The Users & Groups preferences pane is locked by default.

B A typical authentication dialog like this appears when you try to unlock a preferences pane.

C The lock icon changes to an open padlock when a preferences pane is unlocked.

Locking & Unlocking Preference Settings

Many preferences panes include a lock button that enables you to lock the settings. Locking a preferences pane's settings prevent them from being changed accidentally or by users who do not have administrative privileges.

Some preferences panes—for example, Users & Groups **A**—are locked by default. That means you need to unlock it with an administrator's account name and password to make changes.

To unlock a preferences pane:

1. Click the lock button at the bottom of a locked preferences pane window **A**.

2. Enter an administrator's name and password in the authenticate dialog that appears **B** and click Unlock.

   The button changes so that the icon looks like an unlocked padlock **C**.

To lock a preferences pane:

Click the lock button at the bottom of a preferences pane window **C**.

The button changes so that the icon looks like a locked padlock **A**.

Customizing System Preferences

You can now customize the System Preferences window so it only includes the preferences panes you want to see. This can help simplify the interface by removing preferences panes you never use. Because all preferences panes are listed on the View menu, you can still open any of them quickly—even if it doesn't appear in the main window. And, as you might imagine, you can always customize the window again to redisplay any that are hidden.

To customize the System Preferences window:

1. Choose View > Customize.

   The window's view changes to display check marks beside each preferences pane icon .

2. Toggle the check boxes to determine which preferences panes appear.

3. Click Done.

   The System Preferences window displays only the preferences pane icons that were checked when you customized it .

A Toggle the check boxes to determine which preferences pane icons should appear in the System Preferences window.

B In this example, I've hidden Language & Text, Security & Privacy, iCloud, Sharing, Parental Controls, Time Machine, and Accessibility.

Personal Preferences

Personal preferences panes enable you to configure the appearance and operation of OS X to suit your needs. This chapter covers the following System Preferences panes:

- **General** controls general appearance, scrolling, and recent item options.
- **Desktop & Screen Saver** sets the desktop picture and screen saver options.
- **Dock** configures the Dock.
- **Language & Text** controls language, formatting, and input sources.
- **Mission Control** sets options for Mission Control, Exposé, and Spaces.
- **Security & Privacy** controls system-wide security options.
- **Spotlight** customizes the way searching works.
- **Notifications**, which is new in OS X Mountain Lion, customizes the appearance and functionality of Notification Center.

Need to learn the basics of System Preferences? Be sure to read Chapter 32.

In This Chapter:

General

The General preferences pane **A** enables you to set options for color, scroll bar functionality, sidebar icon size, recent items, and text smoothing. These options help customize the Finder so it looks and works the way you prefer.

TIP You can learn more about customizing the Finder in Chapters 30 and 31.

To set General preferences:

In the General preferences pane **A**, set options as desired:

- **Appearance** sets the color for buttons, menus, and windows throughout your computer and its applications. Your options are Blue and Graphite.

- **Highlight Color** sets the highlight color for text in documents, fields, and lists. Choose an option from the pop-up menu **B**.

- **Sidebar icon size** enables you to set the size of sidebar icons to small, medium (the default setting), or large.

- **Show scroll bars** determines whether scroll bars should appear when not in use. You have three options:

  ▸ **Automatically based on mouse or trackpad** displays the scroll bars if you are using a mouse or other device that does not support Multi-Touch gestures.

  ▸ **When scrolling** displays scroll bars only when you are scrolling.

  ▸ **Always** displays scroll bars all the time.

A The General preferences pane.

B Use this pop-up menu to choose a highlight color.

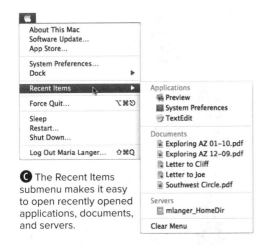

C The Recent Items submenu makes it easy to open recently opened applications, documents, and servers.

12-point text with text smoothing turned on.

12-point text with text smoothing turned off.

D An example of text with text smoothing turned on (top) and off (bottom).

TIP Font or text smoothing uses a process called *antialiasing* to make text more legible onscreen. Antialiasing creates gray pixels between black ones and white ones to eliminate sharp edges **D**.

TIP If you choose other from the Highlight Color pop-up menu **B**, you can use a standard Colors panel **E** to select any color supported by your computer. I explain how to use the Colors panel on the next page.

TIP You can clear the Recent Items submenu by choosing Apple > Recent Items > Clear Menu **C**.

- **Click in the scroll bar to** determines what happens when you click in the scroll track of a scroll bar:
  - ▸ **Jump to the next page** scrolls to the next window or page of the document.
  - ▸ **Jump to the spot that's clicked** scrolls to the relative location in the document. For example, if you click in the scroll track two-thirds of the way between the top and bottom, you'll scroll two-thirds of the way through the document. This is the same as dragging the scroller to that position.

- **Ask to keep changes when closing documents** displays a dialog when you close a document with unsaved changes. With this option enabled, you can override the Auto Save feature (page 144) on a case-by-case basis. This option is new in Mountain Lion.

- **Close windows when quitting an application** prevents an application's open windows from automatically reopening the next time you launch it. This option, which is new in Mountain Lion, overrides the Resume feature (page 144).

- **Recent Items** enables you to specify how many documents, applications, and servers to list on the Recent Items submenu **C** (page 85). Options range from None to 50.

- **Use LCD font smoothing when available** determines how OS X smooths text onscreen for LCD displays. This option varies depending on your computer model and display.

- **Turn off text smoothing for font sizes** enables you to choose a minimum font size for text smoothing. Text in the font size you set and smaller will not be smoothed. Options range from 4 to 12.

To use the Colors panel:

1. Click the icon along the top of the Colors panel to select one of the color models.

2. How you choose a color depends on the model you selected:

   ▸ **Color Wheel** displays a circle of color. Click inside the circle to choose a color. You can drag the vertical slider up or down to change the brightness.

   ▸ **Color Sliders ⑤** displays several sliders you can use to change color values. Start by selecting a slider group from the pop-up menu, and then move the sliders to create a color.

   ▸ **Color Palettes ⑥** displays clickable color samples. Choose a palette from the List pop-up menu, and then click the color you want.

   ▸ **Image Palettes ⑦** displays colors from an image. You can drag an image file onto the sample area and then click a color in the image to select it.

   ▸ **Crayons ⑧** displays different colored crayons. Click a crayon to choose its color.

   The color of the selected item changes immediately.

TIP You can use the color wells at the bottom of the Colors panel to store frequently used colors. Simply drag a color into an empty spot. Then, when you open the Colors panel, you can click a stored color to apply it.

E In most cases, the Colors panel will display as a color wheel like this.

F G H I The Colors panel can also appear as color sliders (top-left), color palettes (top-right), image palettes (bottom-left), and my personal favorite, crayons (bottom-right).

A The Desktop options in the Desktop & Screen Saver preferences pane.

B In this example, I've selected an image of clouds from my Pictures folder.

| ✓ Fill Screen |
| Fit to Screen |
| Stretch to Fill Screen |
| Center |
| Tile |

C You can use this pop-up menu to tell Mac OS how to display the picture onscreen.

| When logging in |
| When waking from sleep |
| |
| Every 5 seconds |
| Every minute |
| Every 5 minutes |
| Every 15 minutes |
| ✓ Every 30 minutes |
| Every hour |
| Every day |

D You can set up your desktop picture to change automatically at a frequency you specify.

Desktop & Screen Saver

The Desktop & Screen Saver preferences pane enables you to set the background color or picture for the OS X desktop and configure a screen saver that appears when your computer is idle.

TIP OS X's built-in screen saver doesn't really "save" anything. All it does is cover the normal screen display with graphics, providing an interesting visual when your computer is inactive.

TIP The Energy Saver preferences pane (page 523) offers more protection for LCD displays than Screen Saver.

To set the desktop picture:

1. In the Desktop & Screen Saver preferences pane, click the Desktop button to display its options **A**.

2. In the collections list on the left side of the window, select an image folder or collection.

   The images in the collection appear on the right side of the window.

3. Click the image you want to use.

   It appears in the image well above the collection list and the desktop's background picture changes **B**.

4. If desired, choose an option from the pop-up menu beside the image preview **C** to indicate how it should appear.

continues on next page

5. To change the picture periodically, turn on the Change picture check box and select a frequency option from the pop-up menu **D**. Turning on the Random order check box beneath this displays the images in the collection in random order.

6. To change the menu bar so it is opaque **E** rather than translucent **B**, turn off the Translucent menu bar check box.

E If you don't like a translucent menu bar, you can make it opaque.

TIP For best results, use pictures that are the same size or larger than your screen resolution. For example, if your screen resolution is set to 1024 x 768, the image should be at least this size. You can check or change your screen resolution in the Displays preferences pane (page 521).

TIP The collections list on the left side of the Desktop pane **A** includes photos installed with OS X, as well as access to your Pictures folder and your iPhoto library and albums (if iPhoto is installed).

TIP In step 2, you can click the + button at the bottom of the collections column and use the dialog that appears to locate and choose another folder that contains images.

TIP Although you can have your desktop display a virtual slide show by setting the picture changing frequency in step 5 to a low value like Every 5 seconds, you may find it distracting to have the background change that often. I know I would!

F The Screen Saver options of the Desktop & Screen Saver preferences pane includes a variety of slideshows...

G ...and screen saver modules.

To configure the screen saver:

1. In the Desktop & Screen Saver preferences pane, click the Screen Saver button to display its options **F** **G**.

2. In the Screen Savers list, select a screen saver module. There are two types:

   ▸ **Slideshows F** display photographs from built-in collections, a folder on your Mac, or your iPhoto photo library.

   ▸ **Screen Savers G** display various graphics or text.

   The preview area changes accordingly.

3. Set options for the type of screen saver you selected:

   ▸ For a slideshow screen saver **F** choose an option from the Source pop-up menu and, if necessary, select a folder or library of photos. To shuffle the order of photos, turn on the Shuffle slide order check box.

   ▸ For a screen saver module **G**, click Screen Saver Options, set options in the dialog that appears, and click OK.

4. To include a clock as part of the screen saver, turn on the Show with clock check box.

5. To see what the screen saver looks like on your screen, click the Preview area.

   The screen goes black and the screen saver kicks in. To go back to work, press Esc.

6. To have the screen saver start automatically after a certain amount of idle time, choose an option from the Start after pop-up menu.

continues on next page

7. To set "hot corners" that activate or deactivate the screen saver, click the Hot Corners button to display the Active Screen Corners dialog **H**. Choose an option from each pop-up menu **I** to specify what should happen when you position the pointer in the corresponding corner. When you're finished, click OK to save your settings.

TIP In step 3, not all screen savers can be configured. The options that are available vary depending on the screen saver you selected in step 2.

TIP The Word of the Day screen saver is interative—pressing the D key while it is displayed opens the Dictionary application (page 221) to the currently displayed word.

TIP In step 7, you can configure the hot corners any way you like. For example, you can set it up so every corner starts the screen saver.

TIP You can use the Active Screen Corners dialog **H** to set up hot corners for Mission Control (page 253), Exposé (page 255), Dashboard (Chapter 17), Notification Center (page XX), and Launchpad (page 140), too.

H Use this dialog to set trigger corners for the screen saver and other OS X features. In this example, moving the pointer to the lower-right corner will activate the screen saver.

I Each pop-up menu in the Active Screen Corners dialog offers these options.

Dock

The Dock preferences pane **Ⓐ** enables you to set options that control the appearance and functionality of the Dock (page 34).

TIP You can learn how to further customize the Dock by adding, rearranging, or removing Dock icons on page 468.

TIP The Dock submenu under the Apple menu **Ⓑ** offers easy access to some of the options found in the Dock preferences pane, as well as a handy way to open the preferences pane.

To set Dock preferences:

Set options as desired in the Dock preferences pane **Ⓐ**:

- **Size** changes the size of the Dock and its icons. Drag the slider to resize.

- **Magnification** magnifies a Dock icon when you point to it **Ⓒ**. Use the slider to specify how much magnification there should be.

Ⓐ The Dock preferences pane.

Ⓑ The Dock submenu under the Apple menu offers several of the options found in the Dock preferences pane.

Ⓒ With magnification enabled, pointing to a Dock icon enlarges it. This is especially useful if you have very small Dock icons.

- **Position on screen** lets you move the Dock to the left side, bottom, or right side of the screen. When positioned on the left or right, the Dock fits vertically down the screen **Ⓓ**.

- **Minimize windows using** enables you to choose one of two special effects to use when minimizing a window to the Dock: Genie Effect or Scale Effect.

Ⓓ If you prefer, you can display the Dock vertically on one side of the screen.

continues on next page

- **Double-click a window's title bar to minimize** enables you to quickly minimize a window by double-clicking its title bar. (This option could be found in the General preferences pane in previous versions of OS X.)

- **Minimize windows into application icon** makes an application's minimized windows accessible from the application's icon in the Dock .

- **Animate opening applications** bounces an application's icon in the Dock as it opens.

- **Automatically hide and show the Dock** hides the Dock until you point to where it is hiding. This is a great way to regain screen real estate normally occupied by the Dock.

- **Show indicator lights for open applications** displays blue "bubbles" beneath Dock icons for applications that are open.

TIP Another way to change the size of the Dock and its icons is to drag the divider line up or down **F**.

E When you minimize windows into the application's Dock icon, you can access those windows from the application's Dock icon.

F Another way to resize the Dock icons is to drag the divider.

A The Language options in the Language & Text preferences pane.

B Drag a language to change its position in the preference order list.

C Toggle check boxes to specify which languages should appear in the list.

Language & Text

The Language & Text preferences pane enables you to set options that control how OS X works in an environment where U.S. English is not the primary language or where multiple languages are used.

Language & Text preferences are broken down into four different categories: Language, Text, Region, and Input Sources.

To set preferred language options:

1. In the Language & Text preferences pane, click the Language button **A**.

2. To set the preferred order for languages to appear in application menus and dialogs, drag languages up or down in the Languages list **B**.

3. To set sort order for text in lists, choose an option from the Order for sorted lists pop-up menu.

TIP The changes you make to the Languages list in step 2 take effect in the Finder the next time you restart or log in. Changes take effect in applications the next time you open them.

TIP The Order for sorted lists pop-up menu referred to in step 3 is very long and includes every language supported by OS X.

TIP You can edit the Languages list. Click the Edit List button in the Language pane **A**. In the dialog that appears **C**, toggle check boxes beside languages to specify which ones should appear in the list and click OK.

To set text substitution options:

1. In the Language & Text preferences pane, click the Text button .

2. In the Symbol and Text Substitution list, toggle check boxes to enable the automatic substitutions you want.

3. To add a new substitution to the list, click the + button at the bottom of the list and, in the new line that appears **E** enter the text you want to replace as well as the text you want to replace it with.

4. Choose options from the pop-up menus on the right side of the preferences pane as desired:

   ▸ **Spelling F** is the language you want to use for spelling checks in your document.

   ▸ **Word Break G** determines how a word is selected when double-clicked. Choose your language style.

   ▸ **Smart Quotes** enables you to specify how quote characters should be displayed. Choose options for double quotes **H** and single quotes **I**.

TIP Text substitution controls automatic text substitution options available in several Apple applications, including TextEdit, Calendar, and iMovie.

D The Text options in the Language & Text preferences pane.

E You can add a text substitution to the bottom of the list.

F Use this pop-up menu to choose the primary language for spelling checks in Apple applications.

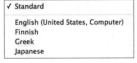

G The Word Break pop-up menu.

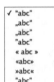

H I The two Smart Quotes pop-up menus.

J The Region options in the Language & Text preferences pane.

K Use this dialog to customize date formats.

L Use this dialog to customize time formats.

To set the date, time & number formats:

1. In the Language & Text preferences pane, click the Region button **J**.

2. Choose an option from the Region pop-up menu.

3. To customize the date or time format, click the Customize button in the appropriate area of the dialog. In the dialogs that appear **K** **L**, drag elements in the edit areas to set the formats and click OK.

4. Use the Calendar and First day of week pop-up menus to set additional calendar options as desired.

5. To customize the number format, click the Customize button in the Numbers area of the dialog, set options in the dialog that appears **M**, and click OK.

6. To change the currency format, choose an option from the Currency pop-up menu.

7. To change the measurement unit, choose an option from the Measurement Units pop-up menu.

TIP Changes in this pane affect how dates, times, and numbers are displayed throughout OS X and applications.

TIP The sample dates, times, and numbers in the Region pane **J** show the effect of your changes.

M Set number format options in this dialog.

To create & customize an input menu:

1. In the Language & Text preferences pane, click the Input Sources button .

2. Turn on the check boxes beside each input method or keyboard layout you may want to use with OS X. If more than one item is selected, an Input menu appears on the menu bar **O**.

3. Select one of the Input source options to determine whether you use the same input method in all documents or allow a different one for each document.

4. To toggle the display of the input menu, set the Show input menu in menu bar check box.

TIP If you're having trouble finding a language in the scrolling list, try entering all or part of its name in the Spotlight search box beneath the list **P**.

TIP To switch from one keyboard or input method to another, select an item from the Input menu **O** or press Option-Command-Spacebar to cycle through all options on the menu, one at a time.

TIP The Input menu may also automatically appear on the menu bar when you use the Special Characters command (page 340) in an application.

TIP Instructions for entering characters in complex languages such as Chinese is far beyond the scope of this book. If you need to use these features, you can find more information in Mac Help. Enter the search phrase *input method* to get started.

N The Input Sources options of the Language & Text preferences pane.

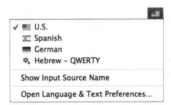

O When you enable several languages, an Input menu with each language you selected appears on the menu bar.

P You can use a Spotlight search field to help find a specific language in the list.

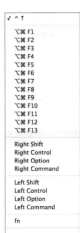

Mission Control

The Mission Control preferences pane **A** enables you to set general options and keyboard shortcuts for Mission Control (page 253), Exposé (page 255), Spaces (page 257), and Dashboard (Chapter 17) to customize the way these features work.

To set Mission Control preferences:

1. In the top part of the Mission Control preferences pane **A**, toggle check boxes to set options as desired:

   ▸ **Show Dashboard as a space** creates a separate space for Dashboard.

   ▸ **Automatically rearrange spaces based on most recent use** places the most recently used spaces to the left of other spaces.

   ▸ **When switching to an application, switch to a space with open windows for the application** switches spaces when you switch to an application that has windows open in a space.

   ▸ **Group windows by application** ensures that all windows for an application appear in the same space.

2. Under Keyboard and Mouse Shortcuts, use pop-up menus to choose keyboard keys **B** and mouse buttons **C** to activate various components of Mission Control and Dashboard.

> **TIP** If you hold down the Shift, Control, Option, or Command key while displaying the keyboard shortcuts or mouse button pop-up menu, the menu changes to reflect the key(s) being held **D**.

> **TIP** Clicking the Hot Corners button enables you to specify screen corners to invoke a Mission Control feature. You can learn more about setting hot corners on page 499.

A The Mission Control preferences pane.

B Use this menu to choose a keystroke to invoke a feature.

C Use this menu to choose a mouse button to invoke a feature.

D Holding down the Option and Command keys (for example) changes the options available in the menu.

Security & Privacy

The Security & Privacy preferences pane includes four panels of options that you can use to enhance security on your Mac:

- **General** offers options for protecting your computer from unauthorized access, primarily in a work environment where your computer is shared with other people. It also offers options for configuring Mountain Lion's new Gatekeeper feature, which can protect your computer from unauthorized apps.

- **FileVault** enables you to encrypt your hard disk's contents, making it virtually impossible for a hacker to access the files on your hard disk. Best of all, it's all done quickly and transparently—files are decrypted automatically when you log in and encrypted again when you log out.

- **Firewall** protects your computer from unauthorized access via a network or Internet connection by blocking your computer's networking ports from incoming traffic. You open only the ports you need to exchange information with various networking services. This helps prevent hackers from gaining access to your computer.

- **Privacy** enables you to set privacy options related to location services, Contacts, Twitter, and diagnostic and usage data.

TIP You must have an administrator user name and password to make changes to Security & Privacy preference pane options.

TIP If your computer never connects to the Internet and is not part of a network, there's no benefit to using the firewall feature.

A The General options in the Security & Privacy preferences pane.

B Use this dialog to enter a message to appear when the computer's screen is locked.

To set General security options:

1. In the Security & Privacy preferences pane, click the General button **A**.

2. If necessary, click the lock icon at the bottom of the window and enter an administrator name and password to unlock the preferences pane options.

3. Set basic options as desired:

   ▸ **Require password after sleep or screen saver begins** displays a login screen when you wake your computer or deactivate the screen saver (page 499). You can choose a time period from the pop-up menu, from immediately to 4 hours.

   ▸ **Show a message when the screen is locked** enables you to enter a message to display onscreen when the computer is locked. Click the Set Lock Message button to display a dialog **B**, enter the message you want, and click OK.

   ▸ **Disable automatic login** turns off the automatic login feature so a password is required to access the computer.

4. Choose one of the Gatekeeper security options to determine what downloaded applications should be allowed:

   ▸ **Mac App Store** allows you to install only apps downloaded from Apple's App Store (Chapter 13).

   ▸ **Mac App Store and identified developers** allows you to install apps downloaded from Apple's App Store (Chapter 13), as well as developers who have registered with Apple.

   ▸ **Anywhere** allows you to install any app you like.

continues on next page

5. To set additional, advanced options, click the Advanced button to display another dialog **C**. Then set options and click OK:

> **Log out after *n* minutes of inactivity** automatically logs out (page 122) a user who has been inactive for the number of minutes you specify.

> **Require an administrator password to access locked preferences** prompts for an administrator password before allowing modification of a locked System Preferences pane (page 491).

> **Automatically update safe downloads list** gets periodic updates about malware from Apple.

To enable FileVault:

1. In the Security & Privacy preferences pane, click the FileVault button **D**.

2. If necessary, click the lock icon at the bottom of the window and enter an administrator name and password to unlock the preferences pane options.

3. Click Turn On FileVault.

4. A dialog listing all of the computer's users appears **E**. For each user you want to access the encrypted disk, click the Enable User button, enter the user's password in the dialog that appears, and click OK.

5. Click Continue.

6. A dialog with a recovery key appears next **F**. Write down the key and put it in a safe place.

7. Click Continue.

C Use this dialog to set a few more advanced security options.

D Before enabling FileVault, the FileVault options look like this.

E Use this dialog to indicate who should have access to the encrypted files.

F Write down the recovery key that appears.

G You can store the recovery key with Apple.

H When your computer restarts, encryption begins.

I When encryption is done, the FileVault panel should look something like this.

8. Another dialog appears, offering to store the recovery key with Apple **G**. If you select the first option, choose three questions and enter three corresponding answers in the dialog.

9. Click Continue.

10. A dialog instructs you to click Restart to begin the encryption process. Click Restart.

11. Your computer restarts and presents a login screen. Enter your password and press Return.

    OS X encrypts your disk. You can monitor progress by opening the FileVault pane of the Security & Privacy preferences pane **H**. When encryption is complete, a message in the FileVault panel tells you **I**.

TIP You can continue working with your computer while it encrypts your hard disk.

TIP When FileVault is enabled, you must log in each time you start or wake your computer.

To turn off FileVault:

1. In the Security & Privacy preferences pane, click the FileVault button **I**.

2. If necessary, click the lock icon at the bottom of the window and enter an administrator name and password to unlock the preferences pane options.

3. Click Turn Off FileVault.

4. A confirmation dialog appears. Click Turn Off Encryption.

    OS X disables FileVault and decrypts your disk.

TIP You can continue working with your computer while it decrypts your hard disk.

To enable the firewall:

1. In the Security & Privacy preferences pane, click the Firewall button .

2. If necessary, click the lock icon at the bottom of the window and enter an administrator name and password to unlock the preferences pane options.

3. Click the Turn On Firewall button.

   The window changes to indicate that the firewall is On and a Turn Off Firewall button appears **K**.

TIP To disable the firewall, click the Turn Off Firewall button in the Firewall panel **K**.

To set advanced firewall options:

1. In the Firewall panel of the Security & Privacy pane **K**, click Firewall Options.

2. Set options in the dialog that appears **L**:

   ▸ **Block all incoming connections** does not allow any outside connections to your computer.

   ▸ To limit incoming connections to specific services and applications click the + button and use the Open dialog that appears to add applications. The Block all incoming connections check box must be turned off.

   ▸ **Automatically allow signed software to receive incoming connections** allows connections for services with a valid certificate of authority.

   ▸ **Enable stealth mode** prevents your computer from responding to access attempts, making it appear as if your computer does not exist.

3. Click OK.

J The Firewall panel looks like this before the firewall feature is turned on.

K Once the firewall is turned on, the Turn On Firewall button turns into a Turn Off Firewall button.

L You can set firewall options in this dialog.

M You can enable or disable location services for your computer or for specific applications.

N Specify which apps can access information in your Contacts database.

O Specify which apps (if any) can access your Twitter account.

P You can help Apple improve its products by sending anonymous information about how you use your Mac.

To set Privacy options:

1. In the Security & Privacy preferences pane, click the Privacy button.

2. If necessary, click the lock icon at the bottom of the window and enter an administrator name and password to unlock the preferences pane options.

3. To enable or disable location services for your computer or specific applications, click Location Services **M**. Then toggle check boxes on the right side of the window.

4. To specify which applications can access your Contacts database, click Contacts **N** and then toggle check boxes on the right side of the window.

5. To specify which applications can access your Twitter account, click Twitter **O** and then toggle check boxes on the right side of the window.

6. To specify whether your computer should send anonymous information to Apple about how you use your computer, click Diagnostics & Usage **P** and toggle the check box on the right side of the window.

Spotlight

You can set options for the way Spotlight works and the results it shows in search results windows. You do this in the two panels of the Spotlight preferences pane:

- **Search Results** enables you to determine which categories of items should appear in search results and what order they should appear in.

- **Privacy** enables you to exclude specific folders or disks from searches.

To set Spotlight Search Results menu preferences:

1. In the Spotlight preferences pane, click the Search Results button **A**.

2. Toggle check boxes to specify which categories of search results should be displayed.

3. To change the order in which categories should appear in search results, drag a category to a new position in the list **B**.

TIP The changes you make in the Spotlight Search Results panel affect the Spotlight search menu **C** only—not the other search features of OS X.

A Use the Search Results panel to specify which categories of items should appear in search results and what order they should appear in.

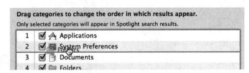

B Changing the order of search results is as easy as dragging categories around in a list.

C Changes affect the Spotlight menu's search results.

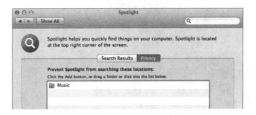

D The Privacy options in the Spotlight preferences pane.

E Use an Open dialog like this to locate, select, and choose folders or disks to exclude.

F Or drag a folder from the Finder into the list in the Spotlight preferences pane.

To exclude locations from search:

1. In the Spotlight preferences pane, click the Privacy button **D**.

2. Do one of the following:

   ▶ Click the + button beneath the list and use the dialog that appears **E** to add the folder or disk you want to exclude from searches.

   ▶ Drag a folder or disk from a Finder window into the list area **F**.

   The item is added to the list **G**.

3. Repeat step 2 for each item you want to exclude from searches.

TIP To remove an item from the list **G**, select the item and click the − button at the bottom of the list. The item is removed from the list and will be included in future searches.

TIP The Privacy panel settings affect all OS X search features—not just the Spotlight menu.

G The folder is added to the list and will be excluded from searches.

To set Spotlight keyboard shortcuts:

1. Display either panel of the Spotlight preferences pane Ⓐ Ⓓ.

2. Toggle the check boxes to enable or disable the two shortcuts:

   ‣ **Spotlight menu keyboard shortcut** displays the Spotlight menu Ⓗ.

   ‣ **Spotlight window keyboard shortcut** displays the Searching window for the results of a Spotlight Search Ⓘ.

3. To set a shortcut key, select an option from the drop-down list or select the list and press the keys you want to assign.

Ⓗ Pressing Command-Spacebar displays the Spotlight search menu.

Ⓘ Pressing Option-Command-Spacebar displays the Searching window.

Notifications

The Notifications preferences pane **A**, which is new in OS X Mountain Lion, enables you to set preferences for the new Notification Center feature (page XX). You can specify which applications appear in Notification Center, as well as how their alerts appear. You can also set the sort order for Notification Center items.

A The Notifications preferences pane.

B A banner is a notification that appears onscreen but disappears after a few moments.

C An alert is a notification that remains onscreen until you dismiss it.

D In this example, I have notifications from two different apps.

To set Notification Center options for applications:

1. In the Notification Center preferences pane, select the application you want to set options for **A**.

2. Click to choose an alert style:

   ▸ **None** does not display any alert.

   ▸ **Banners** displays a message in the upper-right corner of the screen that disappears after a few moments **B**.

   ▸ **Alerts** display a message in the upper-right corner of the screen that must be manually dismissed **C**.

3. Toggle check boxes to set other options:

   ▸ **Show in Notification Center** includes the application's activity in Notification Center **D**. With this option turned on, you can use the pop-up menu to specify how many of the most recent items should appear. If you turn this check box off, the application moves to the bottom of the application list.

   ▸ **Badge app icon** displays a number on the application's icon in the Dock or Finder windows that indicates how many notifications exist for that item.

   ▸ **Play sound when receiving notifications** plays an alert sound each time a new notification is received.

4. Repeat steps 1 through 3 for each application you want to set options for.

5. To specify whether a Share button should appear in Notification Center , select Share Button in the application list and toggle the check box on the right side of the window.

6. To set the sort order for notifications, choose an option from the Sort Notification Center pop-up menu:

▸ **Manually** enables you to set the order by dragging applications up or down in the application list **E**.

▸ **By time** sorts the notifications by time with the most recent on top.

E To manually sort notifications, drag apps up or down in the application list.

Hardware Preferences

Hardware preferences panes enable you to configure the hardware components of your computer system. This chapter covers the following System Preferences panes:

- **CDs & DVDs** controls the way your optical drive works.

- **Displays** controls monitor settings, including resolution and color.

- **Energy Saver** controls energy consumption and schedules.

- **Keyboard** controls USB or Bluetooth keyboard operation and lets you customize keyboard shortcuts.

- **Mouse** controls USB or Bluetooth mouse operation.

- **Trackpad** controls built-in or Bluetooth trackpad options and operation.

- **Print & Scan** enables you to set up printers, scanners, and fax modems.

- **Sound** controls sound input and output options, as well as alert sounds.

Need to learn the basics of System Preferences? Be sure to read Chapter 32.

CDs & DVDs

The CDs & DVDs preferences pane lets you specify what should happen when you insert a CD or DVD disc.

The options that appear vary depending on your computer's CD and DVD capabilities. The illustration here shows how this preferences pane appears for a MacBook Air with a MacBook Air SuperDrive connected. This external drive, which is capable of reading and writing both CDs and DVDs, provides the same capabilities as the internal optical drive available in most recently released Macintosh models.

A The CDs & DVDs preferences pane, as it appears for a MacBook Air with a MacBook Air SuperDrive attached and iPhoto installed.

To specify what should happen when you insert a CD or DVD:

In the CDs & DVDs preferences pane **A**, choose an option from the pop-up menu beside each event that you want to set. The menus are basically the same; **B** and **C** show examples for a blank CD and a music CD. Your options are:

- **Ask what to do** displays a dialog **D** when you insert that type of disc. This enables you to tell your computer what to do on the fly, when a disc is inserted.

- **Open** *application name* always opens the specified application when you insert that type of disc.

- **Open other application** displays a dialog you can use to select the application that should open when you insert that type of disc.

- **Run script** displays a dialog you can use to select an AppleScript applet (page 392) that should open when you insert that type of disc.

- **Ignore** tells your computer not to do anything when you insert that type of disc.

B C The pop-up menu of options for a blank CD (top) and a music CD (bottom). The other pop-up menus are very similar.

D Use this dialog to tell your computer what to do when you insert a disc.

A The Display options of the Displays preferences pane for an 11-inch MacBook Air with the Best for built-in display option selected.

B The Display options of the Displays preferences pane for a 15-inch MacBook Pro with Retina display with the Best for built-in display option selected.

C Display options for a MacBook Air with the Scaled option selected.

Displays

The Displays preferences pane enables you to set the resolution, colors, and other settings for your monitor. Settings are organized into panes; this section covers the Display and Color panes.

The options that are available in the Displays preferences pane vary depending on your computer and monitor. The options shown in this chapter are for an 11-inch MacBook Air and a 15-inch MacBook Pro with Retina display.

To set display options:

1. In the Displays preferences pane, click the Display button **A** **B**.

2. Set options as desired:

   ▶ **Resolution** controls the number of pixels that appear on screen. The higher the resolution, the more pixels. This makes the screen contents smaller but shows more. To choose a specific resolution, if necessary, select Scaled **C** **D** and then choose the resolution you want.

continues on next page

D Display options for a MacBook Pro with Retina display with the Scaled option selected.

- **Brightness** lets you adjust the display's brightness by dragging a slider.

- **Automatically adjust brightness** adjusts brightness based on the brightness of your workspace. This option only appears on computers that support it.

- **Show mirroring options in the menu bar when available** adds a menu you can use to set mirroring options when more than one monitor is connected.

TIP If you have multiple displays connected to your Mac, the Display pane will appear for each one.

TIP On a Retina display, you can point to each of the resolution options to see a preview of it in the preferences pane.

TIP If you have an Apple TV, you can use the AirPlay mirroring pop-up menu **B D** to mirror your display on your television.

To set display color options:

1. In the Displays preferences pane, click the Color button **E**.

2. To limit the selection of color profiles to just those designed to work with your display, turn on the Show profiles for this display only check box.

3. To use a predefined display, select one of the Display Profiles.

4. To get details for a selected display, click the Open Profile button to display a window with information **F**. You can click the window's close button to dismiss it when you're finished.

5. To calibrate your monitor, click the Calibrate button. This launches the Display Calibrator Assistant **G**, which steps you through the process of fine-tuning color options for your display.

E The Color pane of the Displays preferences pane for an 11-inch MacBook Air.

F The details of a color profile. (If you understand this, you qualify as a true Color Geek.)

G The first screen of the Display Calibrator Assistant.

TIP Color profiles and the Display Calibrator Assistant are advanced feature of OS X. They work with ColorSync (page 377) to display colors onscreen as they will appear when printed.

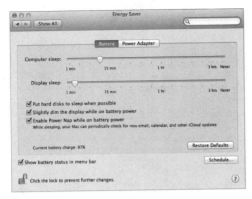

A The Energy Saver preferences pane on a MacBook Air. These are the settings for when on battery power...

B ...and these are the settings for when plugged into a power adapter.

Energy Saver

The Energy Saver preferences pane enables you to specify settings that can reduce the amount of power your computer uses when idle.

Energy Saver settings are especially important for laptop users running on battery power. Because of this, laptops have two panes of settings: one for Battery power **A** and one for when connected to a Power Adapter **B**.

The appearance of and options in the Energy Saver preferences pane vary depending on your computer. The illustrations here are for a MacBook Air.

To set Energy Saver options:

1. If necessary, in the Energy Saver preferences pane, click the button to select the power source you want to configure for: Battery **A** or Power Adapter **B**.

2. To set the amount of inactive time before the computer sleeps, drag the Computer sleep slider to the right or left. Dragging all the way to the right disables computer sleep.

3. To set the amount of inactive time before the display sleeps, drag the Display sleep slider to the left or right. (You cannot set display sleep for longer than computer sleep.) Dragging all the way to the right disables display sleep.

4. Toggle check boxes to set additional options as desired:

   ▸ **Put hard disks to sleep when possible** tells your computer to put any internal or external hard disks to sleep when they aren't needed.

continues on next page

- **Slightly dim the display while on battery power** reduces the brightness of the display when the computer is not plugged in.

- **Wake for Wi-Fi network access** wakes the computer from computer sleep when it detects a Wake-on-LAN packet.

- **Enable Power Nap while on battery power** or **Enable Power Nap while plugged into a power adapter** enables the Power Nap feature, which is new in OS X Mountain Lion. This enables your computer to perform the listed tasks while sleeping.

- **Start up automatically after a power failure** (not shown) automatically restarts the computer when power is restored after a power failure. This option only appears for desktop Macs.

5. To display battery status on a laptop's menu bar **C**, turn on the Show battery status in menu bar check box.

TIP To wake a sleeping display, press any key. A sleeping hard disk wakes automatically when it needs to.

TIP If your computer is being used as a server, it's important to turn on the Restart automatically check box. This ensures that the computer is running whenever possible.

TIP A kernel panic is a computer operating system "crash" that dims the screen and displays a multilanguage message telling you you'll need to restart.

TIP Choosing Show Percentage from the Battery Status menu on the menu bar **C** displays the percentage of battery power left beside the battery icon.

TIP You can click the Restore Defaults button in the Energy Saver preferences pane to revert to Energy Saver "factory settings."

7:54 Remaining
Power Source: Battery

Show Percentage
Open Energy Saver Preferences...

C The Battery Status menu offers a handy way to see how much power is left in your laptop's battery. (Gotta love the battery life in a MacBook Air, huh?)

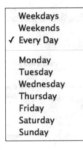

D Use this dialog to schedule automatic startup and shutdown days and times.

E Use this pop-up menu to specify the days of the week your computer should automatically start up or shut down.

| Weekdays |
| Weekends |
| ✓ Every Day |
| Monday |
| Tuesday |
| Wednesday |
| Thursday |
| Friday |
| Saturday |
| Sunday |

| Sleep |
| Restart |
| ✓ Shut Down |

F Use this pop-up menu to specify what it should do at shut down time.

G Your computer will give you a 10-minute warning before shutting down automatically.

To schedule start up & shut down:

1. In the Energy Saver preferences pane, click the Schedule button to display the schedule dialog **D**.

2. To set automatic startup, turn on the Start up or wake check box. Then choose an option from the pop-up menu **E** and enter a time beside it.

3. To set automatic sleep, restart, or shut down, turn on the second check box, choose options from the pop-up menus beside it **E F**, and enter a time beside them.

4. Click OK to save your settings.

TIP Your computer will give you a 10-minute warning for a scheduled shutdown. When the warning dialog appears **G**, you can choose to cancel the shutdown, shut down immediately, or just wrap up your work and let the computer shut down when it's ready.

TIP A laptop will not automatically start unless it is connected to a power adapter.

Keyboard

The Keyboard preferences pane enables you to customize the way the keyboard works. Options can be set in at least two panes:

- **Keyboard** enables you to set keyboard functionality options, such as key repeat rate.

- **Keyboard Shortcuts** enables you to view and assign shortcuts for application menu commands.

The appearance of the Keyboard preferences pane varies depending on the type of computer and keyboard you are using. The illustrations here are for a MacBook Air.

TIP To use a Bluetooth keyboard with your Mac, it must be paired (page 552).

To set keyboard options:

1. In the Keyboard preferences pane, click the Keyboard button **A**.

2. Set options as desired:

   ▸ **Key Repeat** sets how fast a key repeats when held down. (Adjusting this is especially useful for heavy-handed typists.)

   ▸ **Delay Until Repeat** sets how long a key must be pressed before it starts to repeat.

3. Set additional options, if available, for a keyboard:

   ▸ **Use all F1, F2, etc. keys as standard function keys** takes away special functionality for these keys, such as brightness and volume control, and requires you to press the FN key with those keys for the same functionality.

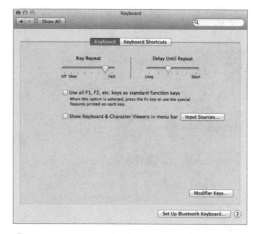

A The Keyboard options in the Keyboard preferences pane on a MacBook Air.

You can display this menu in the menu bar.

C Use the Character Viewer to insert a special character into a document with just a click.

D Use the Keyboard Viewer to enter characters by clicking a keyboard.

For each modifier key listed below, choose the action you want it to perform from the pop-up menu.

Caps Lock (⇪) Key: ⇪ Caps Lock ⬍
Control (^) Key: ^ Control ⬍
Option (⌥) Key: ⌥ Option ⬍
Command (⌘) Key: ⌘ Command ⬍

Restore Defaults   Cancel   **OK**

E You can use this dialog to change the behavior of modifier keys.

- ▶ **Illuminate keyboard in low light conditions** (not shown) turns on backlighting for your keyboard in low light conditions. (Keep in mind that this can reduce battery life.)

- ▶ **Turn off when computer is not used for** (not shown) lets you specify, with a slider, how long before keyboard lighting should be turned off when the computer is idle.

- ▶ **Show Keyboard & Character Viewers in menu bar** displays a menu **B**, which you can use to display the Character Viewer **C** and Keyboard Viewer **D** palettes. These palettes enable you to enter characters into OS X applications by clicking a palette button.

4. To change the behavior of modifier keys such as Command, Option, and Control, click the Modifier Keys button. In the dialog that appears **E**, use the pop-up menus to set the action you want each key to perform and click OK.

TIP Clicking the Input Sources button in the Keyboard pane displays the Input Sources pane of the Language & Text preferences pane (page 503).

TIP Why you'd want to change the behavior of modifier keys is beyond me. It would make a good April Fool's joke, though.

TIP If you have a Bluetooth keyboard paired and connected to your Mac, a battery level indicator will appear in the bottom-left corner of the Keyboard preferences pane.

To customize keyboard shortcuts:

1. In the Keyboard preferences pane, click the Keyboard Shortcuts button **F**.

2. In the list on the left side of the window, select the category or type of shortcut key you want to change.

3. To turn a shortcut on or off, toggle its check box in the list on the right side of the window.

4. To modify keyboard shortcuts in the list on the right side of the window, double-click the shortcut you want to change so it becomes selected **G** and then hold down the new keys to make the change **H**.

5. To set the way the Tab key highlights items in windows and dialogs, select one of the two options at the bottom of the preferences pane: Text boxes and lists only or All controls.

> **TIP** You can also use the Keyboard Shortcuts pane **F** to learn about shortcuts available in the Finder and other applications that do not appear on menus. The ones listed under Keyboard & Text Input are especially interesting and you may find them useful.

> **TIP** When you add a keyboard shortcut for a menu command, the shortcut appears on the menu **I**.

> **TIP** You can click the Restore Defaults button to set all keyboard shortcuts back to "factory settings."

F The Keyboard Shortcuts options of the Keyboard preferences pane on a MacBook Air.

G To change a shortcut, double-click it...

H ...and then press the desired keys.

I Keyboard shortcuts you change or add for menu commands appear on the menus. (You may have to restart the computer to see the change.)

J In this example, I'm adding a shortcut to System Preferences that'll display the Keyboard preferences pane.

K The new shortcut appears in the list.

To add and remove application shortcuts:

1. In the Keyboard preferences pane, click the Keyboard Shortcuts button **F**.

2. In the list on the left side of the window, select Application Shortcuts.

3. Do the following:

   ▸ To add a shortcut, click the + button at the bottom of the list. Then set options in the dialog that appears **J** to specify the application, menu command, and keyboard shortcut you want to add. Click Add and the shortcut is added to the list **K**.

   ▸ To remove a shortcut, select the shortcut you want to add and click the – (minus) button at the bottom of the list. The shortcut is removed.

Mouse

The Mouse preferences pane enables you to set mouse functionality options, such as scroll speed and button assignment.

The appearance of the Mouse preferences pane varies depending on the type of mouse connected to your Macintosh. The illustrations here show settings for a USB Apple Mouse and a Bluetooth Magic Mouse. If you have a different kind of mouse, you'll see different—but likely similar—options.

TIP To use a Bluetooth mouse with your Mac, it must be paired (page 552).

To set Apple Mouse options:

1. Make sure your mouse is properly paired or connected to your Mac.

2. Open the Mouse preferences pane **A**.

3. To determine the scrolling direction toggle the check box at the top of the window. Leaving this check box turned on sets scrolling so content moves in the same direction as your fingers.

4. Use sliders at the top of the pane to set speed options:

   ▸ **Tracking** is the speed of the pointer movement on your screen.

   ▸ **Double-Click** is the amount of time between each click of a double-click.

   ▸ **Scrolling** is how scroll ball movements are translated to window scrolling.

5. Use pop-up menus **B** to assign actions to each mouse button.

6. Select an option from the Scrolling pop-up menu **C** to determine how the scroll ball scrolls window contents.

A The Mouse preferences pane with a USB Apple Mouse connected.

B Use a pop-up menu like this one to assign an action to each button.

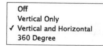

C Use this pop-up menu to specify how scrolling should work.

TIP If you choose Other from any of the button pop-up menus **B**, you can assign that button to an application.

D The Point & Click options of the Mouse preferences pane with a Magic Mouse connected.

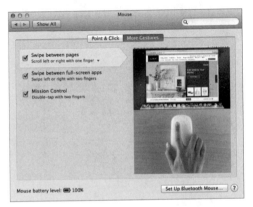

E The More Gestures options of the Mouse preferences pane with a Magic Mouse connected.

TIP You can learn more about the Multi-Touch gestures supported by your Magic Mouse by pointing to an option and watching the video demonstration in the window to the right **D E**.

TIP If you have a Bluetooth mouse paired and connected to your Mac, a battery level indicator will appear in the bottom-left corner of the Mouse preferences pane **D E**.

To set Magic Mouse options:

1. Make sure your mouse is properly paired and connected to your Mac.

2. Open the Mouse preferences pane and, if necessary, click the Point & Click button **D**.

3. To determine the scrolling direction, toggle the Scroll direction: natural check box. Leaving this check box turned on sets scrolling so content moves in the same direction as your fingers.

4. To enable a right-click button, turn on the Secondary click check box and choose an option from the pop-up menu beneath it. Your options are Click on right side or Click on left side.

5. To enable or disable zooming by double-tapping with one finger, toggle the Smart zoom check box.

6. To set the speed of the pointer movement on your screen, drag the Tracking slider to the left or right.

7. Click the More Gestures button **E** and toggle check boxes to enable the gestures you want to use:

   ▸ **Swipe between pages** lets you move from page to page by swiping. If you enable this feature, choose an option from the pop-up menu to specify how many fingers to use for swiping.

   ▸ **Swipe between full-screen apps** enables you to swipe to the left or right with two fingers to switch from one full-screen app to the next.

   ▸ **Mission Control** opens Mission Control (page 253) when you double-tap the mouse with two fingers.

Trackpad

The Trackpad preferences pane, which is only available on computers with a built-in or connected trackpad, enables you to set trackpad functionality options, such as tracking speed and trackpad gestures.

The options that appear in Trackpad preferences vary depending on the computer model and type of trackpad. The illustrations here show options for the trackpad on a MacBook Air; options are identical for recent MacBook Pro models and Apple's Magic Trackpad. Older laptop models may not support all gesture options.

TIP To use a Bluetooth trackpad with your Mac, it must be paired (page 552).

To set trackpad options:

1. Open the Trackpad preferences pane.

2. If necessary, click Point & Click and set options **A**:

   ▸ **Tap to Click** enables you to click with a light tap rather than pressing down hard enough to feel or hear a click.

   ▸ **Secondary click** enables right-clicking (page 13) with one finger. If you enable this option, use the menu to specify whether you'll use two fingers or click in the bottom-right or bottom-left corner of the trackpad.

   ▸ **Look up** enables you to double-tap a word with three fingers to look it up in the Dictionary **B**.

   ▸ **Three Finger Drag** enables you to move items by dragging with three fingers.

   ▸ **Tracking Speed** is the speed of the pointer movement on your screen. Drag the slider to the left or right.

A The Point & Click options in the Trackpad preferences pane for a Multi-Touch trackpad.

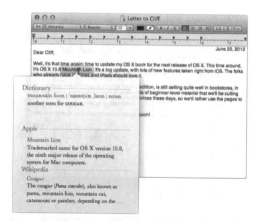

B With the Look up option enabled, you can get information about a word in a document by double-tapping it with three fingers.

⊙ The Scroll & Zoom options in the Trackpad preferences pane for a Multi-Touch trackpad.

⊙ The More Gestures options in the Trackpad preferences pane for a Multi-Touch trackpad.

TIP You can learn more about the Multi-Touch gestures supported by your trackpad by pointing to an option and watching the video demonstration in the window to the right **Ⓐ Ⓒ Ⓓ**.

TIP If you have a Bluetooth trackpad paired and connected to your Mac, a battery level indicator will appear in the bottom-left corner of the Trackpad preferences pane.

3. Click Scroll & Zoom and set options **⊙**:

    ▸ **Scroll direction: natural** sets scrolling so content moves in the same direction as your fingers.

    ▸ **Zoom in or out** enables you to zoom images and other content by pinching with two fingers.

    ▸ **Smart zoom** zooms content when you tap it with two fingers.

    ▸ **Rotate** enables you to rotate images and other content by dragging in a rotating motion with two fingers.

4. Click More Gestures and set options **⊙**:

    ▸ **Swipe between pages** enables you to flip from one document page to another by swiping. Choose the number of fingers from the pop-up menu.

    ▸ **Swipe between full-screen apps** enables you to swipe to the left or right to switch from one full-screen app to the next. Choose the number of fingers from the pop-up menu.

    ▸ **Notification Center** opens Notification Center (page XXX) when you swipe to the left from the right edge with two fingers.

    ▸ **Mission Control** opens Mission Control (page 253) when you swipe up. Choose the number of fingers from the pop-up menu.

    ▸ **App Exposé** opens Exposé (page 255) when you swipe down. Choose the number of fingers from the pop-up menu.

    ▸ **Launchpad** enables you to pinch with your thumb and three fingers to open Launchpad.

    ▸ **Show Desktop** enables you to spread with your thumb and three fingers to view the desktop.

Print & Scan

Before you can print from an OS X application, you must make a printer accessible to OS X. You do this with the Print & Scan preferences pane **Ⓐ**.

OS X is smart. If you connect a printer directly to your Mac and it has an appropriate driver installed, it automatically recognizes the printer and adds it to the Printers list.

However if OS X does not recognize your printer or you want to use a printer accessible via a network (page 343), you may need to manually add the printer to the Print & Scan preferences pane.

The Print & Scan preferences pane enables you to perform the following tasks:

- Add printers, scanners, and fax modems to the Printers list that your Mac consults when printing or scanning.

- Set the default printer and paper size.

- Set printer options.

- Create printer pools (page 343) so your print jobs go to whatever networked printer is available when you're ready to print.

TIP You only have to add a printer if it does not already appear in the Printers list. This needs to be done only once; OS X will remember all printers that you add.

TIP You may have to unlock this preferences pane to set certain options in it. You can learn how on page 491.

TIP To set up printer sharing with the Sharing preferences pane, consult the section titled "To enable & configure printer sharing" on page 556.

Ⓐ The Print & Scan preferences pane with four printers added to the Printers list: a laser printer accessible via Time Capsule with Back to My Mac and a wide area network connection, a Wi-Fi inkjet printer accessible via local area network connection, a laser printer directly connected via USB, and a laser printer connected to another computer and shared over the local area network. This is not a typical setup, but it is possible.

B In this example, all I did was plug in my printer—OS X offered to do the rest.

C In this example, my Mac automatically recognized and set up a printer that was directly connected to it via USB cable.

D If your printer is not automatically added, you can use the + button at the bottom of the printer list to manually add it.

To add a printer that is listed by default:

1. If necessary, connect the printer you want to use with the computer and turn it on.

   If the printer appears in the Print & Scan preferences pane **A**, you're done. You can skip the remaining steps.

2. If a dialog appears, offering to download driver software **B**, click install. Then wait while your computer downloads and installs the print drivers for your printer.

   The printer should appear in the Print & Scan preferences pane **C**; you're done and you can skip the remaining steps.

3. Click the + button beneath the Printers list in the Print & Scan preferences pane **A** to display a menu that lists the printers your computer "sees" locally or on a network you are connected to **D**.

4. Do one of the following:

   ▸ If the printer you want to add appears in the menu, select it.

   ▸ If the printer you want to add does not appear in the menu, skip the remaining steps and follow the instructions in the section titled "To add a printer that is not listed by default" on page 536.

5. Follow steps 1 and 2 to complete the installation.

TIP If you directly connect a printer to your Mac, it may offer to install the software and add the printer without even opening the Print & Scan preferences pane **B**.

TIP In step 3, if the printer you want to use does not appear in the list, double-check to make sure the printer is connected to your computer or network and turned on.

To add a printer that is not listed by default:

1. If you haven't already done so, follow step 3 in the section titled "To add a printer that is listed by default" on page 535.

2. On the pop-up menu **D**, choose Add Printer or Scanner.

   The Add dialog appears.

3. In the dialog's toolbar, click the button for the type of printer you want to add:

   ▸ **Default E** lists the printers your computer sees.

   ▸ **Fax F** lets you add an internal, external, or network fax modem.

   ▸ **IP G** enables you to add a printer at a specific IP address.

   ▸ **Windows H** lets you add a printer connected to a Windows computer or Windows network.

4. Set options in the bottom of the dialog for the printer type and location.

5. Click Add. The printer is added to the Printers list **A**.

TIP In step 3, it may be necessary to log in to a network to access certain types of network printers.

To delete a printer:

1. In the Printers list, select the printer you want to delete **A**.

2. Click the – button beneath the list.

3. Click Delete Printer in the confirmation dialog that appears.

   The printer is removed from the list.

TIP You cannot print to a printer that you have deleted unless you re-add it.

E F G H The Add dialog for default printers, fax modems, IP printers, and Windows printers.

① Use this pop-up menu of printers to choose the one to use by default.

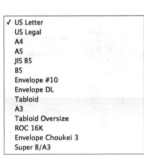

① The word *Default* appears beneath the name of the default printer in the Printers list.

⑥ Use this pop-up menu to choose the printer's default paper size.

To set the default printer:

In the Print & Scan preferences pane, choose one of the printers from the Default Printer pop-up menu **①**.

The word *Default* appears in the Printers list beneath the name of the printer you chose **①**.

TIP The default printer is the one that is automatically chosen when you open the Print dialog (page 345).

TIP If you choose Last Printer Used from the Default Printer pop-up menu **①**, the last printer you used to print becomes the default printer. Thus, the default printer changes every time you choose a different printer for printing.

To set the default paper size:

1. In the Printers list, select the printer you want to set the default paper size for **④**.
2. Choose one of the paper sizes from the Default Paper Size pop-up menu **⑥**.

TIP The default paper size is the one that is automatically chosen when you open the Page Setup dialog (page 344).

To open a print queue:

1. In the Printers list, select the name of the printer queue you want to open **④**.
2. Click Open Print Queue.

   The print queue window opens, displaying status and active print jobs.

TIP The print queue feature is illustrated and discussed in detail on page 355.

To configure a printer:

1. In the Printers list **A**, select the printer you want to configure.

2. Click the Options & Supplies button.

3. Set options or review information in the three or four separate panes of the dialog that appears:

   ▸ **General ①** enables you to set the printer's name and location and provides additional information about the printer's location and driver.

   ▸ **Driver ⓜ** enables you to set the printer driver and set printer-specific options (if available).

   ▸ **Supply Levels ⓝ** enables you to see the ink or toner levels for printers that can communicate this information to your computer. (Only one of my printers can do this, so don't feel slighted if this pane comes up blank for you.)

   ▸ **Utility ⓞ** may give you access to additional installed utilities to work with your printer. This option is only available for some printers.

4. Click OK to save your settings.

TIP The options that appear in each pane of this dialog vary depending on printer type and model. It's not possible to show all configuration options for all printers. The instructions and illustrations here should be enough to get you started with your printer. Consult the manual that came with your printer for more information.

① ⓜ ⓝ ⓞ The Options & Supplies dialog's four possible panes. The first two are for a color HP LaserJet printer; the last two are for an all-in-one color Epson printer. Options vary widely depending on the printer.

① When you select multiple printers, the Create Printer Pool button appears in the Print & Scan dialog.

① A printer pool is added to the Printers list.

② Drag a printer from the Printers list to the desktop or a Finder window.

③ A desktop printer is actually an alias file for a printer.

To create a printer pool:

1. In the Printers list, select the printers you want to include in the printer pool **①**. To select more than one printer at a time, hold down the Command key while clicking the name of each one.

2. Click the Create Printer Pool button **①**.

3. Enter a name for the printer pool in the Name box of the dialog that appears, and click OK.

   The printer pool you created appears in the Printers list window **①**.

TIP When you print to a printer pool, your computer automatically looks at each printer in the pool, in the order they are listed, and prints to the first one available.

To delete a printer pool:

1. In the Printers list, select the printer pool you want to delete **①**.

2. Click the – button beneath the list.

3. Click Delete Printer in the confirmation dialog that appears.

   The printer pool is removed from the list.

TIP Deleting a printer pool does not delete the printers it includes.

To create a desktop printer:

In the Print & Scan preferences pane, drag the icon for the printer you want to create a desktop printer for out of the window and onto the desktop **②**.

When you release the button, an alias icon (page 82) for the printer appears on the desktop **③**.

TIP Using desktop printers is covered on page 355.

Sound

The Sound preferences pane enables you to set options to control the system and alert sounds, output device, and input device. Sound settings can be changed in three panels:

- **Sound Effects** lets you set options for alert sounds and sound effects.
- **Output** allows you to set the output device and balance.
- **Input** enables you to set the input device and volume.

The options that appear in the Sound preferences pane vary depending on your computer and connected audio devices. The options shown here are for a MacBook Air.

To set system volume:

1. Display any panel of the Sound preferences pane **Ⓐ**.
2. If necessary, on a Mac with only one audio port, select an option from the Use audio port for pop-up menu (not shown) to determine whether the audio port is used for Sound Input or Sound Output.
3. Set options in the bottom of the window:
   - ▸ **Output volume** is the overall output volume for all sounds. Drag the slider to the left or right. Each time you move and release the slider, an alert sounds so you can hear a sample of your change.
   - ▸ **Mute** keeps your computer quiet.
   - ▸ **Show volume in menu bar** displays a Sound Volume menu in the menu bar **Ⓑ**.

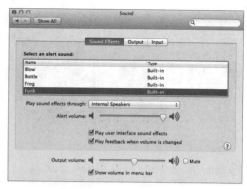

Ⓐ The Sound Effects panel of the Sound preferences pane on a MacBook Air.

Ⓑ You can display a Sound Volume menu in the menu bar.

To set sound effects options:

1. In the Sound preferences pane, click the Sound Effects button Ⓐ.

2. To set the alert sound, select one of the options in the scrolling list. Each time you select a sound, it plays so you can hear what it sounds like.

3. Set other options as desired:

   - **Play sound effects through** enables you to set the output device for alert and sound effect sounds. If you choose Selected sound output device, it will use whatever is set in the Output panel (page 542).

   - **Alert volume** is the volume of alert sounds. Drag the slider to the left or right. Each time you move and release the slider, an alert sounds so you can hear a sample of your change.

   - **Play user interface sound effects** plays sound effects for different system events, such as dragging an icon to the Trash or completing a copy operation.

   - **Play feedback when volume is changed** enables you to hear the volume each time you change it.

TIP Alert volume depends partly on the system volume setting, which is discussed on page 540. An alert sound cannot be louder than the system sound.

To set output device options:

1. In the Sound preferences pane, click the Output button **C**.

2. To set the output device, select one of the options in the scrolling list.

   The options that appear depend on the devices connected to your computer.

3. To set the speaker balance for the selected device, drag the Balance slider to the left or right. Each time you move and release the slider, an alert sounds so you can hear a sample of your change.

To set input device options:

1. In the Sound preferences pane, click the Input button **D**.

2. To set the input device, select one of the options in the scrolling list.

   The options that appear depend on the devices connected to your computer.

3. To set the input volume for the selected device, drag the Input volume slider to the left or right. The further to the right you drag the slider, the more sensitive the microphone will be. You can test this by watching the Input level bars as you speak or make sounds.

4. To filter out ambient sounds, turn on the Use ambient noise reduction check box. (This option is only available for some input devices.)

TIP Input device and volume are especially important if you plan to use OS X's speech recognition features (page 585).

C The Output panel of the Sound preferences pane.

D The Input panel of the Sound preferences pane.

Internet & Wireless Preferences

Internet & Wireless preferences panes enable you to configure your Mac to take advantage of networking, sharing, and Internet-based services. This chapter covers the following System Preferences panes:

- **iCloud** enables you to set up your computer to work with Apple's iCloud suite of cloud-based services.

- **Mail, Contacts & Calendars** helps you configure a variety of Internet-based account services.

- **Network** enables you to fine-tune network connection settings.

- **Bluetooth** enables you to pair and manage Bluetooth devices.

- **Sharing** enables you to set up sharing services, including file sharing and printer sharing.

Need to learn the basics of System Preferences? Be sure to read Chapter 32.

In This Chapter:

iCloud

The iCloud preferences pane enables you to set up your Mac to take advantage of the features of iCloud, an Apple, Inc. cloud-based service. iCloud offers a number of features that can work with computers running OS X and iOS devices such as the iPad, iPhone, and iPod touch. iCloud is free for up to 5 GB of storage space; additional space is available for an annual fee.

You use the iCloud preferences pane to sign your computer into iCloud, choose the services you want to use with it, and monitor your storage space usage.

You can learn more about using iCloud in Chapter 19, which covers its features and use. This part of the chapter concentrates on settings in the iCloud preferences pane.

TIP iCloud replaces MobileMe, a similar service that was discontinued in June 2012.

To sign in to iCloud:

1. In the iCloud preferences pane **Ⓐ**, enter your Apple ID and password in the appropriate boxes.

2. Click Sign In.

   Your Mac goes online to validate your password. It then displays a list of available services and a status bar representing storage use **Ⓑ**.

TIP If, for some reason, you decide you don't want to be connected to iCloud, you can click the Sign Out button in the iCloud preferences pane **Ⓑ**. You can learn more about signing out on page 280.

Ⓐ Before you sign in to iCloud, the iCloud preferences pane looks like this.

Ⓑ Once you've signed in, you can enable services for your account.

C When you enable iCloud services for Contacts, you'll need to merge your existing contacts with any already on iCloud.

D You must allow location sharing to enable Find My Mac.

TIP To manage Photo Stream photos on your Mac, you need iPhoto or Aperture.

TIP You can disable iCloud services by turning off the check boxes. This works similarly to simply signing out of iCloud—but for specific services. Learn more on page 280.

To enable iCloud services:

1. In the iCloud preferences pane **B**, turn on check boxes for the services you want to enable:

   ▸ **Mail** enables your iCloud email address in the Mail application.

   ▸ **Contacts** stores your Contacts application data on iCloud.

   ▸ **Calendars & Reminders** stores your Calendar and Reminders application data on iCloud.

   ▸ **Notes** stores your Notes application data on iCloud.

   ▸ **Safari** stores your Safari bookmarks on iCloud.

   ▸ **Photo Stream** shares recent photos from your iOS devices with your Mac.

   ▸ **Documents & Data** lets you store documents created with compatible applications on iCloud.

   ▸ **Back to My Mac** enables you to share the documents on your Mac with authorized users via the Internet.

   ▸ **Find My Mac** turns on location tracking for your Mac so you can find it if it's lost or stolen.

2. Set additional options, if necessary, for the services you enable:

   ▸ For Contacts, click Merge in the dialog that appears **C** to merge existing contacts with any that might already be stored on iCloud.

   ▸ For Back to My Mac, click More to learn more about the connection and, if necessary, turn on screen or file sharing (page 555) for your Mac.

   ▸ For Find My Mac, click Allow in the dialog that appears **D** to turn on location sharing.

Mail, Contacts & Calendars

The Mail, Contacts & Calendars preferences pane **A** makes it easy to set up your
iCloud (page 544), Microsoft Exchange,
Gmail, Yahoo!, AOL, and other accounts
for use with Mail, Calendar, Messages, and
other applications. Adding an account to
this preferences pane automatically sets
up these accounts in the applications you
specify, eliminating the need to set them
up individually in each application.

TIP You must have an account with a service
before you can set it up in the Mail, Contacts &
Calendars preferences pane.

To add an account:

1. On the right side of the Mail, Contacts
   & Calendars preferences pane **A**, click
   the button for the type of account you
   want to add.

   A dialog prompting you for information
   about that account appears **B**.

2. Enter required information for the
   account.

3. Click Set Up.

4. A dialog may appear with a list of applications **C**. Toggle the check boxes to
   select the applications you plan to use
   with that account.

5. Click Add Account.

   The account is added to the account
   list **D**.

TIP If the list of account types does not
appear on the right side of the Mail, Contacts
& Calendars preferences pane **A**, click the
+ button at the bottom of the account list to
display it.

A The Mail, Contacts & Calendars preferences
pane makes it easy to add accounts to OS X.

B Use the form that appears to enter
information about the account you are
adding.

C Toggle check boxes to indicate which
applications you plan to use with that account.

D The account you added appears in the list.

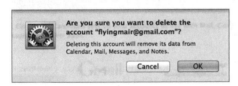

E Use this dialog to make changes to an account's settings.

Are you sure you want to delete the account "flyingmair@gmail.com"?

Deleting this account will remove its data from Calendar, Mail, Messages, and Notes.

Cancel   OK

F Click OK in this dialog to delete the selected account.

To modify an account:

1. In the Mail, Contacts & Calendars preferences pane, select the account you want to modify **D**.

2. Do one or more of the following:

   ► To stop using an account with an application, turn off the application's check box in the right side of the window.

   ► To modify account settings, click the Details button on the right side of the window, make changes in the dialog that appears **E**, and click OK.

   Your changes are saved.

To remove an account:

1. In the Mail, Contacts & Calendars preferences pane, select the account you want to remove **D**.

2. Click the – button at the bottom of the account list.

3. In the confirmation dialog that appears **F**, click OK.

   The account is removed from the list.

TIP Removing an account from the Mail, Contacts & Calendars preferences pane does not delete the account from the associated service. It just removes that service from your computer.

Network

The Network preferences pane enables you to check, change, add, and remove network interfaces (page 396). In most cases, network connections are added automatically when you configure your computer to connect a network, but you can use the Network preferences pane to make changes to automatically added settings, if necessary.

You can also use the Network preferences pane to add and modify location settings. Locations are particularly useful if you travel with your computer and use different connection options at each destination.

TIP Each type of network interface has its own group of settings options. This section looks at the options for a Wi-Fi connection, which is the type of connection you're most likely to use. Options for other connection types are similar.

TIP A complete discussion of the advanced settings for a network interface is beyond the scope of this book. If you're not sure how to change a network setting, don't change it without assistance from someone who does know. Incorrectly setting an option could make it impossible for your computer to connect to the network or the Internet.

TIP Clicking the Help (?) button in the lower-left corner of the Advanced settings dialog can help you learn more about advanced network settings.

A The Network preferences pane for a Wi-Fi connection.

B The Wi-Fi options include preferred networks and some security settings.

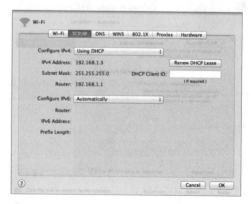

C Use TCP/IP options to set the IP address.

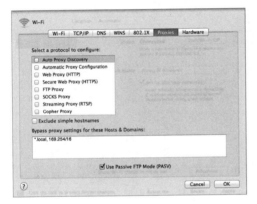

D You can specify DNS servers and search domains.

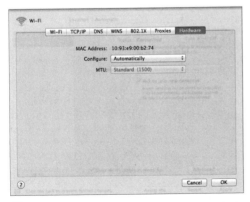

E Enable and configure proxies.

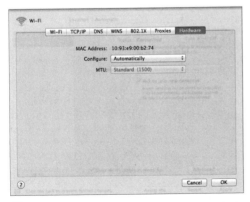

F The Hardware options provide your computer's MAC address and configuration options.

To check or modify Wi-Fi network settings:

1. In the Network preferences pane, select the Wi-Fi network connection you want to check or modify.

   Basic information appears on the right wide of the window **A**.

2. To change the Wi-Fi network you're connected to, choose a different network from the Network Name pop-up menu. The menu includes all networks within range of your computer that your computer has connected to in the past. (You may be prompted to enter a password to connect.)

3. To check or modify advanced options, click Advanced. You can then change options in any of six screens:

   ▸ **Wi-Fi B** lists your preferred networks and includes options for security for your Wi-Fi settings.

   ▸ **TCP/IP C** lets you configure your IP address and related options.

   ▸ **DNS D** enables you to add DNS servers and search domains.

   ▸ **WINS** enables you to set Windows Internet Naming Service options.

   ▸ **802.1X** lets you add 802.1x profiles to your system.

   ▸ **Proxies E** lets you enable and configure proxy protocols.

   ▸ **Hardware F** displays the MAC address and configuration options for your computer's Wi-Fi device.

   Click OK to save your settings and dismiss the advanced settings dialog.

TIP Don't confuse Mac with MAC. A Mac is a computer. MAC is short for Media Access Control and is a unique device ID.

Bluetooth

You can use the Bluetooth preferences pane to do several things:

- Enable or disable Bluetooth on your computer.
- Set Bluetooth preferences.
- Add or remove Bluetooth devices.

This part of the chapter discusses all of these things.

To enable or disable Bluetooth:

Toggle check boxes at the top of the Bluetooth preferences pane :

- **On** enables Bluetooth. Bluetooth must be enabled to connect to Bluetooth devices.
- **Discoverable** makes your computer "visible" to Bluetooth devices you might want to pair with.

TIP Bluetooth must be turned on to use Bluetooth sharing. You enable Bluetooth sharing in the Sharing preferences pane (page 558).

TIP Disabling Bluetooth can help conserve battery power on a laptop when you don't need a Bluetooth connection.

A The Bluetooth preferences pane with three devices paired, two of which are connected.

Advanced Bluetooth preferences.

To set Bluetooth preferences:

1. In the Bluetooth preferences pane Ⓐ, click Advanced to display advanced Bluetooth preferences Ⓑ.

2. Toggle check boxes to set options as desired:

   ▸ **Open Bluetooth Setup Assistant at startup if no keyboard is detected** tells your computer to launch the Bluetooth Setup Assistant if no keyboard is connected; this assumes that you're going to set up a Bluetooth keyboard.

   ▸ **Open Bluetooth Setup Assistant at startup if no mouse or trackpad is detected** tells your computer to launch the Bluetooth Setup Assistant if no mouse or trackpad is connected; this assumes that you're going to set up a Bluetooth input device.

   ▸ **Allow Bluetooth devices to wake this computer** makes it possible for a Bluetooth keyboard or mouse to wake the computer. This option is not supported by all computer models.

   ▸ **Reject incoming audio requests** prevents audio devices such as Bluetooth headphones from connecting to the computer.

   ▸ **Serial ports that devices use to connect to this computer** enables you to add serial port information for devices you will connect via Bluetooth. You normally will not need to make changes to this list unless instructed by a device's installation manual.

3. Click OK.

To pair a device:

1. In the Bluetooth preferences pane ,
   click the + button at the bottom of the
   list of devices.

   The Bluetooth Setup Assistant opens.
   It scans the area for Bluetooth devices
   and lists them **C**.

2. Select the device you want to pair with
   and click Continue.

3. The next screen may display a passkey
   and provide instructions **D**. Enter the
   passkey or confirm that it matches the
   one that appears on the device you
   are pairing to and press Return or click
   Continue.

4. A Conclusion screen appears next. To
   set up another device, click the Set Up
   Another Device button and follow steps
   2 and 3 above. Otherwise, click Quit.

   The paired device appears in the list in
   the Bluetooth preferences pane **E**.

TIP Some devices have predefined passkeys.
If you aren't told the passkey for a pairing and
need one, consult the device's manual for
more information.

TIP If you're not prompted for a passkey at
all, you can skip step 3.

TIP You can rename a Bluetooth device in
the Bluetooth preferences pane **E**. Simply
select the device and choose Rename from the
Action pop-up menu beneath the list. Enter
a new name for the device in the dialog that
appears and click OK.

TIP You can set options for a Bluetooth
keyboard, mouse, or trackpad in the Keyboard
(page 526), Mouse (page 530), or Trackpad (page 532)
preferences pane.

TIP To unpair a device, select it in the Devices
list **E** and click the – button at the bottom
of the list. Click Remove in the confirmation
dialog that appears.

C Select the device you want to pair with.

D If a passkey appears, follow the instructions to
enter it into the device.

E The paired device appears in the list of devices.

Ⓐ The Sharing preferences pane before any sharing services have been enabled. The options for Screen Sharing are shown here.

Sharing

To share files, printers, Internet connection, or other services with other network users, you must set options in the Sharing preferences pane **Ⓐ**. Sharing lets you name your computer, enable sharing for specific services, and control how other users can access your computer.

The Sharing preferences pane includes the following services:

- **DVD or CD Sharing** (not shown) enables other network users to use your computer's CD or DVD drive from their computer.

- **Screen Sharing** enables other users to view and control your computer over the network. This is handy for providing support to novice users.

- **File Sharing** enables other network users to access files on your computer.

- **Printer Sharing** enables other network users to print with your printers.

- **Scanner Sharing** enables other network users to scan with your scanners.

- **Remote Login** enables other network users to access your computer using Secure Shell (SSH) and Unix.

- **Remote Management** enables other network users to operate your computer using Apple Remote Desktop, an application available from Apple, Inc.

- **Remote Apple Events** makes it possible for other network computers to send Apple Events to your computer. Apple Events are scripting commands that perform specific tasks.

- **Internet Sharing** enables you to share an Internet connection with other network users.

continues on next page

- **Bluetooth Sharing** enables you to set options for how other computers can share files with your computer via Bluetooth.

To enable a sharing service, simply turn on its check box. You can then set options in the area to the right of the list. To disable a sharing service, turn off its check box.

This part of the chapter explains how to set sharing options for the following services: File Sharing, Printer Sharing, Internet Sharing, and Bluetooth Sharing. A discussion of the remaining sharing services is beyond the scope of this book.

CAUTION If your computer is on a large network, consult the system administrator before changing any sharing configuration options.

TIP Unless your computer is part of a big network and managed by a system administrator, it's extremely unlikely that you'll need to enable Remote Login, Remote Management, or Remote Apple Events. Leave these options turned off unless you know that you'll need to use them.

To set the computer's identity:

In the Sharing preferences pane 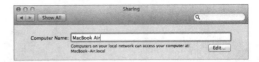, enter a name in the Computer Name text box **B**.

TIP Your computer name is not the same as your hard disk name.

TIP If your computer is on a large network, give your computer a name that can easily distinguish it from others on the network. Ask your system administrator; there may be organization-wide computer naming conventions that you need to follow.

TIP You can also change the identifier for your computer on the local subnet. Click the Edit button in the Sharing preferences pane **A** **B** and enter a new name in the dialog **C**. The name you enter cannot include spaces and must end in .local. Click OK.

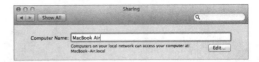

B You can change your computer's network identity by entering a new name in the Computer Name box.

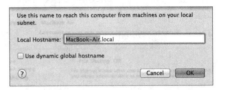

C You can also set a custom name for your computer on the local subnet.

D The Sharing preferences pane with File Sharing enabled.

E Use this dialog to specify a folder to share.

F The folder is added to the list of Shared folders.

G Use a dialog like this to select an existing user or contact.

H You can also create a new user account on the fly.

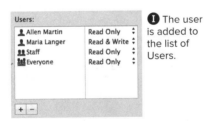

I The user is added to the list of Users.

J Choose a permissions option from the pop-up menu beside a user name.

To enable & configure file sharing:

1. In the Sharing preferences pane, turn on the File Sharing check box **D**.

2. To specify folders to share, click the + button beneath the Shared Folders list. Then use the dialog that appears **E** to locate and select the folder you want to share. Click Add to add it to the list of folders **F**.

3. To specify users who can access a folder, select the folder you want to set access for and click the + button under the Users column. Then use the dialog that appears **G** to select an existing account from Users & Groups or your Contacts database. Or click the New Person button and use the New Person dialog **H** to add a new user account. The additional user is added to the Users list **I**. You'll need to repeat this step for each folder you want to add users for.

4. To set permissions for a user, select the user name and choose an option from the pop-up menu that appears beside it **J**. Repeat this process for each user for each folder as desired.

5. To set more advanced options, click the Options button. Then set options in the dialog that appears **K** to enable specific connection methods, and click Done.

continues on next page

K You can set additional options in this dialog.

TIP By default, your Public folder is always set up to be shared.

TIP In step 3, you may need to enter an administrator password to add a new user.

TIP You can learn more about users, groups, and permissions on page 415. You set up users and groups in the Users & Groups preferences pane (page 560).

TIP To share files with Windows users, you must follow step 5 and enable SMB. Be sure to enable the Windows users' names in the bottom half of the dialog and enter their passwords when prompted.

To enable & configure printer sharing:

1. In the Sharing preferences pane, turn on the Printer Sharing check box **L**.

2. In the Printers list, turn on the check box for each printer you want to share **M**.

3. To specify users who can share the printer, select the printer you want to set access for and click the + button under the Users column. Then use the dialog that appears **G** to select an existing account from Users & Groups or your Contacts database. Or click the New Person button and use the New Person dialog **H** to add a new user account. The additional user is added to the Users list **N**. You'll need to repeat this step for each printer you want to add users for.

4. To prevent unlisted users from sharing a printer, make sure the permissions for the Everyone entry in the Users column is set to No Access **N**.

TIP You add printers in the Print & Scan preferences pane (page 534).

TIP You can learn more about using printers, including shared printers, in Chapter 24.

L The Sharing preferences pane with Printer Sharing enabled.

M Turn on the check box beside each printer you want to share.

N In this example, only one user can share the printer.

O You must set options on the right side of the window before enabling Internet sharing.

P A dialog like this warns you about the possible consequences of sharing an Internet connection.

Q In this example, I'm sharing my Wi-Fi Internet connection with other users via Bluetooth.

To enable & configure Internet sharing:

1. In the Sharing preferences pane, select the Internet Sharing option in the Service list **O**.

2. Choose the source of your computer's Internet connection from the Share your connection from pop-up menu. This menu includes all network connections set up for your computer.

3. Turn on the check box for each port in the To computers using list to indicate how you want to distribute your Internet connection **O**.

4. Turn on the Internet Sharing check box in the Services list.

5. A confirmation dialog may appear **P**. Click Start.

   The Sharing preferences pane indicates that Internet sharing is enabled and how your preferences are set **Q**.

TIP To make changes to Internet Sharing options, you must first turn off the Internet Sharing check box in the Service list.

TIP Internet sharing enables you to share your existing Internet connection with another computer. If you do not have an Internet connection, you can use a connection shared by another network user. Use the Network preferences pane (page 548) to choose the interface on which the shared connection is available to you.

TIP When you share an Internet connection, the total connection throughput is divided among the active connections. So, for example, if two computers are actively sharing a 6 Mbps DSL connection with you, the average throughput of each connection will only be about 2 Mbps.

To enable & configure Bluetooth sharing:

1. In the Sharing preferences pane, turn on the check box for Bluetooth Sharing in the Service list ⓡ.

2. Set options on the right side of the Sharing preferences pane:

   ▸ **When receiving items** lets you specify what your computer should do when receiving items from a Bluetooth device. Your options are Accept and Save, Accept and Open, Ask What to Do, and Never Allow.

   ▸ **Folder for accepted items** lets you select a folder to store items you receive from a Bluetooth device. Choose Other from this pop-up menu to use a dialog to select a folder other than Downloads.

   ▸ **When other devices browse** lets you specify what your computer should do when a Bluetooth device attempts to browse files on your disk. Your options are Always Allow, Ask What to Do, and Never Allow.

   ▸ **Folder others can browse** lets you choose the folder a Bluetooth device can browse. Choose Other from this pop-up menu to use a dialog to select a folder other than Public.

ⓡ The Sharing preferences pane with Bluetooth sharing enabled.

36

System Preferences

System preferences panes enable you to configure the operation of OS X to suit your needs. This chapter covers the following preferences panes:

- **Users & Groups** enables you to set up user accounts and groups for computer and network access.

- **Parental Controls** help you manage the way your children use the computer and Internet.

- **Date & Time** enables you to set the date, time, time zone, and clock options.

- **Software Update** lets you set options for Apple software updates.

- **Dictation & Speech** enables you to set speech-related options.

- **Time Machine** enables you to set up and configure OS X's backup feature.

- **Accessibility** controls options of interest to people with special access needs.

- **Startup Disk** lets you choose a disk for your computer's next start.

Need to learn the basics of System Preferences? Be sure to read Chapter 32.

In This Chapter:

Users & Groups

To take advantage of the multiple users features of OS X, which are discussed in detail in Chapter 10, you need to set up user accounts.

The OS X Setup Assistant, which is discussed in Chapter 1, does part of the setup for you. Immediately after you install OS X, the Setup Assistant prompts you for information to set up the Admin user account.

If you are your computer's only user, you're finished setting up users. But if additional people—coworkers, friends, or family members—will be using your computer, it's in your best interest to set up a separate user account for each one. You can then specify what each user is allowed to do on the computer. You do all this with the Users & Groups preferences pane .

This part of the chapter explains how to add, modify, set capabilities for, and delete user accounts. It also tells you how to use the Users & Groups preferences pane to modify settings for your own account and to set up Login Options and Login Items.

TIP You must unlock the Users & Groups preferences pane (page 491) before you can make changes to it. If you are the person who set up the computer, you are the administrator and can use your own name and password to unlock the preferences pane and make changes.

A The Users & Groups preferences pane with three user accounts configured.

B Select the Guest User account to set options.

To set options for the Guest User account:

1. In the list of users on the left side of the Users & Groups preferences pane, select Guest User **B**.

2. Set options on the right side of the window to specify how guests can access the computer:

   ▸ **Allow guests to log in to this computer** enables the Guest User account for login. This makes it possible for a guest user to access your computer's applications and temporarily store files in a Guest user folder on your hard disk.

   ▸ **Enable parental controls** turns on the Parental Controls feature to limit access for the Guest User account. If you turn on this check box, you can click the Open Parental Controls button to set options in the Parental Controls preferences pane (page 571).

   ▸ **Allow guests to connect to shared folders** enables guest users to log in to your computer via a network connection to access the contents of shared folders (page 418).

   TIP Files created or saved to a Guest User account user folder are deleted when the guest logs out. If you expect a user to regularly log in to your computer, you might find it more convenient to set up a standard account for that user.

   TIP The guest account cannot be used to log in to your computer from a remote location.

   TIP You can disable guest access to your computer by turning off the two Allow check boxes for the guest account in the Users & Groups preferences pane **B**.

To add a new user:

1. In the Users & Groups preferences pane **A**, click the + button at the bottom of the accounts list to display a blank new user dialog **C**.

2. Choose the type of account you want to create from the New Account pop-up menu **D**:

   ▸ **Administrator** is an account that has full administrative access over the computer.

   CAUTION Only give Administrator privileges to individuals you trust and who have a good understanding of how OS X works. An Administrator has access to the entire computer and can make changes that lock you out or prevent the computer from working properly.

   ▸ **Standard** is a normal user account with regular privileges.

   ▸ **Managed with Parental Controls** is an account with limited access and privileges, as set up with parental controls (page 571).

   ▸ **Sharing Only** is an account for file sharing only. A user with this kind of account cannot log in to your computer to access its applications.

   ▸ **Group** is a collection of multiple users. If you choose this option, follow the instructions in the section titled "To create a group" on page 564.

3. Enter information for the user account in each field:

   ▸ **Full Name** is the user's full name.

   ▸ **Account name** is the account name for the user. This name, which is often a shorter variation of the user's full name, should be in lowercase characters and should not include spaces.

C Use this dialog to set options for a new user account.

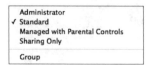

D The New Account pop-up menu offers five different options.

E The new user's account appears in the Users & Groups preferences pane.

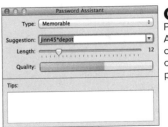

F A home folder for the user account appears in the Users folder.

G The Password Assistant can help you create a secure password.

H When you add a user, you may be prompted to turn off or keep automatic login.

▸ **Password** and **Verify** are the user's password, entered the same way in both fields. The password should be at least six characters long.

▸ **Password hint** is a hint to help the user remember the password.

4. Click Create User.

Two things happen:

▸ The new account appears in the list of accounts on the left side of the Users & Groups preferences pane **E**.

▸ A folder for the new user appears in the Users folder on your hard disk **F**.

TIP In step 3, you can use the Password Assistant to generate a random password. Click the key button beside the Password box to display the Password Assistant **G**, choose an option from the Type pop-up menu, drag the slider to modify the password length, and consider the password that appears in the Suggestion box.

TIP After step 4, a dialog may appear, asking if you want to turn off automatic login **H**. Click the button for the option you prefer.

To create a group:

1. In the Users & Groups preferences pane **A**, click the + button at the bottom of the accounts list to display a blank new user dialog **C**.

2. From the New Account pop-up menu **D**, choose Group.

   The dialog collapses to offer just one field **I**.

3. Enter a name for the group in the Full Name field.

4. Click Create Group.

   The new group appears in the list on the left side of the Users & Groups preferences pane **J**.

5. With the group selected, toggle check boxes in the Membership area on the right side of the preferences pane **K** to indicate which users are part of the group.

TIP You can change the accounts in a group at any time. Just open the Users & Groups preferences pane and repeat step 5.

TIP Groups are used to assign permissions to files and folders, as discussed on page 415.

I There's just one option for creating a new group.

J A new group appears at the bottom of the users list.

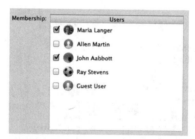

K Toggle check boxes to indicate who is part of the group.

Resetting the account password doesn't reset the password for the user's "login" keychain.

To reset the password for the "login" keychain, use Keychain Access, located in the Utilities folder.

New password:

Verify:

Password hint:
(Recommended)

Cancel   Reset Password

L Use this dialog to change a password.

Apple ID:

Create Apple ID...   Cancel   OK

M Enter a user's Apple ID in this dialog.

To modify a user's settings:

1. In the accounts list of the Users & Groups preferences pane, select the name of the account you want to modify **E**.

2. Make changes as desired on the left side of the window:

   ▸ **Reset Password** displays a dialog you can use to change the user's password **L**. Enter a new password twice and change the password hint, if necessary. Then click Reset Password.

   ▸ **Full Name** is the user's name.

   ▸ **Apple ID** is the user's Apple ID. Click the Set button to display a dialog **M**, enter the Apple ID, and click OK.

   ▸ **Allow user to reset password using Apple ID** makes it possible for a user to reset his password by logging in with his Apple ID.

   ▸ **Allow user to administer this computer** gives the user administrator privileges.

   ▸ **Enable parental controls** lets you limit the user's access based on options in the parental controls feature (page 571).

TIP You cannot modify a user's account settings while he is logged in using fast user switching (page 124).

TIP If the user's Apple ID is already entered, the Set button appears as a Change button; click it to change the Apple ID if necessary.

To change a user's picture:

1. In the Users & Groups preferences pane, select the name of the user you want to change the picture for **E**.

2. Click the picture well to display a menu of pictures and options **N**.

3. Do one of the following:

   ▸ To use an OS X default or recently used image, click Defaults **N** or Recents and then click the image you want to use and click Done. You can skip the remaining steps.

   ▸ To use your computer's built-in camera to take a picture, click Camera to activate the camera **O**, pose in front of the lens, and click the Take a Picture button.

   ▸ To use a picture on disk, drag the icon for an image from a Finder window into the image well **P**.

4. Drag the image into position and drag the slider to zoom the image in or out to frame it **Q**.

5. Click Done.

The picture changes to the image you selected or inserted **R**.

TIP A user's picture appears in his Address Book card, the Login screen, and as his default Messages picture.

N Choose one of the images that are part of OS X.

O You can also use your computer's camera to take a picture. (Yes, that's a dog.)

P You can also drag a picture from the Finder into the image well.

Q Drag the image and slider to frame it the way you like.

R The new image appears in the Users & Groups preferences pane for the user.

S The login items for my account.

T You can add a login item by dragging it into the list.

U You can also use a dialog like this to locate, select, and add an item.

V The item appears in the list.

To specify login items:

1. In the Users & Groups preferences pane, select the name of the account you logged in with. Normally, this will be your account, but if you want to set login items for another user, you must log in with that user's account.

2. Click the Login Items button to display its options **S**.

3. To add a login item, use one of the following techniques:

   ▸ Drag its icon from a Finder window to the list **T**.

   ▸ Click the + button at the bottom of the list and use the dialog that appears **U** to locate and select the item. Then click Add.

   The item you dragged or selected appears in the list **V**.

4. To remove a login item, select it in the list and then click the – button at the bottom of the list. The item is removed.

5. To automatically hide an item when it launches, turn on the Hide check box beside it in the list.

TIP Login items are applications, documents, folders, or other items that are automatically opened when you log in or start up the computer.

TIP Each user can change his own login items, unless his account has Parental Controls (page 571) enabled.

To delete a user's account:

1. In the Users & Groups preferences pane, select the name of the user you want to delete **E**.

2. Click the – button at the bottom of the accounts list.

3. A dialog with three options for dealing with the user's home folder appears :

   ▸ **Save the home folder in a disk image** saves the contents of the user's home folder in a disk image file in the Deleted Users folder. The file can be opened, if necessary, to extract files.

   ▸ **Don't change the home folder** leaves the home folder in the Users folder, without making any changes.

   ▸ **Delete the home folder** removes the user's home folder from the hard disk. If you select this option, you can toggle the **Erase home folder securely** check box to completely remove all data in the home folder in a way that makes it unrecoverable.

   CAUTION If you delete a user's home folder, all the files within it are deleted.

4. Click OK to delete the user.

TIP When you delete a user's account, he can no longer log in to the computer and access his files.

W Use this dialog to specify what should happen to the user's home folder when you delete his account.

X You can set Login Options in the Users & Groups preferences pane.

To set Login Options:

1. In the Users & Groups preferences pane, click the Login Options button at the bottom of the accounts list.

   Login Options appear on the right side of the window **X**.

2. Set options as desired:

   ▸ **Automatic login** enables you to choose a user account for the computer to automatically log in to when you start the computer. To disable this feature, choose Off.

   ▸ **Display login window as** lets you select how the login window (page 123) should appear: as a list of users or as blank fields for user name and password.

   ▸ **Show the Sleep, Restart, and Shut Down buttons** displays these buttons in the login window, making it possible to do any of these things without logging in to the computer.

   ▸ **Show Input menu in login window** displays the Input menu (page 506), which can be used to choose a different keyboard layout for logging in and using the computer.

   ▸ **Show password hints** displays a password hint in the login window (page 123) if the user has unsuccessfully attempted to log in three times.

   ▸ **Show fast user switching menu as** enables the fast user switching feature (page 124). Use the pop-up menu to determine what should display on the far right end of the menu bar: Full Name, Short Name, or Icon.

   continues on next page

- **Use VoiceOver in the login window** activates the VoiceOver feature (page 390) to speak each item in the login window as a user points to it.

- **Network Account Server** enables you to join or edit connection information for a network account server. This is an advanced feature of OS X that is beyond the scope of this book.

TIP With the automatic login feature enabled, the login window (page 123) will not appear when you start the computer.

TIP The login window option to display name and password is more secure than a list of users because it requires unauthorized users to know both a valid user name and the corresponding password.

Parental Controls

Parental controls enable you to limit an account's access to computer features. Designed to help parents protect their children from certain content and activities, it can also be used to limit a user to certain applications, activities, and usage times. In addition, it can keep a log of a user's activities for later review.

Parental controls are broken down into five groups of settings:

- **Apps** control what applications and tasks the user can access. It also allows you to enable Simple Finder, a special version of the Finder for novice users. And it gives you access to logs so you can see what the user has been up to.

- **Web** enables you to control access to websites.

- **People** limits Game Center activity and who the user can communicate with via email or chat.

- **Time Limits** enables you to set the amount of time on weekdays and weekends the user can use the computer and to prevent the user from using the computer at certain times of the day or night.

- **Other** controls access to dictation, profanity in the Dictionary, printer administration, CD and DVD burning, and password changes.

This section explains how to activate parental controls for a user account. It also discusses the available settings you can assign to a user's account.

TIP The Parental Controls preferences pane is normally locked to prevent unauthorized changes. You can learn more about unlocking and locking preferences panes on page 491.

To enable parental controls for a user account:

1. In the Parental Controls preferences pane, select the user you want to enable parental controls for .

2. Click the Enable Parental Controls button.

   Parental controls settings appear **B**.

TIP You cannot set parental controls for a user with administrator privileges.

TIP You can also enable parental controls by turning on the check box beside Enable Parental Controls in the user's account settings in the Users & Groups preferences pane (page 560).

TIP If parental controls settings for the user appear after step 1 **B**, parental controls are already enabled for that user.

TIP The Manage parental controls from another computer option in the Parental Controls preferences pane **A** enables a user on a networked computer running OS X 10.5 or later to log in to the computer and set parental control options. A parent might use this to manage controls on another computer used by her children. A discussion of this feature is beyond the scope of this book.

To disable parental controls for a user account:

1. In the Parental Controls preferences pane, select the user you want to disable parental controls for **B**.

2. Choose Turn off Parental Controls for "*User Name*" from the action pop-up menu at the bottom of the user list **C**.

A The Parental Controls preferences pane looks like this when it's disabled for a selected user account.

B Enabling parental controls for a user displays control options you can set for that account.

C The action pop-up menu in the Parental Controls preferences pane.

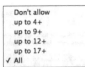

| Don't allow |
| up to 4+ |
| up to 9+ |
| up to 12+ |
| up to 17+ |
| ✓ All |

D If you buy apps from the App Store, you can use a pop-up menu to limit access based on age rating.

E Simple Finder is just that: a simple version of the Finder.

F If a user tries to access an application he's not allowed to, he'll see this.

TIP Simple Finder **E**, as the name suggests, is a highly simplified version of the Finder. Designed for users with little or no knowledge of computers, it offers a safe, highly controlled environment for kids and novices. If you want to try Simple Finder, create a new user with Simple Finder enabled, then log in as that user. If you've been using a Mac for more than a few years, I guarantee you'll go nuts in about five minutes. (I didn't even last two.)

To limit a user's access to applications & system functions:

1. In the Parental Controls preferences pane, select the name of the user you want to set access limitations for.

2. Click the Apps button **B**.

3. To enable Simple Finder for the user, turn on the Use Simple Finder check box.

4. To limit the user's access to applications, turn on the Limit Applications check box. Then set application access options as desired:

   ▸ **Allow App Store Apps** lets you specify a maximum age rating for applications purchased from the App Store. Choose an option from the pop-up menu **D**.

   ▸ **Allowed Apps** lets you specify which applications the user can access. Toggle check boxes in the list. You can click the disclosure triangle to the left of a category to display the individual applications within it. This option is only available if either the Use Simple Finder or Limit Applications check box is turned on.

5. To allow the user to add or remove Dock items for his account, turn on the Allow User to Modify the Dock check box. This option is not available if Simple Finder is enabled for the account.

TIP If a user attempts to access an application he does not have access to, a dialog appears **F**. If the user clicks the Always Allow or Allow Once button, he'll need to enter an administrator's name and password to continue.

To limit access to the Web:

1. In the Parental Controls preferences pane, select the name of the user you want to limit Web access for.

2. Click the Web button .

3. Select one of the three Website Restrictions options:

   ▸ **Allow unrestricted access to websites** does not apply restrictions.

   ▸ **Try to limit access to adult websites automatically** uses a built-in filter to prevent access to adult content websites. If you select this option, you can click the Customize button to create and maintain a list of websites the user can and can't access **H**. Just use the + and – buttons beneath each list to add or remove URLs.

   ▸ **Allow access to only these websites** displays a list of websites that the user can access. These are the only sites the user can access. Use the + and – buttons beneath the list to add or remove URLs.

TIP Customizing the content filter does not prevent access to content not listed in the dialog. For example, given the settings in **H**, if the user attempted to access my website (www.marialanger.com), he would not be stopped, since the site is not forbidden and has no objectionable content. (Well, at least I don't think so.)

TIP If a website is blocked, the browser window remains empty when viewing that site.

G Use the Web options to limit access to Web sites.

H In this example, I've listed two kid-friendly websites and two that might not be appropriate for young kids.

O Use the People options to limit communication to certain email and chat accounts.

J You can manually add accounts in a dialog like this one.

K You can also add accounts directly from your Contacts database.

To limit access to Game Center, email, & chat:

1. In the Parental Controls preferences pane, select the name of the user you want to set access limitations for.

2. Click the People button **O**.

3. To control access to Game Center, toggle check boxes:

   ▸ **Allow joining Game Center multiplayer games** allows the user to play games with other players on Game Center.

   ▸ **Allow adding Game Center friends** allows the user to add friends in Game Center.

4. Turn on the check box for the application you want to limit:

   ▸ **Limit Mail** restricts the addresses the user can exchange email with.

   ▸ **Limit Messages** restricts the instant messaging addresses the user can enter into a chat session with.

5. If you checked either of the options in step 4, build a list of the allowed email or instant messaging addresses in the Allowed Contacts list. Click the + button and use one or both of the following techniques to add people:

   ▸ Manually add the name, email address, and AIM account information for a person **O**. Then click Add.

   ▸ Click the disclosure triangle beside the Last Name field to display a list of contacts in your Contacts database **K** (Chapter 20). Then hold down the Command key and click the names of the people you want to allow. Click Add to add them.

continues on next page

6. To receive an email message from anyone not on the list who attempts to email the user, turn on the Send permission requests to check box and enter your email address in the box beside it. This makes it possible to see who is trying to send email to the user and what that email contains.

TIP Parental Controls for Mail and Messages are a good way to prevent your children from getting email from or chatting with people you don't know.

To limit a user's time on the computer:

1. In the Parental Controls preferences pane, select the name of the user you want to set access limitations for.

2. Click the Time Limits button .

3. Turn on the check boxes and set options for each of the times you want to limit:

▸ **Weekday time limits** controls the amount of time the user can spend on the computer on Monday through Friday.

▸ **Weekend time limits** controls the amount of time the user can spend on the computer on Saturdays and Sundays.

▸ **School nights** enables you to specify what times the computer can't be used on Sunday through Thursday nights.

▸ **Weekend** enables you to specify what times the computer can't be used on Friday and Saturday nights.

TIP Although this feature is designed to limit the time a child spends on a computer, I sometimes wish someone would set it for me!

L You can set Time Limit options to limit the amount of time and time of day your child uses the computer.

M The Other options cover a few additional Parental Control features.

To set other control options:

1. In the Parental Controls preferences pane, select the name of the user you want to set access limitations for.

2. Click the Other button **M**.

3. Toggle check boxes to set other control options:

   ▸ **Disable use of Dictation** prevents the user from using the dictation feature.

   ▸ **Hide profanity in Dictionary** hides "bad words" in OS X's Dictionary application and widget.

   ▸ **Limit printer administration** prevents the user from changing printer settings, adding printers, or removing printers.

   ▸ **Limit CD and DVD burning** prevents the user from copying data, music, or other material to disc in the Finder.

   ▸ **Disable changing the password** prevents the user from changing his password.

TIP The Hide profanity in Dictionary check box setting does not affect non-Apple application dictionaries, like the one that comes with Microsoft Word.

To review access logs for a user:

1. In the Parental Controls preferences pane, select the name of the user you want to view logs for.

2. Click the Apps **B**, Web **G**, or People **I** button.

3. Click the Logs button to display the logs dialog **N**.

4. In the Log Collections column, click the name of the log you want to view.

5. Choose a time period from the Show activity for pop-up menu. The options range from Today to All.

6. Choose an option from the Group by pop-up menu to specify how the log should be arranged. The options that appear vary based on what you selected in step 4.

7. View log details in the Logs column. You can click disclosure triangles to display more information about items.

8. To open an item in the log, select it and click the Open button at the bottom of the window.

9. To allow or restrict a site, application, or contact, select the item in the log and click the Restrict or Allow button at the bottom of the window. (The button that appears varies based on what is selected.)

TIP Although it might seem sneaky, it's a good idea to review this information periodically to see what your children have been doing with the computer.

N Here's an example of the Websites Visited log.

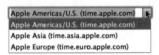

A The Date & Time options in the Date & Time preferences pane.

B Use this drop-down list to choose the time server closest to you.

Date & Time

The Date & Time preferences pane includes three panes for setting the system time and clock options:

- **Date & Time** enables you to automatically or manually set the date and time.

- **Time Zone** enables you to set your time zone and specify whether daylight savings time is in effect.

- **Clock** enables you to set options for the appearance of the menu bar clock.

TIP To change the formats of dates and times throughout OS X, use the Language & Text preferences pane (page 503).

To set the date & time automatically:

1. In the Date & Time preferences pane, click the Date & Time button **A**.

2. If necessary, turn on the Set date and time automatically check box.

3. Choose the closest time server from the drop-down list **B**.

TIP With the network time server feature enabled, your computer will use its Internet connection to periodically get the date and time from a time server and update the system clock automatically. This ensures that your computer's clock is always correct.

To set the date & time manually:

1. In the Date & Time preferences pane, click the Date & Time button **A**.

2. If necessary, turn off the Set date and time automatically check box.

3. Use any combination of the following techniques:

   ▸ Click the numbers you want to change in the date and time boxes and enter new values **C**.

   ▸ Click the calendar and clock images to set the correct values.

4. Click Save to save your settings.

To set the time zone automatically:

1. In the Date & Time preferences pane, click the Time Zone button **D**.

2. If necessary, turn on the Set time zone automatically using current location check box.

3. Wait while your computer attempts to determine your current location.

   One of two things happens:

   ▸ If your computer can determine your location, your time zone is set.

   ▸ If your computer cannot determine your location, it displays a message telling you so **E**. You'll need to set your time zone manually.

TIP An Internet connection is required to automatically set your time zone. This feature uses OS X's location services capabilities.

C You can manually set the date and time by clicking, dragging, and entering values in the clock and calendar area.

D The Time Zone options of the Date & Time preferences pane.

E If your computer can't figure out where it is, it tells you.

Portland, OR – United States ▾
Portland, OR – United States
Redding, CA – United States
Reno, NV – United States
Richmond – Canada
Roseville, CA – United States
Sacramento, CA – United States
Salem, OR – United States
Seattle, WA – United States
Sparks, NV – United States
Spokane, WA – United States

F Although I clicked closest to Portland, I'm really closer to Seattle, which I can choose from this list.

To set the time zone manually:

1. In the Date & Time preferences pane, click the Time Zone button **D**.

2. If necessary, turn off the Set time zone automatically using current location check box.

3. Click the map at your approximate location.

   A light gray bar indicates the time zone area **D**.

4. Choose the name of a city in your time zone from the Closest City drop-down list beneath the map **F**.

TIP When manually setting the time zone, only those cities in or near the light gray bar on the map are listed in the drop-down list **F**. If a nearby city does not appear, make sure you clicked the correct area in the map.

TIP If you prefer, in step 4 you can type the name of a city in the text box. If it's included on the list, it'll appear in the box. Press Return to accept it.

TIP It's a good idea to choose the correct time zone, since OS X uses this information with the network time server (if utilized) and to properly change the clock for daylight saving time.

To set clock options:

1. In the Date & Time preferences pane, click the Clock button 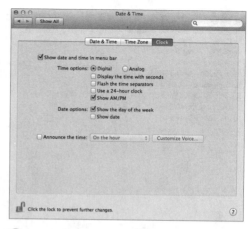.

2. To enable the menu bar clock, turn on the Show date and time in menu bar check box.

3. Set Time options:

   ▸ **Digital** and **Analog** lets you choose between displaying the date and time with letters and numbers ⓗ or as an analog clock ①. If you choose Analog, the remaining Time and Date options turn gray; skip to step 4.

   ▸ **Display the time with seconds** displays the seconds as part of the time.

   ▸ **Flash the time separators** blinks the colon(s) in the time every second.

   ▸ **Use a 24-hour clock** displays the time as a 24-hour (rather than 12-hour) clock.

   ▸ **Show AM/PM** displays AM or PM after the time.

4. Set Date options:

   ▸ **Show the day of the week** displays the three-letter abbreviation for the day of the week before the time.

   ▸ **Show date** displays the date before the time.

5. To instruct your computer to vocally announce the time periodically, turn on the Announce the time check box and choose a frequency option from the pop-up menu: On the hour, On the half hour, or On the quarter hour. You can also click the Customize Voice button and set voice options in the dialog that appears ⓙ.

TIP The menu bar clock is also a menu that displays the full date and offers options for changing the clock display.

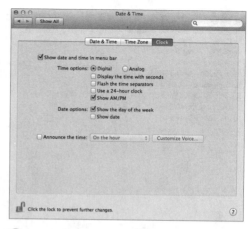

G The Clock options in the Date & Time preferences pane.

ⓗ ① The far right end of the menu bar on my MacBook Air displaying the digital clock with settings in **G** (top) and the analog clock (bottom).

ⓙ If you set your computer to announce the time, you can also set options for the voice it uses to do so.

A The Scheduled Checks options of the Software Update preferences pane.

B When Software Update finds updates, it displays a notification window like this.

Software Update

The Software Update preferences pane enables you to configure the software update feature of OS X. This feature checks Apple's servers for updates to your Apple software and apps purchased from the App Store. If it finds updates, it can automatically download and install them.

To set automatic update options:

In the Software Update preferences pane **A**, toggle check boxes to set options as desired:

- **Automatically check for updates** periodically checks Apple's servers for updates to all of your installed Apple software. With this option enabled, you can set two additional options:

  ▸ **Download newly available updates in the background** automatically downloads updates when they are available and alerts you when they are ready to be installed.

  ▸ **Install system data files and security updates** automatically downloads and installs system and security updates as they become available.

- **Automatically download apps purchased on other Macs** keeps track of your App Store purchases on other Macs and downloads them to this Mac.

TIP When your computer checks for updates and finds one, it displays a notification window **B**. Follow the instructions in the section titled "To install updates" to install the updates.

To manually check for updates:

1. In the Software Update preferences pane **A**, click Check Now.

   Your computer opens the App Store application, switches to the Updates window, and checks for updates to installed applications.

2. When the check is complete, one of two things happens:

   ▸ If updates are available, they are listed in the App Store Updates window **C**. Follow the instructions in the section titled "To install updates."

   ▸ If no updates are available, a message in the App Store Updates window tells you. Choose App Store > Quit App Store, or press Command-Q to quit.

To install updates:

1. Do one of the following:

   ▸ In the Update notification window **B**, click Update.

   ▸ In the App Store Updates window **C**, click the Update button for the update you want to install or click Update All.

2. If a License Agreement window appears, read the license agreement (or at least pretend to) and click Agree.

3. If an authentication dialog appears, enter an administrator name and password and click OK.

4. If you'll need to restart your computer after installing the software, a dialog tells you. Click Restart.

5. Wait while your computer downloads (if necessary) and installs the update from Apple's server.

C If updates are available, they appear in a list in the Updates window.

D You can click the More link to learn all about an update.

TIP You can usually continue working with your Mac as updates are downloaded and installed.

TIP You can learn about an update before you install it by clicking the More link at the bottom of the short description. The description expands to provide additional details about the update **D**.

TIP If you don't install a listed update, it will appear in the App Store Updates window **C** again the next time you check for updates.

A The Dictation options in the Dictation & Speech preferences pane.

B You must agree to let Apple transcribe your dictation.

C If you have multiple microphones, you can select the one you want to use from this menu.

Off
✓ Press Fn (Function) Key Twice
Press Right Command Key Twice
Press Left Command Key Twice
Press Either Command Key Twice
Customize...

D Use this menu to choose the keystroke you want to use to start the dictation feature.

English (Australia)
English (United Kingdom)
✓ English (United States)
French
German
Japanese

E Be sure to choose the language you will use to dictate.

Dictation & Speech

OS X's Dictation & Speech preferences pane includes two groups of options:

- **Dictation** lets you enable and configure the dictation feature.

- **Text to Speech** lets you set the default system voice and enable and configure talking alerts and other spoken items.

In this section, I explain how to enable and configure these features.

TIP Dictation requires a sound input device, such as a built-in or external microphone or FaceTime camera.

TIP You can learn more about using the dictation feature on page 192.

To enable & configure dictation:

1. In the Dictation & Speech preferences pane, click the Dictation button **A**.

2. Select the On radio button.

3. A dialog explains that what you dictate is sent to Apple for conversion to text **B**. Click Enable Dictation.

4. If your Mac has more than one microphone, click the menu beneath the microphone icon to select the one you want to use for dictation **C**.

5. Use the pop-up menu to set options:

   ▶ **Shortcut D** is the keystroke to start dictation. Choose Customize to use a keystroke of your choice.

   ▶ **Language E** is the language you will be using to dictate.

TIP An external microphone—especially one on a headset—will work more reliably than a built-in microphone, such as the one on the front of the computer.

To set Text to Speech options:

1. In the Dictation & Speech preferences pane, click the Text to Speech button **F**.

2. Select one of the voices in the System Voice list **G**.

3. To change the speed at which the voice speaks, use the Speaking Rate slider.

4. To test the settings, click the Play button.

5. To speak alerts, turn on the Announce when alerts are displayed check box. Then click the Set Alert Options button, set options in the dialog that appears **H**, and click OK:

   ▸ **Voice** enables you to choose the System Voice or another voice.

   ▸ **Phrase** **I** is text that should be spoken before the alert.

   ▸ **Delay** is the amount of time that should elapse between when the dialog appears and the alert is spoken. Use the slider to set the delay.

6. To get a verbal alert when an application needs your attention, turn on the Announce when an application requires your attention check box. (Normally, the icon for an application needing attention bounces in the Dock.)

7. To have your computer speak selected text, turn on the Speak selected text when the key is pressed check box. The default keystroke is Option-Esc, but you can change the keystroke by clicking the Change Key button and using the dialog that appears **J** to set a new one.

F The Text to Speech options in the Dictation & Speech preferences pane.

G Choose a voice from this menu.

H Set options for speaking alerts.

I Use this menu to choose a phrase that should be spoken before alert text.

J You can set a different keystroke for speaking selected text.

OS X includes dozens of voices for many different languages. Toggle check boxes to add or remove them from the Voices menu.

 You can add your own alert phrases if you don't like the ones that are part of OS X.

TIP You can list additional voices by choosing Customize from the Voices menu **G**. This displays a dialog you can use to check off the voices you want on the menu **K**. This list includes many for languages other than English.

TIP The settings you make in the Text to Speech pane affect any application that can speak text.

TIP In step 5, you can choose Edit Phrase List from the Phrase pop-up menu **I** to display the Alert Phrases dialog **L**. Click the Add or Remove buttons to add a new phrase or remove a selected one. When you're finished, click OK to save your changes.

TIP To speak the time, click the Open Date & Time Preferences button. This displays the Clock options of the Date & Time preferences pane (page 582) so you can set options.

TIP To change VoiceOver settings, click the Open Accessibility Preferences button. This displays the Accessibility preferences pane (page 590) so you can set options.

Time Machine

The Time Machine preferences pane allows you to enable and configure Time Machine (page 115), OS X's built-in backup and restore feature.

This section explains how to set Time Machine options.

To set Time Machine options:

1. If necessary, follow the instructions on page 116 to enable Time Machine backups.

2. In the Time Machine preferences pane **A** click the Options button.

   A dialog with a list of items that should not be included in the backup, as well as one or more option check boxes, appears **B**.

3. To exclude an item from backup, click the + button and use the dialog that appears to locate and select the disk or folder you want to exclude **C**. Then click Exclude.

   The item is added to the list of items that will not be backed up **D**. Repeat this process for each item you want to exclude from the backup.

4. Toggle check boxes to set other options as desired:

   ▶ **Back up while on battery power** tells your laptop to create a Time Machine backup while not plugged in.

   ▶ **Notify after old backups are deleted** displays a warning when your backup disk is full and old backups need to be deleted to make room for new ones.

5. Click Save.

A The Time Machine preferences pane, with Time Machine already enabled.

B Use this dialog to set Time Machine backup options.

C Use this dialog to select disks, folders, or individual items to exclude from the backup.

D Items you exclude appear in the list.

E The Time Machine menu offers access to Time Machine features and the Time Machine preferences pane.

6. To include the Time Machine menu on the menu bar **E**, in the main window of the Time Machine preferences pane **A**, turn on the Show Time Machine in menu bar check box.

TIP You may have to unlock the Time Machine preferences pane (page 491) before you can make changes to it.

TIP If you change your mind and want to start backing up an item you have previously excluded, in the list of items to exclude **D**, select the item you want to start backing up and click the – button at the bottom of the list. The item is removed from the list and will be backed up from that point forward.

Accessibility

The Accessibility preferences pane enables you to set options for making your computer easier to use by people with special access needs.

Accessibility's features can be set in seven different screens:

- **Display** enables you to set options that control how the display appears.

- **Zoom** enables you to set options for zooming content onscreen.

- **VoiceOver** lets you set up the OS X VoiceOver feature, which speaks descriptions of onscreen items and makes it possible to control the computer with the keyboard.

- **Audio** enables you to set options for sound output.

- **Keyboard** Ⓔ lets you configure Sticky Keys and Slow Keys, two features that can make using the keyboard easier.

Ⓐ You can set Display options to make the screen easier for someone with visual impairments to see.

Ⓑ The Zoom options control screen zooming features that can benefit someone with visual impairments.

Ⓒ To have your computer speak the items you point to onscreen, enable and configure VoiceOver.

Ⓓ The Audio options make it possible to flash the screen when an alert sounds and play stereo sound as mono.

E Set the Keyboard options to make the keyboard easier to use.

F Set options in the Mouse & Keyboard screen to use the keyboard to move the pointer and change the double-click speed.

G You can use the Speakable Items settings to configure your computer to accept voice commands.

- **Mouse & Trackpad ⑤** enables you to set options that can make it easier to use a mouse or trackpad.

- **Speakable Items ⑥** lets you configure your computer to accept spoken commands for controlling a variety of computer functions.

A complete discussion of OS X's accessibility features is beyond the scope of this book. To learn more about these features and how they work, click the Help button in any screen of the Accessibility preferences pane.

TIP Accessibility was called Universal Access in previous versions of OS X. It could be found among the Personal preferences in the System Preferences window.

Startup Disk

The Startup Disk preferences pane enables you to select a startup disk and, if desired, restart your computer. You might find this helpful if you want to start your computer under Windows using Boot Camp (page 376) or from a bootable CD or DVD disc, such as an OS X installer disc.

> **TIP** OS X's **Target Disk Mode feature**, which is supported by some Mac models, lets you use your computer's hard disk as an external hard disk when connected to another computer via FireWire. If your computer supports it, you can enable this option in the Startup Disk preferences pane **B**.

> **TIP** To decide "on the fly" which startup disk to use, hold down the Option key at startup to display icons for each startup disk and the Recovery Partition (page 119). Click the disk you want and then press Return to complete the startup process from the disk you selected.

> **TIP** Holding down the C key while restarting your computer with a bootable optical disc inserted usually starts the computer from the System folder on that disc.

To select a startup disk:

1. Display the Startup Disk preferences pane **A**.

2. Click the icon for the startup disk you want to use.

3. Do one of the following:
   - ▸ To immediately restart your computer, click the Restart button. The startup disk you selected in step 2 will be used to start the computer.
   - ▸ Quit System Preferences. The next time you start the computer, the startup disk you selected in step 2 (if available) will be used to start the computer.

A The Startup Disk preferences pane on my MacBook Air with a USB Drive containing the OS X 10.8 installer plugged in. Note that because this computer does not have a FireWire port there is no Target Disk Mode option.

B My MacBook Pro does have a FireWire port, so the Target Disk Mode button appears in the Startup Disk preferences pane.

References

In This Part

Menus & Keyboard Shortcuts

This appendix illustrates all of OS X's Finder menus and provides a list of corresponding keyboard shortcuts.

To use a keyboard shortcut, hold down the modifier key (usually Command) while pressing the keyboard key for the command.

Menus and keyboard commands are discussed in detail in Chapter 2.

In This Appendix:

Apple Menu

Option-Command-D	Dock > Turn Hiding On/Off
Option-Command-Esc	Force Quit
Option-Command-Media Eject	Sleep
Shift-Command-Q	Log Out

Finder Menu

Command-,	Preferences
Shift-Command-Delete	Empty Trash
Command-H	Hide Finder
Option-Command-H	Hide Others

```
File
New Finder Window                        ⌘N
New Folder                              ⇧⌘N
New Folder with Selection (3 Items)      ^⌘N
New Smart Folder                        ⌥⌘N
New Burn Folder
Open                                     ⌘O
Open With                                 ▶
Print                                    ⌘P
Close Window                             ⌘W

Get Info                                 ⌘I

Compress 3 Items

Duplicate                                ⌘D
Make Alias                               ⌘L
Quick Look 3 Items                       ⌘Y
Show Original                            ⌘R
Add to Sidebar                           ⌘T

Move to Trash                           ⌘⌫
Eject                                    ⌘E
Burn 3 Items to Disc...

Find                                     ⌘F

Label:
☒ ■ ■ ■ ■ ■ ■ ■
```

File Menu

Command-N	New Finder Window
Shift-Command-N	New Folder
Control-Command-N	New Folder with Selection
Option-Command-N	New Smart Folder
Command-O	Open
Option-Command-O	Open and Close Window
Control-Command-O	Open in New Window
Command-W	Close Window
Option-Command-W	Close All
Command-I	Get Info
Option-Command-I	Show Inspector
Control-Command-I	Get Summary Info
Command-D	Duplicate
Option-Shift-Command-D	Duplicate Exactly
Command-L	Make Alias
Command-Y	Quick Look
Option-Command-Y	Slideshow
Command-R	Show Original
Command-T	Add to Sidebar
Shift-Command-T	Add to Dock
Command-Delete	Move to Trash
Option-Command-Delete	Move to Trash
Command-E	Eject
Option-Command-E	Eject
Control-Command-E	Eject
Command-F	Find
Control-Command-F	Find by Name

Edit Menu

Command-Z	Undo
Shift-Command-Z	Redo
Command-X	Cut
Command-C	Copy
Command-V	Paste
Option-Command-V	Move Items Here
Command-A	Select All
Option-Command-A	Deselect All
fn fn	Start Dictation

Edit

Undo	⌘Z
Redo	⇧⌘Z
Cut	⌘X
Copy	⌘C
Paste	⌘V
Select All	⌘A
Show Clipboard	
Start Dictation	fn fn
Special Characters...	

View Menu

Command-1	as Icons
Command-2	as List
Command-3	as Columns
Command-4	as Cover Flow
Option-Command-1	Clean Up By > Name
Option-Command-2	Clean Up By > Kind
Option-Command-5	Clean Up By > Date Modified
Option-Command-6	Clean Up By > Size
Option-Command-7	Clean Up By > Label
Control-Command-1	Arrange By > Name
Control-Command-2	Arrange By > Kind
Control-Command-3	Arrange By > Date Last Opened
Control-Command-4	Arrange By > Date Added
Control-Command-5	Arrange By > Date Modified
Control-Command-6	Arrange By > Size
Control-Command-7	Arrange By > Label
Control-Command-0	Arrange By > None
Control-Option-Command-0	Sort By > None

View

✓ as Icons	⌘1
as List	⌘2
as Columns	⌘3
as Cover Flow	⌘4
Clean Up Selection	
Clean Up By	▶
Arrange By	▶
Show Path Bar	
Hide Status Bar	⌘/
Hide Sidebar	⌥⌘S
Hide Toolbar	⌥⌘T
Customize Toolbar...	
Show View Options	⌘J

Control-Option-Command-1	Sort By > Name
Control-Option-Command-2	Sort By > Kind
Control-Option-Command-3	Sort By > Date Last Opened
Control-Option-Command-4	Sort By > Date Added
Control-Option-Command-5	Sort By > Date Modified
Control-Option-Command-6	Sort By > Size
Control-Option-Command-7	Sort By > Label
Command-/	Show/Hide Status Bar
Option-Command-S	Show/Hide Sidebar
Option-Command-T	Show/Hide Toolbar
Command-J	Show/Hide View Options

Go Menu

Go	
Back	⌘[
Forward	⌘]
Enclosing Folder	⌘↑
📄 All My Files	⇧⌘F
📄 Documents	⇧⌘O
🖥 Desktop	⇧⌘D
⬇ Downloads	⌥⌘L
🏠 Home	⇧⌘H
💻 Computer	⇧⌘C
📡 AirDrop	⇧⌘R
🌐 Network	⇧⌘K
📂 Applications	⇧⌘A
✂ Utilities	⇧⌘U
Recent Folders	▶
Go to Folder...	⇧⌘G
Connect to Server...	⌘K

Command-[	Back
Command-]	Forward
Command-Up Arrow	Enclosing Folder
Shift-Command-Up Arrow	Select Startup Disk on Desktop
Option-Command-Up Arrow	Enclosing Folder
Control-Command-Up Arrow	Enclosing Folder in New Window
Shift-Command-F	All My Files
Shift-Command-O	Documents
Shift-Command-D	Desktop

continues on next page

Option-Command-L	Downloads
Shift-Command-H	Home
Shift-Command-C	Computer
Shift-Command-R	AirDrop
Shift-Command-K	Network
Shift-Command-A	Applications
Shift-Command-U	Utilities
Shift-Command-G	Go to Folder
Command-K	Connect to Server

Window Menu

Command-M	Minimize
Option-Command-M	Minimize All
Command-`	Cycle Through Windows

Help Menu

Shift-Command-/	Display Mac Help menu

Index

Trash, file management, 48–50
trash icons, 19
troubleshooting, help advice, 74
Try to limit access to adult websites
    automatically option (Parent Controls
    preferences pane), 574
Turn Bluetooth Off command (Status menu), 412
Turn off text smoothing for font sizes option
    (General preferences pane), 495
Turn off when computer is not used for option
    (Keyboard preferences pane), 527
turning off. *See also* quitting
    FaceTime, 455
tweets, Notification Center, 261
Twitter, xxi
two-button mouse, 14

U

Undo command (Edit menu), 92
uninstalling
    font, 330
    Launchpad, 141
Unit Converter, 248
unlocking System Preferences, 491
unsaved documents, 163
updates
    apps, 176
    options (software), 583–584
    OS X Mountain Lion, 5
    security, xxii
    Snow Leopard, 5
URLs, viewing, 457
USB Apple Mouse, 13
Use all F1, F2, etc. keys as standard function keys
    option (Keyboard preferences pane), 526
Use iCloud for Find My Mac window, 10
Use LCD font smoothing when available option
    (General preferences pane), 495
Use relative dates option, 480
Use VoiceOver in the login window option
    (Users & Groups preferences pane), 570
users, 415
    access, limiting with parental controls, 573
    accounts
        adding users, 562–563
        deleting, 568
        disabling parental controls, 572
        enabling parental controls, 572
        login items, 567
        pictures, 566
        setting up, 560

settings, 565
    adding, 562–563
    groups, help advice, 74
    names, 415
Users & Groups pane (System preferences
    panes), 560–570
Users & Groups preference pane, 123
Users & Groups preferences pane, 415
Users folder, 38
utility applications, 131, 373
    Activity Monitor, 374–375
    automation tools, 392
    Boot Camp Assistant, 374–375
    ColorSync Utility, 377–379
    Console, 380
    DigitalColor Meter, 381
    Grab, 382–383
    Grapher, 384
    Keychain Access, 385–386
    Migration Assistant, 387
    System Information, 388
    Terminal, 389

V

vCards
    creating, 287–288
    importing, 287–288
Versions, 144
videos
    chat, 449–450
    DVD Player, 215–216
    Photo Booth, 230–232
View buttons, 29
View menu commands, 30
    active window only, 53
    Clean Up, 54
    Show Toolbar, 53
Viewer window, DVD Player, 215
views
    full-screen, 142–143
    options, setting, 476–482
VIPs, xxiii
Voice option (text to speech), 586
voice options, 586–587
VoiceOver, 10, 390–391
    settings, 587
VoiceOver option (Accessibility preferences
    pane), 590
volume
    icons, 19
    sound, 540